THE COMPL
AUST
TEST CRICK
1877

Ross Dundas has been compiling and producing cricket statistics commercially for nearly six years. His clients include PBL (the Australian Cricket Board marketing company), the ABC, Channel 9, and numerous authors of cricket books. Dundas is currently the cricket statistician for the New South Wales Cricket Association.

Jack Pollard is Australia's best-known sports journalist. Sales of works he has written or edited have exceeded one million copies and a dozen of these titles are still in regular circulation. His *Australian Cricket* (1982) won the Great Britain Cricket Society's prestigious Jubilee Award in 1984. He has since written a tribute to Dennis Lillee and Greg Chappell, commemorating their retirement from first-class cricket. This is his thirty-fifth book.

THE COMPLETE BOOK OF
AUSTRALIAN TEST CRICKET RECORDS
1877-1987

Includes International One Day Records

Ross Dundas
Jack Pollard

Published by ABC Enterprises for the
AUSTRALIAN BROADCASTING CORPORATION
20 Atchison Street (Box 4444) Crows Nest NSW 2065

First published 1987

National Library of Australia
Cataloguing-in-Publication entry
Dundas, Ross.
 The complete book of Australian test
 cricket records, 1877-1987.
 ISBN 0 642 53058 0.
 1. Cricket—Australia—Records. 2.
 Test matches (Cricket). I. Pollard,
 Jack, 1926- . II. Australian
 Broadcasting Corporation. III. Title.
796.35′875

Edited by Bryony Cosgrove
Designed by Neil Carlyle
Set in 8½/13 Plantin by Midland Typesetters, Victoria
Printed and bound in Australia by Australian Print Group, Victoria
15-1495

CONTENTS

Italics denote articles by Jack Pollard

ABBREVIATIONS

avrge ... average
b ...... bowled
cap .... captain
c&b .... caught and bowled
ct ...... caught
d ...... declared
dis ..... dismissed
HS .... highest score
HW .... hit wicket
inns .... innings
LBW ... leg before wicket

M ..... matches
mdns ... maidens
mins ... minutes
NO .... not out
opp .... opponent
RO .... run out
st ...... stumped
stk/rt ... strike rate
W/I .... wickets per innings
wkts ... wickets
W/M ... wickets per match

COUNTRIES

AUS ... Australia
CAN ... Canada
EA ..... East Africa
ENG ... England
IND ... India
NZ .... New Zealand

PAK ... Pakistan
SA ..... South Africa
SHJ .... Sharjah (UAE)
SL ..... Sri Lanka
WI ..... West Indies
ZIM ... Zimbabwe

THE GROUNDS

Bombay2 .... Brabourne Stadium
Bombay3 .... Wankhede Stadium

Brisbane1 ...... Exhibition Ground
Brisbane2 ...... Woolloongabba

Colombo1 ...... Sinhalese Sports Club Ground
Colombo2 ...... Saravanamuttu Stadium

Durban1 .... Lord's
Durban2 .... Kingsmead

Johannesburg1 .. Old Wanderers
Johannesburg2 .. Ellis Park
Johannesburg3 .. New Wanderers Stadium

Lahore2 .... Gaddafi Stadium

Madras1 .... Chepauk (Chidambaram Stadium)
Madras2 .... Corporation (Nehru) Stadium

SYMBOLS

* not out (unless otherwise noted)
+ retired hurt (unless otherwise noted)

SOURCES OF ILLUSTRATIONS

Adelaide *Advertiser* p. 51; Melbourne *Age* pp. xvi-xvii; Wally Allen p. 62; Herald & Weekly Times p. 356; News Ltd p. 354; Pollard Publishing Company p. 4, p. 7, p. 52, p. 65, p. 75, p. 89, p. 102, p. 216, p. 218, p. 230, p. 305, p. 308, p. 310; *Sunday Observer* p. 302; West Australian Newspapers Ltd pp. 90-91.

The first tied Test—Australia's Lindsay Kline turns to see Ian Meck.

g run out by a return from West Indies fieldsman Joe Solomon.

PART 1:

AUSTRALIA'S TEST CRICKET RECORDS
1876-77 to 1986-87

THE GAMES

SUMMARY OF TESTS
to 1 September 1987

Opponent	Played	Won	Lost	Drawn	Tied
England	639	229	169	241	–
Australia	473	194	139	138	2
West Indies	252	92	62	97	1
India	246	40	84	121	1
New Zealand	183	26	76	81	–
South Africa	172	38	77	57	–
Pakistan	170	39	40	91	–
Sri Lanka	25	2	13	10	–
Total	**1080**	**660**	**660**	**418**	**2**

AUSTRALIAN TESTS

Opponent	Played	Won	Lost	Drawn	Tied
England	263	97	88	78	–
West Indies	62	27	19	15	1
South Africa	53	29	11	13	–
India	45	20	8	16	1
Pakistan	28	11	8	9	–
New Zealand	21	9	5	7	–
Sri Lanka	1	1	–	–	–
Total	**473**	**194**	**139**	**138**	**2**

John McCarthy Blackham, a member of the Australian Team, 1877-94.

THE FIRST TEST

When James Lillywhite brought the fourth English team to Australia in the summer of 1876-77, he found that cricket standards had improved dramatically. The coaching of the shrewd English professionals William Caffyn and Charles Lawrence,who had remained in Australia instead of returning to England with the first and second touring teams, had helped develop a crop of outstanding players. Competition between the States, which had begun in 1850-51, and the growing strength of club cricket in all the major centres, had also lifted playing skills.

Lillywhite's touring party was an all-professional outfit comprising players from Nottinghamshire, Surrey, Sussex and Yorkshire, strongly dedicated to boosting match profits so that each man could go home with a handsome bonus. At Adelaide they found the groundsman was afraid of using a roller for fear of bruising the turf. At Arrarat the only available roller was made of wood and was 25 centimetres in diameter. At Goulburn, kangaroos joined players on the field.

At Sydney, a Fifteen of New South Wales defeated Lillywhite's team by two wickets and then by 13 wickets, and at Melbourne when a Fifteen of Victoria also beat the "tourists" it was decided that the time had come for a match between the countries on level terms. Lillywhite realised that such a match would lift tour profits and he agreed to it being added to the tour program before he left to fulfill the New Zealand part of his itinerary.

Arrangements for an All England versus All Australia match were left in the hands of the Victorian Cricketers' Association, who in turn relied on Lillywhite's Australian agent, John Conway, the South Melbourne all-rounder, to pick the Australian team. Conway gave no thought to approaching the New South Wales Cricket Association and went straight to the players. He encountered unexpected problems when fast bowler Fred Spofforth refused to play unless he could have Billy Murdoch as his wicket-keeper. Edwin Evans, then Australia's finest all-rounder, declined to play for personal reasons.

Conway stuck with his selection of John McCarthy Blackham as wicket-keeper, which prevented Spofforth from playing. Then the clever bowler Frank Allan broke his promise to play, saying he preferred to be with friends at the Warrnambool Show during the days set down for the match. To replace the dropouts Conway brought in Tom Kendall, a left-arm bowler, Billy Midwinter, one of the most amazing of all international cricketers, and Tom Garrett, son of a Sydney MP and at 18 the youngest ever to play for Australia against England.

Lillywhite's team returned from New Zealand without their wicket-keeper, Edward Pooley, who had been left in gaol to face charges of malicious damage. This resulted from a pub brawl after Pooley bet a Christchurch man he could forecast each player's score against England. The man agreed to pay one pound for each prediction Pooley got right. Pooley wrote down a duck against each name and made a tidy profit. Pooley was acquitted of all charges when the court sorted out the ensuing melee, but England was left without an experienced 'keeper for the big match in Melbourne.

The Englishmen arrived from New Zealand only the day before the match and some were still suffering the effects of sea-sickness when Dave Gregory won the toss for Australia. At 1 pm on 15 March 1877, Charles Bannerman and Nat Thompson strode to the crease to open for Australia and initiate Test cricket. Bannerman, like five of his team-mates, had been born in England. He faced the first ball in Test cricket from Alfred Shaw, which he blocked, and then took a single from the second ball. In the second over, Thompson, who also had taken a single from Shaw, was bowled by Allen Hill, the first wicket to fall in Tests.

Play continued before 1000 spectators until 5 pm with a 50-minute spell for lunch and no tea-break.

Bannerman's partners realised he had the measure of the English bowling, and they dug in at the other end while he scored freely. At the end of the day Australia was 6 for 166, with Bannerman on 126, the first Test century and one of the great innings in all cricket. He punished the Yorkshire lob-bowler Tom Armitage so severely that Armitage had to resort to grubbers. In the midst of pugnacious Australian batting, Ned Gregory made Test cricket's first duck.

Bannerman continued to 165 on the second day, before a ball from George Ulyett split a finger open and he was compelled to retire. All out for 245, Australia then dismissed Lillywhite's side for 196. England looked dangerous at 1 for 79 when Blackham brilliantly caught Henry Charlwood for 36. Henry Jupp topscored for England with 63, though the Australians claimed he broke his own wicket early on and the umpire missed it.

With a first innings lead of 49, Australia managed only 104 in its second innings, Paddy Horan topscoring with 20 and Billy Midwinter contributing an invaluable 17. Set to score 154 to win, England was hot favourite, but Tom Kendall produced a fine spell of fast left-arm bowling to bundle England out for 108. John Selby topscored with 38. Kendall was the match-winner with 7 for 55, from 33.1 four-ball overs. The Victorian Cricket Association was so thrilled by Australia's 45-run win they gave all the players gold medals. Dave Gregory received a slightly bigger medal than the rest for leading the team so skillfully.

Edward Pooley, the wicket-keeper who missed the first Test.

THE TESTS

Intl test No.	Series	Toss	Australia 1st	2nd	Opponent	Opponents 1st	2nd	Result	Australia Captains	Opponent
1876-77 in Australia										
1	Melbourne	AUS	245*	104	England	196	108	AUS by 45 runs	Gregory, DW	Lillywhite, J
2	Melbourne	AUS	122*	259	England	261	6-122	ENG by 4 wkts	Gregory, DW	Lillywhite, J
1878-79 in Australia										
3	Melbourne	ENG	256	0-19	England	113*	160	AUS by 10 wkts	Gregory, DW	Lord Harris
1880 in England										
4	The Oval	ENG	149	327	England	420*	5-57	ENG by 5 wkts	Murdoch, WL	Lord Harris
1881-82 in Australia										
5	Melbourne	ENG	320	3-127	England	294*	308	Drawn	Murdoch, WL	Shaw, A
6	Sydney	ENG	197	5-169	England	133*	232	AUS by 5 wkts	Murdoch, WL	Shaw, A
7	Sydney	ENG	260	4-66	England	188*	134	AUS by 6 wkts	Murdoch, WL	Shaw, A
8	Melbourne	ENG	300	–	England	309*	2-234	Drawn	Murdoch, WL	Shaw, A
1882 in England										
9	The Oval	AUS	63*	122	England	101	77	AUS by 7 runs	Murdoch, WL	Hornby, AN

1882-83 in Australia

No.	Venue							Result		
10	Melbourne	AUS	291*	1-58	England	177	169	AUS by 9 wkts	Murdoch, WL	Bligh, Hon IFW
11	Melbourne	ENG	114	153	England	294*	–	ENG by an inns & 27 runs	Murdoch, WL	Bligh, Hon IFW
12	Sydney	ENG	218	83	England	247*	123	ENG by 69 runs	Murdoch, WL	Bligh, Hon IFW
13	Sydney	ENG	262	6-199	England	263*	197	AUS by 4 wkts	Murdoch, WL	Bligh, Hon IFW

1884 in England

No.	Venue							Result		
14	Manchester	ENG	182	–	England	95*	180	Drawn	Murdoch, WL	Hornby, AN
15	Lord's	AUS	229*	145	England	379	–	ENG by an inns & 5 runs	Murdoch, WL	Lord Harris
16	The Oval	AUS	551*	–	England	346	2-85	Drawn	Murdoch, WL	Lord Harris

1884-85 in Australia

No.	Venue							Result		
17	Adelaide	AUS	243*	191	England	369	2-67	ENG by 8 wkts	Murdoch, WL	Shrewsbury, A
18	Melbourne	ENG	279	126	England	401*	0-7	ENG by 10 wkts	Horan, TP	Shrewsbury, A
19	Sydney	AUS	181*	165	England	133	207	AUS by 6 runs	Massie, HH	Shrewsbury, A
20	Sydney	ENG	309	2-38	England	269*	77	AUS by 8 wkts	Blackham, JM	Shrewsbury, A
21	Melbourne	AUS	163*	125	England	386	–	ENG by an inns & 98 runs	Horan, TP	Shrewsbury, A

Intl test No.	Series	Toss	Australia 1st	Australia 2nd	Opponent	Opponents 1st	Opponents 2nd	Result	Captains Australia	Captains Opponent
1886 in England										
22	Manchester	AUS	205*	123	England	223	6-107	ENG by 4 wkts	Scott, HJH	Steel, AG
23	Lord's	ENG	121	126	England	353*	–	Eng by an inns & 106 runs	Scott, HJH	Steel, AG
24	The Oval	ENG	68	149	England	434*	–	ENG by an inns & 217 runs	Scott, HJH	Steel, AG
1886-87 in Australia										
25	Sydney	AUS	119	97	England	45	184	ENG by 13 runs	McDonnell, PS	Shrewsbury, A
26	Sydney	ENG	84	150	England	151	154	ENG by 71 runs	McDonnell, PS	Shrewsbury, A
1887-88 in Australia										
27	Sydney	AUS	42	82	England	113	137	ENG by 126 runs	McDonnell, PS	Read, RR
1888 in England										
28	Lord's	AUS	116*	60	England	53	62	AUS by 61 runs	McDonnell, PS	Steel, AG
29	The Oval	AUS	80*	100	England	317	–	ENG by an inns & 137 runs	McDonnell, PS	Grace, WG
30	Manchester	ENG	81	70	England	172*	–	ENG by an inns & 21 runs	McDonnell, PS	Grace, WG
1890 in England										
33	Lord's	AUS	132*	176	England	173	3-137	ENG by 7 wkts	Murdoch, WL	Grace, WG

34	The Oval	AUS	92*	102	England	100	8-95	ENG by 2 wkts	Murdoch, WL	Grace, WG
1891-92 in Australia										
35	Melbourne	AUS	240*	236	England	264	158	AUS by 54 runs	Blackham, JM	Grace, WG
36	Sydney	AUS	145*	391	England	307	157	AUS by 72 runs	Blackham, JM	Grace, WG
38	Adelaide	ENG	100	169	England	499*	–	ENG by an inns & 230 runs	Blackham, JM	Grace, WG
1893 in England										
39	Lord's	ENG	269	–	England	334*	8d-234	Drawn	Blackham, JM	Stoddart, AE
40	The Oval	ENG	91	349	England	483*	–	ENG by an inns & 43 runs	Blackham, JM	Grace, WG
41	Manchester	AUS	204*	236	England	243	4-118	Drawn	Blackham, JM	Grace, WG
1894-95 in Australia										
42	Sydney	AUS	586*	166	England	325	437	ENG by 10 runs	Blackham, JM	Stoddart, AE
43	Melbourne	AUS	123	333	England	75*	475	ENG by 94 runs	Giffen, G	Stoddart, AE
44	Adelaide	AUS	238*	411	England	124	143	AUS by 382 runs	Giffen, G	Stoddart, AE
45	Sydney	ENG	284*	–	England	65	72	AUS by an inns & 147 runs	Giffen, G	Stoddart, AE
46	Melbourne	AUS	414*	267	England	385	4-298	ENG by 6 wkts	Giffen, G	Stoddart, AE
1896 in England										
50	Lord's	AUS	53*	347	England	292	4-111	ENG by 6 wkts	Trott, GHS	Grace, WG
51	Manchester	AUS	412*	7-125	England	231	305	AUS by 3 wkts	Trott, GHS	Grace, WG

Intl test No.	Series	Toss	Australia 1st	Australia 2nd	Opponent	Opponents 1st	Opponents 2nd	Result	Captains Australia	Captains Opponent
52	The Oval	ENG	119	44	England	145	84	ENG by 66 runs	Trott, GHS	Grace, WG

1897-98 in Australia

53	Sydney	ENG	237	408	England	551*	1-96	ENG by 9 wkts	Trott, GHS	MacLaren, AC
54	Melbourne	AUS	520*	–	England	315	150	AUS by an inns & 55 runs	Trott, GHS	MacLaren, AC
55	Adelaide	AUS	573*	–	England	278*	282	AUS by an inns & 13 runs	Trott, GHS	Stoddart, AE
56	Melbourne	AUS	323*	2-115	England	174	263	AUS by 8 wkts	Trott, GHS	Stoddart, AE
57	Sydney	ENG	239	4-276	England	335*	178	AUS by 6 wkts	Trott, GHS	MacLaren, AC

1899 in England

60	Nottingham	AUS	252*	8d-230	England	193	7-155	Drawn	Darling, J	Grace, WG
61	Lord's	ENG	421	0-28	England	206*	240	AUS by 10 wkts	Darling, J	MacLaren, AC
62	Leeds	AUS	172*	224	England	220	0-19	Drawn	Darling, J	MacLaren, AC
63	Manchester	ENG	196	7d-346	England	372*	3-94	Drawn	Darling, J	MacLaren, AC
64	The Oval	ENG	352	5-254	England	576*	–	Drawn	Darling, J	MacLaren, AC

1901-02 in Australia

65	Sydney	ENG	168	172	England	464*	–	ENG by an inns & 124 runs	Darling, J	MacLaren, AC
66	Melbourne	ENG	112*	353	England	61	175	AUS by 229 runs	Darling, J	MacLaren, AC

67	Adelaide	ENG	321	6-315	England	388*	247	AUS by 4 wkts	Darling, J	MacLaren, AC
68	Sydney	ENG	299	3-121	England	317*	99	AUS by 7 wkts	Trumble, H	MacLaren, AC
69	Melbourne	AUS	144*	255	England	189	178	AUS by 32 runs	Trumble, H	MacLaren, AC

1902 in England

70	Birmingham	ENG	36	2-46	England	9d-376*	–	Drawn	Darling, J	MacLaren, AC
71	Lord's	ENG	–	–	England	2-102*	–	Drawn	Darling, J	MacLaren, AC
72	Sheffield	AUS	194*	289	England	145	195	AUS by 143 runs	Darling, J	MacLaren, AC
73	Manchester	AUS	299*	86	England	262	120	AUS by 3 runs	Darling, J	MacLaren, AC
74	The Oval	AUS	324*	121	England	183	9-263	ENG by 1 wkt	Darling, J	MacLaren, AC

1902-03 in South Africa

75	Johannesburg1	SA	296	7d-372	South Africa	454*	4-101	Drawn	Darling, J	Taberer, HM
76	Johannesburg1	AUS	175*	309	South Africa	240	85	AUS by 159 runs	Darling, J	Anderson, JH
77	Cape Town	AUS	252*	0-59	South Africa	85	225	AUS by 10 wkts	Darling, J	Halliwell, EA

1903-04 in Australia

78	Sydney	AUS	285*	485	England	577	5-194	ENG by 5 wkts	Noble, MA	Warner, PF
79	Melbourne	ENG	122	111	England	315*	103	ENG by 185 runs	Noble, MA	Warner, PF
80	Adelaide	AUS	388*	351	England	245	278	AUS by 216 runs	Noble, MA	Warner, PF
81	Sydney	ENG	131	171	England	249*	210	ENG by 157 runs	Noble, MA	Warner, PF
82	Melbourne	AUS	247*	133	England	61	9-101	AUS by 218 runs	Noble, MA	Warner, PF

Intl test No.	Series	Toss	Australia 1st	Australia 2nd	Opponent	Opponents 1st	Opponents 2nd	Result	Captains Australia	Opponent
1905 in England										
83	Nottingham	ENG	9-221	9-188	England	196*	5d-426	ENG by 213 runs	Darling, J	Jackson, Hon FS
84	Lord's	ENG	181	–	England	282*	5-151	Drawn	Darling, J	Jackson, Hon FS
85	Leeds	ENG	195	7-224	England	301*	5d-295	Drawn	Darling, J	Jackson, Hon FS
86	Manchester	ENG	197	169	England	446*	–	ENG by an inns & 80 runs	Darling, J	Jackson, Hon FS
87	The Oval	ENG	363	4-124	England	430*	6-261	Drawn	Darling, J	Jackson, Hon FS
1907-08 in Australia										
96	Sydney	ENG	300	8-275	England	273*	300	AUS by 2 wkts	Noble, MA	Fane, FL
97	Melbourne	AUS	266*	397	England	382	9-282	ENG by 1 wkt	Noble, MA	Fane, FL
98	Adelaide	AUS	285*	506	England	363	183	AUS by 245 runs	Noble, MA	Fane, FL
99	Melbourne	AUS	214*	385	England	105	186	AUS by 308 runs	Noble, MA	Jones, AO
100	Sydney	ENG	137*	422	England	281	229	AUS by 49 runs	Noble, MA	Jones, AO
1909 in England										
101	Birmingham	AUS	74*	151	England	121	0-105	ENG by 10 wkts	Noble, MA	MacLaren, AC
102	Lord's	AUS	350	1-41	England	269*	121	AUS by 9 wkts	Noble, MA	MacLaren, AC

#	Venue							Result		
103	Leeds	AUS	188*	207	England	182	87	AUS by 126 runs	Noble, MA	MacLaren, AC
104	Manchester	AUS	147*	9d-279	England	119	3-108	Drawn	Noble, MA	MacLaren, AC
105	The Oval	AUS	325*	5d-339	England	352	3-104	Drawn	Noble, MA	MacLaren, AC

1910-11 in Australia

#	Venue							Result		
111	Sydney	AUS	528*	–	South Africa	174	240	AUS by an inns & 114 runs	Hill, C	Sherwell, PW
112	Melbourne	AUS	348*	327	South Africa	506	80	AUS by 86 runs	Hill, C	Sherwell, PW
113	Adelaide	SA	465	339	South Africa	482*	360	SA by 38 runs	Hill, C	Sherwell, PW
114	Melbourne	SA	328*	578	South Africa	205	171	AUS by 530 runs	Hill, C	Sherwell, PW
115	Sydney	SA	364*	3-198	South Africa	160	401	AUS by 7 wkts	Hill, C	Sherwell, PW

1911-12 in Australia

#	Venue							Result		
116	Sydney	AUS	447*	308	England	318	219	AUS by 146 runs	Hill, C	Douglas, JWHT
117	Melbourne	AUS	184*	299	England	265	2-219	ENG by 8 wkts	Hill, C	Douglas, JWHT
118	Adelaide	AUS	133*	476	England	501	3-112	ENG by 7 wkts	Hill, C	Douglas, JWHT
119	Melbourne	ENG	191*	173	England	589	–	ENG by an inns & 225 runs	Hill, C	Douglas, JWHT
120	Sydney	ENG	176	292	England	324*	214	ENG by 70 runs	Hill, C	Douglas, JWHT

1912 in England

#	Venue							Result		
121	Manchester	AUS	448*	–	South Africa	265	95	AUS by an inns & 88 runs	Gregory, SE	Mitchell, F
123	Lord's	ENG	7-282	–	England	7d-310*	–	Drawn	Gregory, SE	Fry, CB
125	Lord's	SA	390	0-48	South Africa	263*	173	AUS by 10 wkts	Gregory, SE	Mitchell, F

Intl test No.	Series	Toss	Australia 1st	Australia 2nd	Opponent	Opponents 1st	Opponents 2nd	Result	Captains Australia	Opponent
126	Manchester	ENG	0-14	–	England	203*	–	Drawn	Gregory, SE	Fry, CB
127	Nottingham	SA	219	–	South Africa	329*	–	Drawn	Gregory, SE	Tancred, LJ
129	The Oval	ENG	111	65	England	245*	175	ENG by 244 runs	Gregory, SE	Fry, CB
1920-21 in Australia										
135	Sydney	AUS	267*	581	England	190	281	AUS by 377 runs	Armstrong, WW	Douglas, JWHT
136	Melbourne	AUS	499*	–	England	251	157	AUS by an inns & 91 runs	Armstrong, WW	Douglas, JWHT
137	Adelaide	AUS	354*	582	England	447	370	AUS by 119 runs	Armstrong, WW	Douglas, JWHT
138	Melbourne	ENG	389	2-211	England	284*	315	AUS by 8 wkts	Armstrong, WW	Douglas, JWHT
139	Sydney	ENG	392	1-93	England	204*	280	AUS by 9 wkts	Armstrong, WW	Douglas, JWHT
1921 in England										
140	Nottingham	ENG	232	0-30	England	112*	147	AUS by 10 wkts	Armstrong, WW	Douglas, JWHT
141	Lord's	ENG	342	2-131	England	187*	283	AUS by 8 wkts	Armstrong, WW	Douglas, JWHT
142	Leeds	AUS	407*	7d-273	England	259	202	AUS by 219 runs	Armstrong, WW	Tennyson, Hon LH
143	Manchester	ENG	175	–	England	4d-362*	1-44	Drawn	Armstrong, WW	Tennyson, Hon LH
144	The Oval	ENG	389	–	England	8d-403*	2-244	Drawn	Armstrong, WW	Tennyson, Hon LH

1921-22 in South Africa

145	Durban1	AUS	299*	7d-324	South Africa	232	7-184	Drawn	Collins, HL	Taylor, HW
146	Johannesburg1	AUS	450*	0-7	South Africa	243	8d-472	Drawn	Collins, HL	Taylor, HW
147	Cape Town	SA	396	0-1	South Africa	180	216	AUS by 10 wkts	Collins, HL	Taylor, HW

1924-25 in Australia

158	Sydney	AUS	450*	452	England	298	411	AUS by 193 runs	Collins, HL	Gilligan, AER
159	Melbourne	AUS	600*	250	England	479	290	AUS by 81 runs	Collins, HL	Gilligan, AER
160	Adelaide	AUS	489*	250	England	365	363	AUS by 11 runs	Collins, HL	Gilligan, AER
161	Melbourne	ENG	269	250	England	548*	–	ENG by an inns & 29 runs	Collins, HL	Gilligan, AER
162	Sydney	AUS	295*	325	England	167	146	AUS by 307 runs	Collins, HL	Gilligan, AER

1926 in England

163	Nottingham	ENG	–	–	England	0-32*	–	Drawn	Collins, HL	Carr, AW
164	Lord's	AUS	383*	5-194	England	3d-475	–	Drawn	Collins, HL	Carr, AW
165	Leeds	ENG	494*	–	England	294	3-254	Drawn	Bardsley, W	Carr, AW
166	Manchester	AUS	335*	–	England	5-305	–	Drawn	Bardsley, W	Carr, AW
167	The Oval	ENG	302	125	England	280*	436	ENG by 289 runs	Collins, HL	Chapman, APF

1928-29 in Australia

176	Brisbane1	ENG	122	66	England	521*	8d-342	ENG by 675 runs	Ryder, J	Chapman, APF
177	Sydney	AUS	253*	397	England	636	2-16	ENG by 8 wkts	Ryder, J	Chapman, APF
178	Melbourne	AUS	397*	351	England	417	7-332	ENG by 3 wkts	Ryder, J	Chapman, APF

Intl test No.	Series	Toss	Australia 1st	Australia 2nd	Opponent	Opponents 1st	Opponents 2nd	Result	Captains Australia	Captains Opponent
179	Adelaide	ENG	369	336	England	334*	383	ENG by 12 runs	Ryder, J	Chapman, APF
180	Melbourne	ENG	491	5-287	England	519*	257	AUS by 5 wkts	Ryder, J	White, JC

1930 in England

Intl test No.	Series	Toss	Australia 1st	Australia 2nd	Opponent	Opponents 1st	Opponents 2nd	Result	Captains Australia	Captains Opponent
194	Nottingham	ENG	144	335	England	270*	302	ENG by 93 runs	Woodfull, WM	Chapman, APF
195	Lord's	ENG	6d-729	3-72	England	425*	375	AUS by 7 wkts	Woodfull, WM	Chapman, APF
196	Leeds	AUS	566*	–	England	391	3-95	Drawn	Woodfull, WM	Chapman, APF
197	Manchester	AUS	345*	–	England	8-251	–	Drawn	Woodfull, WM	Chapman, APF
198	The Oval	ENG	695	–	England	405*	251	AUS by an inns & 39 runs	Woodfull, WM	Wyatt, RES

1930-31 in Australia

Intl test No.	Series	Toss	Australia 1st	Australia 2nd	Opponent	Opponents 1st	Opponents 2nd	Result	Captains Australia	Captains Opponent
199	Adelaide	WI	376	0-172	West Indies	296*	249	AUS by 10 wkts	Woodfull, WM	Grant, GC
201	Sydney	AUS	369*	–	West Indies	107	90	AUS by an inns & 172 runs	Woodfull, WM	Grant, GC
203	Brisbane1	AUS	558*	–	West Indies	193	148	AUS by an inns & 217 runs	Woodfull, WM	Grant, GC
205	Melbourne	WI	8d-328*	–	West Indies	99	107	AUS by an inns & 122 runs	Woodfull, WM	Grant, GC
208	Sydney	WI	224	220	West Indies	6d-350*	5d-124	WI by 30 runs	Woodfull, WM	Grant, GC

1931-32 in Australia

No	Venue	Team	1st	2nd	Opponent	1st	2nd	Result	Captain	Captain
212	Brisbane2	AUS	450*	–	South Africa	170	117	AUS by an inns & 163 runs	Woodfull, WM	Cameron, HB
213	Sydney	SA	469	–	South Africa	153*	161	AUS by an inns & 155 runs	Woodfull, WM	Cameron, HB
214	Melbourne	AUS	198*	554	South Africa	358	225	AUS by 169 runs	Woodfull, WM	Cameron, HB
215	Adelaide	SA	513	0-73	South Africa	308*	274	AUS by 10 wkts	Woodfull, WM	Cameron, HB
216	Melbourne	SA	153	–	South Africa	36*	45	AUS by an inns & 72 runs	Woodfull, WM	Cameron, HB

1932-33 in Australia

No	Venue	Team	1st	2nd	Opponent	1st	2nd	Result	Captain	Captain
220	Sydney	AUS	360*	164	England	524	0-1	ENG by 10 wkts	Woodfull, WM	Jardine, DR
221	Melbourne	AUS	228*	191	England	169	139	AUS by 111 runs	Woodfull, WM	Jardine, DR
222	Adelaide	ENG	222	193	England	341*	412	ENG by 338 runs	Woodfull, WM	Jardine, DR
223	Brisbane2	AUS	340*	175	England	356	4-162	ENG by 6 wkts	Woodfull, WM	Jardine, DR
224	Sydney	AUS	435*	182	England	454	2-168	ENG by 8 wkts	Woodfull, WM	Jardine, DR

1934 in England

No	Venue	Team	1st	2nd	Opponent	1st	2nd	Result	Captain	Captain
233	Nottingham	AUS	374*	8d-273	England	268	141	AUS by 238 runs	Woodfull, WM	Walters, CF
234	Lord's	ENG	284	118	England	440*	–	ENG by an inns & 38 runs	Woodfull, WM	Wyatt, RES
235	Manchester	ENG	491	1-66	England	9d-627*	0-123	Drawn	Woodfull, WM	Wyatt, RES
236	Leeds	ENG	584	–	England	200*	6-229	Drawn	Woodfull, WM	Wyatt, RES
237	The Oval	AUS	701*	327	England	321	145	AUS by 562 runs	Woodfull, WM	Wyatt, RES

Intl test No.	Series	Toss	Australia 1st	2nd	Opponent	Opponents 1st	2nd	Result	Captains Australia	Opponent
1935-36 in South Africa										
247	Durban2	SA	429	1-102	South Africa	248*	282	AUS by 9 wkts	Richardson, VY	Wade, HF
248	Johannesburg1	SA	250	2-274	South Africa	157*	491	Drawn	Richardson, VY	Wade, HF
249	Cape Town	AUS	8d-362*	–	South Africa	102	182	AUS by an inns & 78 runs	Richardson, VY	Wade, HF
250	Johannesburg1	SA	439	–	South Africa	157*	98	AUS by an inns & 184 runs	Richardson, VY	Wade, HF
251	Durban2	SA	455	–	South Africa	222*	227	AUS by an inns & 6 runs	Richardson, VY	Wade, HF
1936-37 in Australia										
255	Brisbane2	ENG	234	9-58	England	358*	256	ENG by 322 runs	Bradman, DG	Allen, GOB
256	Sydney	ENG	9-80	324	England	6d-426*	–	ENG by an inns & 22 runs	Bradman, DG	Allen, GOB
257	Melbourne	AUS	200*	564	England	9d-76	323	AUS by 365 runs	Bradman, DG	Allen, GOB
258	Adelaide	AUS	288*	433	England	330	243	AUS by 148 runs	Bradman, DG	Allen, GOB
259	Melbourne	AUS	604*	–	England	239	165	AUS by an inns & 200 runs	Bradman, DG	Allen, GOB
1938 in England										
263	Nottingham	ENG	411	6d-427	England	8d-658*	–	Drawn	Bradman, DG	Hammond, WR
264	Lord's	ENG	422	6-204	England	494*	8d-242	Drawn	Bradman, DG	Hammond, WR

265	Leeds	ENG	242	5-107	England	223*	123	AUS by 5 wkts	Bradman, DG	Hammond, WR
266	The Oval	ENG	201	123	England	7d-903*	–	ENG by an inns & 579 runs	Bradman, DG	Hammond, WR

1945-46 in New Zealand

275	Wellington	NZ	8d-199	–	New Zealand	42*	54	AUS by an inns & 103 runs	Brown, WA	Hadlee, WA

1946-47 in Australia

279	Brisbane2	AUS	645*	–	England	141	172	AUS by an inns & 332 runs	Bradman, DG	Hammond, WR
280	Sydney	ENG	8d-659	–	England	255*	371	AUS by an inns & 33 runs	Bradman, DG	Hammond, WR
281	Melbourne	AUS	365*	536	England	351	7-310	Drawn	Bradman, DG	Hammond, WR
282	Adelaide	ENG	487	1-215	England	460*	8d-340	Drawn	Bradman, DG	Hammond, WR
283	Sydney	ENG	253	5-214	England	280*	186	AUS by 4 wkts	Bradman, DG	Yardley, NWD

1947-48 in Australia

290	Brisbane2	AUS	8d-382*	–	India	58	98	AUS by an inns & 226 runs	Bradman, DG	Amarnath, L
291	Sydney	IND	107	–	India	188*	7-61	Drawn	Bradman, DG	Amarnath, L
292	Melbourne	AUS	394*	4d-255	India	9d-291	125	AUS by 233 runs	Bradman, DG	Amarnath, L
294	Adelaide	AUS	674*	–	India	381	277	AUS by an inns & 16 runs	Bradman, DG	Amarnath, L
295	Melbourne	AUS	8d-575*	–	India	331	67	AUS by an inns & 177 runs	Bradman, DG	Amarnath, L

Intl test No.	Series	Toss	Australia 1st	Australia 2nd	Opponent	Opponents 1st	Opponents 2nd	Result	Captains Australia	Captains Opponent
1948 in England										
299	Nottingham	ENG	509	2-98	England	165*	441	AUS by 8 wkts	Bradman, DG	Yardley, NWD
300	Lord's	AUS	350*	7d-460	England	215	186	AUS by 409 runs	Bradman, DG	Yardley, NWD
301	Manchester	ENG	221	1-92	England	363*	3d-174	Drawn	Bradman, DG	Yardley, NWD
302	Leeds	ENG	458	3-404	England	496*	8d-365	AUS by 7 wkts	Bradman, DG	Yardley, NWD
303	The Oval	ENG	389	–	England	52*	188	AUS by an inns & 149 runs	Bradman, DG	Yardley, NWD
1949-50 in South Africa										
318	Johannesburg2	AUS	413*	–	South Africa	137	191	AUS by an inns & 85 runs	Hassett, AL	Nourse, AD
319	Cape Town	AUS	7d-526*	2-87	South Africa	278	333	AUS by 8 wkts	Hassett, AL	Nourse, AD
320	Durban2	SA	75	5-336	South Africa	311*	99	AUS by 5 wkts	Hassett, AL	Nourse, AD
321	Johannesburg2	AUS	8d-465*	2-259	South Africa	352	–	Drawn	Hassett, AL	Nourse, AD
322	Port Elizabeth	AUS	7d-549*	–	South Africa	158	132	AUS by an inns & 259 runs	Hassett, AL	Nourse, AD
1950-51 in Australia										
327	Brisbane2	AUS	228*	7d-32	England	7d-68	122	AUS by 70 runs	Hassett, AL	Brown, FR
328	Melbourne	AUS	194*	181	England	197	150	AUS by 28 runs	Hassett, AL	Brown, FR
329	Sydney	ENG	426	–	England	290*	123	AUS by an inns & 13 runs	Hassett, AL	Brown, FR

No.	Venue	Team	1st	2nd	Opponent	1st	2nd	Result		
330	Adelaide	AUS	371*	8d-403	England	272	228	AUS by 274 runs	Hassett, AL	Brown, FR
331	Melbourne	AUS	217*	197	England	320	2-95	ENG by 8 wkts	Hassett, AL	Brown, FR

1951-52 in Australia

No.	Venue	Team	1st	2nd	Opponent	1st	2nd	Result		
340	Brisbane2	WI	226	7-236	West Indies	216*	245	AUS by 3 wkts	Hassett, AL	Goddard, JDC
341	Sydney	AUS	517	3-137	West Indies	362*	290	AUS by 7 wkts	Hassett, AL	Goddard, JDC
343	Adelaide	AUS	82*	255	West Indies	105	4-233	WI by 6 wkts	Morris, AR	Goddard, JDC
345	Melbourne	WI	216	9-260	West Indies	272*	203	AUS by 1 wkt	Hassett, AL	Goddard, JDC
347	Sydney	AUS	116*	377	West Indies	78	213	AUS by 202 runs	Hassett, AL	Stollmeyer, JB

1952-53 in Australia

No.	Venue	Team	1st	2nd	Opponent	1st	2nd	Result		
359	Brisbane2	AUS	280*	277	South Africa	221	240	AUS by 96 runs	Hassett, AL	Cheetham, JE
361	Melbourne	SA	243	290	South Africa	227*	388	SA by 82 runs	Hassett, AL	Cheetham, JE
362	Sydney	SA	443	–	South Africa	173*	232	AUS by an inns & 38 runs	Hassett, AL	Cheetham, JE
364	Adelaide	AUS	530*	3d-233	South Africa	387	6-177	Drawn	Hassett, AL	Cheetham, JE
365	Melbourne	AUS	520*	209	South Africa	435	4-297	SA by 6 wkts	Hassett, AL	Cheetham, JE

1953 in England

No.	Venue	Team	1st	2nd	Opponent	1st	2nd	Result		
372	Nottingham	AUS	249*	123	England	144	1-120	Drawn	Hassett, AL	Hutton, L
373	Lord's	AUS	346*	368	England	372	7-282	Drawn	Hassett, AL	Hutton, L
374	Manchester	AUS	318*	8-35	England	276	–	Drawn	Hassett, AL	Hutton, L
375	Leeds	AUS	266	4-147	England	167*	275	Drawn	Hassett, AL	Hutton, L
376	The Oval	AUS	275*	162	England	306	2-132	ENG by 8 wkts	Hassett, AL	Hutton, L

Intl test No.	Series	Toss	Australia 1st	Australia 2nd	Opponent	Opponents 1st	Opponents 2nd	Result	Captains Australia	Opponent
1954-55 in Australia										
391	Brisbane2	ENG 8d-601*	–	England	190	257	AUS by an inns & 154 runs	Johnson, IW	Hutton, L
392	Sydney	AUS 228	184	England	154*	296	ENG by 38 runs	Morris, AR	Hutton, L
393	Melbourne	ENG 231	111	England	191*	279	ENG by 128 runs	Johnson, IW	Hutton, L
396	Adelaide	AUS 323*	111	England	341	5-97	ENG by 5 wkts	Johnson, IW	Hutton, L
399	Sydney	AUS 221	6-118	England	7d-371*	–	Drawn	Johnson, IW	Hutton, L
1954-55 in West Indies										
403	Kingston	AUS 9d-515*	1-20	West Indies	259	275	AUS by 9 wkts	Johnson, IW	Atkinson, DE
404	Port-of-Spain	WI 9d-600	–	West Indies	382*	4-273	Drawn	Johnson, IW	Stollmeyer, JB
405	Georgetown	WI 257	2-133	West Indies	182*	207	AUS by 8 wkts	Johnson, IW	Stollmeyer, JB
406	Bridgetown	AUS 668*	249	West Indies	510	6-234	Drawn	Johnson, IW	Atkinson, DE
407	Kingston	WI 8d-758	–	West Indies	357*	319	AUS by an inns & 82 runs	Johnson, IW	Atkinson, DE
1956 in England										
425	Nottingham	ENG 148	3-120	England	8d-217*	3d-188	Drawn	Johnson, IW	May, PBH
426	Lord's	AUS 285*	257	England	171	186	AUS by 185 runs	Johnson, IW	May, PBH
427	Leeds	ENG 143	140	England	325*	–	ENG by an inns & 42 runs	Johnson, IW	May, PBH

No.	Venue							Result		
428	Manchester	ENG	84	205	England	459*	–	ENG by an inns & 170 runs	Johnson, IW	May, PBH
429	The Oval	ENG	202	5-27	England	247*	3d-182	Drawn	Johnson, IW	May, PBH

1956-57 in Pakistan

No.	Venue							Result		
430	Karachi	AUS	80*	187	Pakistan	199	1-69	PAK by 9 wkts	Johnson, IW	Kardar, AH

1956-57 in India

No.	Venue							Result		
431	Madras2	IND	319	–	India	161*	153	AUS by an inns & 5 runs	Johnson, IW	Umrigar, PR
432	Bombay2	IND	7d-523	–	India	251	5-250	Drawn	Lindwall, RR	Umrigar, PR
433	Calcutta	IND	177*	9d-189	India	136	136	AUS by 94 runs	Johnson, IW	Umrigar, PR

1957-58 in South Africa

No.	Venue							Result		
444	Johannesburg3	SA	368	3-162	South Africa	9d-470*	201	Drawn	Craig, ID	McGlew, DJ
445	Cape Town	AUS	449*	–	South Africa	209	99	AUS by an inns & 141 runs	Craig, ID	van Ryneveld, CB
446	Durban2	AUS	163*	7-292	South Africa	384	–	Drawn	Craig, ID	van Ryneveld, CB
449	Johannesburg3	AUS	401*	0-1	South Africa	203	198	AUS by 10 wkts	Craig, ID	van Ryneveld, CB
451	Port Elizabeth	SA	291	2-68	South Africa	214*	144	AUS by 8 wkts	Craig, ID	van Ryneveld, CB

1958-59 in Australia

No.	Venue							Result		
460	Brisbane2	ENG	186	2-147	England	134*	198	AUS by 8 wkts	Benaud, R	May, PBH

Intl test No.	Series	Toss	Australia 1st	Australia 2nd	Opponent	Opponents 1st	Opponents 2nd	Result	Captains Australia	Captains Opponent
462	Melbourne	ENG	308	2-42	England	259*	87	AUS by 8 wkts	Benaud, R	May, PBH
464	Sydney	ENG	357	2-54	England	219*	7d-287	Drawn	Benaud, R	May, PBH
466	Adelaide	ENG	476*	0-36	England	240	270	AUS by 10 wkts	Benaud, R	May, PBH
468	Melbourne	AUS	351	1-69	England	205*	214	AUS by 9 wkts	Benaud, R	May, PBH

1959-60 in Pakistan

Intl test No.	Series	Toss	Australia 1st	Australia 2nd	Opponent	Opponents 1st	Opponents 2nd	Result	Captains Australia	Captains Opponent
479	Dacca	AUS	225	2-112	Pakistan	200*	134	AUS by 8 wkts	Benaud, R	Fazal Mahmood
480	Lahore2	PAK	9d-391	3-123	Pakistan	146*	366	AUS by 7 wkts	Benaud, R	Imtiaz Ahmed
481	Karachi	PAK	257	2-83	Pakistan	287*	8d-194	Drawn	Benaud, R	Imtiaz Ahmed

1959-60 in India

Intl test No.	Series	Toss	Australia 1st	Australia 2nd	Opponent	Opponents 1st	Opponents 2nd	Result	Captains Australia	Captains Opponent
482	Delhi	IND	468	–	India	135*	206	AUS by an inns & 127 runs	Benaud, R	Ramchand, GS
483	Kanpur	IND	219	105	India	152*	291	IND by 119 runs	Benaud, R	Ramchand, GS
484	Bombay2	IND	8d-387	1-34	India	289*	5d-226	Drawn	Benaud, R	Ramchand, GS
486	Madras2	AUS	342*	–	India	149	138	AUS by an inns & 55 runs	Benaud, R	Ramchand, GS
487	Calcutta	IND	331	2-121	India	194*	339	Drawn	Benaud, R	Ramchand, GS

1960-61 in Australia

Intl test No.	Series	Toss	Australia 1st	Australia 2nd	Opponent	Opponents 1st	Opponents 2nd	Result	Captains Australia	Captains Opponent
498	Brisbane2	WI	505	232	West Indies	453*	284	Tied	Benaud, R	Worrell, FMM
500	Melbourne	AUS	348*	3-70	West Indies	181	233	AUS by 7 wkts	Benaud, R	Worrell, FMM

502	Sydney	WI	202		West Indies	339*	326	WI by 222 runs	Benaud, R	Worrell, FMM
504	Adelaide	WI	366	9-273	West Indies	393*	6d-432	Drawn	Benaud, R	Worrell, FMM
506	Melbourne	AUS	356	8-258	West Indies	292*	321	AUS by 2 wkts	Benaud, R	Worrell, FMM

1961 in England

507	Birmingham	ENG	9d-516*	–	England	195	4-401	Drawn	Benaud, R	Cowdrey, MC
508	Lord's	ENG	340	5-71	England	206*	202	AUS by 5 wkts	Benaud, R	Cowdrey, MC
509	Leeds	AUS	237*	120	England	299	2-62	ENG by 8 wkts	Benaud, R	May, PBH
510	Manchester	AUS	190*	432	England	367	201	AUS by 54 runs	Benaud, R	May, PBH
511	The Oval	ENG	494	–	England	256*	8-370	Drawn	Benaud, R	May, PBH

1962-63 in Australia

535	Brisbane2	AUS	404*	4d-362	England	389	6-278	Drawn	Benaud, R	Dexter, ER
536	Melbourne	AUS	316*	248	England	331	3-237	ENG by 7 wkts	Benaud, R	Dexter, ER
537	Sydney	ENG	319	2-67	England	279*	104	AUS by 8 wkts	Benaud, R	Dexter, ER
538	Adelaide	AUS	393*	293	England	331*	4-223	Drawn	Benaud, R	Dexter, ER
539	Sydney	ENG	349	4-152	England	321*	8d-268	Drawn	Benaud, R	Dexter, ER

1963-64 in Australia

548	Brisbane2	AUS	435*	1d-144	South Africa	346	1-13	Drawn	Benaud, R	Goddard, TL
549	Melbourne	AUS	447	2-136	South Africa	274*	306	AUS by 8 wkts	Simpson, RB	Goddard, TL
550	Sydney	AUS	260*	9d-450	South Africa	302	5-326	Drawn	Simpson, RB	Goddard, TL
553	Adelaide	AUS	345*	331	South Africa	595	0-82	SA by 10 wkts	Simpson, RB	Goddard, TL
555	Sydney	SA	311*	270	South Africa	411	0-76	Drawn	Simpson, RB	Goddard, TL

Intl test No.	Series	Toss	Australia 1st	2nd	Opponent	Opponents 1st	2nd	Result	Captains Australia	Opponent
1964 in England										
561	Nottingham	ENG	168	2-40	England	8d-216*	9d-193	Drawn	Simpson, RB	Dexter, ER
562	Lord's	ENG	176*	4-168	England	246	–	Drawn	Simpson, RB	Dexter, ER
563	Leeds	ENG	389	3-111	England	268*	229	AUS by 7 wkts	Simpson, RB	Dexter, ER
564	Manchester	AUS	8d-656*	0-4	England	611	–	Drawn	Simpson, RB	Dexter, ER
565	The Oval	AUS	379	–	England	182*	4-381	Drawn	Simpson, RB	Dexter, ER
1964-65 in India										
566	Madras2	AUS	211*	397	India	276	193	AUS by 139 runs	Simpson, RB	Nawab of Pataudi jr
567	Bombay2	AUS	320*	274	India	341	8-256	IND by 2 wkts	Simpson, RB	Nawab of Pataudi jr
568	Calcutta	IND	174*	1-143	India	235	–	Drawn	Simpson, RB	Nawab of Pataudi jr
1964-65 in Pakistan										
569	Karachi	PAK	352	2-227	Pakistan	414*	8d-279	Drawn	Simpson, RB	Hanif Mohammad
1964-65 in Australia										
570	Melbourne	AUS	448	2-88	Pakistan	287*	326	Drawn	Simpson, RB	Hanif Mohammad

1964-65 in West Indies

No	Venue							Result		
580	Kingston	WI	217	216	West Indies	239*	373	WI by 179 runs	Simpson, RB	Sobers, GA
584	Port-of-Spain	AUS	516	–	West Indies	429*	386	Drawn	Simpson, RB	Sobers, GA
588	Georgetown	WI	179	144	West Indies	355*	180	WI by 212 runs	Simpson, RB	Sobers, GA
589	Bridgetown	AUS	6d-650*	4d-175	West Indies	573	5-242	Drawn	Simpson, RB	Sobers, GA
590	Port-of-Spain	WI	294	0-63	West Indies	224*	131	AUS by 10 wkts	Simpson, RB	Sobers, GA

1965-66 in Australia

No	Venue							Result		
597	Brisbane2	AUS	6d-443*	–	England	280	3-186	Drawn	Booth, BC	Smith, MJK
598	Melbourne	AUS	358*	426	England	558	0-5	Drawn	Simpson, RB	Smith, MJK
599	Sydney	ENG	221	174	England	488*	–	ENG by an inns & 93 runs	Booth, BC	Smith, MJK
600	Adelaide	ENG	516*	–	England	241	266	AUS by an inns & 9 runs	Simpson, RB	Smith, MJK
601	Melbourne	ENG	8d-543	–	England	9d-485*	3-69	Drawn	Simpson, RB	Smith, MJK

1966-67 in South Africa

No	Venue							Result		
611	Johannesburg3	SA	325	261	South Africa	199*	620	SA by 233 runs	Simpson, RB	van der Merwe, PL
613	Cape Town	AUS	542*	4-180	South Africa	353	367	AUS by 6 wkts	Simpson, RB	van der Merwe, PL
615	Durban2	AUS	147	334	South Africa	300*	2-185	SA by 8 wkts	Simpson, RB	van der Merwe, PL
616	Johannesburg3	AUS	143*	8-148	South Africa	9d-332	–	Drawn	Simpson, RB	van der Merwe, PL

Intl test No.	Series	Toss	Australia 1st	2nd	Opponent	Opponents 1st	2nd	Result	Captains Australia	Opponent
617	Port Elizabeth	SA	173*	278	South Africa	276	3-179	SA by 7 wkts	Simpson, RB	van der Merwe, PL
1967-68 in Australia										
624	Adelaide	AUS	335*	369	India	307	251	AUS by 146 runs	Simpson, RB	Borde, CG
625	Melbourne	IND	529	–	India	173*	352	AUS by an inns & 4 runs	Simpson, RB	Borde, CG
626	Brisbane2	IND	379*	294	India	279	355	AUS by 39 runs	Lawry, WM	Nawab of Pataudi jr
628	Sydney	IND	317*	292	India	268	197	AUS by 144 runs	Lawry, WM	Nawab of Pataudi jr
1968 in England										
637	Manchester	AUS	357*	220	England	165	253	AUS by 159 runs	Lawry, WM	Cowdrey, MC
638	Lord's	ENG	78*	4-127	England	7d-351	–	Drawn	Lawry, WM	Cowdrey, MC
639	Birmingham	ENG	222	1-68	England	409*	3d-142	Drawn	Lawry, WM	Cowdrey, MC
640	Leeds	AUS	315*	312	England	302	4-230	Drawn	Lawry, WM	Graveney, TR
641	The Oval	ENG	324	125	England	494*	181	ENG by 226 runs	Lawry, WM	Cowdrey, MC
1968-69 in Australia										
642	Brisbane2	WI	284	240	West Indies	296*	353	WI by 125 runs	Lawry, WM	Sobers, GA
643	Melbourne	AUS	510	–	West Indies	200*	280	AUS by an inns & 30 runs	Lawry, WM	Sobers, GA

No.	Venue						Result		
644	Sydney	WI	547	0-42	West Indies	264*	324	AUS by 10 wkts	Lawry, WM	Sobers, GA
645	Adelaide	WI	533	9-339	West Indies	276*	616	Drawn	Lawry, WM	Sobers, GA
646	Sydney	WI	619*	8d-394	West Indies	279	352	AUS by 382 runs	Lawry, WM	Sobers, GA

1969-70 in India

665	Bombay2	IND	345	2-67	India	271*	137	AUS by 8 wkts	Lawry, WM	Nawab of Pataudi jr
666	Kanpur	IND	348	0-95	India	320*	7d-312	Drawn	Lawry, WM	Nawab of Pataudi jr
667	Delhi	AUS	296*	107	India	223	3-181	IND by 7 wkts	Lawry, WM	Nawab of Pataudi jr
668	Calcutta	AUS	335	0-42	India	212*	161	AUS by 10 wkts	Lawry, WM	Nawab of Pataudi jr
669	Madras1	AUS	258*	153	India	163	171	AUS by 77 runs	Lawry, WM	Nawab of Pataudi jr

1969-70 in South Africa

670	Cape Town	SA	164	280	South Africa	382*	232	SA by 170 runs	Lawry, WM	Bacher, A
671	Durban2	SA	157	336	South Africa	9d-622*	–	SA by an inns & 129 runs	Lawry, WM	Bacher, A
672	Johannesburg3	SA	202	178	South Africa	279*	408	SA by 307 runs	Lawry, WM	Bacher, A
673	Port Elizabeth	SA	212	246	South Africa	311*	8d-470	SA by 323 runs	Lawry, WM	Bacher, A

1970-71 in Australia

| 674 | Brisbane2 | AUS | 433* | 214 | England | 464 | 1-39 | Drawn | Lawry, WM | Illingworth, R |
| 675 | Perth | AUS | 440 | 3-100 | England | 397* | 6d-287 | Drawn | Lawry, WM | Illingworth, R |

Intl test No.	Series	Toss	Australia 1st	Australia 2nd	Opponent	Opponents 1st	Opponents 2nd	Result	Captains Australia	Opponent
676	Melbourne	ENG	-*	-	England	-	-	Drawn	Lawry, WM	Illingworth, R
677	Sydney	ENG	236	116	England	332*	5d-319	ENG by 299 runs	Lawry, WM	Illingworth, R
678	Melbourne	ENG	9d-493*	4d-169	England	392	0-161	Drawn	Lawry, WM	Illingworth, R
679	Adelaide	ENG	235	3-328	England	470*	4d-233	Drawn	Lawry, WM	Illingworth, R
680	Sydney	AUS	264	160	England	184*	302	ENG by 62 runs	Chappell, IM	Illingworth, R

1972 in England

Intl test No.	Series	Toss	Australia 1st	Australia 2nd	Opponent	Opponents 1st	Opponents 2nd	Result	Captains Australia	Opponent
699	Manchester	ENG	142	252	England	249*	234	ENG by 89 runs	Chappell, IM	Illingworth, R
700	Lord's	ENG	308	2-81	England	272*	116	AUS by 8 wkts	Chappell, IM	Illingworth, R
701	Nottingham	ENG	315*	4d-324	England	189	4-290	Drawn	Chappell, IM	Illingworth, R
702	Leeds	AUS	146*	136	England	263	1-21	ENG by 9 wkts	Chappell, IM	Illingworth, R
703	The Oval	ENG	399	5-242	England	284*	356	AUS by 5 wkts	Chappell, IM	Illingworth, R

1972-73 in Australia

Intl test No.	Series	Toss	Australia 1st	Australia 2nd	Opponent	Opponents 1st	Opponents 2nd	Result	Captains Australia	Opponent
705	Adelaide	PAK	585	-	Pakistan	257*	214	AUS by an inns & 114 runs	Chappell, IM	Intikhab Alam
706	Melbourne	AUS	5d-441*	425	Pakistan	8d-574	200	AUS by 92 runs	Chappell, IM	Intikhab Alam
708	Sydney	PAK	334*	184	Pakistan	360	106	AUS by 52 runs	Chappell, IM	Intikhab Alam

1972-73 in West Indies

Intl test No.	Series	Toss	Australia 1st	Australia 2nd	Opponent	Opponents 1st	Opponents 2nd	Result	Captains Australia	Opponent
715	Kingston	AUS	7d-428*	2d-260	West Indies	428	3-67	Drawn	Chappell, IM	Kanhai, RB
717	Bridgetown	AUS	324*	2d-300	West Indies	391	0-36	Drawn	Chappell, IM	Kanhai, RB

719	Port-of-Spain	AUS	332*	281	West Indies	280	289	AUS by 44 runs	Chappell, IM	Kanhai, RB
721	Georgetown	WI	341	0-135	West Indies	366*	109	AUS by 10 wkts	Chappell, IM	Kanhai, RB
722	Port-of-Spain	AUS	8d-419*	7d-218	West Indies	319	5-135	Drawn	Chappell, IM	Kanhai, RB

1973-74 in Australia

729	Melbourne	AUS	8d-462*	–	New Zealand	237	200	AUS by an inns & 25 runs	Chappell, IM	Congdon, BE
730	Sydney	AUS	162	2-30	New Zealand	312*	9d-305	Drawn	Chappell, IM	Congdon, BE
731	Adelaide	AUS	477*	–	New Zealand	218	202	AUS by an inns & 57 runs	Chappell, IM	Congdon, BE

1973-74 in New Zealand

734	Wellington	AUS	6d-511*	8-460	New Zealand	484	–	Drawn	Chappell, IM	Congdon, BE
736	Christchurch	NZ	223*	259	New Zealand	255	5-230	NZ by 5 wkts	Chappell, IM	Congdon, BE
737	Auckland	NZ	221*	346	New Zealand	112	158	AUS by 297 runs	Chappell, IM	Congdon, BE

1974-75 in Australia

747	Brisbane2	AUS	309*	5d-288	England	265	166	AUS by 166 runs	Chappell, IM	Denness, MH
749	Perth	AUS	481	1-23	England	208*	293	AUS by 9 wkts	Chappell, IM	Denness, MH
750	Melbourne	AUS	241	8-238	England	242*	244	Drawn	Chappell, IM	Denness, MH
752	Sydney	AUS	405*	4d-289	England	295	228	AUS by 171 runs	Chappell, IM	Edrich, JH
755	Adelaide	ENG	304*	5d-272	England	172	241	AUS by 163 runs	Chappell, IM	Denness, MH
756	Melbourne	AUS	152*	373	England	529	–	ENG by an inns & 4 runs	Chappell, IM	Denness, MH

Intl test No.	Series	Toss	Australia 1st	Australia 2nd	Opponent	Opponents 1st	Opponents 2nd	Result	Captains Australia	Opponent
1975 in England										
761	Birmingham	ENG	359*	–	England	101	173	AUS by an inns & 85 runs	Chappell, IM	Denness, MH
762	Lord's	ENG	268	3-329	England	315*	7d-436	Drawn	Chappell, IM	Greig, AW
763	Leeds	ENG	135	3-220	England	288*	291	Drawn	Chappell, IM	Greig, AW
764	The Oval	AUS	9d-532*	2-40	England	191	538	Drawn	Chappell, IM	Greig, AW
1975-76 in Australia										
765	Brisbane2	WI	366	2-219	West Indies	214*	370	AUS by 8 wkts	Chappell, GS	Lloyd, CH
766	Perth	AUS	329*	169	West Indies	585	–	WI by an inns & 87 runs	Chappell, GS	Lloyd, CH
767	Melbourne	AUS	485	2-55	West Indies	224*	312	AUS by 8 wkts	Chappell, GS	Lloyd, CH
768	Sydney	AUS	405	3-82	West Indies	355*	128	AUS by 7 wkts	Chappell, GS	Lloyd, CH
769	Adelaide	AUS	418*	7d-345	West Indies	274	299	AUS by 190 runs	Chappell, GS	Lloyd, CH
771	Melbourne	AUS	351*	3d-300	West Indies	160	326	AUS by 165 runs	Chappell, GS	Lloyd, CH
1976-77 in Australia										
790	Adelaide	PAK	454	6-261	Pakistan	272*	466	Drawn	Chappell, GS	Mushtaq Mohammad
791	Melbourne	AUS	8d-517	8d-315	Pakistan	333	151	AUS by 348 runs	Chappell, GS	Mushtaq Mohammad
793	Sydney	PAK	211*	180	Pakistan	360	2-32	PAK by 8 wkts	Chappell, GS	Mushtaq Mohammad

1976-77 in New Zealand

797	Christchurch	NZ	552*	4d-154	New Zealand	357	8-293	Drawn	Chappell, GS	Turner, GM
798	Auckland	AUS	377	0-28	New Zealand	229*	175	AUS by 10 wkts	Chappell, GS	Turner, GM

1976-77 in Australia

801	Melbourne	ENG	138*	9d-419	England	95	417	AUS by 45 runs	Chappell, GS	Greig, AW

1977 in England

805	Lord's	ENG	296	6-114	England	216*	305	Drawn	Chappell, GS	Brearley, JM
806	Manchester	AUS	297*	218	England	437	1-82	ENG by 9 wkts	Chappell, GS	Brearley, JM
807	Nottingham	AUS	243*	309	England	364	3-189	ENG by 7 wkts	Chappell, GS	Brearley, JM
808	Leeds	ENG	103	248	England	436*	–	ENG by an inns & 85 runs	Chappell, GS	Brearley, JM
809	The Oval	AUS	385	–	England	214*	0-57	Drawn	Chappell, GS	Brearley, JM

1977-78 in Australia

810	Brisbane2	AUS	166*	327	India	153	324	AUS by 16 runs	Simpson, RB	Bedi, BS
812	Perth	IND	394	8-342	India	402*	9d-330	AUS by 2 wkts	Simpson, RB	Bedi, BS
813	Melbourne	IND	213	164	India	256*	343	IND by 222 runs	Simpson, RB	Bedi, BS
815	Sydney	AUS	131*	263	India	8d-396	–	IND by an inns & 2 runs	Simpson, RB	Bedi, BS
817	Adelaide	AUS	505*	256	India	269	445	AUS by 47 runs	Simpson, RB	Bedi, BS

1977-78 in West Indies

820	Port-of-Spain	WI	90*	209	West Indies	405	–	WI by an inns & 106 runs	Simpson, RB	Lloyd, CH

Intl test No.	Series	Toss	Australia 1st	2nd	Opponent	Opponents 1st	2nd	Result	Captains Australia	Opponent
822	Bridgetown	WI	250*	178	West Indies	288	1-141	WI by 9 wkts	Simpson, RB	Lloyd, CH
823	Georgetown	WI	286	7-362	West Indies	205*	439	AUS by 3 wkts	Simpson, RB	Kallicharran, AI
824	Port-of-Spain	AUS	290	94	West Indies	292*	290	WI by 198 runs	Simpson, RB	Kallicharran, AI
825	Kingston	AUS	343*	3d-304	West Indies	280	9-258	Drawn	Simpson, RB	Kallicharran, AI

1978-79 in Australia

Intl test No.	Series	Toss	Australia 1st	2nd	Opponent	Opponents 1st	2nd	Result	Captains Australia	Opponent
835	Brisbane2	AUS	116*	339	England	286	3-170	ENG by 7 wkts	Yallop, GN	Brearley, JM
837	Perth	AUS	190	161	England	309*	208	ENG by 166 runs	Yallop, GN	Brearley, JM
839	Melbourne	AUS	258*	167	England	143	179	AUS by 103 runs	Yallop, GN	Brearley, JM
841	Sydney	ENG	294	111	England	152*	346	ENG by 93 runs	Yallop, GN	Brearley, JM
843	Adelaide	AUS	164	160	England	169*	360	ENG by 205 runs	Yallop, GN	Brearley, JM
847	Sydney	AUS	198*	143	England	308	1-35	ENG by 9 wkts	Yallop, GN	Brearley, JM
850	Melbourne	AUS	168	310	Pakistan	196*	9d-353	PAK by 71 runs	Yallop, GN	Mushtaq Mohammad
851	Perth	AUS	327	3-236	Pakistan	277*	285	AUS by 7 wkts	Hughes, KJ	Mushtaq Mohammad

1979-80 in India

Intl test No.	Series	Toss	Australia 1st	2nd	Opponent	Opponents 1st	2nd	Result	Captains Australia	Opponent
856	Madras1	AUS	390*	7-212	India	425	–	Drawn	Hughes, KJ	Gavaskar, SM
857	Bangalore	AUS	333*	3-77	India	5d-457	–	Drawn	Hughes, KJ	Gavaskar, SM
858	Kanpur	IND	304	125	India	271*	311	IND by 153 runs	Hughes, KJ	Gavaskar, SM
859	Delhi	IND	298*	413	India	7d-510	–	Drawn	Hughes, KJ	Gavaskar, SM

No	Venue							Result		
860	Calcutta	AUS	442*	6d-151	India	347	4-200	Drawn	Hughes, KJ	Gavaskar, SM
861	Bombay3	IND	160*	198	India	8d-458	–	IND by an inns & 100 runs	Hughes, KJ	Gavaskar, SM

1979-80 in Australia

No	Venue							Result		
863	Brisbane2	WI	268*	6d-448	West Indies	441	3-40	Drawn	Chappell, GS	Murray, DL
865	Perth	ENG	244*	337	England	228	215	AUS by 138 runs	Chappell, GS	Brearley, JM
868	Melbourne	AUS	156*	259	West Indies	397	0-22	WI by 10 wkts	Chappell, GS	Lloyd, CH
869	Sydney	AUS	145	4-219	England	123*	237	AUS by 6 wkts	Chappell, GS	Brearley, JM
871	Adelaide	AUS	203	165	West Indies	328*	448	WI by 408 runs	Chappell, GS	Lloyd, CH
873	Melbourne	ENG	477	2-103	England	306*	273	AUS by 8 wkts	Chappell, GS	Brearley, JM

1979-80 in Pakistan

No	Venue							Result		
877	Karachi	AUS	225*	140	Pakistan	292	3-76	PAK by 7 wkts	Chappell, GS	Javed Miandad
879	Faisalabad	AUS	617*	–	Pakistan	2-382	–	Drawn	Chappell, GS	Javed Miandad
880	Lahore2	AUS	7d-407*	8-391	Pakistan	9d-420	–	Drawn	Chappell, GS	Javed Miandad

1980 in England

No	Venue							Result		
886	Lord's	AUS	5d-385*	4d-189	England	205	3-244	Drawn	Chappell, GS	Botham, IT

1980-81 in Australia

No	Venue							Result		
888	Brisbane2	AUS	305	0-63	New Zealand	225*	142	AUS by 10 wkts	Chappell, GS	Howarth, GP
890	Perth	AUS	265	2-55	New Zealand	196*	121	AUS by 8 wkts	Chappell, GS	Howarth, GP
892	Melbourne	NZ	321*	188	New Zealand	317	6-128	Drawn	Chappell, GS	Howarth, GP

Intl test No.	Series	Toss	Australia 1st	2nd	Opponent	Opponents 1st	2nd	Result	Captains Australia	Opponent
894	Sydney	IND	406	–	India	201*	201	AUS by an inns & 4 runs	Chappell, GS	Gavaskar, SM
895	Adelaide	IND	528*	7d-221	India	419	8-135	Drawn	Chappell, GS	Gavaskar, SM
896	Melbourne	AUS	419	83	India	237*	324	IND by 59 runs	Chappell, GS	Gavaskar, SM

1981 in England

Intl test No.	Series	Toss	Australia 1st	2nd	Opponent	Opponents 1st	2nd	Result	Captains Australia	Opponent
904	Nottingham	AUS	179	6-132	England	185*	125	AUS by 4 wkts	Hughes, KJ	Botham, IT
905	Lord's	AUS	345	4-90	England	311*	8d-265	Drawn	Hughes, KJ	Botham, IT
906	Leeds	AUS	9d-401*	111	England	174	356	ENG by 18 runs	Hughes, KJ	Brearley, JM
907	Birmingham	ENG	258	121	England	189*	219	ENG by 29 runs	Hughes, KJ	Brearley, JM
908	Manchester	ENG	130	402	England	231*	404	ENG by 103 runs	Hughes, KJ	Brearley, JM
909	The Oval	ENG	352*	9d-344	England	314	7-261	Drawn	Hughes, KJ	Brearley, JM

1981-82 in Australia

Intl test No.	Series	Toss	Australia 1st	2nd	Opponent	Opponents 1st	2nd	Result	Captains Australia	Opponent
910	Perth	PAK	180*	8d-424	Pakistan	62	256	AUS by 286 runs	Chappell, GS	Javed Miandad
911	Brisbane2	AUS	9d-512	0-3	Pakistan	291*	223	AUS by 10 wkts	Chappell, GS	Javed Miandad
914	Melbourne	PAK	293	125	Pakistan	8d-500*	–	PAK by an inns & 82 runs	Chappell, GS	Javed Miandad
916	Melbourne	AUS	198*	222	West Indies	201	161	AUS by 58 runs	Chappell, GS	Lloyd, CH
918	Sydney	WI	267	4-200	West Indies	384*	255	Drawn	Chappell, GS	Lloyd, CH
920	Adelaide	WI	238*	386	West Indies	389	5-239	WI by 5 wkts	Chappell, GS	Lloyd, CH

1981-82 in New Zealand

No.	Venue	Team			Opponent			Result	Captain	Captain
923	Wellington	AUS	1-85	–	New Zealand	7d-266*	–	Drawn	Chappell, GS	Howarth, GP
925	Auckland	NZ	210*	280	New Zealand	387	5-109	NZ by 5 wkts	Chappell, GS	Howarth, GP
927	Christchurch	NZ	353*	2-69	New Zealand	149	272	AUS by 8 wkts	Chappell, GS	Howarth, GP

1982-83 in Pakistan

No.	Venue	Team			Opponent			Result	Captain	Captain
936	Karachi	AUS	284*	179	Pakistan	419	1-47	PAK by 9 wkts	Hughes, KJ	Imran Khan
937	Faisalabad	PAK	168	330	Pakistan	6d-501*	–	PAK by an inns & 3 runs	Hughes, KJ	Imran Khan
938	Lahore2	PAK	316*	214	Pakistan	7d-467	1-64	PAK by 9 wkts	Hughes, KJ	Imran Khan

1982-83 in England

No.	Venue	Team			Opponent			Result	Captain	Captain
939	Perth	AUS	9d-424	2-73	England	411*	358	Drawn	Chappell, GS	Willis, RGD
940	Brisbane2	AUS	341	4-190	England	219*	309	AUS by 7 wkts	Chappell, GS	Willis, RGD
941	Adelaide	ENG	438*	2-83	England	216	304	AUS by 8 wkts	Chappell, GS	Willis, RGD
944	Melbourne	AUS	287	288	England	284*	294	ENG by 3 runs	Chappell, GS	Willis, RGD
945	Sydney	AUS	314*	382	England	237	7-314	Drawn	Chappell, GS	Willis, RGD

1982-83 in Sri Lanka

No.	Venue	Team			Opponent			Result	Captain	Captain
957	Kandy	AUS	4d-514*	–	Sri Lanka	271	205	AUS by an inns & 38 runs	Chappell, GS	Mendis, LRD

1983-84 in Australia

No.	Venue	Team			Opponent			Result	Captain	Captain
967	Perth	PAK	9d-436*	–	Pakistan	129	298	AUS by an inns & 9 runs	Hughes, KJ	Zaheer Abbas

Intl test No.	Series	Toss	Australia 1st	Australia 2nd	Opponent	Opponents 1st	Opponents 2nd	Result	Captains Australia	Opponent
970	Brisbane2	PAK	7d-509	–	Pakistan	156*	3-82	Drawn	Hughes, KJ	Zaheer Abbas
971	Adelaide	AUS	465*	7-310	Pakistan	624	–	Drawn	Hughes, KJ	Zaheer Abbas
974	Melbourne	PAK	555	–	Pakistan	470*	7-238	Drawn	Hughes, KJ	Imran Khan
975	Sydney	AUS	6d-454	0-35	Pakistan	278*	210	AUS by 10 wkts	Hughes, KJ	Imran Khan
1983-84 in West Indies										
980	Georgetown	AUS	279*	9d-273	West Indies	230	0-250	Drawn	Hughes, KJ	Lloyd, CH
984	Port-of-Spain	WI	255*	9-299	West Indies	8d-468	–	Drawn	Hughes, KJ	Richards, IVA
987	Bridgetown	WI	429*	97	West Indies	509	0-21	WI by 10 wkts	Hughes, KJ	Lloyd, CH
988	St. John's	AUS	262*	200	West Indies	498	–	WI by an inns & 36 runs	Hughes, KJ	Lloyd, CH
989	Kingston	WI	199*	160	West Indies	305	0-55	WI by 10 wkts	Hughes, KJ	Lloyd, CH
1984-85 in Australia										
998	Perth	AUS	76	228	West Indies	416*	–	WI by an inns & 112 runs	Hughes, KJ	Lloyd, CH
1000	Brisbane2	WI	175*	271	West Indies	424	2-26	WI by 8 wkts	Hughes, KJ	Lloyd, CH
1003	Adelaide	WI	284	173	West Indies	356*	7d-292	WI by 191 runs	Border, AR	Lloyd, CH
1006	Melbourne	AUS	296	8-198	West Indies	479*	5d-186	Drawn	Border, AR	Lloyd, CH
1007	Sydney	AUS	9d-471*	–	West Indies	163	253	AUS by an inns & 55 runs	Border, AR	Lloyd, CH

1985 in England

No.	Venue	Team			Opponent			Result	Captain	Captain
1018	Leeds	AUS	331*	324	England	533	5-123	ENG by 5 wkts	Border, AR	Gower, DI
1019	Lord's	AUS	425	6-127	England	290*	261	AUS by 4 wkts	Border, AR	Gower, DI
1020	Nottingham	ENG	539	–	England	456*	2-196	Drawn	Border, AR	Gower, DI
1021	Manchester	ENG	257*	5-340	England	9d-482	–	Drawn	Border, AR	Gower, DI
1022	Birmingham	ENG	335*	142	England	5d-595	–	ENG by an inns & 118 runs	Border, AR	Gower, DI
1023	The Oval	ENG	241	129	England	464*	–	ENG by an inns & 94 runs	Border, AR	Gower, DI

1985-86 in Australia

No.	Venue	Team			Opponent			Result	Captain	Captain
1030	Brisbane2	NZ	179*	333	New Zealand	7d-553	–	NZ by an inns & 41 runs	Border, AR	Coney, JV
1031	Sydney	AUS	227	6-260	New Zealand	293*	193	AUS by 4 wkts	Border, AR	Coney, JV
1032	Perth	NZ	203*	259	New Zealand	299	4-164	NZ by 6 wkts	Border, AR	Coney, JV
1033	Adelaide	AUS	381*	0-17	India	520	–	Drawn	Border, AR	Kapil Dev
1034	Melbourne	IND	262*	308	India	445	2-59	Drawn	Border, AR	Kapil Dev
1035	Sydney	IND	396	6-119	India	4d-600*	–	Drawn	Border, AR	Kapil Dev

1985-86 in New Zealand

No.	Venue	Team			Opponent			Result	Captain	Captain
1036	Wellington	NZ	435*	–	New Zealand	6-379	–	Drawn	Border, AR	Coney, JV
1039	Christchurch	NZ	364*	7d-219	New Zealand	339	1-16	Drawn	Border, AR	Coney, JV
1041	Auckland	AUS	314*	103	New Zealand	258	2-160	NZ by 8 wkts	Border, AR	Coney, JV

1986-87 in India

No.	Venue	Team			Opponent			Result	Captain	Captain
1053	Madras1	AUS	7d-574*	5d-170	India	397	347	Tied	Border, AR	Kapil Dev

Intl test No.	Series	Toss	Australia 1st	Australia 2nd	Opponent	Opponents 1st	Opponents 2nd	Result	Captains Australia	Captains Opponent
1054	Delhi	AUS	3d-207*	–	India	3-107	–	Drawn	Border, AR	Kapil Dev
1055	Bombay3	AUS	345*	2-216	India	5d-517	–	Drawn	Border, AR	Kapil Dev
1986-87 in Australia										
1058	Brisbane2	AUS	248	282	England	456*	3-77	ENG by 7 wkts	Border, AR	Gatting, MW
1060	Perth	ENG	401	4-197	England	8d-592*	8d-199	Drawn	Border, AR	Gatting, MW
1061	Adelaide	AUS	5d-514*	3d-201	England	455	2-39	Drawn	Border, AR	Gatting, MW
1063	Melbourne	ENG	141*	194	England	349	–	ENG by an inns & 14 runs	Border, AR	Gatting, MW
1066	Sydney	AUS	343*	251	England	275	264	AUS by 55 runs	Border, AR	Gatting, MW

* Denotes team batting first

RESULTS OF ALL SERIES

Years	Opponent	Venue	Tests	Aust. Won	Aust. Lost	Aust. Drew	Aust. Tied	Series result	
1876-77	England	Australia	2	1	1	–	–	Drawn	1-1
1878-79	England	Australia	1	1	–	–	–	Won	1-0
1880	England	England	1	–	1	–	–	Lost	1-0
1881-82	England	Australia	4	2	–	2	–	Won	2-0
1882	England	England	1	1	–	–	–	Won	1-0
1882-83	England	Australia	4	2	2	–	–	Drawn	2-2
1884	England	England	3	–	1	2	–	Lost	1-0
1884-85	England	Australia	5	2	3	–	–	Lost	3-2
1886	England	England	3	–	3	–	–	Lost	3-0
1886-87	England	Australia	2	–	2	–	–	Lost	2-0
1887-88	England	Australia	1	–	1	–	–	Lost	1-0
1888	England	England	3	1	2	–	–	Lost	2-1
1890	England	England	2	–	2	–	–	Lost	2-0
1891-92	England	Australia	3	2	1	–	–	Won	2-1
1893	England	England	3	–	1	2	–	Lost	1-0
1894-95	England	Australia	5	2	3	–	–	Lost	3-2
1896	England	England	3	1	2	–	–	Lost	2-1
1897-98	England	Australia	5	4	1	–	–	Won	4-1
1899	England	England	5	1	–	4	–	Won	1-0
1901-02	England	Australia	5	4	1	–	–	Won	4-1
1902	England	England	5	3	1	1	–	Won	3-1
1902	South Africa	South Africa	3	2	–	1	–	Won	2-0
1903-04	England	Australia	5	2	3	–	–	Lost	3-2
1905	England	England	5	–	2	3	–	Lost	2-0
1907-08	England	Australia	5	4	1	–	–	Won	4-1
1909	England	England	5	2	1	2	–	Won	2-1
1910-11	South Africa	Australia	5	4	1	–	–	Won	4-1
1911-12	England	Australia	5	1	4	–	–	Lost	4-1
1912	South Africa	England	3	2	–	1	–	Won	2-0
1912	England	England	3	–	1	2	–	Lost	1-0
1920-21	England	Australia	5	5	–	–	–	Won	5-0
1921	England	England	5	3	–	2	–	Won	3-0
1921-22	South Africa	South Africa	3	1	–	2	–	Won	1-0
1924-25	England	Australia	5	4	1	–	–	Won	4-1
1926	England	England	5	–	1	4	–	Lost	1-0
1928-29	England	Australia	5	1	4	–	–	Lost	4-1

Years	Opponent	Venue	Tests	Aust. Won	Aust. Lost	Aust. Drew	Aust. Tied	Series result	
1930	England	England	5	2	1	2	–	Won	2-1
1930-31	West Indies	Australia	5	4	1	–	–	Won	4-1
1931-32	South Africa	Australia	5	5	–	–	–	Won	5-0
1932-33	England	Australia	5	1	4	–	–	Lost	4-1
1934	England	England	5	2	1	2	–	Won	2-1
1935-36	South Africa	South Africa	5	4	–	1	–	Won	4-0
1936-37	England	Australia	5	3	2	–	–	Won	3-2
1938	England	England	5	1	1	2	–	Drawn	1-1
1945-46	New Zealand	New Zealand	1	1	–	–	–	Won	1-0
1946-47	England	Australia	5	3	–	2	–	Won	3-0
1947-48	India	Australia	5	4	–	1	–	Won	4-0
1948	England	England	5	4	–	1	–	Won	4-0
1949-50	South Africa	South Africa	5	4	–	1	–	Won	4-0
1950-51	England	Australia	5	4	1	–	–	Won	4-1
1951-52	West Indies	Australia	5	4	1	–	–	Won	4-1
1952-53	South Africa	Australia	5	2	2	1	–	Drawn	2-2
1953	England	England	5	–	1	4	–	Lost	1-0
1954-55	England	Australia	5	1	3	1	–	Lost	3-1
1954-55	West Indies	West Indies	5	3	–	2	–	Won	3-0
1956	England	England	5	1	2	2	–	Lost	2-1
1956-57	Pakistan	Pakistan	1	–	1	–	–	Lost	1-0
1956-57	India	India	3	2	–	1	–	Won	2-0
1957-58	South Africa	South Africa	5	3	–	2	–	Won	3-0
1958-59	England	Australia	5	4	–	1	–	Won	4-0
1959-60	Pakistan	Pakistan	3	2	–	1	–	Won	2-0
1959-60	India	India	5	2	1	2	–	Won	2-1
1960-61	West Indies	Australia	5	2	1	1	1	Won	2-1
1961	England	England	5	2	1	2	–	Won	2-1
1962-63	England	Australia	5	1	1	3	–	Drawn	1-1
1963-64	South Africa	Australia	5	1	1	3	–	Drawn	1-1
1964	England	England	5	1	–	4	–	Won	1-0
1964-65	India	India	3	1	1	1	–	Drawn	1-1
1964-65	Pakistan	Pakistan	1	–	–	1	–	Drawn	0-0
1964-65	Pakistan	Pakistan	1	–	–	1	–	Drawn	0-0
1964-65	West Indies	West Indies	5	1	2	2	–	Lost	2-1
1965-66	England	Australia	5	1	1	3	–	Drawn	1-1
1966-67	South Africa	South Africa	5	1	3	1	–	Lost	3-1
1967-68	India	Australia	4	4	–	–	–	Won	4-0

Years	Opponent	Venue	Tests	Aust. Won	Aust. Lost	Aust. Drew	Aust. Tied	Series result	
1968	England	England	5	1	1	3	–	Drawn	1-1
1968-69	West Indies	Australia	5	3	1	1	–	Won	3-1
1969-70	India	India	5	3	1	1	–	Won	3-1
1969-70	South Africa	South Africa	4	–	4	–	–	Lost	4-0
1970-71	England	Australia	7	–	2	5	–	Lost	2-0
1972	England	England	5	2	2	1	–	Drawn	2-2
1972-73	Pakistan	Australia	2	2	–	–	–	Won	2-0
1972-73	West Indies	West Indies	5	2	–	3	–	Won	2-0
1973-74	New Zealand	Australia	3	2	–	1	–	Won	2-0
1973-74	New Zealand	New Zealand	3	1	1	1	–	Drawn	1-1
1974-75	England	Australia	6	4	1	1	–	Won	4-1
1975	England	England	4	1	–	3	–	Won	1-0
1975-76	West Indies	Australia	6	5	1	–	–	Won	5-1
1976-77	Pakistan	Australia	3	1	1	1	–	Drawn	1-1
1976-77	New Zealand	New Zealand	2	1	–	1	–	Won	1-0
1976-77	England	Australia	1	1	–	–	–	Won	1-0
1977	England	England	5	–	3	2	–	Lost	3-0
1977-78	India	Australia	5	3	2	–	–	Won	3-2
1977-78	West Indies	West Indies	5	1	3	1	–	Lost	3-1
1978-79	England	Australia	6	1	5	–	–	Lost	5-1
1978-79	Pakistan	Australia	2	1	1	–	–	Drawn	1-1
1979-80	India	India	6	–	2	4	–	Lost	2-0
1979-80	West Indies	Australia	3	–	2	1	–	Lost	2-0
1979-80	England	Australia	3	3	–	–	–	Won	3-0
1979-80	Pakistan	Pakistan	3	–	1	2	–	Lost	1-0
1980	England	England	1	–	–	1	–	Drawn	0-0
1980-81	New Zealand	Australia	3	2	–	1	–	Won	2-0
1980-81	India	Australia	3	1	1	1	–	Drawn	1-1
1981	England	England	6	1	3	2	–	Lost	3-1
1981-82	Pakistan	Australia	3	2	1	–	–	Won	2-1
1981-82	West Indies	Australia	3	1	1	1	–	Drawn	1-1
1981-82	New Zealand	New Zealand	3	1	1	1	–	Drawn	1-1
1982-83	Pakistan	Pakistan	3	–	3	–	–	Lost	3-0
1982-83	England	Australia	5	2	1	2	–	Won	2-1
1982-83	Sri Lanka	Sri Lanka	1	1	–	–	–	Won	1-0
1983-84	Pakistan	Australia	5	2	–	3	–	Won	2-0
1983-84	West Indies	West Indies	5	–	3	2	–	Lost	3-0
1984-85	West Indies	Australia	5	1	3	1	–	Lost	3-1

Years	Opponent	Venue	Tests	Aust. Won	Aust. Lost	Aust. Drew	Aust. Tied	Series result	
1985	England	England	6	1	3	2	–	Lost	3-1
1985-86	New Zealand	Australia	3	1	2	–	–	Lost	2-1
1985-86	India	Australia	3	–	–	3	–	Drawn	0-0
1985-86	New Zealand	New Zealand	3	–	1	2	–	Lost	1-0
1986-87	India	India	3	–	–	2	1	Lost	2-0
1986-87	England	Australia	5	1	2	2	–	Lost	2-1
Total			**473**	**194**	**139**	**138**	**2**		

SERIES SUMMARY

Venue	Series	Aust. Won	Aust. Lost	Aust. Drawn
Australia	57	31	15	11
England	31	12	15	4
India	6	3	2	1
New Zealand	5	2	1	2
Pakistan	6	1	3	2
South Africa	7	5	2	–
Sri Lanka	1	1	–	–
West Indies	5	2	3	–
Total	**118**	**57**	**41**	**20**

Opponent	Series	Aust. Won	Aust. Lost	Aust. Drew
England	62	27	27	8
India	11	6	2	3
New Zealand	8	4	2	2
Pakistan	11	4	3	4
South Africa	12	8	2	2
Sri Lanka	1	1	–	–
West Indies	13	7	5	1
Total	**118**	**57**	**41**	**20**

SUMMARY OF TEST MATCHES
ON ALL GROUNDS

Venue	Date of 1st Test	Tests	Won	Lost	Drawn	Tie
In Australia:						
Adelaide	12 Dec 1884	45	21	13	11	–
Brisbane1	30 Nov 1928	2	1	1	–	–
Brisbane2	10 Feb 1933	29	15	7	6	1
Melbourne	15 Mar 1877	80	42	25	13	–
Perth	11 Dec 1970	14	7	4	3	–
Sydney	17 Feb 1882	73	39	24	10	–
Total		**243**	**125**	**74**	**43**	**1**
In England:						
Birmingham	29 May 1902	7	1	3	3	–
Leeds	29 Jun 1899	19	5	6	8	–
Lord's	21 Jly 1884	29	11	5	13	–
Manchester	10 Jly 1884	25	5	7	13	–
Nottingham	1 Jun 1899	16	4	3	9	–
Sheffield	3 Jly 1902	1	1	–	–	–
The Oval	6 Sep 1880	29	5	13	11	–
Total		**126**	**32**	**37**	**57**	**—**
In India:						
Bangalore	19 Sep 1979	1	–	–	1	–
Bombay2	26 Sep 1956	4	1	1	2	–
Bombay3	3 Nov 1979	2	–	1	1	–
Calcutta	2 Nov 1956	5	2	–	3	–
Delhi	12 Dec 1959	4	1	1	2	–
Kanpur	19 Dec 1959	3	–	2	1	–
Madras1	24 Dec 1969	3	1	–	1	1
Madras2	19 Oct 1956	3	3	–	–	–
Total		**25**	**8**	**5**	**11**	**1**
In New Zealand:						
Auckland	22 Mar 1974	4	2	2	–	–
Christchurch	8 Mar 1974	4	1	1	2	–
Wellington	29 Mar 1946	4	1	–	3	–
Total		**12**	**4**	**3**	**5**	**—**

Venue	Date of 1st Test	Tests	Won	Lost	Drawn	Tie
In Pakistan:						
Dacca	13 Nov 1959	1	1	–	–	–
Faisalabad	6 Mar 1979	2	–	1	1	–
Karachi	11 Oct 1956	5	–	3	2	–
Lahore2	21 Nov 1959	3	1	1	1	–
Total		**11**	**2**	**5**	**4**	**—**
In South Africa:						
Cape Town	8 Nov 1902	7	6	1	–	–
Durban1	5 Nov 1921	1	–	–	1	–
Durban2	14 Dec 1935	6	3	2	1	–
Johannesburg1	11 Oct 1902	5	2	–	3	–
Johannesburg2	24 Dec 1949	2	1	–	1	–
Johannesburg3	23 Dec 1957	5	1	2	2	–
Port Elizabeth	3 Mar 1950	4	2	2	–	–
Total		**30**	**15**	**7**	**8**	**—**
In Sri Lanka:						
Kandy	22 Apr 1983	1	1	–	–	–
Total		**1**	**1**	**—**	**—**	**—**
In West Indies:						
Bridgetown	14 May 1955	5	–	2	3	–
Georgetown	26 Apr 1955	5	3	1	1	–
Kingston	26 Mar 1955	6	2	2	2	–
Port-of-Spain	11 Apr 1955	8	2	2	4	–
St. John's	7 Apr 1984	1	–	1	–	–
Total		**25**	**7**	**8**	**10**	**—**
Total in Australia		243	125	74	43	1
Total abroad		230	69	65	95	1
Grand total		**473**	**194**	**139**	**138**	**2**

RUNS SCORED ON EACH TEST GROUND

Venue	Tests	Australia Batting			Australia Bowling		
		Runs	Wkts	Avrge	Runs	Wkts	Avrge
In Australia:							
Adelaide	45	27814	730	38.10	26782	791	33.86
Brisbane1	2	746	27	27.63	1204	38	31.68
Brisbane2	29	15123	434	34.85	13406	493	27.19
Melbourne	80	40885	1309	31.23	38240	1373	27.85
Perth	14	6994	219	31.94	7525	245	30.71
Sydney	73	35389	1192	29.69	34701	1278	27.15
Total	**243**	**126951**	**3911**	**32.46**	**121858**	**4218**	**28.89**
In England:							
Birmingham	7	2328	101	23.05	3026	91	33.25
Leeds	19	9080	311	29.20	8877	292	30.40
Lord's	29	12377	408	30.34	12819	442	29.00
Manchester	25	10083	385	26.19	10458	335	31.22
Nottingham	16	6832	226	30.23	6907	227	30.43
Sheffield	1	483	20	24.15	340	20	17.00
The Oval	29	12688	470	27.00	14371	443	32.44
Total	**126**	**53871**	**1921**	**28.04**	**56798**	**1850**	**30.70**
In India:							
Bangalore	1	410	13	31.54	457	5	91.40
Bombay2	4	1950	46	42.39	2021	68	29.72
Bombay3	2	919	31	29.65	975	13	75.00
Calcutta	5	2105	68	30.96	1960	84	23.33
Delhi	4	1789	53	33.75	1362	43	31.67
Kanpur	3	1196	49	24.41	1657	57	29.07
Madras1	3	1757	49	35.86	1503	49	30.67
Madras2	3	1269	40	31.73	1070	60	17.83
Total	**25**	**11395**	**349**	**32.65**	**11005**	**379**	**29.04**
In New Zealand:							
Auckland	4	1879	70	26.84	1588	67	23.70
Christchurch	4	2193	63	34.81	1911	64	29.86
Wellington	4	1690	33	51.21	1225	43	28.49
Total	**12**	**5762**	**166**	**34.71**	**4724**	**174**	**27.15**

Venue	Tests	Australia Batting			Australia Bowling		
		Runs	Wkts	Avrge	Runs	Wkts	Avrge
In Pakistan:							
Dacca	1	337	12	28.08	334	20	16.70
Faisalabad	2	1115	30	37.17	883	8	110.38
Karachi	5	2014	84	23.98	2276	70	32.51
Lahore2	3	1842	47	39.19	1463	37	39.54
Total	**11**	**5308**	**173**	**30.68**	**4956**	**135**	**36.71**
In South Africa:							
Cape Town	7	3298	81	40.72	3243	140	23.16
Durban1	1	623	17	36.65	416	17	24.47
Durban2	6	2826	93	30.39	2880	91	31.65
Johannesburg1	5	2572	69	37.28	2498	92	27.15
Johannesburg2	2	1137	20	56.85	680	30	22.67
Johannesburg3	5	2189	81	27.02	2910	88	33.07
Port Elizabeth	4	1817	59	30.80	1884	71	26.54
Total	**30**	**14462**	**420**	**34.43**	**14511**	**529**	**27.43**
In Sri Lanka:							
Kandy	1	514	4	128.50	476	20	23.80
Total	**1**	**514**	**4**	**128.50**	**476**	**20**	**23.80**
In West Indies:							
Bridgetown	5	3320	82	40.49	2945	61	48.28
Georgetown	5	2389	77	31.03	2523	90	28.03
Kingston	6	3421	79	43.30	3215	102	31.52
Port-of-Spain	8	3960	122	32.46	4303	125	34.42
St. John's	1	462	20	23.10	498	10	49.80
Total	**25**	**13552**	**380**	**31.65**	**13484**	**388**	**34.75**
Total in Australia	243	126951	3911	32.46	121858	4218	28.89
Total abroad	230	104864	3413	30.72	105954	3475	30.49
Grand total	**473**	**231815**	**7324**	**31.65**	**227812**	**7693**	**29.61**

THE FIRST TIED TEST

The 1960-61 series between Australia and the West Indies began with cricket administration in disarray. Three summers of controversy over bowlers who chucked had failed to produce a definition of a throw. A conference in London of all the cricket nations made a brave, but inadequate, attempt, and the public felt officials were succumbing to an hysteria whipped up by Fleet Street over bowlers like Ian Meckiff and Gordon Rorke. A series in which both sides concentrated on the game's virtues and forgot the bickering was needed urgently, and that is what the Tests between Frank Worrell's West Indians and Richie Benaud's Australians produced.

The 498th game of Test cricket at the Woolloongabba Ground in Brisbane, from 9 to 14 December, produced the first tie, a result in which justice was done after exhilarating performances from both sides. There were records galore and the two sides matched each other with cricket skills of the highest level.

The West Indians batted first, and when Alan Davidson had their first three batsmen out for 65 they looked to be in dire trouble. Then Garfield St Auburn Sobers played an innings of majestic quality, and in partnership with his captain, Worrell, (65) took the West Indies to 239 before the fourth wicket fell. Sobers' 132 in his first Test in Australia was studded with magnificent drives and legside sweeps and pulls that gave fieldsmen little hope of preventing fours. Joe Solomon (65), Gerry Alexander (60) and Wes Hall (50) carried on Sobers' work to take the West Indies to 453.

Australia responded with a fine opening stand of 84 by Colin McDonald and Bob Simpson, who took his score to 92 before he was bowled by Sonny Ramadhin. Norman O'Neill then showed why he had been hailed as "another Bradman" in a vigorous knock of 181, which took Australia to 505 and a first innings lead of 48.

Here, Davidson, who had matured into a superfine opening bowler, gave Australia what appeared to be a match-winning advantage by taking 6 for 87 to have a match analysis of 11 for 222, moving the ball either way off the pitch and through the air. Worrell topscored with another 65 in the West Indies' total of 284, and Rohan Kanhai played some glorious strokes for 54.

Set to score 233 in 310 minutes, Australia lost 2 for 7, and at 6 for 92 looked in danger of defeat. Davidson then took the West Indian spin bowlers Ramadhin and Alf Valentine apart in a thrilling innings of 80, to become the first player to take more than ten wickets and score more than 100 runs in a Test. He had made 44 in the first innings.

With four wickets left, Australia needed seven runs, but these four wickets all fell for only six runs, the score slumping from 7 for 226 to all out for 232. The result looked so clearly to end in Australia's favour that some prominent commentators left the Press box and were on their way home to southern States when play ended.

The Australians began the last over needing six runs to win from eight deliveries. They got a single from the first ball and Benaud was caught off Wes Hall for 52 from the second. Needing five runs to win with two wickets in hand, Australia failed to score from the third ball but got a bye off the fourth. A single came from the fifth ball when Wally Grout was dropped. Three to win with three deliveries left.

Meckiff hit Hall's sixth ball for 2 but Grout was run out attempting a third run. Last man Lindsay Kline went to the crease with Australia requiring a run to win with two balls left. Kline played the seventh ball away to square leg but as he and Meckiff set off for a run, Joe Solomon scooped up the ball and with only one stump t aim at threw down the stumps at Ian Meckiff's end. In the Australian dressing-room a bewildered "Slasher" Mackay asked team-mates: "Who won?"

This remained the only tie in Test history until 1986 when Australia and India tied at Madras after Australia had declared in both innings and Dean Jones scored a memorable double century. Hall's 6 for 63 in Australia's second innings at Brisbane gave him 10 for 203 for the match and set up what proved a magnificent series which saw the teams go into the Fifth Test all square. Never again would some of the distinguished commentators who missed the first tie ever leave a Test until the last ball was bowled.

THE INNINGS

HIGHEST INNINGS TOTAL FOR EACH TEST GROUND

Venue	Runs	Opponent	Series
In Australia:			
Adelaide	674	India	1947-48
Brisbane1	558	West Indies	1930-31
Brisbane2	645	England	1946-47
Melbourne	604	England	1936-37
Perth	481	England	1974-75
Sydney	8d-659	England	1946-47
In England:			
Birmingham	9d-516	England	1961
Leeds	584	England	1934
Lord's	6d-729	England	1930
Manchester	8d-656	England	1964
Nottingham	539	England	1985
Sheffield	289	England	1902
The Oval	701	England	1934
In India:			
Bangalore	333	India	1979-80
Bombay2	7d-523	India	1956-57
Bombay3	345	India	1986-87
Calcutta	442	India	1979-80
Delhi	468	India	1959-60
Kanpur	348	India	1969-70

Venue	Runs	Opponent	Series
Madras1	7d-574	India	1986-87
Madras2	397	India	1964-65

In New Zealand:

Auckland	377	New Zealand	1976-77
Christchurch	552	New Zealand	1976-77
Wellington	6d-511	New Zealand	1973-74

In Pakistan:

Dacca	225	Pakistan	1959-60
Faisalabad	617	Pakistan	1979-80
Karachi	352	Pakistan	1964-65
Lahore2	7d-407	Pakistan	1979-80

In South Africa:

Cape Town	542	South Africa	1966-67
Durban1	7d-324	South Africa	1921-22
Durban2	455	South Africa	1935-36
Johannesburg1	450	South Africa	1921-22
Johannesburg2	8d-465	South Africa	1949-50
Johannesburg3	401	South Africa	1957-58
Port Elizabeth	7d-549	South Africa	1949-50

In Sri Lanka:

Kandy	4d-514	Sri Lanka	1982-83

In West Indies:

Bridgetown	668	West Indies	1954-55
Georgetown	7-362	West Indies	1977-78
Kingston	8d-758	West Indies	1954-55
Port-of-Spain	9d-600	West Indies	1954-55
St. John's	262	West Indies	1983-84

INNINGS OF 500 OR MORE

Score	Opponent	Venue	Series
8d-758	West Indies	Kingston	1954-55
6d-729	England	Lord's	1930
701	England	The Oval	1934
695	England	The Oval	1930
674	India	Adelaide	1947-48
668	West Indies	Bridgetown	1954-55
8d-659	England	Sydney	1946-47
8d-656	England	Manchester	1964
6d-650	West Indies	Bridgetown	1964-65
645	England	Brisbane	1946-47
619	West Indies	Sydney	1968-69
617	Pakistan	Faisalabad	1979-80
604	England	Melbourne	1936-37
8d-601	England	Brisbane2	1954-55
600	England	Melbourne	1924-25
9d-600	West Indies	Port-of-Spain	1954-55
586	England	Sydney	1894-95
585	Pakistan	Adelaide	1972-73
584	England	Leeds	1934
582	England	Adelaide	1920-21
581	England	Sydney	1920-21
578	South Africa	Melbourne	1910-11
8d-575	India	Melbourne	1947-48
7d-574	India	Madras1	1986-87
573	England	Adelaide	1897-98
566	England	Leeds	1930
564	England	Melbourne	1936-37
558	West Indies	Brisbane1	1930-31
555	Pakistan	Melbourne	1983-84
554	South Africa	Melbourne	1931-32
552	New Zealand	Christchurch	1976-77
551	England	The Oval	1884
7d-549	South Africa	Port Elizabeth	1949-50
547	West Indies	Sydney	1968-69
8d-543	England	Melbourne	1965-66
542	South Africa	Cape Town	1966-67

Score	Opponent	Venue	Series
539	England	Nottingham	1985
536	England	Melbourne	1946-47
533	West Indies	Adelaide	1968-69
9d-532	England	The Oval	1975
530	South Africa	Adelaide	1952-53
529	India	Melbourne	1967-68
528	South Africa	Sydney	1910-11
528	India	Adelaide	1980-81
7d-526	South Africa	Cape Town	1949-50
7d-523	India	Bombay2	1956-57
520	England	Melbourne	1897-98
520	South Africa	Melbourne	1952-53
517	West Indies	Sydney	1951-52
8d-517	Pakistan	Melbourne	1976-77
516	West Indies	Port-of-Spain	1964-65
516	England	Adelaide	1965-66
9d-515	West Indies	Kingston	1954-55
4d-514	Sri Lanka	Kandy	1982-83
5d-514	England	Adelaide	1986-87
513	South Africa	Adelaide	1931-32
9d-512	Pakistan	Brisbane2	1981-82
6d-511	New Zealand	Wellington	1973-74
510	West Indies	Melbourne	1968-69
509	England	Nottingham	1948
7d-509	Pakistan	Brisbane2	1983-84
506	England	Adelaide	1907-08
505	West Indies	Brisbane2	1960-61
505	India	Adelaide	1977-78

HIGHEST SECOND INNINGS TOTALS

Score	Opponent	Venue	Series
582	England	Adelaide	1920-21
581	England	Sydney	1920-21
578	South Africa	Melbourne	1910-11
564	England	Melbourne	1936-37
554	South Africa	Melbourne	1931-32

Score	Opponent	Venue	Series
536	England	Melbourne	1946-47
506	England	Adelaide	1907-08
485	England	Sydney	1903-04
476	England	Adelaide	1911-12
7d-460	England	Lord's	1948
8d-460	New Zealand	Wellington	1973-74
452	England	Sydney	1924-25
9d-450	South Africa	Sydney	1963-64
6d-448	West Indies	Brisbane2	1979-80
433	England	Adelaide	1936-37
432	England	Manchester	1961
6d-427	England	Nottingham	1938
426	England	Melbourne	1965-66
425	Pakistan	Melbourne	1972-73
8d-424	Pakistan	Perth	1981-82
422	England	Sydney	1907-08
9d-419	England	Melbourne	1976-77
413	India	Delhi	1979-80
411	England	Adelaide	1894-95
408	England	Sydney	1897-98
3d-404	England	Leeds	1948
8d-403	England	Adelaide	1950-51
402	England	Manchester	1981

LOWEST COMPLETED INNINGS
TOTAL FOR EACH TEST GROUND

Venue	Score	Opponent	Series
In Australia:			
Adelaide	82	West Indies	1951-52
Brisbane1	66¢	England	1928-29
Brisbane2	58	England	1936-37
Melbourne	83	India	1980-81
Perth	76	West Indies	1984-85
Sydney	42	England	1887-88

Venue	Score	Opponent	Series
In England:			
Birmingham	36	England	1902
Leeds	103	England	1977
Lord's	53	England	1896
Manchester	70	England	1888
Nottingham	123	England	1953
Sheffield	194	England	1902
The Oval	44	England	1896
In India:			
Bangalore	333	India	1979-80
Bombay2	274¢	India	1964-65
Bombay3	160	India	1979-80
Calcutta	174	India	1964-65
Delhi	107	India	1969-70
Kanpur	105¢	India	1959-60
Madras1	153	India	1969-70
Madras2	211	India	1964-65
In New Zealand:			
Auckland	103	New Zealand	1985-86
Christchurch	223	New Zealand	1973-74
Wellington	9d-199	New Zealand	1945-46
In Pakistan:			
Dacca	225	Pakistan	1959-60
Faisalabad	168	Pakistan	1982-83
Karachi	80	Pakistan	1956-57
Lahore2	214	Pakistan	1982-83
In South Africa:			
Cape Town	164	South Africa	1969-70
Durban1	299¢	South Africa	1921-22
Durban2	75	South Africa	1949-50
Johannesburg1	175	South Africa	1902-03
Johannesburg2	413	South Africa	1949-50
Johannesburg3	143	South Africa	1966-67
Port Elizabeth	173	South Africa	1966-67

Venue	Score	Opponent	Series
In Sri Lanka:			
Kandy	4d-514	Sri Lanka	1982-83
In West Indies:			
Bridgetown	97	West Indies	1983-84
Georgetown	144	West Indies	1964-65
Kingston	160¢	West Indies	1983-84
Port-of-Spain	90	West Indies	1977-78
St. John's	200	West Indies	1983-84

¢ Denotes 1 man absent

LOWEST COMPLETED INNINGS TOTALS

Score	Opponent	Venue	Series
36	England	Birmingham	1902
42	England	Sydney	1887-88
44	England	The Oval	1896
53	England	Lord's	1896
58¢	England	Brisbane2	1935-36
60	England	Lord's	1888
63	England	The Oval	1882
65	England	The Oval	1912
66¢¢	England	Brisbane1	1928-29
68	England	The Oval	1886
70	England	Manchester	1888
74	England	Birmingham	1909
75	South Africa	Durban2	1949-50
76	West Indies	Perth	1984-85
78	England	Lord's	1968
80	England	The Oval	1888
80¢	England	Sydney	1936-37
80	Pakistan	Karachi	1956-57
81	England	Manchester	1888

Score	Opponent	Venue	Series
82	England	Sydney	1888
82	West Indies	Adelaide	1951-52
83	England	Sydney	1882-83
83	India	Melbourne	1980-81
84	England	Sydney	1886-87
84	England	Manchester	1956
86	England	Manchester	1902
90	West Indies	Port-of-Spain	1977-78
91	England	The Oval	1893
92	England	The Oval	1890
94	West Indies	Port-of-Spain	1977-78
97	England	Sydney	1887-88
97	West Indies	Bridgetown	1983-84
100	England	The Oval	1888
100	England	Adelaide	1891-92

¢ Denotes one man absent
¢¢ Denotes two men absent

HIGHEST FOURTH INNINGS TOTALS

To Win:

Score	Opponent	Venue	Series
3-404	England	Leeds	1948
7-362	West Indies	Georgetown	1977-78
8-342	India	Perth	1977-78
5-336	South Africa	Durban2	1949-50
6-315	England	Adelaide	1901-02
5-287	England	Melbourne	1928-29
4-276	England	Sydney	1897-98
8-275	England	Sydney	1907-08
9-260	West Indies	Melbourne	1951-52
6-260	New Zealand	Sydney	1985-86
8-258	West Indies	Melbourne	1960-61
5-242	England	The Oval	1972
7-236	West Indies	Brisbane2	1951-52
3-236	Pakistan	Perth	1978-79
2-219	West Indies	Brisbane2	1975-76
5-214	England	Sydney	1946-47
2-211	England	Melbourne	1920-21

To Draw:

Score	Opponent	Venue	Series	Runs set in 4th inns
9-339	West Indies	Adelaide	1968-69	360
3-329	England	Lord's	1975	484
3-328	England	Adelaide	1970-71	469
2-274	South Africa	Johannesburg1	1935-36	399
9-273	West Indies	Adelaide	1960-61	460
6-261	Pakistan	Adelaide	1976-77	285
8-238	England	Melbourne	1974-75	246
2-227	Pakistan	Karachi	1964-65	342
7-224	England	Leeds	1905	402
3-220	England	Leeds	1975	445
1-215	England	Adelaide	1946-47	304
6-204	England	Lord's	1938	315
4-200	West Indies	Adelaide	1979-80	373

To Lose:

Score	Opponent	Venue	Series	Losing margin
402	England	Manchester	1981	103
339	South Africa	Adelaide	1910-11	38
336	England	Adelaide	1928-29	12
335	England	Nottingham	1930	93
310	Pakistan	Melbourne	1978-79	71
292	England	Sydney	1911-12	70
290	South Africa	Melbourne	1952-53	82
288	England	Melbourne	1982-83	3
280	South Africa	Cape Town	1969-70	170
261	South Africa	Johannesburg3	1966-67	495
252	England	Manchester	1972	89
246	South Africa	Port Elizabeth	1966-67	323
241	West Indies	Sydney	1960-61	222
240	West Indies	Brisbane2	1968-69	125
220	West Indies	Sydney	1930-31	30
216	West Indies	Kingston	1964-65	396

To Tie:

Score	Opponent	Venue	Series
232	West Indies	Brisbane2	1960-61

The Australian Team to play the West Indies, 1964-65.

THE "WINDIES"

The 1964-65 series in the West Indies between Australia and the West Indies was marred throughout by accusations that Charlie Griffiths was a chucker. The wonderful spirit that had prevailed between the teams in 1954-55 was replaced by a simmering bitterness.

Australian captain Bob Simpson was restrained and diplomatic in his comments about Griffiths during the tour but later was outspoken in his belief that Griffiths should have been no-balled. Most of those who followed the series from the Press box agreed that Griffiths threw an average of two balls an over, sometimes more.

Australia lost the First and Third Tests largely because of the failure to bat sensibly against Griffiths. His figures were far from remarkable but his very presence provided problems the Australians could not handle.

Trailing by two Tests to nil after the Second Test had been drawn, the Australians went into the Fourth knowing they had to win both the remaining Tests to share the series. They began in determined fashion,with openers Bill Lawry and Bob Simpson batting throughout the first day to set up a splendid batting reversal.

They continued on next day until both reached double centuries, the first opening pair to achieve this in the same innings. Their stand of 382 was Australia's highest-ever for the first wicket and was only 31 runs short of the world record by Vinoo Mankad and Pankaj Roy in 1955-56. Bob Cowper carried on the heavy scoring and Australia's second wicket fell at 522. Lawry made 210, Simpson 201 and Cowper 102, and after a quick 51 from Norm O'Neill Australia declared at 6 for 650.

The Australian bowlers lacked hostility on such a perfect pitch and the West Indies scored freely from all eight bowlers used. Rohan Kanhai made 129 and Seymour Nurse scored the third double century of the Test: 201. The West Indies total of 573 gave Australia a lead of 77, far less than they must have expected when Lawry and Simpson were involved in their big stand.

Simpson was out with only seven runs on the board in Australia's second innings. But a fine 74 not out from O'Neill, and 58 from Lawry before he retired hurt, enabled Simpson to declare at 4 for 175 and set the West Indies to score 253 runs in 270 minutes.

The West Indian batsmen took up the challenge, putting on 145 in entertaining style for the first wicket. Two wickets then fell for one run and when the third went at 183 Simpson was able to curb the scoring rate. But his bowlers just could not break through, although Peter Philpott and Graham McKenzie tried desperately, knowing the series was up for grabs.

The Australian fielding in the closing overs reached a very high standard and was mainly responsible for the West Indies falling 11 runs short on 242, with five wickets left, when time ran out. Both sides suffered nasty injuries. Conrad Hunte retired for a period when he was hit in the face attempting to hook Hawke in the West Indies' first innings. Lawry was hurt in Australia's second innings.

Significantly, in a tense encounter between two evenly matched teams, Charlie Griffiths did not take a wicket. His figures were 0 for 131 and 0 for 38 from a total of 42 overs. He made amends, however, in the Fifth Test when he took 6 for 46 in Australia's first innings. Australia recovered through some outstanding bowling by McKenzie to win the Fifth Test by ten wickets, but the West Indies had already gained their first victory in a rubber against Australia.

Griffiths took only 15 wickets in the series, and apart from his coup in the Fifth Test did not appear likely to blast through an Australian innings. But at the end of the series, Norman O'Neill produced a series of articles damning Griffiths' action and the umpires who allowed him to bowl unchecked through the entire Caribbean summer. The pity of it was that in the angry debate that followed, the record-breaking opening partnership by Simpson and Lawry at Bridgetown was virtually forgotten.

Australian Captain Bob Simpson.

HIGHEST AGGREGATE IN A TEST

Aggregate	1st inns	2nd inns	Opponent	Venue	Series
20 for 1028	701	327	England	The Oval	1934
18 for 1013	619	8d-394	West Indies	Sydney	1968-69
14 for 971	6d-511	8-460	New Zealand	Wellington	1973-74
20 for 936	354	582	England	Adelaide	1920-21
20 for 917	668	249	West Indies	Bridgetown	1954-55
20 for 906	328	578	South Africa	Melbourne	1910-11
20 for 902	450	452	England	Sydney	1924-25
20 for 901	365	536	England	Melbourne	1946-47
19 for 872	533	9-339	West Indies	Adelaide	1968-69
15 for 866	5d-441	425	Pakistan	Melbourne	1972-73
13 for 862	458	3-404	England	Leeds	1948
20 for 850	600	250	England	Melbourne	1924-25
20 for 848	267	581	England	Sydney	1920-21
16 for 838	411	6d-427	England	Nottingham	1938
16 for 832	8d-517	8d-315	Pakistan	Melbourne	1976-77
10 for 825	6d-650	4d-175	West Indies	Bridgetown	1964-65
17 for 810	350	7d-460	England	Lord's	1948
20 for 804	465	339	South Africa	Adelaide	1910-11
9 for 801	6d-729	3-72	England	Lord's	1930

LOWEST AGGREGATE IN A COMPLETED TEST

Aggregate	1st inns	2nd inns	Opponent	Venue	Series
20 for 124	42	82	England	Sydney	1887-88
20 for 151	81	70	England	Old Trafford	1888
20 for 163	119	44	England	The Oval	1896
20 for 176	116	60	England	Lord's	1888
20 for 176	111	65	England	The Oval	1912
20 for 180	80	100	England	The Oval	1888
20 for 185	63	122	England	The Oval	1882
17 for 188	122*	66†	England	Brisbane1	1928-29
20 for 194	92	102	England	The Oval	1890
20 for 216	119	97	England	Sydney	1886-87
20 for 217	68	149	England	The Oval	1886

Aggregate	1st inns	2nd inns	Opponent	Venue	Series
20 for 225	74	151	England	Birmingham	1909
20 for 233	122	111	England	Melbourne	1903-04
20 for 234	84	150	England	Sydney	1886-87
20 for 247	121	126	England	Lord's	1886

* 1 man absent
† 2 men absent

HIGHEST MATCH AGGREGATE

Aggregate	Opponent	Venue	Series	Result
39 for 1764	West Indies	Adelaide	1968-69	Drawn
40 for 1753	England	Adelaide	1920-21	AUS by 119 runs
31 for 1723	England	Leeds	1948	AUS by 7 wkts
36 for 1661	West Indies	Bridgetown	1954-55	Drawn
40 for 1646	South Africa	Adelaide	1910-11	SA by 38 runs
38 for 1644	West Indies	Sydney	1968-69	AUS by 382 runs
24 for 1640	West Indies	Bridgetown	1964-65	Drawn
33 for 1640	Pakistan	Melbourne	1972-73	AUS by 92 runs
40 for 1619	England	Melbourne	1924-25	AUS by 81 runs
40 for 1611	England	Sydney	1924-25	AUS by 193 runs
29 for 1601	England	Lord's	1930	AUS by 7 wkts
37 for 1562	England	Melbourne	1946-47	Drawn
35 for 1554	England	Melbourne	1928-29	AUS by 5 wkts
35 for 1541	England	Sydney	1903-04	ENG by 5 wkts
40 for 1514	England	Sydney	1894-95	ENG by 10 runs
29 for 1502	England	Adelaide	1946-47	Drawn

LOWEST COMPLETED MATCH AGGREGATE

Aggregate	Opponent	Venue	Series	Result
29 for 234	South Africa	Melbourne	1931-32	AUS by an inns & 32 runs
40 for 291	England	Lord's	1888	AUS by 61 runs
28 for 295	New Zealand	Wellington	1946-47	AUS by an inns & 103 runs
30 for 323	England	Manchester	1888	ENG by an inns & 21 runs
40 for 363	England	The Oval	1882	AUS by 7 runs
40 for 374	England	Sydney	1887-88	ENG by 126 runs

Aggregate	Opponent	Venue	Series	Result
38 for 389	England	The Oval	1890	ENG by 2 wkts
40 for 392	England	The Oval	1896	ENG by 66 runs
28 for 421	England	Sydney	1894-95	AUS by an inns & 147 runs
40 for 445	England	Sydney	1886-87	ENG by 13 runs
34 for 450	England	Brisbane2	1950-51	AUS by 70 runs
30 for 451	England	Birmingham	1909	ENG by 10 wkts
29 for 457	England	Manchester	1884	ENG by 4 wkts
30 for 497	England	The Oval	1888	ENG by an inns & 137 runs

THE RESULTS

LARGEST MARGINS OF VICTORY

Opponent	Margin	Venue	Series
England	inns & 332 runs	Brisbane2	1946-47
South Africa	inns & 259 runs	Port Elizabeth	1949-50
India	inns & 226 runs	Brisbane2	1947-48
West Indies	inns & 217 runs	Brisbane1	1930-31
England	inns & 200 runs	Melbourne	1936-37
South Africa	inns & 184 runs	Johannesburg1	1935-36
India	inns & 177 runs	Melbourne	1947-48
West Indies	inns & 172 runs	Sydney	1930-31
South Africa	inns & 163 runs	Brisbane2	1931-32
South Africa	inns & 155 runs	Sydney	1931-32
England	inns & 154 runs	Brisbane2	1954-55
England	inns & 149 runs	The Oval	1948
England	inns & 147 runs	Sydney	1894-95
South Africa	inns & 141 runs	Cape Town	1957-58
India	inns & 127 runs	Delhi	1959-60
West Indies	inns & 122 runs	Melbourne	1930-31
South Africa	inns & 114 runs	Sydney	1910-11
Pakistan	inns & 114 runs	Adelaide	1972-73
New Zealand	inns & 103 runs	Wellington	1945-46
England	562 runs	The Oval	1934
South Africa	530 runs	Melbourne	1910-11
England	409 runs	Lord's	1948
England	382 runs	Adelaide	1894-95
West Indies	382 runs	Sydney	1968-69

Opponent	Margin	Venue	Series
England	377 runs	Sydney	1920-21
England	365 runs	Melbourne	1936-37
Pakistan	348 runs	Melbourne	1976-77
England	308 runs	Melbourne	1907-08
England	307 runs	Sydney	1924-25
New Zealand	297 runs	Auckland	1973-74
Pakistan	286 runs	Perth	1981-82
England	274 runs	Adelaide	1950-51
England	245 runs	Adelaide	1907-08
England	238 runs	Nottingham	1934
India	233 runs	Melbourne	1947-48
India	229 runs	Melbourne	1901-02
England	219 runs	Leeds	1921
England	218 runs	Melbourne	1903-04
England	216 runs	Adelaide	1903-04
West Indies	202 runs	Sydney	1951-52

NARROWEST WINNING MARGINS

Winning Team	Losing Team	Venue	Date
Tied Test Matches:			
Australia *505 & 232*	West Indies *453 & 284*	Brisbane2	1960-61
Australia *7d-574 & 5d-170*	India *397 & 347*	Madras1	1986-87
Won by one wicket:			
Australia	West Indies	Melbourne	1951-52
Won by two wickets:			
Australia	West Indies	Melbourne	1960-61
Australia	India	Perth	1977-78
Won by three wickets:			
Australia	England	Manchester	1896
Australia	West Indies	Georgetown	1977-78
Australia	West Indies	Brisbane2	1951-52

Winning Team	Losing Team	Venue	Date
Won by less than thirty runs:			
Australia	England 3 runs	Manchester	1902
Australia	England 6 runs	Sydney	1884-85
Australia	England 7 runs	The Oval	1882
Australia	England 11 runs	Adelaide	1924-25
Australia	India 16 runs	Brisbane2	1977-78
Australia	England 28 runs	Melbourne	1950-51

VICTORY LOSING FEWEST WICKETS

Winning Team	Losing Team	Venue	Date
Four Wickets:			
Australia *4d-514*	Sri Lanka *271 & 205*	Kandy	1982-83
Six Wickets:			
Australia *6d-454 & 0-35*	Pakistan *278 & 210*	Sydney	1983-84
Seven Wickets:			
Australia *7d-549*	South Africa *158 & 132*	Port Elizabeth	1949-50

LARGEST MARGINS OF DEFEAT

Opponent	Margin	Venue	Series
England	inns & 579 runs	The Oval	1938
England	inns & 230 runs	Adelaide	1891-92
England	inns & 225 runs	Melbourne	1911-12
England	inns & 217 runs	The Oval	1886
England	inns & 170 runs	Manchester	1956
England	inns & 137 runs	The Oval	1888
South Africa	inns & 129 runs	Durban2	1969-70
England	inns & 124 runs	Sydney	1901-02
England	inns & 118 runs	Birmingham	1985
West Indies	inns & 112 runs	Perth	1984-85

Opponent	Margin	Venue	Series
West Indies	inns & 106 runs	Port-of-Spain	1977-78
England	inns & 106 runs	Lord's	1886
India	inns & 100 runs	Bombay3	1979-80
England	675 runs	Brisbane1	1928-29
West Indies	408 runs	Adelaide	1979-80
England	338 runs	Adelaide	1932-33
South Africa	323 runs	Port Elizabeth	1969-70
England	322 runs	Brisbane2	1936-37
South Africa	307 runs	Johannesburg3	1969-70
England	299 runs	Sydney	1970-71
England	289 runs	The Oval	1926
England	244 runs	The Oval	1912
South Africa	233 runs	Johannesburg3	1966-67
England	226 runs	The Oval	1968
West Indies	222 runs	Sydney	1960-61
India	222 runs	Melbourne	1977-78
England	213 runs	Nottingham	1905
West Indies	212 runs	Georgetown	1964-65
England	205 runs	Adelaide	1978-79

NARROWEST LOSING MARGINS

Losing Team	Winning Team	Margin	Venue	Date
Lost by one wicket:				
Australia	England		The Oval	1902
Australia	England		Melbourne	1907-08
Lost by two wickets:				
Australia	England		The Oval	1890
Australia	India		Bombay2	1964-65
Lost by three wickets:				
Australia	England		Melbourne	1928-29
Lost by less than thirty runs:				
Australia	England	3 runs	Melbourne	1982-83
Australia	England	10 runs	Sydney	1894-95

Losing Team	Winning Team	Margin	Venue	Date
Australia	England	12 runs	Adelaide	1928-29
Australia	England	13 runs	Sydney	1886-87
Australia	England	18 runs	Leeds	1981
Australia	England	29 runs	Birmingham	1981
Australia	West Indies	30 runs	Sydney	1930-31

OPPONENT'S VICTORY LOSING FEWEST WICKETS

Losing Team	Winning Team	Venue	Date
Five Wickets:			
Australia *335 & 142*	England *5d-595*	Birmingham	1985
Six Wickets:			
Australia *9-80 & 324*	England *6d-426*	Sydney	1936-37
Australia *168 & 330*	Pakistan *6d-501*	Faisalabad	1982-83
Seven Wickets:			
Australia *8-201 & 8-123*	England *7d-903*	The Oval	1938
Australia *179 & 333*	New Zealand *7d-553*	Brisbane2	1985-86

MATCHES COMPLETED IN TWO DAYS

	Opponent	Venue	Series
Australia *63 & 122*	defeated England *101 & 77*	The Oval	1882
Australia *116 & 60*	defeated England *53 & 62*	Lord's	1888
Australia *80 & 100*	lost to England *317*	The Oval	1888
Australia *81 & 70*	lost to England *172*	Manchester	1888
Australia *92 & 102*	lost to England *100 & 8-95*	The Oval	1890
Australia *448*	defeated South Africa *265 & 95*	Manchester	1912
Australia *232 & 0-30*	defeated England *112 & 147*	Nottingham	1921
Australia *8d-328*	defeated West Indies *99 & 107*	Melbourne	1930-31
Australia *439*	defeated South Africa *157 & 98*	Johannesburg1	1935-36
Australia *8d-199*	defeated New Zealand *42 & 54*	Wellington	1945-46

THE ASHES

Until the Ninth Test at The Oval in August 1882, English cricket fans had taken it for granted that England would triumph whenever she cared to field her best team, whatever the calibre of the opposition. Defeats in Australia and against earlier Australian teams in England always were excused on the grounds that Australia had the advantage of playing against second-rate England sides.

Now as Billy Murdoch's Australian side produced almost daily demonstrations of their skill in batting, bowling and fielding, it became obvious that when the two countries met England's prestige would be at stake. Murdoch's side arrived to learn that the main English counties intended to avoid playing them. Lord Harris, still upset at the manner in which he had been treated in the Sydney riot of 1879, listened sympathetically to the Australians' arguments for big matches, but for weeks they were denied on the grounds that they were shameless bonus-seeking professionals.

The Australians were told they had arrived too late to get major fixtures and that the itineraries of the stronger counties had all been finalised before they got to England. A weak Canadian team that arrived after the Australians, however, were given big games. Reduced to advertising for matches, the Australians spent weeks in remote towns and villages playing any teams that would give them a match. Manager George Alexander even offered to play either the Gentlemen or the Players and give all proceeds to charity, but without any change in the English attitude.

Murdoch appealed to his friend W.G. Grace, who had toured Australia in 1873-74, in an attempt to overcome the Australians' humiliation. Grace promised to do all he could, and his pressure finally convinced Lord Harris to forget the irritations of the Sydney riot and helped stage a match between All England and the Australians.

The match began at The Oval on 28 August 1882, on a rain-soaked pitch. Australia won the toss and made the mistake of batting first; they were dismissed in 135 minutes for 63. Slow left-arm Yorkshire bowler Edmund Peate, and Lancashire left-arm medium-pacer Richard Barlow exploited the conditions superbly; only three Australians reached double figures.

The Ashes, the 'body of English cricket'.

England lost six wickets before passing Australia's score, thanks to equally impressive bowling from Fred Spofforth, Tom Garrett and Harry Boyle. Only a stubborn 26 by George Ulyett took England to 101 and a lead of 38. With rain imminent England looked to be in a sound position.

The next morning Hugh Massie attacked all the England bowlers, and in a masterly display of controlled hitting took care of the arrears, while Alick Bannerman defended as if his life hung on it. Massie, who earlier in the tour had made a magnificent double century against Oxford University, rushed to 50 in 41 minutes out of 61, but when Allan Steel bowled Massie only Murdoch offered any resistance.

England needed only 85 to win, but in the Australian dressing-room Spofforth kept telling his team-mates: "This thing can be done. We can get them out." This seemed very unlikely when England took her score to 51 for the loss of only two wickets, but then the most celebrated collapse in the history of cricket followed.

The England batsmen were shackled, unable to get the ball past the fieldsmen, whose nerve was unbroken as Spofforth bowled his break-backs at his spiteful best, cleverly mixing his pace. At the other end Harry Boyle kept an immaculate length with his right-hand round-armers. Behind the stumps John Blackham took every ball that passed the batsmen centimetres from the bails.

The struggle became so intense that one spectator dropped dead, another gnawed pieces from his umbrella handle, and the scorer's hand trembled so much he finished with something like "Geese" when he tried to write Peate. Horan wrote later that England's batsmen became so parched they could barely speak. Maiden over followed maiden over and the ground was so quiet the bowlers' approach runs could be heard.

Spofforth began the collapse when he forced Ulyett to edge his straight one to Blackham, and two runs later W.G. Grace mishit a drive to Bannerman at mid-off. The score edged to 60 with Alfred Lyttelton and Alfred "Bunny" Lucas together. Twelve successive maidens followed before Spofforth spoke to Bannerman, who deliberately misfielded to give Lyttelton a single and bring him to face Spofforth. Four more maidens followed before Spofforth scattered Lyttelton's stumps. England was 5 for 66, and 19 were still required.

Lucas broke the Australian stranglehold by hitting Boyle for four, but Spofforth struck back at once by dismissing Steel and Read in one over. England was 7 for 70, with 15 needed. Then came a 2 and three byes off Spofforth because Lucas edged Spofforth into his stumps.

C.T. Studd, who earlier in the season had scored two centuries against the Australians, came in, so the Australians concentrated all their efforts at the other end. Murdoch caught Syd Barnes off his glove from a Boyle delivery that kicked. Last man Peate swung the first ball for 2, slashed and missed at the next two, and had his stumps broken by the last ball of Boyle's over. Australia had won by 7 runs.

Spofforth had bowled his last 11 overs for 2 runs and four wickets and had finished the match with 14 for 90. As Peate's stumps were knocked over to give Australia victory, the ground went silent for an instant. Then wild cheering broke over the ground. Spofforth was carried shoulder-high to the dressing-room. Three days later the *Sporting Times* published the mock obituary stating that the body of English cricket would be cremated and "the ashes" taken to Australia. One of the great sporting legends had begun.

VICTORY AFTER ENFORCING FOLLOW-ON

Losing Team	Winning Team	Venue	Date
Australia 586 & 166	England 325 & 437	Sydney	1894-95
Australia 9d-401 & 111	England 174 & 356	Leeds	1981

LONGEST MATCHES

Days	Opponent	Venue	Series
8 days	England	Melbourne	1928-29
7 days	England	Sydney	1924-25
7 days	England	Melbourne	1924-25
7 days	England	Adelaide	1924-25
7 days	England	Melbourne	1928-29
7 days	England	Adelaide	1928-29

MOST RUNS SCORED IN ONE DAY

Runs	Opponent	Venue	Day	Series
6-494	South Africa	Sydney	1	1910-11
2-475	England	The Oval	1	1934
3-458	England	Leeds	1	1930
1-455	England	Leeds	2	1934

FEWEST RUNS IN A FULL DAY'S PLAY

Runs		Venue	Day	Series
95	Australia 80 & Pakistan 2-15	Karachi	1	1956-57
104	Pakistan 5-104	Karachi	4	1959-60
106	England 2-92 to 198	Brisbane2	4	1958-59
112	Australia 6-138 to 187	Karachi	4	1956-57
117	India 5-117	Madras2	1	1956-57

WINNING EVERY TEST IN A SERIES

Series	Opponent	Venue	No of tests	Australia Captain	Opponent Captain
1920-21	England	Australia	5	Armstrong, WW	Douglas, JWHT
1931-32	South Africa	Australia	5	Woodfull, WM	Cameron, HB
1967-68	India	Australia	4	Simpson, RB & Lawry, WM	Borde, CG & Nawab of Pataudi jr
1972-73	Pakistan	Australia	3	Chappell, IM	Intikhab Alam
1979-80	England	Australia	3	Chappell, GS	Brearley, JM

LOSING EVERY TEST IN A SERIES

Series	Opponent	Venue	No of tests	Australia Captain	Opponent Captain
1886	England	England	3	Scott, HJH	Steel, AG
1886-87	England	Australia	2	McDonnell, PS	Shrewsbury, A
1890	England	England	2	Murdoch, WL	Grace, WG
1969-70	South Africa	South Africa	4	Lawry, WM	Bacher, A
1982-83	Pakistan	Pakistan	3	Hughes, KJ	Imran Khan

DRAWN EVERY TEST IN A SERIES

Series	Opponent	Venue	No of tests	Australia Captain	Opponent Captain
1985-86	India	Australia	3	Border, AR	Kapil Dev

MOST CONSECUTIVE DEFEATS

No of Tests	From	To
7	Melbourne 1884-85	Sydney 1887-88
6	Bridgetown 1983-84	Adelaide 1984-85
5	Adelaide 1926	Adelaide 1928-29

TEST CRICKET'S SECOND TIED MATCH — MADRAS 1986

When umpire Vikram Raju lifted his finger to rule India's number 11 batsman, Maninder Singh, out leg-before-wicket at the Chidambaram stadium in Madras, Australian cricket supporters around the world could scarcely believe it.

The decision produced Test cricket's second tied match — historic in itself —, but to get an LBW decision in India which decided a Test match was almost beyond the belief of any Australian cricketer who had toured that country.

From the first ball this match, played from 18 to 22 September 1986, was a most unusual affair. Temperatures hovered around 40 degrees Celsius amid exceptionally high humidity readings, and the wildly excited crowds of spectators averaged 30,000 each day. Unlike the initial tied Test at Brisbane in December 1960, this was probably the most acrimonious Test ever played, with fist fights between players being only narrowly avoided.

Australia declared its innings closed twice in the match and would have been unlucky to lose, but throughout most of the last day defeat appeared certain. As in Brisbane, only a sensational collapse in the final innings prevented the batting side (India) from winning.

A remarkable 210 by Dean Jones — the first double century by an Australian in India — and centuries by David Boon (122) and Allan Border (106) enabled Australia to score 574 in the first innings. Jones's knock in the oppressive heat and humidity was one of the best in Test history. His body reached such a stage of dehydration that he could not keep down any fluids and he repeatedly vomited beside the pitch. When it was over Jones was rushed to hospital and put on a drip until his moisture level returned to normal.

Bob Simpson, the only man to have been involved in both tied Tests (he made 92 and 0 as an opener in Brisbane), said: "I doubt whether any cricketer has had to push his body as hard as Jones did for nearly eight and a half hours in Madras. I'm not sure he had fully recovered by the end of the tour."

India responded to Australia's fine start with some spirited batting. Krishnamachari Srikkanth (53), Mohammed Azharuddin (50), Ravis

Shastri (62) and Kapil Dev, who made a splendid 119, all hit out vigorously without knocking the indomitable Greg Matthews out of the attack. Matthews took 5 for 103 from 28.2 overs.

Australia made 5 for 170 to lift Australia's overall lead to 347 by stumps at the end of the second last day. The next morning Border boldly closed the Australian innings, leaving India to score 348 off 87 overs for a win. This gamble appeared to have backfired at tea, when India was 2 for 193 and needed 155 runs off 30 overs, with Ravis Shastri and Chetan Sharma handling the Australian attack comfortably.

Tempers frayed on both sides as the Australians constantly clashed with umpires and opposing batsmen. Sunil Gavaskar (90) and Mohinder Armanath (51) appeared to set up an easy Indian win with their second wicket stand of 103, but then Australia made a notable breakthrough when Kapil Dev was caught at short fine leg trying to hook for a duck. Shastri took over as India's mainstay, hooking the ball savagely and driving with superb timing as he farmed the strike.

India, with four wickets in hand, required 57 off the last ten overs. But in the 84th over Chetan Sharma was caught in the deep to take India to 7 for 331. In the same over, wicket-keeper Kiran More was out LBW for a duck, leaving India at 8 for 334 with three overs left.

Matthews and fellow spinner Ray Bright were superb in the final moments, bowling with great composure and skill. Even when Shastri smashed Matthews high over long-on for six, the Australians did not falter, doggedly chasing every ball. During a drinks break Matthews had to be led away from Indians with whom he exchanged words and gestures. At one point umpire Dara Dotiwalla shouted at Border and waved a finger at him. When Tim Zoehrer unsuccessfully appealed for a stumping Zoehrer hurled the ball into the dust in disgust.

Bright bowled Shivlal Yadav off the last ball of the second last over to set up the dramatic last over. With India needing four runs to win, Maninder Singh meandered out in his yellow *patka*. Despite the heat, he appeared to be shivering. Shastri got two runs with an on-drive. On the third ball he made the mistake of taking a single, exposing Maninder to Matthews. He patted the first ball back but completely misread the second last delivery of the match and was given out LBW.

Maninder Singh had appeared plumb as he was close to his stumps but to be given such a decision in India was probably the most extraordinary thing in an extraordinary match. India had lost its last four wickets for 16 runs off 22 balls, and Matthews had finished with 5 for 146 for a match analysis of 10 for 249 from 68.1 overs.

MOST CONSECUTIVE WINS

No of Tests	From	To
8	Sydney 1920-21	Leeds 1921
5	The Oval 1930	Melbourne 1930-31
5	Brisbane2 1931-32	Melbourne 1931-32
5	Melbourne 1947-48	Lord's 1948
5	Leeds 1948	Durban2 1949-50
5	Port Elizabeth 1949-50	1950-51
5	Adelaide 1967-68	Manchester 1968

MOST CONSECUTIVE TESTS
WITHOUT DEFEAT

No of Tests	From	To
25	Wellington 1946-47	Adelaide 1950-51
17	Madras2 1956-57	Delhi 1959-60
16	Sydney 1920-21	Adelaide 1924-25
13	The Oval 1972	Wellington 1973-74

MOST CONSECUTIVE TESTS
WITHOUT VICTORY

No of Tests	From	To
14	Perth 1985-86	Melbourne 1986-87
12	Cape Town 1969-70	Manchester 1972
9	Nottingham 1926	Adelaide 1928-29
9	Georgetown 1983-84	Melbourne 1984-85
8	Bombay2 1964-65	Bridgetown 1964-65
7	Melbourne 1884-85	Sydney 1887-88
7	Adelaide 1952-53	The Oval 1953
7	Madras1 1979-80	Brisbane1 1979-80
6	Adelaide 1891-92	Melbourne 1894-95

MOST CONSECUTIVE DRAWS

No of Tests	From	To
5	Adelaide 1985-86	Christchurch 1985-86
4	Manchester 1921	Johannesburg1 1921-22
4	Nottingham 1926	Manchester 1926
4	Nottingham 1953	Leeds 1953

MOST CONSECUTIVE TESTS ENDING IN A RESULT

No of Tests	From	To	Australia Won	Lost
19	Adelaide 1884-85	Adelaide 1891-92	5	12
18	The Oval 1930	Lord's 1934	12	6
14	Port Elizabeth 1949-50	Sydney 1952-53	11	3
13	Sydney 1894-95	Sydney 1897-98	7	6
11	Sydney 1910-11	Manchester 1912	6	5

BATTING

HIGHEST SCORES
FOR EACH BATTING ORDER

Order	Score	Batsman	Opponent	Venue	Series
1	225	Simpson, RB	England	Adelaide	1965-66
	210	Lawry, WM	West Indies	Bridgetown	1964-65
	203	Collins, HL	South Africa	Johannesburg1	1921-22
2	311	Simpson, RB	England	Manchester	1964
	266	Ponsford, WH	England	The Oval	1964
	207	Stackpole, KR	England	Brisbane2	1970-71
3	334	Bradman, DG	England	Leeds	1930
	299	Bradman, DG	South Africa	Adelaide	1931-32
	268	Yallop, GN	Pakistan	Melbourne	1983-84
4	307	Cowper, RM	England	Melbourne	1965-66
	247*	Chappell, GS	New Zealand	Wellington	1973-74
	235	Chappell, GS	Pakistan	Faisalabad	1979-80
5	304	Bradman, DG	England	Leeds	1934
	242	Walters, KD	West Indies	Sydney	1968-69
	214*	Trumper, VT	South Africa	Adelaide	1910-11
6	250	Walters, KD	New Zealand	Christchurch	1976-77
	234	Bradman, DG	England	Sydney	1946-47
	201	Gregory, SE	England	Sydney	1894-95
7	270	Bradman, DG	England	Melbourne	1936-37
	201*	Ryder, J	England	Adelaide	1924-25
	158	Armstrong, WW	England	Sydney	1920-21
8	128	Bonnor, GJ	England	Sydney	1884-85
	121	Benaud, R	West Indies	Kingston	1954-55
	120	Phillips, WB	West Indies	Bridgetown	1983-84
9	160	Hill, C	England	Adelaide	1907-08
	100	Lindwall, RR	England	Melbourne	1946-47
	100	Gregory, JM	England	Melbourne	1920-21
10	104	Duff, RA	England	Melbourne	1901-02
	74	Blackham, JM	England	Sydney	1894-95
	73*	Lillee, DK	England	Lord's	1975

Order	Score	Batsman	Opponent	Venue	Series
11	52	Hogg, RM	West Indies	Georgetown	1983-84
	50	Spofforth, FR	England	Melbourne	1884-85
	46*	Mailey, AA	England	Sydney	1924-25

CENTURIES SCORED
ON TEST MATCH GROUNDS

Venue	ENG	IND	NZ	PAK	SA	SL	WI	Total
In Australia:								
Adelaide	29	11	1	7	5	–	5	58
Brisbane1	–	–	–	–	–	–	2	2
Brisbane2	14	1	3	3	3	–	7	31
Melbourne	38	10	2	10	7	–	10	77
Perth	7	2	–	3	–	–	1	13
Sydney	30	3	–	1	7	–	11	52
Total	**118**	**27**	**6**	**24**	**22**	**–**	**36**	**233**
In England:								
Birmingham	1	–	–	–	–	–	–	1
Leeds	14	–	–	–	–	–	–	14
Lord's	22	–	–	–	2	–	–	24
Manchester	13	–	–	–	2	–	–	15
Nottingham	12	–	–	–	–	–	–	12
Sheffield	1	–	–	–	–	–	–	1
The Oval	22	–	–	–	–	–	–	22
Total	**85**	**–**	**–**	**–**	**4**	**–**	**–**	**89**
In India:								
Bangalore	–	–	–	–	–	–	–	–
Bombay2	–	5	–	–	–	–	–	5
Bombay3	–	1	–	–	–	–	–	1
Calcutta	–	2	–	–	–	–	–	2
Delhi	–	2	–	–	–	–	–	2
Kanpur	–	1	–	–	–	–	–	1
Madras1	–	6	–	–	–	–	–	6
Madras2	–	1	–	–	–	–	–	1
Total	**–**	**18**	**–**	**–**	**–**	**–**	**–**	**18**

Venue	ENG	IND	NZ	PAK	SA	SL	WI	Total
In New Zealand:								
Auckland	–	–	4	–	–	–	–	4
Christchurch	–	–	5	–	–	–	–	5
Wellington	–	–	5	–	–	–	–	5
Total	–	–	**14**	–	–	–	–	**14**
In Pakistan:								
Dacca	–	–	–	–	–	–	–	–
Faisalabad	–	–	–	3	–	–	–	3
Karachi	–	–	–	2	–	–	–	2
Lahore2	–	–	–	3	–	–	–	3
Total	–	–	–	**8**	–	–	–	**8**
In South Africa:								
Cape Town	–	–	–	–	7	–	–	7
Durban1	–	–	–	–	1	–	–	1
Durban2	–	–	–	–	4	–	–	4
Johannesburg1	–	–	–	–	6	–	–	6
Johannesburg2	–	–	–	–	6	–	–	6
Johannesburg3	–	–	–	–	2	–	–	2
Port Elizabeth	–	–	–	–	3	–	–	3
Total	–	–	–	–	**29**	–	–	**29**
In Sri Lanka:								
Kandy	–	–	–	–	–	2	–	2
Total	–	–	–	–	–	**2**	–	**2**
In West Indies:								
Bridgetown	–	–	–	–	–	–	9	9
Georgetown	–	–	–	–	–	–	3	3
Kingston	–	–	–	–	–	–	9	9
Port-of-Spain	–	–	–	–	–	–	7	7
St. John's	–	–	–	–	–	–	–	–
Total	–	–	–	–	–	–	**28**	**28**
Total in Australia	118	27	6	24	22	–	36	233
Total abroad	85	18	14	8	33	2	28	188
Grand total	203	45	20	32	55	2	64	421

DON BRADMAN

Donald George Bradman was the most successful batsman in the history of Australian cricket. He scored a century at an average better than every third time he batted. He made 117 first-class centuries, 74 of them chanceless and a further 20 which were chanceless up to 100. He deliberately threw his innings away 46 times, but he still finished with 28,067 runs at an average of 95.14.

In Tests, Bradman was just four runs short of averaging 100, finishing with 6996 runs from his 52 Tests at an average of 99.94. When he went to the crease for his last Test innings at The Oval in 1948, spectators cheered from the time he went through the gate until he reached the pitch. He was clean bowled for a duck.

Bradman was not born at Bowral as legend has it. He was born on 27 August 1908, at 89 Adam Street, Cootamundra, in the house of the local midwife, Mrs Eliza Schultz. His father, George Bradman, was the son of an English migrant from an area on the border of Cambridgeshire and Suffolk formed by the villages of Horseneath and Haverhill. Don's grandfather was a farm labourer who was drawn to New South Wales by the gold strikes near Bathurst. Don's mother was a Whatman, a family with a long history in the Bowral – Mittagong district.

After his birth Bradman was taken home to the family cottage at Yeo Yeo, between Stockingbal and Wallendbean, where his father owned a wheat and sheep farm. Don was the youngest and smallest in a family of five children. When he was two years old, the family moved to Bowral from Yeo Yeo to benefit his mother's health.

Don's father turned to carpentry in Bowral; he was one of the men who did the form work for the concrete bicycle track around the Sydney Cricket Ground. One of Bowral's leading builders, Alf Stephens, often used Bradman's father on building projects, and it was Stephens, captain of the Bowral Cricket Club, who helped stimulate Don's interest in the game.

Bradman attended Bowral Intermediate High School, but the school was not involved in organised sport. At the weekends Don scored for the Bowral Cricket Club, riding to their matches in the back of a truck. When the team was short, he filled in, but he was so small one of the players took pity on him and presented him with a bat that had a large piece cut off the bottom.

In 1921, Don's father took him to Sydney to watch the England v. Australia Test in which Charlie Macartney scored a spectacular 170. In the train back to Bowral, Don knew that he wanted to be a great batsman like Macartney.

Bradman sang in the church choir and took piano lessons from his sister Islet. Each afternoon he practised cricket in the backyard, hitting a golf ball with a stump against the concrete base of a water tank. Sometimes his mother bowled left-armers to him.

At 17, Bradman scored 234 not out for Bowral on the Wingello ground and he followed this with an innings of 300 against Moss Vale in a match in which his brother Victor was out for one run. These innings brought him publicity in Sydney newspapers and an invitation to attend a trial at the Sydney Cricket Ground nets before the State selectors.

On 27 November 1926, Bradman made his first appearance in Sydney, scoring 110 in even time for the St George Club. He travelled

Don Bradman, posing for a promotional photograph for a bat manufacturing company.

Don Bradman at the practice nets, Perth 1930.

back and forth from Bowral to Sydney for grade matches. At the end of the 1927 season he made 320 not out for Bowral against Moss Vale in the final of the district competition.

He went to Adelaide for his first State match with the New South Wales side in the 1927-28 season. He batted at number 7 and made 118 in a chanceless knock. In the last match of that season he made 134 not out for New South Wales against Victoria, the first of many centuries on the SCG. Over the next 20 years he filled that ground many times, his batting attracting spectators who had never previously been interested in cricket.

A few days after his twentieth birthday Bradman left Bowral to live in Sydney. He made 131 and 133 not out for New South Wales against Queensland, which won him a place in the State side to play the touring England side captained by Percy Chapman.

He scored 87 in the first innings against England, and in the second innings saved the match for New South Wales with an unbroken partnership of 249 for the fourth wicket with Alan Kippax. For a 20-year-old, his innings of 132 not out was a wonderful effort and it won him a place in the Australian team for the First Test in Brisbane. On the first sticky wicket he had ever seen he made 18 and 1, and England won by 675 runs.

For the only time in his life, Bradman was dropped for the Second Test in Sydney, fielding for 11 hours as twelfth man when Bill Ponsford was hurt. Recalled for the Third Test, he scored 79 and 112. Bradman went on to triumphant tours of England in 1930, 1934, 1938 and 1948. With Arthur Mailey's team, Bradman toured America in 1932, when he was on his honeymoon with his wife Jessie. He scored 18 centuries in his 51 innings, including 260 against Western Ontario and 150 not out against Edmonton (when he put on 50 in seven minutes at one stage). He never toured the West Indies or South Africa. In 1949, he became the only Australian to be knighted for his services to cricket. In 1981, he was made a Companion of the Order of Australia, which ranks six places higher than a knighthood in the Order Of Precedence.

MOST HUNDREDS IN A SERIES

100's	Tests	Series	Opponent	Venue	Players
12	5	1954-55	West Indies	West Indies	Harvey, RN (3) Miller, KR (3) McDonald, CC (2) Archer, RG Benaud, R Lindwall, RR Morris, AR
10	5	1920-21	England	Australia	Armstrong, WW (3) Collins, HL (2) Pellew, CE (2) Gregory, JM Kelleway, C Macartney, CG
10	5	1946-47	England	Australia	Morris, AR (3) Bradman, DG (2) Barnes, SG Hassett, AL Lindwall, RR McCool, CL Miller, KR
10	5	1968-69	West Indies	Australia	Walters, KD (4) Lawry, WM (3) Chappell, IM (2) Redpath, IR
10	5	1975-76	West Indies	Australia	Chappell, GS (3) Redpath, IR (3) Chappell, IM Cosier, GJ McCosker, RB Turner, A
8	5	1947-48	India	Australia	Bradman, DG (4) Barnes, SG Harvey, RN Hassett, AL Morris, AR
8	5	1948	England	England	Morris, AR (3) Bradman, DG (2) Barnes, SG Harvey, RN Hassett, AL

MOST HUNDREDS IN AN INNINGS

100's Scores		Batsmen	Opponent	Venue	Series
5	204	Harvey, RN	West Indies	Kingston	1954-55
	128	Archer, RG			
	127	McDonald, CC			
	121	Benaud, R			
	109	Miller, KR			
3	211	Murdoch, WL	England	The Oval	1884
	103	McDonnell, PS			
	102	Scott, HJH			
3	147	Kelleway, C	England	Adelaide	1920-21
	121	Armstrong, WW			
	104	Pellew, CE			
3	151	Macartney, CG	England	Leeds	1926
	141	Woodfull, WM			
	100	Taylor, JM			
3	169	Bradman, DG	England	Melbourne	1936-37
	118	McCabe, SJ			
	118	Badcock, CL			
3	201	Bradman, DG	India	Adelaide	1947-48
	198	Hassett, AL			
	112	Barnes, SG			
3	167	Hassett, AL	South Africa	Port Elizabeth	1949-50
	157	Morris, AR			
	116	Harvey, RN			
3	133	Harvey, RN	West Indies	Port-of-Spain	1954-55
	111	Morris, AR			
	110	McDonald, CC			
3	210	Lawry, WM	West Indies	Bridgetown	1964-65
	201	Simpson, RB			
	102	Cowper, RM			
3	151	Chappell, IM	India	Melbourne	1967-68
	109	Simpson, RB			
	100	Lawry, WM			
3	210	Jones, DM	India	Madras2	1986-87
	122	Boon, DC			
	106	Border, AR			

MOST HUNDREDS IN A MATCH

100's	Inns	Scores	Batsmen	Opponent	Venue	Series
5	1st	204	Harvey, RN	West Indies	Kingston	1954-55
		127	McDonald, CC			
		128	Archer, RG			
		121	Benaud, R			
		109	Miller, KR			
4	1st	162	Collins, HL	England	Adelaide	1920-21
	2nd	147	Kelleway, C			
		121	Armstrong, WW			
		104	Pellew, CE			
4	1st	112	Ryder, J	England	Melbourne	1928-29
		100	Kippax, AF			
	2nd	112	Bradman, DG			
		107	Woodfull, WM			
4	1st	118	Moroney, J	South Africa	Johannesburg2	1949-50
		111	Morris, AR			
	2nd	101*	Moroney, J			
		100	Harvey, RN			
4	1st	242	Walters, KD	West Indies	Sydney	1968-69
		151	Lawry, WM			
	2nd	132	Redpath, IR			
		103	Walters, KD			
4	1st	135	Redpath, IR	Pakistan	Melbourne	1972-73
		116*	Chappell, GS			
	2nd	142	Benaud, J			
		127	Sheahan, AP			
4	1st	247*	Chappell, GS	New Zealand	Wellington	1973-74
		145	Chappell, IM			
	2nd	133	Chappell, GS			
		121	Chappell, IM			

MOST FIFTIES IN AN INNINGS
(Without a Century)

50's	Scores	Batsmen	Opponent	Venue	Series
5	77	Armstrong, WW	England	Melbourne	1907-08
	64	Noble, MA			
	64	Macartney, CG			
	63	Trumper, VT			
	53	Carter, H			
5	76	Chappell, IM	West Indies	Adelaide	1968-69
	62	Lawry, WM			
	62	Stackpole, KR			
	59	McKenzie, GD			
	51	Sheahan, AP			

MOST FIFTIES IN A MATCH
(Without a Century)

50's	Inns	Scores	Batsmen	Opponent	Venue	Series
6	1st	74	Darling, J	England	Melbourne	1894-95
		70	Gregory, SE			
		57	Giffen, G			
		55	Lyons, JJ			
	2nd	51	Giffen, G			
		50	Darling, J			
6	1st	98	Hill, C	England	Adelaide	1901-02
		65	Trumper, VT			
		55	Gregory, SE			
	2nd	97	Hill, C			
		69	Darling, J			
		62*	Trumble, H			
6	1st	61	Noble, MA	England	Melbourne	1907-08
	2nd	77	Armstrong, WW			
		64	Noble, MA			
		64	Macartney, CG			
		63	Trumper, VT			
		53	Carter, C			
6	1st	85	Darling, LS	England	Sydney	1932-33
		73	McCabe, SJ			
		61	O'Brien, LPJ			
		52	Oldfield, WAS			
	2nd	71	Bradman, DG			
		67	Woodfull, WM			
6	1st	75	Booth, BC	South Africa	Sydney	1963-64
		58	Simpson, RB			
	2nd	90	Benaud, R			
		89	Lawry, WM			
		88	O'Neill, NC			
		76	McKenzie, GD			
6	1st	91	Burge, PJP	South Africa	Sydney	1963-64
		78	Simpson, RB			
		70	Shepherd, BK			
		58	Booth, BC			
	2nd	78	Shepherd, BK			
		66	O'Neill, NC			
6	1st	80	Burge, PJP	India	Bombay1	1964-65
		78	Jarman, BN			
		67	Vievers, TR			
	2nd	81	Cowper, RM			
		74	Booth, BC			
		68	Lawry, WM			

50's	Inns	Scores	Batsmen	Opponent	Venue	Series
6	1st	93	Walters, KD	India	Brisbane2	1967-68
		64	Lawry, WM			
		58	Sheahan, AP			
		51	Cowper, RM			
	2nd	79	Redpath, IR			
		62*	Walters, KD			
6	1st	99	Edwards, R	England	Lord's	1975
		73*	Lillee, DK			
	2nd	86	Chappell, IM			
		79	McCosker, RB			
		73*	Chappell, GS			
		52*	Edwards, R			

MOST FIFTIES IN A SERIES
(Excluding Centuries)

50's	Tests	Series	Opponent	Venue	Players
20	5	1960-61	West Indies	Australia	Simpson, RB (4)
					McDonald, CC (3)
					O'Neill, NC (3)
					Burge, PJP (2)
					Benaud, R (2)
					Mackay, KD (2)
					Harvey, RN
					Davidson, AK
					Favell, LE
					Martin., JW
20	6	1974-75	England	Australia	Chappell, GS (5)
					Chappell, IM (4)
					Walters, KD (3)
					Redpath, IR (3)
					McCosker, RB (2)
					Edwards, R
					Marsh, RW
					Jenner, TJ
19	5	1910-11	South Africa	Australia	Bardsley, W (5)
					Ransford, VS (4)
					Gehrs, DRA (2)
					Kelleway, C (2)
					Trumper, VT (2)
					Armstrong, WW
					Hill, C
					Hordern, HV
					Macartney, CG

50's	Tests	Series	Opponent	Venue	Players
19	6	1979-80	India	India	Hughes, KJ (5)
					Border, AR (3)
					Hilditch, AMJ (3)
					Yallop, GN (2)
					Whatmore, DF (2)
					Yardley, B
					Wright, KJ
					Sleep, PR
					Darling, WM
18	5	1972-73	West Indies	West Indies	Chappell, IM (3)
					Walters, KD (3)
					Marsh, RW (3)
					Redpath, IR (3)
					Chappell, GS (2)
					Stackpole, KR (2)
					Edwards, R (2)

FIFTY OR MORE IN AN INNINGS
(Including Centuries)

50's	Scores	Batsmen	Opponent	Venue	Series
6	158	Armstrong, WW	England	Sydney	1920-21
	104	Collins, HL			
	78	Kelleway, C			
	69	Macartney, CG			
	57	Bardsley, W			
	51	Taylor, JM			
6	232	Bradman, DG	England	The Oval	1930
	110	Ponsford, WH			
	73	Jackson, A			
	54	Woodfull, WM			
	54	McCabe, SJ			
	53*	Fairfax, AG			
6	137	Miller, KR	West Indies	Bridgetown	1954-55
	118	Lindwall, RR			
	98	Archer, RG			
	74	Harvey, RN			
	72	Favell, LE			
	53	Langley, GRA			
6	110	Walters, KD	West Indies	Adelaide	1968-69
	76	Chappell, IM			
	62	Lawry, WM			
	62	Stackpole, KR			
	59	McKenzie, GD			
	51	Sheahan, AP			

FIFTY OR MORE IN A MATCH
(Including Centuries)

50's	Inns	Scores	Batsmen	Opponent	Venue	Series
8	1st	137	Miller, KR	West Indies	Bridgetown	1954-55
		118	Lindwall, RR			
		98	Archer, RG			
		74	Harvey, RN			
		72	Favell, LE			
		53	Langley, GRA			
	2nd	57	Johnson, IW			
		53	Favell, LE			
8	1st	112	Booth, BC	England	Brisbane2	1962-63
		86*	Mackay, KD			
		51	Benaud, R			
		50	Simpson, RB			
	2nd	98	Lawry, WM			
		71	Simpson, RB			
		57	Harvey, RN			
		56	O'Neill, NC			
7	1st	118	Moroney, J	South Africa	Johannesburg2	1949-50
		111	Morris, AR			
		84	Miller, KR			
		56*	Harvey, RN			
		53	Hassett, AL			
	2nd	101*	Moroney, J			
		100	Harvey, RN			

FIFTY OR MORE IN A SERIES
(Including Centuries)

Total	50's	100's	No of tests	Series	Opponent	Venue
27	17	10	5	1920-21	England	Australia
26	19	7	5	1910-11	South Africa	Australia
26	16	10	5	1968-69	West Indies	Australia
26	20	6	6	1974-75	England	Australia
24	12	12	5	1954-55	West Indies	Australia

MOST RUNS IN A TEST MATCH

Runs	Batsman		Opponent	Venue	Series
380	Chappell, GS	(247* & 133)	New Zealand	Wellington	1973-74
345	Walters, KD	(242 & 103)	West Indies	Sydney	1968-69
334	Bradman, DG	(334 & —)	England	Headingley	1930
321	Bradman, DG	(244 & 77)	England	The Oval	1934
315	Simpson, RB	(311 & 4*)	England	Manchester	1964
307	Cowper, RM	(307 & —)	England	Melbourne	1965-66
304	Bradman, DG	(304 & —)	England	Headingley	1934
303	Border, AR	(150* & 153)	Pakistan	Lahore2	1979-80
299	Bradman, DG	(299* & —)	South Africa	Adelaide	1931-32
289	Ryder, J	(201* & 88)	England	Adelaide	1924-25
288	Ponsford, WH	(266 & 22)	England	The Oval	1934
283	Bradman, DG	(13 & 270)	England	Melbourne	1936-37
271	McCabe, SJ	(232 & 39)	England	Nottingham	1938
270	Walters, KD	(250 & 20*)	New Zealand	Christchurch	1976-77
268	Simpson, RB	(153 & 115)	Pakistan	Karachi	1964-65
268	Lawry, WM	(210 & 58®)	West Indies	Bridgetown	1964-65
268	Yallop, GN	(268 & —)	Pakistan	Melbourne	1983-84
266	Bardsley, W	(136 & 130)	England	The Oval	1909
266	Chappell, IM	(145 & 121)	New Zealand	Wellington	1973-74
266	Hughes, KJ	(213 & 53)	India	Adelaide	1980-81
259	Bradman, DG	(132 & 127*)	India	Melbourne	1947-48
255	Bradman, DG	(254 & 1)	England	Lord's	1930
254	Border, AR	(140 & 114*)	New Zealand	Christchurch	1985-86

ALLAN BORDER

Most Test cricketers face a showdown at some time in their careers, a match or a series that proved the turning point and established them as players of undoubted international calibre.

For Allan Robert Border, the compact, sometimes bearded, left-hander from the Sydney suburb of Cremorne, the big challenge came on tour in Pakistan in 1980. When he went to the crease in the first innings of the Test at Lahore, Border still had to confirm his Test position.

Border had first come to attention at North Sydney Boys' High School, when he won selection in the Combined High Schools XI for the interstate carnival in 1972-73. He played baseball for Mosman Firsts, whose number 1 pitcher was his brother John, and cricket for Mosman, where his brother Brett was in a lower grade team.

Allan was an established first-grade cricketer when he went to play for Gloucestershire Second XI in 1977, and after a season for East Lancashire in the Lancashire League in 1978, he made the jump from the New South Wales team to the Australian side.

Like most left-handers he frequently succumbed to deliveries outside his off-stump, a frailty cleverly exploited by the England bowlers. But at Perth he showed the first signs of his high quality by scoring 115 on the usually lively WACA pitch. He showed his courage by continuing after sustaining a nasty cut near the eye, when he tried to hook after passing his century. That knock proved a match winner, Australia winning by 138 runs. At Melbourne in the same series he made 63 in the Third Test of that series, Australia winning by eight wickets.

Border did reasonably well on tour in India in 1979, scoring 749 runs at 39.42, but his place in the Test team was still open to challengers when he went to Pakistan in 1980 under Greg Chappell's captaincy.

The Pakistanis served up pitches that ideally suited their spinners Iqbal Qasim and Tauseef Ahmad but did nothing to help an Australian attack based on the pace of Dennis Lillee. To try and get a faster pitch, Dennis Lillee feigned injury before the Lahore Test while his team-mates put round the story that Ashley Mallett was to be flown from

Allan Border in full swing.

Australia to reinforce the Australian attack with his off-spinners. The Pakistanis did not fall for this ploy and the match was played on the usual flat pitch that nullified Lillee's pace.

The Pakistani spinners bowled well on a pitch suited to them, but from the time he took guard Border never allowed them to dictate. His judgment was sustained and faultless in both innings. When he went forward to kill the spin of the ball he placed the half-volleys immaculately through gaps between fieldsmen. When he played back he had time to pull and cut with authority.

Abdul Qadir became annoyed at his inability to force Border into error. Indeed, Border made batting look so easy it was puzzling how team-mates were being dismissed at the other end. He never appeared likely to miss out on a century in the first innings, finishing on 150 not out. He continued this superb form in the second innings, playing every ball on its merit and again with supreme judgment.

In oppressive heat and high humidity, Border's stamina was as impressive as his shot selection. He always picked the right stroke for every ball sent down to him and when he had frustrated the spinners he sustained his run rate against the medium-pacers, showing none of his old weakness outside the off-stump.

His 153 in the second innings of a match that petered out to a draw rightly earned Border the reputation of one of the world's best players of spin-bowling. On a worn dusty pitch that helped Qadir and Ahmad more than in the first innings, Border had to work harder for his runs, but again his judgement was flawless.

Border's effort at Lahore took his average for the three-Test series to 131.66 and firmly established him in the Australian side for as long as he cared to play Test cricket. He returned home with a maturity he had previously lacked, a batsman fit to be ranked with Joe Darling, Clem Hill, Warren Bardsley, Arthur Morris, and Neil Harvey among the greatest Australian left-handed batsmen, a player renowned for his reliability in a crisis.

HIGHEST AGGREGATES IN A SERIES

Batsman	Opponent	Venue	Series	M	Inn	NO	Runs	H.S	50	100	Avrge
Bradman, DG	ENG	ENG	1930	5	7	–	974	334	–	4	139.14
Harvey, RN	SA	AUS	1952-53	5	9	–	834	205	3	4	92.66
Bradman, DG	ENG	AUS	1936-37	5	9	–	810	270	1	3	90.00
Bradman, DG	SA	AUS	1931-32	5	5	1	806	299*	–	4	201.50
Bradman, DG	ENG	ENG	1934	5	8	–	758	304	1	2	94.75
Bradman, DG	IND	AUS	1947-48	5	6	2	715	201	1	4	178.75
Chappell, GS	WI	AUS	1975-76	6	11	5	702	182*	3	3	117.00
Walters, KD	WI	AUS	1968-69	4	6	–	699	242	2	4	116.50
Morris, AR	ENG	ENG	1948	5	9	1	696	196	3	3	87.00
Bradman, DG	ENG	AUS	1946-47	5	8	1	680	234	3	2	97.14
Lawry, WM	WI	AUS	1968-69	5	8	–	667	205	2	3	83.38
Trumper, VT	SA	AUS	1910-11	5	9	2	661	214*	2	2	94.43
Harvey, RN	SA	SA	1949-50	5	8	3	660	178	1	4	132.00
Harvey, RN	WI	WI	1954-55	5	7	1	650	204	1	3	108.33
Stackpole, KR	ENG	AUS	1970-71	7	12	–	627	207	2	2	52.25
Chappell, GS	ENG	AUS	1974-75	6	11	–	608	144*	5	2	55.27
Border, AR	ENG	ENG	1985	6	11	2	597	196	1	2	66.33
Hughes, KJ	IND	IND	1979-80	6	12	2	594	100	5	1	59.40
Lawry, WM	ENG	AUS	1965-66	5	7	–	592	166	2	3	84.57
Redpath, IR	WI	AUS	1975-76	6	11	–	575	103	2	3	52.27

Trumper, VT	ENG	AUS	1903-04	5	10	1	574	185*	3	2	63.77
Bardsley, W	SA	AUS	1910-11	5	9	–	573	132	5	1	63.67
Ponsford, WH	ENG	ENG	1934	4	7	1	569	266	1	2	94.83
Collins, HL	ENG	AUS	1920-21	5	9	–	557	162	3	2	61.89
Yallop, GN	PAK	AUS	1983-84	5	6	–	554	268	1	2	92.33
Chappell, IM	WI	AUS	1968-69	5	8	–	548	165	3	2	68.50
Chappell, IM	WI	WI	1972-73	5	9	2	542	109	3	2	77.43
Taylor, JM	ENG	AUS	1924-25	5	10	–	541	108	4	1	54.10
Simpson, RB	IND	AUS	1977-78	5	10	–	539	176	2	2	53.90
Darling, J	ENG	AUS	1897-98	5	8	–	537	178	–	3	67.13
Border, AR	ENG	ENG	1981	6	12	3	533	123*	3	2	59.22
Booth, BC	SA	AUS	1963-64	4	7	1	531	169	3	2	88.50
O'Neil, NC	WI	AUS	1960-61	5	10	–	522	181	3	1	52.20
Border, AR	IND	IND	1979-80	6	12	–	521	162	3	1	43.42
Border, AR	WI	WI	1983-84	5	10	3	521	100*	4	1	74.43
Hill, C	ENG	AUS	1901-02	5	10	–	521	99	4	–	52.10
McDonald, CC	ENG	AUS	1958-59	5	9	1	519	170	1	2	64.88
Brown, WA	ENG	ENG	1938	4	8	1	512	206*	1	2	73.14
Jones, DM	ENG	AUS	1986-87	5	10	1	511	184*	3	1	56.78
Bradman, DG	ENG	ENG	1948	5	9	2	508	173*	1	2	72.57
Wessels, KC	WI	AUS	1984-85	5	9	–	505	173	4	1	56.11
Morris, AR	ENG	AUS	1946-47	5	8	1	503	155	1	3	71.86

LEADING RUN-SCORERS

Batsman	M	Inn	No	Runs	H.S	50	100	Avrge	ENG	IND	NZ	PAK	SA	SL	WI
Chappell, GS	88	151	19	7110	247*	31	24	53.86	2619	368	1076	1581	–	66	1400
Bradman, DG	52	80	10	6996	334	13	29	99.94	5028	715	–	–	806	–	447
Border, AR	89	157	26	6917	196	33	21	52.80	2342	1292	713	1302	–	47	1221
Harvey, RN	79	137	10	6149	205	24	21	48.42	2416	775	–	279	1625	–	1054
Walters, KD	75	125	14	5357	250	33	15	48.26	1981	756	901	265	258	–	1196
Chappell, IM	76	136	10	5345	196	26	14	42.42	2138	536	486	352	288	–	1545
Lawry, WM	68	123	12	5234	210	27	13	47.15	2233	892	–	89	985	–	1035
Simpson, RB	62	111	7	4869	311	27	10	46.82	1405	1125	–	316	980	–	1043
Redpath, IR	67	120	11	4737	171	31	8	43.46	1512	475	413	299	791	–	1247
Hughes, KJ	70	124	6	4415	213	22	9	37.42	1499	988	138	1016	–	–	774
Marsh, RW	97	150	13	3633	132	16	3	26.52	1633	83	486	724	–	–	707
Morris, AR	46	79	3	3533	206	12	12	46.49	2080	209	–	–	792	–	452
Hill, C	49	89	2	3412	191	19	7	39.22	2660	–	–	–	752	–	–
Trumper, VT	48	89	8	3163	214*	13	8	39.05	2263	–	–	–	900	–	–
Wood, GM	53	101	5	3109	172	13	8	32.39	1063	287	393	463	–	4	899
McDonald, CC	47	83	4	3107	170	17	5	39.33	1043	224	–	174	786	–	880
Hassett, AL	43	69	3	3073	198*	11	10	46.56	1572	332	19	–	748	–	402
Miller, KR	55	87	7	2958	147	13	7	36.98	1511	185	30	32	399	–	801
Armstrong, WW	50	84	10	2863	159*	8	6	38.69	2172	–	–	–	691	–	–
Stackpole, KR	44	80	5	2807	207	14	7	37.43	1164	368	197	37	441	–	600

O'Neill, NC	42	69	8	2779	181	15	6	45.56	1072	416	–	218	285	–	788
Yallop, GN	39	70	3	2756	268	9	8	41.13	709	568	–	882	–	98	499
McCabe, SJ	39	62	5	2748	232	13	6	48.21	1931	–	–	–	621	–	196
Bardsley, W	41	66	5	2469	193*	14	6	40.48	1487	–	–	–	82	–	–
Woodfull, WM	35	54	4	2300	161	13	7	46.00	1675	–	–	–	421	–	204
Burge, PJP	42	68	8	2290	181	12	4	38.17	1179	457	–	94	331	–	229
Gregory, SE	58	100	7	2282	201	8	4	24.54	2193	–	–	–	89	–	–
Benaud, R	63	97	7	2201	122	9	3	24.46	767	144	–	144	684	–	462
Macartney, CG	35	55	4	2131	170	9	7	41.78	1640	–	–	–	491	–	–
Ponsford, WH	29	48	4	2122	266	6	7	48.23	1558	–	–	–	97	–	467
Cowper, RM	27	46	2	2061	307	10	5	46.84	686	604	–	99	255	–	417
Noble, MA	42	73	7	1997	133	16	1	30.26	1905	–	–	–	92	–	–
Booth, BC	29	48	6	1773	169	10	5	42.21	824	112	–	72	531	–	234
Wessels, KC	24	42	1	1761	179	9	4	42.95	754	–	73	256	–	141	537
Ritchie, GM	30	53	5	1690	146	7	3	35.21	666	231	344	205	–	–	244
Darling, J	34	60	2	1657	178	8	3	28.57	1632	–	–	–	25	–	–
McCosker, RB	25	46	5	1622	127	9	4	39.56	977	–	198	228	–	–	219
Sheahan, AP	31	53	6	1594	127	7	2	33.91	341	506	49	194	247	–	257
Brown, WA	22	35	1	1592	206*	9	4	46.82	980	128	67	–	417	–	–
Mackay, KD	37	52	7	1507	89	13	–	33.49	497	273	–	73	375	–	289
Lindwall, RR	61	84	13	1502	118	5	2	21.15	795	173	–	29	107	–	398
Phillips, WB	27	48	2	1485	159	7	2	32.28	350	67	312	362	–	–	394
Oldfield, WAS	54	80	17	1427	65*	4	–	22.65	1116	–	–	–	221	–	90

Batsman	M	Inn	No	Runs	H.S	50	100	Avrge	ENG	IND	NZ	PAK	SA	SL	WI
Kelleway, C	26	42	4	1422	147	6	3	37.42	874	–	–	–	548	–	–
Boon, DC	23	42	2	1399	131	7	4	34.98	268	648	351	–	–	–	132
Ryder, J	20	32	5	1394	201*	9	3	51.63	1060	–	–	–	334	–	–
Dyson, J	30	58	7	1359	127*	5	2	26.65	489	178	229	220	–	–	243
Collins, HL	19	31	1	1352	203	6	4	45.07	1012	–	–	–	340	–	–
Laird, BM	21	40	2	1341	92	11	–	35.29	162	–	147	492	–	–	540
Davidson, AK	44	61	7	1328	80	5	–	24.59	750	109	–	130	127	–	212
Duff, RA	22	40	3	1317	146	6	2	35.59	1079	–	–	–	238	–	–
Hookes, DW	23	41	3	1306	143*	8	1	34.37	700	76	59	–	–	143	328
Burke, JW	24	44	7	1280	189	5	3	34.59	676	183	–	14	389	–	18
Giffen, G	31	53	–	1238	161	6	1	23.36	1238	–	–	–	–	–	–
Ransford, VS	20	38	6	1211	143*	7	1	37.84	893	–	–	–	318	–	–
Kippax, AF	22	34	1	1192	146	8	2	36.12	753	–	–	–	162	–	277
Fingleton, JHW	18	29	1	1189	136	3	5	42.46	671	–	–	–	518	–	–
Edwards, R	20	32	3	1171	170*	9	2	40.38	805	–	–	161	–	–	205
Gregory, JM	24	34	3	1146	119	7	2	36.97	941	–	–	–	205	–	–
Bannerman, AC	28	50	2	1108	94	8	–	23.08	1108	–	–	–	–	–	–
Hilditch, AMJ	18	34	–	1073	119	6	2	31.56	428	313	12	135	–	–	185
Barnes, SG	13	19	2	1072	234	5	3	63.06	846	172	54	–	–	–	–
Matthews, GRJ	21	34	6	1031	130	4	3	36.82	236	282	395	97	–	–	21
Johnson, IW	45	66	12	1000	77	6	–	18.52	485	124	7	13	117	–	254

LEADING BATTING AVERAGES

	M	Inn	NO	Runs	H.S	50	100	Avrge
Trott, AE	3	5	3	205	85*	2	–	102.50
Bradman, DG	52	80	10	6996	334	13	29	99.94
Barnes, SG	13	19	2	1072	234	5	3	63.06
Moss, JK	1	2	1	60	38*	–	–	60.00
Bannerman, C	3	6	2	239	165*	–	1	59.75
Jones, DM	10	19	2	947	210	4	2	55.71
Chappell, GS	88	151	19	7110	247*	31	24	53.86
Border, AR	89	157	26	6917	196	33	21	52.80
Ryder, J	20	32	5	1394	201*	9	3	51.63
Fairfax, AG	10	12	4	410	65	4	–	51.25
Gregory, RG	2	3	–	153	80	2	–	51.00

FASTEST TO 1000 RUNS

Inn	Batsman	Inn	Batsman
13	Bradman, DG	26	Chappell, GS
14	Harvey, RN	26	Yallop, GN
17	Barnes, SG	26	Border, AR
18	Collins, HL	26	Wessels, KC
18	Walters, KD	27	Kippax, AF
19	Morris, AR	27	Miller, KR
20	Fingleton, JHW	28	Darling, J
20	O'Neill, NC	28	Edwards, R
20	Booth, BC	28	Hookes, DW
21	Bardsley, W	29	Gregory, JM
21	Woodfull, WM	29	Kelleway, C
21	Hassett, AL	29	Laird, BM
21	McDonald, CC	29	Hilditch, AMJ
21	Lawry, WM	30	Ransford, VS
21	Cowper, RM	30	McCabe, SJ
23	Brown, WA	30	Hughes, KJ
24	Hill, C	30	Boon, DC
24	McCosker, RB	31	Simpson, RB
25	Ponsford, WH	31	Redpath, IR
26	Ryder, J	31	Wood, GM

Inn	Batsman	Inn	Batsman
32	Burke, JW	38	Armstrong, WW
32	Burge, PJP	39	Noble, MA
32	Ritchie, RM	41	Gregory, SE
32	Matthews, GRJ	43	Dyson, J
33	Chappell, IM	44	Giffen, G
33	Stackpole, KR	45	Davidson, AK
33	Marsh, RW	46	Benaud, R
34	Duff, RA	48	Bannerman, AC
34	Mackay, KD	53	Lindwall, RR
34	Sheahan, AP	54	Oldfield, WAS
35	Trumper, VT	66	Johnson, IW
37	Macartney, CG		

FASTEST TO 2000 RUNS

Inn	Batsman	Inn	Batsman
22	Bradman, DG	54	McDonald, CC
35	Walters, KD	54	Hughes, KJ
36	Morris, AR	55	Simpson, RB
37	Harvey, RN	55	Stackpole, KR
43	Cowper, RM	57	Miller, KR
44	Chappell, GS	58	Burge, PJP
45	Woodfull, WM	58	Yallop, GN
45	Hassett, AL	60	Redpath, IR
45	O'Neill, NC	61	Trumper, VT
46	Bardsley, W	61	Chappell, IM
47	Hill, C	63	Armstrong, WW
47	Ponsford, WH	63	Wood, GM
48	Border, AR	64	Marsh, RW
49	McCabe, SJ	87	Gregory, SE
53	Macartney, CG	91	Benaud, R
53	Lawry, WM		

FASTEST TO 3000 RUNS

Inn	Batsman	Inn	Batsman
33	Bradman, DG	76	Hill, C
54	Harvey, RN	77	McDonald, CC
64	Morris, AR	80	Trumper, VT
65	Lawry, WM	81	Hughes, KJ
65	Chappell, GS	83	Redpath, IR
66	Hassett, AL	84	Chappell, IM
68	Walters, KD	97	Wood, GM
72	Border, AR	118	Marsh, RW
74	Simpson, RB		

FASTEST TO 4000 RUNS

Inn	Batsman	Inn	Batsman
48	Bradman, DG	90	Simpson, RB
80	Harvey, RN	99	Border, AR
87	Chappell, GS	101	Chappell, IM
89	Walters, KD	105	Redpath, IR
90	Lawry, WM	105	Hughes, KJ

FASTEST TO 5000 RUNS

Inn	Batsman	Inn	Batsman
56	Bradman, DG	118	Walters, KD
105	Harvey, RN	120	Border, AR
106	Chappell, GS	121	Chappell, IM
117	Lawry, WM		

FASTEST TO 6000 RUNS

Inn	Batsman	Inn	Batsman
68	Bradman, DG	134	Harvey, RN
129	Chappell, GS	140	Border, AR

FASTEST TO 7000 RUNS

Inn	Batsman
151	Chappell, GS

1000 RUNS IN A CALENDAR YEAR

Batsman	Year	M	Inn	NO	Runs	H.S	100	Avrge
Simpson, RB	1964	14	26	3	1381	311	3	60.04
Hughes, KJ	1979	15	28	4	1163	130*	2	48.45
Border, AR	1985	12	20	3	1099	196	4	64.65
Border, AR	1979	14	27	3	1073	162	3	44.70
Hill, C	1902	12	21	2	1061	142	2	55.78
Lawry, WM	1964	14	27	2	1056	157	2	42.24
Bradman, DG	1948	8	13	4	1025	201	5	113.88
Border, AR	1986	11	19	3	1000	140	5	62.50

LEADING CENTURY MAKERS

Batsman	M	Inn	100s	ENG	IND	NZ	Opponents PAK	SA	SL	WI
Bradman, DG	52	80	29	19	4	–	–	4	–	2
Chappell, GS	88	151	24	9	1	3	6	–	–	5
Harvey, RN	79	137	21	6	4	–	–	8	–	3
Border, AR	89	157	21	7	4	3	5	–	–	2
Walters, KD	75	125	15	4	1	3	1	–	–	6
Chappell, IM	76	136	14	4	2	2	1	–	–	5
Lawry, WM	68	123	13	7	1	–	–	1	–	4
Morris, AR	46	79	12	8	1	–	–	2	–	1
Hassett, AL	43	69	10	4	1	–	–	3	–	2
Simpson, RB	62	111	10	2	4	–	2	1	–	1

INNINGS PER HUNDREDS

Batsman	M	Inn	100s	Inns per 100s
Bradman, DG	52	80	29	2.76
Hartigan, RJ	2	4	1	4.00
Benaud, R	3	5	1	5.00
Graham, H	6	10	2	5.00
Fingleton, JHW	18	29	5	5.80
Bannerman, C	3	6	1	6.00
Moroney, J	7	12	2	6.00
Chappell, GS	88	151	24	6.29
Barnes, SG	13	19	3	6.33
Harvey, RN	79	137	21	6.52
Morris, AR	46	79	12	6.58
Ponsford, WH	29	48	7	6.86
Hassett, AL	43	69	10	6.90
Pellew, CE	10	14	2	7.00
Border, AR	89	157	21	7.48
Woodfull, WM	35	54	7	7.71
Collins, HL	19	31	4	7.75
Macartney, CG	35	55	7	7.86

INNINGS OF FIFTY OR MORE

Batsman	M	Inn	50s	Inns per 50s
Gregory, RG	2	3	2	1.50
Bradman, DG	52	80	42	1.90
Hartkopf, AEV	1	2	1	2.00
Barnes, SG	13	19	8	2.38
Trott, AE	3	5	2	2.50
Walters, KD	75	125	48	2.60
Ryder, J	20	32	12	2.67
Brown, WA	22	35	13	2.69
Woodfull, WM	35	54	20	2.70
Chappell, GS	88	151	55	2.75
Shepherd, BK	9	14	5	2.80
Edwards, R	20	32	11	2.91

Batsman	M	Inn	50s	Inns per 50s
Border, AR	89	157	54	2.91
Fairfax, AG	10	12	4	3.00
Kent, MF	3	6	2	3.00
Simpson, RB	62	111	37	3.00
Harvey, RN	79	137	45	3.00

LEADING HALF-CENTURY SCORERS
(Scores between 50 and 100)

Batsman	M	Inn	100s	Opponents ENG	IND	NZ	PAK	SA	SL	WI
Border, AR	89	157	33	11	6	1	6	–	–	9
Walters, KD	75	125	33	13	7	4	1	3	–	5
Redpath, IR	67	120	31	10	4	3	1	7	–	6
Chappell, GS	88	151	31	12	2	3	6	–	1	7
Simpson, RB	62	111	27	9	6	–	–	6	–	6
Lawry, WM	68	123	27	13	7	–	–	4	–	3
Chappell, IM	76	136	26	16	1	1	1	–	–	7
Harvey, RN	79	137	24	12	2	–	2	5	–	3
Hughes, KJ	70	124	22	6	6	1	7	–	–	2
Hill, C	49	89	19	16	–	–	–	3	–	–
McDonald, CC	47	83	17	5	1	–	–	5	–	6
Marsh, RW	97	150	16	9	–	1	2	–	–	4
Noble, MA	42	73	16	15	–	–	–	1	–	–
O'Neill, NC	42	69	15	7	–	–	–	3	–	5

LEADING SCORERS OF FIFTY OR MORE
(Scores above fifty)

Batsman	M	Inn	100s	50s	Total	Opponents ENG	IND	NZ	PAK	SA	SL	WI
Chappell, GS	88	151	31	24	55	21	3	6	–	1	1	12
Border, AR	89	157	33	21	54	18	10	4	11	–	–	11
Walters, KD	75	125	33	15	48	17	8	7	2	3	–	11
Harvey, RN	79	137	24	21	45	18	6	–	2	13	–	6
Bradman, DG	52	80	29	13	42	31	5	–	–	4	–	2
Lawry, WM	68	123	27	13	40	20	8	–	–	5	–	7
Chappell, IM	76	136	26	14	40	20	3	3	2	–	–	12
Redpath, IR	67	120	31	8	39	12	4	4	2	7	–	10
Simpson, RB	62	111	27	10	37	11	10	–	2	7	–	7
Hughes, KJ	70	124	22	9	31	9	8	1	9	–	–	4
Hill, C	49	89	19	7	26	20	–	–	–	6	–	–
Morris, AR	46	79	12	12	24	16	1	–	–	5	–	2
McDonald, CC	47	83	17	5	22	7	1	–	–	6	–	8
Hassett, AL	43	69	10	11	21	10	2	–	–	6	–	3
O'Neill, NC	42	69	15	6	21	9	2	–	1	3	–	6
Stackpole, KR	44	80	14	7	21	10	2	1	–	2	–	6
Bardsley, W	41	66	14	6	20	11	–	–	–	9	–	–
Woodfull, WM	35	54	13	7	20	14	–	–	–	4	–	2

CARRIED BAT THROUGH COMPLETED INNINGS

Batsman	Score	Inns total	Opponent	Venue	Series
Barrett, JE	67*	176	England	Lord's	1890
Armstrong, WW	159*	309	South Africa	Johannesburg1	1902-03
Bardsley, W	193*	383	England	Lord's	1926
Woodfull, WM	30*	66 +	England	Brisbane1	1928-29
Woodfull, WM	73*	193 + +	England	Adelaide	1932-33
Brown, WA	206*	422	England	Lord's	1938
Lawry, WM	49*	107	India	Delhi	1969-70
Lawry, WM	60*	116 +	England	Sydney	1970-71
Redpath, IR	159*	346	New Zealand	Auckland	1973-74
Boon, DC	58*	103	New Zealand	Auckland	1985-86

+ Denotes 1 man absent
+ + Denotes 2 men absent

HIGHEST INDIVIDUAL INNINGS

Batsman	Venue	Series	Opponent ENG	IND	NZ	PAK	SA	SL	WI
Bradman, DG	Leeds	1930	334	—	—	—	—	—	—
Simpson, RB	Manchester	1964	311	—	—	—	—	—	—
Cowper, RM	Melbourne	1965-66	307	—	—	—	—	—	—
Bradman, DG	Leeds	1934	304	—	—	—	—	—	—
Bradman, DG	Adelaide	1931-32	—	—	—	—	299*	—	—
Bradman, DG	Melbourne	1936-37	270	—	—	—	—	—	—
Yallop, GN	Melbourne	1983-84	—	—	—	268	—	—	—
Ponsford, WH	The Oval	1934	266	—	—	—	—	—	—
Bradman, DG	Lord's	1930	254	—	—	—	—	—	—
Walters, KD	Christchurch	1976-77	—	—	250	—	—	—	—
Chappell, GS	Wellington	1973-74	—	—	247*	—	—	—	—
Bradman, DG	The Oval	1934	244	—	—	—	—	—	—
Walters, KD	Sydney	1968-69	—	—	—	—	—	—	242
Chappell, GS	Faisalabad	1979-80	—	—	—	235	—	—	—
Barnes, SG	Sydney	1946-47	234	—	—	—	—	—	—
Bradman, DG	Sydney	1946-47	234	—	—	—	—	—	—
Bradman, DG	The Oval	1930	232	—	—	—	—	—	—

Batsman	Venue	Series	Opponent ENG	IND	NZ	PAK	SA	SL	WI
McCabe, SJ	Nottingham	1938	232	–	–	–	–	–	–
Bradman, DG	Brisbane2	1931-32	–	–	–	–	226	–	–
Simpson, RB	Adelaide	1965-66	225	–	–	–	–	–	–
Bradman, DG	Brisbane1	1930-31	–	–	–	–	–	–	223
Trumper, VT	Adelaide	1910-11	–	–	–	–	214*	–	–
Hughes, KJ	Adelaide	1980-81	–	213	–	–	–	–	–
Bradman, DG	Adelaide	1936-37	212	–	–	–	–	–	–
Murdoch, WL	The Oval	1884	211	–	–	–	–	–	–
Lawry, WM	Bridgetown	1964-65	–	–	–	–	–	–	210
Jones, DM	Madras2	1986-87	–	210	–	–	–	–	–
Stackpole, KR	Brisbane2	1970-71	207	–	–	–	–	–	–
Brown, WA	Lord's	1938	206*	–	–	–	–	–	–
Morris, AR	Adelaide	1950-51	206	–	–	–	–	–	–
Harvey, RN	Melbourne	1952-53	–	–	–	–	–	–	205
Lawry, WM	Melbourne	1968-69	–	–	–	–	–	–	205
Harvey, RN	Kingston	1954-55	–	–	–	–	–	–	204
Chappell, GS	Sydney	1980-81	–	204	–	–	–	–	–
Collins, HL	Johannesburg2	1921-22	–	–	–	–	203	–	–
Gregory, SE	Sydney	1894-95	201	–	–	–	–	–	–
Ryder, J	Adelaide	1924-25	201*	–	–	–	–	–	–
Bradman, DG	Adelaide	1947-48	–	201	–	–	–	–	–
Simpson, RB	Bridgetown	1964-65	–	–	–	–	–	–	201
Chappell, GS	Faisalabad	1979-80	–	–	–	201	–	–	–
Hassett, AL	Adelaide	1947-48	–	198*	–	–	–	–	–
Morris, AR	The Oval	1948	196	–	–	–	–	–	–
Chappell, IM	Adelaide	1972-73	–	–	–	196	–	–	–
Border, AR	Lord's	1985	196	–	–	–	–	–	–
Bardsley, W	Lord's	1926	193*	–	–	–	–	–	–
Chappell, IM	The Oval	1975	192	–	–	–	–	–	–
Hill, C	Sydney	1910-11	–	–	–	–	191	–	–
Harvey, RN	Sydney	1952-53	–	–	–	–	190	–	–
McCabe, SJ	Johannesburg1	1935-36	–	–	–	–	189*	–	–
Burke, JW	Cape Town	1957-58	–	–	–	–	189	–	–
Hill, C	Melbourne	1897-98	188	–	–	–	–	–	–
McCabe, SJ	Sydney	1932-33	187*	–	–	–	–	–	–
Bradman, DG	Brisbane2	1946-47	187	–	–	–	–	–	–
Trumper, VT	Sydney	1903-04	185*	–	–	–	–	–	–
Bradman, DG	Brisbane2	1947-48	–	185	–	–	–	–	–

Batsman	Venue	Series	Opponent ENG	IND	NZ	PAK	SA	SL	WI
Jones, DM	Sydney	1986-87	184*	–	–	–	–	–	–
Ponsford, WH	Sydney	1930-31	–	–	–	–	–	–	183
Chappell, GS	Sydney	1975-76	–	–	–	–	–	–	182*
Morris, AR	Leeds	1948	182	–	–	–	–	–	–
Chappell, GS	Sydney	1983-84	–	–	–	182	–	–	–
Ponsford, WH	Leeds	1934	181	–	–	–	–	–	–
O'Neill, NC	Brisbane2	1960-61	–	–	–	–	–	–	181
Burge, PJP	The Oval	1961	181	–	–	–	–	–	–
Wessels, KC	Adelaide	1983-84	–	–	–	179	–	–	–
Darling, J	Adelaide	1897-98	178	–	–	–	–	–	–
Harvey, RN	Cape Town	1949-50	–	–	–	–	178	–	–
Simpson, RB	Perth	1977-78	–	176	–	–	–	–	–
Chappell, GS	Christchurch	1981-82	–	–	176	–	–	–	–

CENTURIES IN MOST CONSECUTIVE INNINGS

Batsman	Runs	Inn	Opponent	Venue	Series
Four:					
Fingleton, JHW	112	1	South Africa	Cape Town	1935-36
	108	1	South Africa	Johannesburg1	1935-36
	118	1	South Africa	Durban2	1935-36
	100	1	England	Brisbane2	1936-37
Three:					
Bardsley, W	136	1	England	The Oval	1909
	130	2			
	132	1	South Africa	Sydney	1910-11
Bradman, DG	132	1	India	Melbourne	1947-48
	127*	2			
	201	1	India	Adelaide	1947-48
Macartney, CG	133*	2	England	Lord's	1926
	151	1	England	Leeds	1926
	109	1	England	Manchester	1926
Morris, AR	155	2	England	Melbourne	1946-47
	122	1	England	Adelaide	1946-47
	124*	2			

MOST DOUBLE CENTURIES IN A SERIES

Batsman	Times achieved	Opponent	Venue	Series
Three:				
Bradman, DG	1	England	England	1930
Two:				
Bradman, DG	3	South Africa	Australia	1931-32
		England	England	1934
		England	Australia	1936-37

MOST CENTURIES IN A SERIES

Batsman	Times achieved	Opponent	Venue	Series
Four:				
Bradman, DG	3	England	England	1930
		South Africa	Australia	1931-32
		India	Australia	1947-48
Harvey, RN	2	South Africa	South Africa	1949-50
		South Africa	Australia	1952-53
Walters, KD	1	West Indies	Australia	1968-69
Three:				
Bradman, DG	2	England	Australia	1936-37
		England	England	1938
Morris, AR	2	England	England	1946-47
		England	England	1948
Lawry, WM	2	England	Australia	1965-66
		West Indies	Australia	1968-69
Darling, J	1	England	Australia	1897-98
Armstrong, WW	1	England	Australia	1920-21
Macartney, CG	1	England	England	1926
Woodfull, WM	1	England	Australia	1928-29
Fingleton, JHW	1	South Africa	South Africa	1935-36
Harvey, RN	1	West Indies	West Indies	1954-55
Miller, KR	1	West Indies	West Indies	1954-55
Chappell, GS	1	West Indies	Australia	1975-76
Redpath, IR	1	West Indies	Australia	1975-76

JOHN "FINGO" FINGLETON

John Henry Webb Fingleton was the son of a member of the New South Wales parliament, educated at Waverly Christian Brothers College, who married Phillippa, daughter of Sir Kenneth Street, Chief Justice of New South Wales. These impressive connections did not help him much when he batted against Harold Larwood and Bill Voce in the infamous Bodyline series; Fingleton had to endure a fearsome hiding.

He made his debut for New South Wales in 1930-31 and his first appearance in international cricket in the Fifth Test against South Africa in 1931-32. But the Bodyline series was his first full Test series. He took an awful battering for New South Wales against England in the match before the Tests began, and in an effort that began his reputation for courage batted through the innings for 119 not out.

In the first three Tests of the Bodyline summer, Fingleton was hit repeatedly all round the body, finishing each match covered in bruises despite special padding aimed to protect his heart and ribs on the side facing the bowlers. He made 83 in the Test Australia won at Melbourne, but after securing ducks in both innings at Adelaide he was dropped.

His entire Test future appeared in jeopardy and it was no surprise that he missed the 1934 tour of England, although his omission rankled with him for the rest of his life. His chance to regain prestige came on the 1935-36 Australian tour of South Africa, which Bradman missed because of injury, with Bill Woodfull and Bill Ponsford in retirement.

Fingleton began quietly with 2 and 36 not out in the First Test, followed by 62 and 40 in the Second Test. Then at Cape Town, in the Third Test, he hit a splendid 121, to which he added 108 in the Fourth Test at Johannesburg, and 118 in the Fifth Test at Durban. Australia won each of these matches by an innings; the speed with which Fingleton got his runs as well as his freedom from error made such big margins possible.

He was a tremendous cutter of the ball in this form. He drove with power and freedom on both sides of the wicket, glanced delicately and was always watchful for the ball to hook or pull. In the field he was super fast to the ball, immaculate in his gathering and throwing, and he helped produce many run-outs.

In scoring his three successive centuries in South Africa, Fingleton had opening partnerships of 233, 99 and 162 with Billy Brown. On the entire South African tour Fingleton made 1192 runs at 79.16, by far the best performance in a team that scored heavily.

Until he shrugged aside his reputation as a stonewaller and produced this wonderful sequence of heavy scoring, Fingleton admitted he had not enjoyed big cricket. The Bodyline tour had soured him, as it had most of the Australians who took part in it.

But on his return from South Africa, Australians saw a more relaxed and confident stroke-maker. He had always been a devastating performer in the practice nets and now he took that form into matches, batting with delightful freedom in club cricket for Waverley.

Fingleton made his fourth Test century in a row against England at Brisbane in December 1936, in the First Test against Gubby Allen's England team. He made an even 100 before he was bowled by Hedley Verity. This was the first instance on record of a batsman scoring four Test hundreds in successive innings, but the sequence came to a sudden end in Australia's second innings when Voce bowled him first ball.

Fingleton made 73 in the Second Test at Sydney and 136 in the Third Test at Melbourne to consolidate his selection in the Australian team which toured England in 1938. He made four centuries on the English tour, 124 against Oxford University, 123 not out against Hampshire, 121 against the Gentlemen, and 111 against Cambridge University, but averaged only 20.50 in the Tests. He was remembered more for his action in refusing to bat in the Nottingham Test when spectators heckled him for slow scoring. He removed his gloves and sat beside the pitch, an extraordinary reaction to barracking that *Wisden* said was never more than mild and never hostile, and was unwarranted as only a small proportion of the crowd objected to his tactics in trying to save Australia.

Fingleton, a trained journalist, worked as press secretary for Billy Hughes and Ben Chifley. He helped his old Bodyline foe Harold Larwood migrate to Australia.

CENTURIES IN EACH INNINGS OF A MATCH

Batsman	1st Inns	2nd Inns	Opponent	Venue	Series
Bardsley, W	136	130	England	The Oval	1909
Morris, AR	122	124*	England	Adelaide	1946-47
Bradman, DG	132	127*	India	Melbourne	1947-48
Moroney, J	118	101*	South Africa	Johannesburg2	1949-50
Simpson, RB	153	115	Pakistan	Karachi	1964-65
Walters, KD	242	103	West Indies	Sydney	1968-69
Chappell, IM	145	121	New Zealand	Wellington	1973-74
Chappell, GS	247*	133	New Zealand	Wellington	1973-74
Chappell, GS	123	109*	West Indies	Brisbane2	1975-76
Border, AR	150*	153	Pakistan	Lahore2	1979-80

CENTURIES IN MOST CONSECUTIVE TESTS

Batsman	Runs	Inn	Opponent	Venue	Series
Six:					
Bradman, DG	270	–	England	Melbourne	1936-37
	212	–	England	Adelaide	1936-37
	169	–	England	Melbourne	1936-37
	144*	–	England	Trent Bridge	1938
	102*	–	England	Lord's	1938
	103	–	England	Headingley	1938

Bradman was injured and unable to bat in the next Test.
In the following two Tests he scored 187 and 234.

Batsman	Runs	Inn	Opponent	Venue	Series
Four:					
Bradman, DG	123	–	England	Melbourne	1928-29
	131	–	England	Nottingham	1930
	254	–	England	Lord's	1930
	334	–	England	Leeds	1930
Bradman, DG	226	–	South Africa	Brisbane2	1931-32
	112	–	South Africa	Sydney	1931-32
	167	–	South Africa	Melbourne	1931-32
	299*	–	South Africa	Adelaide	1931-32

Bradman was injured and unable to bat in next Test.
In the following Test he scored 103.

Batsman	*Runs*	*Inn*	*Opponent*	*Venue*	*Series*
Fingleton, JHW	112	–	South Africa	Cape Town	1935-36
	108	–	South Africa	Johannesburg1	1935-36
	118	–	South Africa	Durban2	1935-36
	100	–	England	Brisbane2	1936-37
Harvey, RN	178	–	South Africa	Cape Town	1949-50
	151*	–	South Africa	Durban2	1949-50
	100	–	South Africa	Johannesburg2	1949-50
	116	–	South Africa	Port Elizabeth	1949-50

Three:

Batsman	*Runs*	*Inn*	*Opponent*	*Venue*	*Series*
Bardsley, W	136	1	England	The Oval	1909
	130	2			
	132	–	South Africa	Sydney	1910-11
Armstrong, WW	158	–	England	Sydney	1920-21
	121	–	England	Adelaide	1920-21
	123*	–	England	Melbourne	1920-21
Macartney, CG	133*	–	England	Lord's	1926
	151	–	England	Leeds	1926
	109	–	England	Manchester	1926
Harvey, RN	190	–	South Africa	Sydney	1952-53
	116	–	South Africa	Adelaide	1952-53
	205	–	South Africa	Melbourne	1952-53
Walters, KD	118	–	West Indies	Sydney	1968-69
	110	–	West Indies	Adelaide	1968-69
	242	1	West Indies	Sydney	1968-69
	103	2			

MOST FIFTIES
IN CONSECUTIVE INNINGS

Batsman	*1st inns*	*2nd inns*	*Opponent*	*Venue*	*Series*
Six:					
Ryder, J	78*	58	South Africa	Durban1	1921-22
	56	–	South Africa	Johannesburg1	1921-22
	142	–	South Africa	Cape Town	1921-22
	201*	88	England	Adelaide	1924-25
Walters, KD	76	–	West Indies	Brisbane2	1968-69
	118	–	West Indies	Sydney	1968-69
	110	50	West Indies	Adelaide	1968-69
	242	103	West Indies	Sydney	1968-69
Chappell, GS	68	54*	West Indies	Melbourne	1975-76
	52	70	Pakistan	Adelaide	1976-77
	121	67	Pakistan	Melbourne	1976-77

Batsman	1st inns	2nd inns	Opponent	Venue	Series
Five:					
Harvey, RN	2	151*	South Africa	Durban2	1949-50
	56*	100	South Africa	Johannesburg2	1949-50
	116	–	South Africa	Port Elizabeth	1949-50
	74	12	England	Brisbane2	1950-51
Harvey, RN	11	60	South Africa	Melbourne	1952-53
	190	–	South Africa	Sydney	1952-53
	84	116	South Africa	Adelaide	1952-53
	205	7	South Africa	Melbourne	1952-53
Bradman, DG	132	127*	India	Melbourne	1947-48
	201	–	India	Adelaide	1947-48
	57	–	India	Melbourne	1947-48
	138	0	England	Nottingham	1948

Noble, MA scored 60* & 59* on the second day of 3rd Test v England, Manchester

MOST FIFTIES
IN CONSECUTIVE MATCHES

Batsman	1st inns	2nd inns	Opponent	Venue	Series
Seven:					
Bradman, DG	0	82	England	Sydney	1936-37
	13	270	England	Melbourne	1936-37
	26	212	England	Adelaide	1936-37
	169	–	England	Melbourne	1936-37
	51	144*	England	Nottingham	1938
	18	102*	England	Lord's	1938
	103	16	England	Leeds	1938

Bradman was injured in the next Test and did not bat. In the following 6 Tests he surpassed 50 in at least 1 innings of each of the Tests.

Batsman	1st inns	2nd inns	Opponent	Venue	Series
Fingleton, JHW	62	40	South Africa	Johannesburg1	1935-36
	112	–	South Africa	Cape Town	1935-36
	108	–	South Africa	Johannesburg1	1935-36
	118	–	South Africa	Durban2	1935-36
	100	0	England	Brisbane2	1936-37
	12	72	England	Sydney	1936-37
	38	136	England	Adelaide	1936-37
Stackpole, KR	87	136	England	Adelaide	1970-71
	6	67	England	Sydney	1970-71
	53	67	England	Manchester	1972
	5	57	England	Lord's	1972
	114	12	England	Nottingham	1972
	52	28	England	Leeds	1972
	18	79	England	The Oval	1972

CENTURY ON TEST DEBUT

Batsman	Runs	2nd inns	Opponent	Venue	Series
In 1st innings:					
Bannerman, C	165 +	4	England	Melbourne	1876-77
Graham, H	107	–	England	Lord's	1893
Ponsford, WH	110	27	England	Sydney	1924-25
Jackson, A	164	36	England	Adelaide	1928-29
Walters, KD	155	–	England	Brisbane2	1965-66
Chappell, GS	108	–	England	Perth	1970-71
Cosier, GJ	109	–	West Indies	Melbourne	1975-76
Wessels, KC	162	46	England	Brisbane2	1982-83
Phillips, WB	159	–	Pakistan	Perth	1983-84
In 2nd innings:					
Duff, RA	32	104	England	Melbourne	1901-02
Hartigan, RJ	48	116	England	Adelaide	1907-08
Collins, HL	70	104	England	Sydney	1920-21
Burke, JW	12	101*	England	Adelaide	1950-51
Wellham, DM	24	103	England	The Oval	1981

NINETIES ON TEST DEBUT

Batsman	Runs	2nd inns	Opponent	Venue	Series
In 1st innings:					
Chipperfield, AG	99	4	England	Nottingham	1934
Redpath, IR	97	25	South Africa	Melbourne	1963-64
Laird, BM	92	75	West Indies	Brisbane2	1979-80
Minnett, RB	90	17	England	Sydney	1911-12
In 2nd innings:					
Richardson, AJ	22	98	England	Sydney	1924-25

ARTHUR "CHIPPER" CHIPPERFIELD

Arthur Chipperfield went to England with the Australian team in 1934 after only three first-class matches. He had scored consistently for several seasons in the Sydney first-grade competition for Western Suburbs, but he had only one outstanding innings in his record on which to attribute his selection—152 for Northern New South Wales against England during the acrimonious Bodyline tour.

Chipperfield's inclusion in the Australian side was widely reported to have come through the recommendation of former Test opener Warren Bardsley, who rated Chipperfield the finest slips fieldsman he had seen. Bardsley had had plenty of time to study Chipperfield when they had played in the Western Suburbs side.

Chipperfield, who was to be troubled all his life by sinusitis, missed early matches on the Australian tour in 1934 because of influenza, but recovered to score a splendid century against Hampshire. This and a fighting 37 not out at Lord's on a wet wicket—Neville Cardus said it was worth a century under normal conditions—won him a place in the First Test at Nottingham.

Australia, who began with an opening stand of 77 between Bill Woodfull and Bill Ponsford, had lost 6 for 234 when Chipperfield went in at number 7. He made 17 runs by the end of the first day and next morning became involved in useful partnerships with Bert Oldfield and Clarrie Grimmett.

Grimmett was then aged 42, a factor Chipperfield was mindful of in their running between wickets. At lunch Chipperfield had added 82 to his overnight score and went to the break on 99. His friend Ben Barnett, the Victorian wicket-keeper, said he should already have passed his century had he not missed one or two singles.

It never occurred to Chipperfield that he would not score his century. The England attack was without the two destroyers of the previous series in Australia, Harold Larwood and Bill Voce, and Cyril Walters had taken over as captain from the enigmatic Douglas Jardine. Ken Farnes, in his debut as England's fast bowler, found the pitch a difficult one from which to extract life. George Geary, Wally Hammond and Hedley Verity all had been made to appear innocuous in the face of sound, determined Australian batting.

Grimmett advised Chipperfield, as they went out to resume the innings, to play back at all costs until he had picked up the single needed for his century. Instead, Chipperfield played forward to the third ball after lunch from Farnes, confident he could drive it, edged it, and turned to see wicket-keeper Les Ames toss the ball up after completing the catch.

Chipperfield was the first batsman to miss a century on debut by one run, but he had the satisfaction of figuring in an Australian victory in that Test by 238 runs. Australia's first innings of 374 was followed by an innings of 268 by England. Australia then declared at 8 for 273. England appeared likely to save the match until Grimmett and Norm O'Reilly came together and spun them out for 141.

Chipperfield's impressive Test debut assured him of a place in the remaining Tests of that series, Australia clinching The Ashes in the Fifth Test, following the memorable second wicket stand of 451 by Don Bradman (244) and Bill Ponsford (266).

Chipperfield went to South Africa with the Australian team in 1935-36 and at Durban scored the century that had eluded him at Nottingham: 109 in an Australian score of 429, which was enough to set up victory by nine wickets. Throughout a series that Australia won 4-0 his slips catching remained a joy, for he took the catches without falling down or somersaulting and seldom had a mark on his trousers at the finish of play. When his career ended he could not recall ever having been embraced by a team-mate.

Arthur Chipperfield played 14 Tests in all, scoring 522 runs at 32.47. In a first-class career that spanned 96 first-class matches, he held 91 catches and took 65 wickets with his right-arm leg-spinners, his best figures being 8 for 66 for New South Wales against England in 1936. He made a second visit to England with Bradman's team in 1938 but did not appear in a Test. He made nine first-class centuries, but it was the one that got away at Nottingham when he was 29 that made him a unique cricketer.

MOST RUNS ON TEST DEBUT

Runs	Batsman	1st inns	2nd inns	Opponent	Venue	Series
208	Wessels, KC	162	46	England	Brisbane2	1982-83
200	Jackson, A	164	36	England	Adelaide	1928-29
174	Collins, HL	70	104	England	Sydney	1920-21
169	Bannerman, C	165 +	4	England	Melbourne	1976-77
167	Laird, BM	92	75	West Indies	Brisbane2	1979-80
164	Hartigan, RJ	48	116	England	Adelaide	1907-08
159	Phillips, WB	159	–	Pakistan	Perth	1983-84
155	Walters, KD	155	–	England	Brisbane2	1965-66

FIRST CLASS AND TEST DEBUT IN THE SAME SEASON

Player	Season	Player	Season
Garrett, TW	1876-77	McKibbon, TR	1894-95
Hodges, JH	1876-77	Fairfax, AG	1928-29
Bonnor, GJ	1880	Toshack, ERH	1945-46
Pope, RJ	1884-85	Meuleman, KD	1945-46
Robertson, WR	1884-85	Dell, AR	1970-71
Cottam, JT	1886-87	Thomson, JR	1972-73
Ferris, JJ	1886-87	Davis, IC	1973-74

MAIDEN FIRST-CLASS CENTURY IN A TEST MATCH

Batsman	Runs	Opponent	Venue	Series
Bannerman, C	165 +	England	Melbourne	1876-77
Murdoch, WL	153*	England	The Oval	1880
McDonnell, PS	147	England	Sydney	1881-82
Graham, H	107	England	Lord's	1893

Bannerman's 165 was his only hundred in first-class cricket. Bannerman & Graham scored their hundreds on Test debut. Graham also scored his 2nd first-class century in a Test. 105 v England at Sydney, 1894-95.

YOUNGEST PLAYERS
TO SCORE A CENTURY

Years	Days	Batsman	Runs	Opponent	Venue	Series
19	121	Harvey, RN	153	India	Melbourne	1947-48
19	152	Jackson, A	164	England	Adelaide	1928-29
19	357	Walters, KD	155	England	Brisbane2	1965-66
20	129	Bradman, DG	112	England	Melbourne	1928-29
20	240	Burke, JW	101	England	Adelaide	1950-51
20	317	Hill, C	188	England	Melbourne	1897-98
21	149	Wood, GM	126	West Indies	Georgetown	1977-78
21	226	Trumper, VT	135*	England	Lord's	1899
21	231	Archer, RG	128	England	Kingston	1954-55

YOUNGEST PLAYERS TO SCORE
A DOUBLE CENTURY

Years	Days	Batsman	Runs	Opponent	Venue	Series
21	307	Bradman, DG	254	England	Lord's	1930
23	65	Walters, KD	242	West Indies	Sydney	1968-69

PLAYERS TO SCORE
A TRIPLE CENTURY

Years	Days	Batsman	Runs	Opponent	Venue	Series
21	318	Bradman, DG	334	England	Leeds	1930
25	127	Cowper, RM	307	England	Melbourne	1965-66
28	175	Simpson, RB	311	England	Manchester	1964

OLDEST PLAYERS
TO SCORE A CENTURY

Years	Days	Batsman	Runs	Opponent	Venue	Series
43	201	Bardsley, W	193*	England	Lord's	1926
42	360	Simpson, RB	100	India	Adelaide	1977-78
41	268	Armstrong, WW	123*	England	Melbourne	1920-21
40	29	Macartney, CG	109	England	Manchester	1926
39	334	Bradman, DG	173*	England	Leeds	1948
39	301	Hassett, AL	104	England	Lord's	1953
39	143	Ryder, J	112	England	Melbourne	1928-29
37	351	Richardson, AJ	100	England	Leeds	1926
35	332	Collins, HL	114	England	Sydney	1924-25
35	262	Giffen, G	161	England	Sydney	1894-95
35	197	Miller, KR	109	West Indies	Kingston	1954-55
35	152	Chappell, GS	182	Pakistan	Sydney	1983-84
35	5	Walters, KD	107	New Zealand	Melbourne	1980-81

HIGHEST INDIVIDUAL INNINGS
FOR EACH TEST GROUND

Venue	Runs	Batsman	Opponent	Series
Australia:				
Adelaide	299*	Bradman, DG	South Africa	1931-32
Brisbane1	223	Bradman, DG	West Indies	1930-31
Brisbane2	226	Bradman, DG	South Africa	1931-32
Melbourne	307	Cowper, RM	England	1965-66
Perth	176	Simpson, RB	India	1977-78
Sydney	242	Walters, KD	West Indies	1968-69
England:				
Birmingham	114	Harvey, RN	England	1961
Leeds	334	Bradman, DG	England	1930
Lord's	254	Bradman, DG	England	1930
Manchester	311	Simpson, RB	England	1964
Nottingham	232	McCabe, SJ	England	1938
Sheffield	119	Hill, C	England	1902
The Oval	266	Ponsford, WH	England	1934

Venue	Runs	Batsman	Opponent	Series
India:				
Bangalore	86	Hughes, KJ	India	1979-80
Bombay2	163	O'Neill, NC	India	1959-60
Bombay3	101	Marsh, GR	India	1986-87
Calcutta	167	Yallop, GN	India	1979-80
Delhi	138	Chappell, IM	India	1969-70
Kanpur	114	Sheahan, AP	India	1969-70
Madras1	210	Jones, DM	India	1986-87
Madras2	101	Favell, LE	India	1959-60
New Zealand:				
Auckland	159*	Redpath, IR	New Zealand	1973-74
Christchurch	250	Walters, KD	New Zealand	1976-77
Wellington	247*	Chappell, GS	New Zealand	1973-74
Pakistan:				
Dacca	96	Harvey, RN	Pakistan	1959-60
Faisalabad	235	Chappell, GS	Pakistan	1979-80
Karachi	166	Simpson, RB	Pakistan	1964-65
Lahore2	153	Border, AR	Pakistan	1979-80
South Africa:				
Cape Town	189	Burke, JW	South Africa	1957-58
Durban1	116	Macartney, CG	South Africa	1921-22
Durban2	151*	Harvey, RN	South Africa	1949-50
Johannesburg1	203	Collins, HL	South Africa	1921-22
Johannesburg2	118	Moroney,J	South Africa	1949-50
Johannesburg3	122	Benaud, R	South Africa	1957-58
Port Elizabeth	167	Hassett, AL	South Africa	1949-50
Sri Lanka:				
Kandy	143*	Hookes, DW	Sri Lanka	1982-83
West Indies:				
Bridgetown	210	Lawry, WM	West Indies	1964-65
Georgetown	126	Wood, GM	West Indies	1977-78
Kingston	204	Harvey, RN	West Indies	1954-55
Port-of-Spain	143	Cowper, RM	West Indies	1964-65
St. John's	98	Border, AR	West Indies	1983-84

TEST CENTURIES

Batsman	100s	Runs	Inns	Opponent	Venue	Series
Archer, RG		128		West Indies	Kingston	1954-55
Armstrong, WW	6	159*		South Africa	Johannesburg1	1902-03
		133*		England	Melbourne	1907-08
		132		South Africa	Melbourne	1910-11
		158		England	Sydney	1920-21
		121		England	Adelaide	1920-21
		123*		England	Melbourne	1920-21
Badcock, CL		118		England	Melbourne	1936-37
Bannerman, C		165 + d		England	Melbourne	1876-77
Bardsley, W	6	136	1	England	The Oval	1909
		130	2			
		132		South Africa	Sydney	1910-11
		121		South Africa	Manchester	1912
		164		South Africa	Lord's	1912
		193*		England	Lord's	1926
Barnes, SG	3	234		England	Sydney	1946-47
		112		India	Adelaide	1947-48
		141		England	Lord's	1948
Benaud, J		142		Pakistan	Melbourne	1972-73
Benaud, R	3	121		West Indies	Kingston	1954-55
		122		South Africa	Johannesburg3	1957-58
		100		South Africa	Johannesburg3	1957-58
Bonnor, GJ		128		England	Sydney	1884-85
Boon, DC	4	123		India	Adelaide	1985-86
		131		India	Sydney	1985-86
		122		India	Madras3	1986-87
		103		England	Adelaide	1986-87
Booth, BC	5	112		England	Brisbane2	1962-63
		103		England	Melbourne	1962-63
		169		South Africa	Brisbane2	1963-64
		102*		South Africa	Sydney	1963-64
		117		West Indies	Port-of-Spain	1964-65
Border, AR	21	105		Pakistan	Melbourne	1978-79
		162		India	Madras1	1979-80
		115		England	Perth	1979-80
		150*	1	Pakistan	Lahore2	1979-80
		153	2			

Batsman	*100s*	*Runs*	*Inns*	*Opponent*	*Venue*	*Series*
Border, AR		124		India	Melbourne	1980-81
		123*		England	Manchester	1981
		106*		England	The Oval	1981
		126		West Indies	Adelaide	1981-82
		118		Pakistan	Brisbane2	1983-84
		117*		Pakistan	Adelaide	1983-84
		100*		West Indies	Port-of-Spain	1983-84
		196		England	Lord's	1985
		146*		England	Manchester	1985
		152*		New Zealand	Brisbane2	1985-86
		163		India	Melbourne	1985-86
		140 114*	1 2	New Zealand	Christchurch	1985-86
		106		India	Madras1	1986-87
		125		England	Perth	1986-87
		100*		England	Adelaide	1986-87
Bradman, DG	29	112		England	Melbourne	1928-29
		123		England	Melbourne	1928-29
		131		England	Nottingham	1930
		254		England	Lord's	1930
		334		England	Leeds	1930
		232		England	The Oval	1930
		223		West Indies	Brisbane1	1930-31
		152		West Indies	Melbourne	1930-31
		226		South Africa	Brisbane2	1931-32
		112		South Africa	Sydney	1931-32
		167		South Africa	Melbourne	1931-32
		299*		South Africa	Adelaide	1931-32
		103*		England	Melbourne	1932-33
		304		England	Leeds	1934
		244		England	The Oval	1934
		270		England	Melbourne	1936-37
		212		England	Adelaide	1936-37
		169		England	Melbourne	1936-37
		144*		England	Nottingham	1938
		102*		England	Lord's	1938
		103		England	Leeds	1938
		187		England	Brisbane2	1946-47
		234		England	Sydney	1946-47

Batsman	100s	Runs	Inns	Opponent	Venue	Series
Bradman, DG		185		India	Brisbane2	1947-48
		132	1	India	Melbourne	1947-48
		127*	2			
		201		India	Adelaide	1947-48
		138		England	Nottingham	1948
		173*		England	Leeds	1948
Brown, WA	4	105		England	Lord's	1934
		121		South Africa	Cape Town	1935-36
		133		England	Nottingham	1938
		206*		England	Lord's	1938
Burge, PJP	4	181		England	The Oval	1961
		103		England	Sydney	1962-63
		160		England	Leeds	1964
		120		England	Melbourne	1965-66
Burke, JW	3	101*	d	England	Adelaide	1950-51
		161		India	Bombay2	1956-57
		189		South Africa	Cape Town	1957-58
Chappell, GS	24	108d		England	Perth	1970-71
		131		England	Lord's	1972
		113		England	The Oval	1972
		116*		Pakistan	Melbourne	1972-73
		106		West Indies	Bridgetown	1972-73
		247*	1	New Zealand	Wellington	1973-74
		133	2			
		144		England	Sydney	1974-75
		102		England	Melbourne	1974-75
		123	1	West Indies	Brisbane2	1975-76
		109*	2			
		182*		West Indies	Sydney	1975-76
		121		Pakistan	Melbourne	1976-77
		112		England	Manchester	1977
		124		West Indies	Brisbane2	1979-80
		114		England	Melbourne	1979-80
		235		Pakistan	Faisalabad	1979-80
		204		India	Sydney	1980-81
		201		Pakistan	Brisbane2	1981-82
		176		New Zealand	Christchurch	1981-82
		117		England	Perth	1982-83
		115		England	Adelaide	1982-83

Batsman	100s	Runs	Inns	Opponent	Venue	Series
Chappell, GS		150*		Pakistan	Brisbane2	1983-84
		182		Pakistan	Sydney	1983-84
Chappell, IM	14	151		India	Melbourne	1967-68
		117		West Indies	Brisbane2	1968-69
		165		West Indies	Melbourne	1968-69
		138		India	Delhi	1969-70
		111		England	Melbourne	1970-71
		104		England	Adelaide	1970-71
		118		England	The Oval	1972
		196		Pakistan	Adelaide	1972-73
		106*		West Indies	Bridgetown	1972-73
		109		West Indies	Georgetown	1972-73
		145	1	New Zealand	Wellington	1973-74
		121	2			
		192		England	The Oval	1975
		156		West Indies	Perth	1975-76
Chipperfield, AG		109		South Africa	Durban2	1935-36
Collins, HL	4	104d		England	Sydney	1920-21
		162		England	Adelaide	1920-21
		203		South Africa	Johannesburg1	1921-22
		114		England	Sydney	1924-25
Cosier, GJ	2	109d		West Indies	Melbourne	1975-76
		168		Pakistan	Melbourne	1976-77
Cowper, RM	5	143		West Indies	Port-of-Spain	1964-65
		102		West Indies	Bridgetown	1964-65
		307		England	Melbourne	1965-66
		108		India	Adelaide	1967-68
		165		India	Sydney	1967-68
Darling, J	3	101		England	Sydney	1897-98
		178		England	Adelaide	1897-98
		160		England	Sydney	1897-98
Davis, IC		105		Pakistan	Adelaide	1976-77
Duff, RA	2	104d		England	Melbourne	1901-02
		146		England	The Oval	1905
Dyson, J	2	102		England	Leeds	1981
		127*		West Indies	Sydney	1981-82
Edwards, R	2	170*		England	Nottingham	1972
		115		England	Perth	1974-75

Batsman	100s	Runs	Inns	Opponent	Venue	Series
Favell, LE		101		India	Madras2	1959-60
Fingleton, JHW	5	112		South Africa	Cape Town	1935-36
		108		South Africa	Johannesburg1	1935-36
		118		South Africa	Durban2	1935-36
		100		England	Brisbane2	1936-37
		136		England	Melbourne	1936-37
Giffen, G		161		England	Sydney	1894-95
Gilmour, GJ		101		New Zealand	Christchurch	1976-77
Graham, H	2	107d		England	Lord's	1893
		105		England	Sydney	1894-95
Gregory, JM	2	100		England	Melbourne	1920-21
		119		South Africa	Johannesburg1	1921-22
Gregory, SE	4	201		England	Sydney	1894-95
		103		England	Lord's	1896
		117		England	The Oval	1899
		112		England	Adelaide	1903-04
Hartigan, RJ		116d		England	Adelaide	1907-08
Harvey, RN	21	153		India	Melbourne	1947-48
		112		England	Leeds	1948
		178		South Africa	Cape Town	1949-50
		151*		South Africa	Durban2	1949-50
		100		South Africa	Johannesburg2	1949-50
		116		South Africa	Port Elizabeth	1949-50
		109		South Africa	Brisbane2	1952-53
		190		South Africa	Sydney	1952-53
		116		South Africa	Adelaide	1952-53
		205		South Africa	Melbourne	1952-53
		122		England	Manchester	1953
		162		England	Brisbane2	1954-55
		133		West Indies	Kingston	1954-55
		133		West Indies	Port-of-Spain	1954-55
		204		West Indies	Kingston	1954-55
		140		India	Bombay2	1956-57
		167		England	Melbourne	1958-59
		114		India	Delhi	1959-60
		102		India	Bombay2	1959-60
		114		England	Birmingham	1961
		154		England	Adelaide	1962-63

Batsman	100s	Runs	Inns	Opponent	Venue	Series
Hassett, AL	10	128		England	Brisbane2	1946-47
		198*		India	Adelaide	1947-48
		137		England	Nottingham	1948
		112		South Africa	Johannesburg2	1949-50
		167		South Africa	Port Elizabeth	1949-50
		132		West Indies	Sydney	1951-52
		102		West Indies	Melbourne	1951-52
		163		South Africa	Adelaide	1952-53
		115		England	Nottingham	1953
		104		England	Lord's	1953
Hendry, HSTL		112		England	Sydney	1928-29
Hilditch, AMJ	2	113		West Indies	Melbourne	1984-85
		119		England	Leeds	1985
Hill, C	7	188		England	Melbourne	1897-98
		135		England	Lord's	1899
		119		England	Sheffield	1902
		142		South Africa	Johannesburg1	1902-03
		160		England	Adelaide	1907-08
		191		South Africa	Sydney	1910-11
		100		South Africa	Melbourne	1910-11
Hookes, DW		143*		Sri Lanka	Kandy	1982-83
Horan, TP		124		England	Melbourne	1881-82
Hughes, KJ	9	129		England	Brisbane2	1978-79
		100		India	Madras1	1979-80
		130*		West Indies	Brisbane2	1979-80
		117		England	Lord's	1980
		213		India	Adelaide	1980-81
		106		Pakistan	Perth	1981-82
		100*		West Indies	Melbourne	1981-82
		137		England	Sydney	1982-83
		106		Pakistan	Adelaide	1983-84
Iredale, FA	2	140		England	Adelaide	1884-85
		108		England	Manchester	1896
Jackson, A		164d		England	Adelaide	1928-29
Jones, DM	2	210		India	Madras1	1986-87
		184*		England	Sydney	1986-87

Batsman	100s	Runs	Inns	Opponent	Venue	Series
Kelleway, C	3	114		South Africa	Manchester	1912
		102		South Africa	Lord's	1912
		147		England	Adelaide	1920-21
Kippax, AF	2	100		England	Melbourne	1928-29
		146		West Indies	Adelaide	1930-31
Lawry, WM	13	130		England	Lord's	1961
		102		England	Manchester	1961
		157		South Africa	Melbourne	1963-64
		106		England	Manchester	1964
		210		West Indies	Bridgetown	1964-65
		166		England	Brisbane2	1965-66
		119		England	Adelaide	1965-66
		108		England	Melbourne	1965-66
		100		India	Melbourne	1967-68
		135		England	The Oval	1968
		105		West Indies	Brisbane2	1968-69
		205		West Indies	Melbourne	1968-69
		151		West Indies	Sydney	1968-69
Lindwall, RR	2	100		England	Melbourne	1946-47
		118		West Indies	Bridgetown	1954-55
Loxton, SJE		101		South Africa	Johannesburg2	1949-50
Lyons, JJ		134		England	Sydney	1892-93
Macartney, CG	7	137		South Africa	Sydney	1910-11
		170		England	Sydney	1920-21
		115		England	Leeds	1921
		116		South Africa	Durban1	1921-22
		133*		England	Lord's	1926
		151		England	Leeds	1926
		109		England	Manchester	1926
Mann, AL		105		India	Perth	1977-78
Marsh, GR	3	118		New Zealand	Auckland	1985-86
		101		India	Bombay3	1986-87
		110		England	Brisbane2	1986-87
Marsh, RW	3	118		Pakistan	Adelaide	1972-73
		132		New Zealand	Adelaide	1973-74
		110*		England	Melbourne	1976-77
Matthews, GRJ	3	115		New Zealand	Brisbane2	1985-86
		100*		India	Melbourne	1985-86
		130		New Zealand	Wellington	1985-86

Batsman	100s	Runs	Inns	Opponent	Venue	Series
McCabe, SJ	6	187*		England	Sydney	1932-33
		137		England	Manchester	1934
		149		South Africa	Durban2	1935-36
		189*		South Africa	Johannesburg1	1935-36
		112		England	Melbourne	1936-37
		232		England	Nottingham	1938
McCool, CL		104*		England	Melbourne	1946-47
McCosker, RB	4	127		England	The Oval	1975
		109*		West Indies	Melbourne	1975-76
		105		Pakistan	Melbourne	1976-77
		107		England	Nottingham	1977
McDonald, CC	5	154		South Africa	Adelaide	1952-53
		110		West Indies	Port-of-Spain	1954-55
		127		West Indies	Kingston	1954-55
		170		England	Adelaide	1958-59
		133		England	Melbourne	1958-59
McDonnell, PS	3	147		England	Sydney	1881-82
		103		England	The Oval	1884
		124		England	Adelaide	1884-85
McLeod, CE		112		England	Melbourne	1897-98
Miller, KR	7	141*		England	Adelaide	1946-47
		145*		England	Sydney	1950-51
		129		West Indies	Sydney	1951-52
		109		England	Lord's	1953
		147		West Indies	Kingston	1954-55
		137		West Indies	Bridgetown	1954-55
		109		West Indies	Kingston	1954-55
Moroney, J	2	118	1	South Africa	Johannesburg2	1949-50
		101*	2			
Morris, AR	12	155		England	Melbourne	1946-47
		122	1	England	Adelaide	1946-47
		124*	2			
		100*		India	Melbourne	1947-48
		105		England	Lord's	1948
		182		England	Leeds	1948
		196		England	The Oval	1948
		111		South Africa	Johannesburg2	1949-50
		157		South Africa	Port Elizabeth	1949-50
		206		England	Adelaide	1950-51

Batsman	100s	Runs	Inns	Opponent	Venue	Series
Morris, AR		153		England	Brisbane2	1954-55
		111		West Indies	Port-of-Spain	1954-55
Murdoch, WL	2	153*		England	The Oval	1880
		211		England	The Oval	1884
Noble, MA		133		England	Sydney	1903-04
O'Neill, NC	6	134		Pakistan	Lahore2	1959-60
		163		India	Bombay2	1959-60
		113		India	Calcutta	1959-60
		181		West Indies	Brisbane2	1960-61
		117		England	The Oval	1961
		100		England	Adelaide	1962-63
Pellew, CE	2	116		England	Melbourne	1920-21
		104		England	Adelaide	1920-21
Phillips, WB	2	159d		Pakistan	Perth	1983-84
		120		West Indies	Bridgetown	1983-84
Ponsford, WH	7	110d		England	Sydney	1924-25
		128		England	Melbourne	1924-25
		110		England	The Oval	1930
		183		West Indies	Sydney	1930-31
		109		West Indies	Brisbane1	1930-31
		181		England	Leeds	1934
		266		England	The Oval	1934
Ransford, VS		143*		England	Lord's	1909
Redpath, IR	8	132		West Indies	Sydney	1968-69
		171		England	Perth	1970-71
		135		Pakistan	Melbourne	1972-73
		159*		New Zealand	Auckland	1973-74
		105		England	Sydney	1974-75
		102		West Indies	Melbourne	1975-76
		103		West Indies	Adelaide	1975-76
		101		West Indies	Melbourne	1975-76
Richardson, AJ		100		England	Leeds	1926
Richardson, VY		138		England	Melbourne	1924-25
Rigg, KE		127		South Africa	Sydney	1931-32
Ritchie, GM	3	106*		Pakistan	Faisalabad	1982-83
		146		England	Nottingham	1985
		128		India	Adelaide	1985-86

Batsman	100s	Runs	Inns	Opponent	Venue	Series
Ryder, J	3	142		South Africa	Cape Town	1920-21
		201*		England	Adelaide	1924-25
		112		England	Melbourne	1928-29
Scott, HJH		102		England	The Oval	1884
Serjeant, CS		124		West Indies	Georgetown	1977-78
Sheahan, AP	2	114		India	Kanpur	1969-70
		127		Pakistan	Melbourne	1972-73
Simpson, RB	10	311		England	Manchester	1964
		153	1	Pakistan	Karachi	1964-65
		115	2			
		201		West Indies	Bridgetown	1964-65
		225		England	Adelaide	1965-66
		153		South Africa	Cape Town	1966-67
		103		India	Adelaide	1967-68
		109		India	Melbourne	1967-68
		176		India	Perth	1977-78
		100		India	Adelaide	1977-78
Stackpole, KR	7	134		South Africa	Cape Town	1966-67
		103		India	Bombay2	1969-70
		207		England	Brisbane2	1970-71
		136		England	Adelaide	1970-71
		114		England	Nottingham	1972
		142		West Indies	Kingston	1972-73
		122		New Zealand	Melbourne	1973-74
Taylor, JM		108		England	Sydney	1924-25
Toohey, PM		122		West Indies	Kingston	1977-78
Trott, GHS		143		England	Lord's	1896
Trumper, VT	8	135*		England	Lord's	1899
		104		England	Manchester	1902
		185*		England	Sydney	1903-04
		113		England	Adelaide	1903-04
		166		England	Sydney	1907-08
		159		South Africa	Melbourne	1910-11
		214*		South Africa	Adelaide	1910-11
		113		England	Sydney	1911-12
Turner, A		136		West Indies	Adelaide	1975-76
Walters, KD	15	155d		England	Brisbane2	1965-66
		115		England	Melbourne	1965-66

Batsman	100s	Runs	Inns	Opponent	Venue	Series
Walters, KD		118		West Indies	Sydney	1968-69
		110		West Indies	Adelaide	1968-69
		242	1	West Indies	Sydney	1968-69
		103	2			
		102		India	Madras1	1969-70
		112		England	Brisbane2	1970-71
		102*		West Indies	Bridgetown	1972-73
		112		West Indies	Port-of-Spain	1972-73
		104*		New Zealand	Auckland	1973-74
		103		England	Perth	1974-75
		107		Pakistan	Adelaide	1976-77
		250		New Zealand	Christchurch	1976-77
		107		New Zealand	Melbourne	1980-81
Wellham, DM		103d		England	The Oval	1981
Wessels, KC	4	162d		England	Brisbane2	1982-83
		141		Sri Lanka	Kandy	1982-83
		179		Pakistan	Adelaide	1983-84
		173		West Indies	Sydney	1984-85
Wood, GM	8	126		West Indies	Georgetown	1977-78
		100		England	Melbourne	1978-79
		112		England	Lord's	1980
		111		New Zealand	Brisbane2	1980-81
		125		India	Adelaide	1980-81
		100		Pakistan	Melbourne	1981-82
		100		New Zealand	Auckland	1981-82
		172		England	Nottingham	1985
Woodfull, WM	7	141		England	Leeds	1926
		117		England	Manchester	1926
		111		England	Sydney	1928-29
		107		England	Melbourne	1928-29
		102		England	Melbourne	1928-29
		155		England	Lord's	1930
		161		South Africa	Melbourne	1931-32
Yallop, GN	8	121		India	Adelaide	1977-78
		102		England	Brisbane2	1978-79
		121		England	Sydney	1978-79
		167		India	Calcutta	1979-80
		172		Pakistan	Faisalabad	1979-80

Batsman	100s	Runs	Inns	Opponent	Venue	Series
Yallop, GN		114		England	Manchester	1981
		141		Pakistan	Perth	1983-84
		268		Pakistan	Melbourne	1983-84
Total		**421**				

d Denotes on debut

LARGE PERCENTAGE
OF A COMPLETED INNINGS TOTAL

Percentage	Batsman	Runs	Inns Total	Opponent	Venue	Series
67.35	Bannerman, C	165	245	England	Melbourne	1876-77
61.11	Yallop, GN	121	198	England	Sydney	1978-79
60.66	Trumper, VT	74	122	England	Melbourne	1903-04
59.01	Bradman, DG	334	566	England	Leeds	1930
58.28	Bradman, DG	299	513	South Africa	Adelaide	1931-32
58.20	Hill, C	188	323	England	Melbourne	1897-98
56.54	McDonnell, PS	147	260	England	Sydney	1881-82
56.51	Cowper, RM	165	292	India	Sydney	1967-68
56.45	McCabe, SJ	232	411	England	Nottingham	1938
56.31	Boon, DC	58*	103	New Zealand	Auckland	1985-86

LARGE PERCENTAGE OF INCOMPLETE
INNINGS TOTAL

Percentage	Batsman	Runs	Inns Total	Opponent	Venue	Series
73.91	McDonald	51*	1-69	England	Melbourne	1958-59
70.37	Stackpole	57*	2-81	England	Lord's	1972
68.98	McCabe	189*	2-274	South Africa	Johannesburg1	1934-35
68.89	Wood	62*	4-90	England	Lord's	1981
68.56	Macartney	133*	5-194	England	Lord's	1926
65.31	Barnes	64*	2-98	England	Nottingham	1948
64.41	Trumper	38*	0-59	South Africa	Cape Town	1902-03
63.50	Dyson	127*	4-200	West Indies	Sydney	1981-82
60.42	Lawry	87*	1d-144	South Africa	Brisbane2	1963-64
58.95	Lawry	56*	0-95	India	Kanpur	1969-70

DUCK AND A CENTURY
IN THE SAME MATCH

Batsman	1st inns	2nd inns	Opponent	Venue	Series
Murdoch, WL	0	153*	England	The Oval	1880
Trott, GHS	0	143	England	Lord's	1896
Hill, C	188	0	England	Melbourne	1897-98
Bradman, DG	0	103*	England	Melbourne	1932-33
Fingleton, JHW	100	0	England	Brisbane2	1936-37
Bradman, DG	138	0	England	Nottingham	1948
Barnes, SG	0	141	England	Lord's	1948
Harvey, RN	122	0	England	Manchester	1953
Redpath, IR	0	132	West Indies	Sydney	1968-69
Chappell, IM	138	0	India	Delhi	1969-70
Davis, IC	105	0	Pakistan	Adelaide	1976-77
McCosker, RB	0	105	Pakistan	Melbourne	1976-77
Serjeant, CS	0	124	West Indies	Georgetown	1977-78
Yallop, GN	0	114	England	Manchester	1981
Marsh, GR	118	0	New Zealand	Auckland	1985-86
Boon, DC	103	0	England	Adelaide	1986-87

NERVOUS NINETIES

Batsman		Opponent	Venue	Series
Ninety-nine:				
Hill, C	Ct	England	Melbourne	1901-02
Macartney, CG	Ct	England	Lord's	1912
Chipperfield, AG	Ct	England	Nottingham	1934
Brown, WA	RO	India	Melbourne	1947-48
Miller, KR	B	England	Adelaide	1950-51
Morris, AR	RO	South Africa	Melbourne	1952-53
McDonald, CC	Ct	South Africa	Cape Town	1957-58
Cowper, RM	Ct	England	Melbourne	1965-66
Chappell, IM	Ct	India	Calcutta	1969-70
Edwards, R	LBW	England	Lord's	1975
Hughes, KJ	Ct	England	Perth	1979-80

Chipperfield reached 99 on debut

Batsman		Opponent	Venue	Series
Ninety-eight:				
Hill, C	Ct	England	Adelaide	1901-02
Hill, C	Ct	England	Adelaide	1911-12
Richardson, AJ	C&B	England	Sydney	1924-25
Archer, RG	B	West Indies	Bridgetown	1954-55
Lawry, WM	Ct	England	Brisbane2	1962-63
Booth, BC	C&B	England	Nottingham	1964
Lawry, WM	Ct	South Africa	Johannesburg3	1966-67
Yallop, GN	LBW	Sri Lanka	Kandy	1982-83
Border, AR	Ct	West Indies	St. John's	1983-84
Wessels, KC	B	West Indies	Adelaide	1984-85
Ninety-seven:				
Hill, C	B	England	Adelaide	1901-02
Benaud, R	Ct	England	Lord's	1956
Redpath, IR	B	South Africa	Melbourne	1963-64
Marsh, RW	HW	West Indies	Kingston	1972-73
Chappell, IM	C&B	West Indies	Port-of-Spain	1972-73
Toohey, PM	Stp	West Indies	Kingston	1977-78
Ninety-six:				
Hill, C	B	England	Sydney	1897-98
Harvey, RN	B	Pakistan	Dacca	1959-60
Shepherd, BK	Ct	South Africa	Melbourne	1963-64
Chappell, IM	LBW	West Indies	Adelaide	1968-69
Ninety-five:				
Trott, GHS	C&B	England	Melbourne	1894-95
Ransford, VS	B	South Africa	Melbourne	1910-11
McCool, CL	LBW	England	Brisbane	1946-47
Gilmour, GJ	Ct	West Indies	Adelaide	1975-76

DISMISSED IN NERVOUS NINETIES

Batsman	Score		Opponent	Venue	Series
Five times:					
Hill, C	99	Ct	England	Melbourne	1901-02
	98	Ct	England	Adelaide	1901-02
	98	Ct	England	Adelaide	1911-12
	97	B	England	Adelaide	1901-02
	96	B	England	Sydney	1897-98
Four times:					
Simpson, RB	94	LBW	South Africa	Durban	1966-67
	92	B	West Indies	Brisbane2	1960-61
	92	B	West Indies	Melbourne	1960-61
	91	B	England	Sydney	1962-63
Chappell, IM	99	Ct	India	Calcutta	1969-70
	97	C&B	West Indies	Port-of-Spain	1972-73
	96	LBW	West Indies	Adelaide	1968-69
	90	Ct	England	Brisbane2	1974-75
Three times:					
Lawry, WM	98	Ct	South Africa	Johannesburg3	1966-67
	98	Ct	England	Brisbane2	1962-63
	94	Ct	England	The Oval	1964
Redpath, IR	97	B	South Africa	Melbourne	1963-64
	93	Ct	New Zealand	Wellington	1973-74
	92	B	England	Leeds	1968
Marsh, RW	97	HW	West Indies	Kingston	1972-73
	91	Ct	New Zealand	Perth	1980-81
	91	Ct	England	Manchester	1972
Hughes, KJ	99	Ct	England	Perth	1979-80
	94	LBW	Pakistan	Melbourne	1983-84
	92	LBW	India	Calcutta	1979-80

Hill was dismissed on 99, 98 & 97 in consecutive innings v England 1901-02.
He was the first Test player from any country to be dismissed on 99.

NOT OUT IN THE NINETIES

Batsman	Score	Opponent	Venue	Series
Chappell, GS	98	England	Sydney	1979-80
Border, AR	98	West Indies	Port-of-Spain	1983-84
McCosker, RB	95	England	Leeds	1975
Walters, KD	94	India	Sydney	1967-68
Ponsford, WH	92	West Indies	Adelaide	1930-31
Harvey, RN	92	England	Sydney	1954-55
Marsh, RW	92	England	Melbourne	1970-71
Hill, C	91	South Africa	Cape Town	1902-03

MOST RUNS FROM STROKES WORTH FOUR OR MORE IN AN INNINGS

Total	6s	5s	4s	Batsman	Runs	Opponent	Venue	Series
184	–	–	46	Bradman, DG	334	England	Leeds	1930
184	2	–	43	Bradman, DG	304	England	Leeds	1934
142	1	–	34	McCabe, SJ	232	England	Nottingham	1938
134	1	–	32	Bradman, DG	244	England	The Oval	1934
132	–	–	33	Morris, AR	182	England	Leeds	1948
132	–	–	33	Morris, AR	206	England	Adelaide	1950-51
132	2	–	30	Walters, KD	250	New Zealand	Christchurch	1976-77
126	1	–	30	Chappell, GS	247*	New Zealand	Wellington	1973-74
120	–	–	30	Darling, J	160	England	Sydney	1897-98
120	2	–	27	Jones, DM	210	India	Madras2	1986-87
116	–	–	29	McCabe, SJ	189*	South Africa	Johannesburg	1935-36
116	–	–	29	Bradman, DG	173*	England	Leeds	1948
116	–	–	29	Yallop, GN	268	Pakistan	Melbourne	1983-84
113	–	1	27	Ponsford, WH	181	England	Leeds	1934
112	–	–	28	Gregory, SE	201	England	Sydney	1894-95
112	2	–	25	Lawry, WM	210	West Indies	Bridgetown	1964-65
111	1	1	25	Darling, J	178	England	Adelaide	1897-98
108	4	–	21	Chappell, IM	196	Pakistan	Adelaide	1972-73
108	–	–	27	Chappell, GS	204	India	Sydney	1980-81
104	–	–	26	Collins, HL	203	South Africa	Johannesburg1	1921-22
104	2	–	23	Chappell, GS	176	New Zealand	Christchurch	1981-82

Total	6s	5s	4s	Batsman	Runs	Opponent	Venue	Series
102	1	–	24	Harvey, RN	204	West Indies	Kingston	1954-55
102	1	–	24	Stackpole, KR	207	England	Brisbane2	1970-71
102	1	–	24	Wessels, KC	179	Pakistan	Adelaide	1983-84
100	–	–	25	Trumper, VT	185*	England	Sydney	1903-04
100	–	–	25	Bradman, DG	254	England	Lord's	1930
100	–	–	25	McCabe, SJ	187*	England	Sydney	1932-33

MOST FOURS IN AN INNINGS

4s	Batsman	Runs	Opponent	Venue	Series
46	Bradman, DG	334	England	Leeds	1930
43	Bradman, DG	304	England	Leeds	1934
34	McCabe, SJ	232	England	Nottingham	1938
33	Morris, AR	182	England	Leeds	1948
33	Morris, AR	206	England	Adelaide	1950-51
32	Bradman, DG	244	England	The Oval	1934
30	Chappell, GS	247*	New Zealand	Wellington	1973-74
30	Darling, J	160	England	Sydney	1897-98
30	Walters, KD	250	New Zealand	Christchurch	1976-77

MOST SIXES IN AN INNINGS

6s	Batsman	Runs	Opponent	Venue	Series
5	Loxton, SJE	93	England	Leeds	1948
5	Border, AR	153	Pakistan	Lahore2	1979-80
4	Connolly, AN	31	India	Calcutta	1969-70
4	Marsh, RW	91	England	Manchester	1972
4	Chappell, IM	196	Pakistan	Adelaide	1972-73
4	Marsh, RW	118	Pakistan	Adelaide	1972-73
4	Phillips, WB	120	West Indies	Bridgetown	1983-84
3	O'Reilly, WJ	56	South Africa	Johannesburg2	1935-36
3	Lawry, WM	106	England	Manchester	1964
3	Lawry, WM	81	England	Manchester	1968
3	Freeman, EW	76	West Indies	Sydney	1968-69
3	Lillee, DK	73*	England	Lord's	1972

6s	Batsman	Runs	Opponent	Venue	Series
3	Hughes, KJ	117	England	Lord's	1980
3	Hughes, KJ	137	England	Sydney	1982-83

MOST FOURS OFF CONSECUTIVE BALLS

4s	Batsman	Bowler	Opponent	Venue	Series
4	Hookes, DW	Greig, AW	England	Melbourne	1976-77

LONGEST INNINGS

Mins	Batsman	Runs	Opponent	Venue	Series
762	Simpson, RB	311	England	Manchester	1964
727	Cowper, RM	307	England	Melbourne	1965-66
716	Yallop, GN	268	Pakistan	Melbourne	1983-84
642	Barnes, SG	234	England	Sydney	1946-47
601	Wood, GM	172	England	Nottingham	1985
547	Simpson, RB	225	England	Adelaide	1965-66
546	Jones, DM	184*	England	Sydney	1986-87
544	Lawry, WM	210	West Indies	Bridgetown	1964-65
526	Chappell, GS	182	Pakistan	Sydney	1983-84
520	Yallop, GN	167	India	Calcutta	1979-80
504	Yallop, GN	172	Pakistan	Faisalabad	1979-80
504	Jones, DM	210	India	Madras2	1986-87
503	Lawry, WM	151	West Indies	Sydney	1968-69
487	McDonald, CC	170	England	Adelaide	1958-59
485	Murdoch, WL	211	England	The Oval	1884
484	Redpath, IR	171	England	Perth	1970-71
482	Walters, KD	242	West Indies	Sydney	1968-69

FASTEST FIFTIES

Mins	Batsman	Runs	Opponent	Venue	Series
35	Macartney, CG	56	England	The Oval	1921
35	Gregory, JM	119	South Africa	Johannesburg1	1921-22

FASTEST HUNDREDS

Mins	Batsman	Runs	Opponent	Venue	Series
70	Gregory, JM	119	South Africa	Johannesburg1	1921-22
78	Benaud, R	121	West Indies	Kingston	1954-55
91	Darling, J	160	England	Sydney	1897-98
91	McCabe, SJ	189*	South Africa	Johannesburg1	1935-36
94	Trumper, VT	185*	England	Sydney	1903-04
99	Bradman, DG	334	England	Leeds	1930

FASTEST DOUBLE HUNDREDS

Mins	Batsman	Runs	Opponent	Venue	Series
214	Bradman, DG	334	England	Leeds	1930
223	McCabe, SJ	232	England	Nottingham	1938
226	Trumper, VT	214*	South Africa	Adelaide	1910-11
234	Bradman, DG	254	England	Lord's	1930
241	Gregory, SE	201	England	Sydney	1894-95
251	Bradman, DG	223	West Indies	Brisbane1	1930-31
253	Bradman, DG	226	South Africa	Brisbane2	1931-32

FASTEST TRIPLE HUNDREDS

Mins	Batsman	Runs	Opponent	Venue	Series
336	Bradman, DG	334	England	Leeds	1930

Bradman scored his three 100s in 99, 115 & 122 minutes respectively and reached 309* at the end of the first day.

MOST RUNS IN A DAY

Runs		Batsman	Score	Opponent	Venue	Series
309	(0-309*)	Bradman, DG	334	England	Leeds	1930
271	(0-271*)	Bradman, DG	304	England	Leeds	1934

Runs		Batsman	Score	Opponent	Venue	Series
244	(0-244)	Bradman, DG	244	England	The Oval	1934
233	(0-223*)	Bradman, DG	223	West Indies	Brisbane1	1930-31
213	(19*-232)	McCabe, SJ	232	England	Nottingham	1938
208	(20*-228*)	Trumper, VT	214*	South Africa	Adelaide	1910-11
205	(0-205*)	Ponsford, WH	266	England	The Oval	1934
203	(0-203)	Collins, HL	203	South Africa	Johannesburg1	1921-22
201	(0-201)	Bradman, DG	201	India	Adelaide	1947-48
200	(0-200*)	Bradman, DG	226	South Africa	Brisbane2	1931-32

FASTEST INNINGS

Runs	Mins	Batsman	Opponent	Venue	Series
35	14	Howell, WP	England	Sydney	1901-02
62	50	Trumper, VT	England	Sheffield	1902
63	50	Trumper, VT	South Africa	Johannesburg1	1902-03
61	63	Lindwall, RR	West Indies	Brisbane	1951-52
67	64	Gehrs, DRA	South Africa	Sydney	1910-11
59	67	Macartney, CG	South Africa	Durban2	1921-22
74	73	Yardley, B	West Indies	Bridgetown	1977-78
79	89	Duff, RA	England	Adelaide	1903-04
88	97	McCabe, SJ	England	Nottingham	1934
121	96	Benaud, R	West Indies	Kingston	1954-55
119	97	Gregory, JM	South Africa	Johannesburg1	1921-22
113	126	Trumper, VT	England	Sydney	1911-12
116	114	Macartney, CG	South Africa	Durban2	1921-22
128	115	Bonnor, GJ	England	Sydney	1884-85
116	130	Harvey, RN	South Africa	Port Elizabeth	1949-50
151	170	Macartney, CG	England	Leeds	1926
160	175	Darling, J	England	Sydney	1897-98
189*	165	McCabe, SJ	South Africa	Johannesburg1	1935-36
191	202	Hill, C	South Africa	Sydney	1910-11
232	235	McCabe, SJ	England	Nottingham	1938

SID BARNES' BATTING MARATHON

Sid Barnes had backed himself to get a hundred in the Second Test against England at Sydney in December 1946. Australia had already established ascendancy by winning the First Test at Brisbane by an innings and 332 runs, and despite stubborn batting by Bill Edrich (71) and John Ikin (60) had England out for 255 on a good Sydney pitch. Now as Barnes went to the crease with Arthur Morris a thunderstorm approached.

Barnes appealed against the light three times in Alec Bedser's opening over, the first time before Bedser bowled a ball, and as he played for time to get the storm directly overhead he did more gardening than batting. In the second over Morris had difficulty sighting deliveries from Edrich and the umpires upheld the fourth light appeal. Barnes sprinted for the gate and was first off.

Ten minutes later the storm broke fiercely over the ground. The Saturday crowd of 44,000 was saturated. Puddles littered the field as spectators tried to find cover against the wind and rain. At Mascot airport, only a few kilometres away, the wind was timed at 125 kilometres an hour. Two further inspections of the pitch followed and finally the umpires, George Borwick and Jack Scott, brought the players back on to the field after a three-hour delay.

Only one run had been scored when a shower arrived, with Barnes again leading the race from the field. By the time he opened the dressing-room door, however, the shower had eased and the umpires recalled the players. Spectators booed Barnes as he reappeared, and he responded by sprinting all the way back to the crease. For the next half hour, every time the ball marked the soggy pitch, Barnes patted the mark, and when spectators heckled him he simply stepped further along the pitch and gave it extra taps. He did not look like a man who wanted to win a bet.

After 45 minutes Edrich bowled Morris for 5 and surprisingly, Ian Johnson appeared instead of Don Bradman. Following instructions, Johnson appealed against the light twice in one over. Barnes, who hd scored 21 out of 27 without difficulty, took the cue and added an appeal of his own. The umpires yielded to the fifth appeal in nine minutes and play ended for the day an hour before the scheduled time.

Later, in a radio broadcast, Barnes explained that the Australians could have batted on, but that they might have lost three wickets. "It was a Test match and we just had to win," he said. "So I appealed after every second ball, complained of people moving about, the light, in fact, everything." The comment drew heavy criticism of Barnes.

After a rest day on the Sunday the pitch rolled out well on Monday, and Barnes took the score along with Johnson, Lindsay Hassett and Keith Miller, until Australia reached 4 for 159 when Bradman appeared. By the close on Monday night they had taken the total to 4 for 252, with Barnes 109 after six hours and Bradman passed his 50. Barnes had batted the entire day for 88.

The partnership continued for most of the fourth day until Bradman began to hit out and was out for 234 after six and a half hours' batting. Barnes' 200 was the slowest double century in Anglo-Australian Tests. The Barnes-Bradman stand of 405 was a world record for the fifth wicket. Barnes let the fouth-day crowd see the beautiful drives he had found somewhere between Monday night and Tuesday afternoon.

When he drew level with Bradman's score of 234, Barnes had seen Australia's score rise from 0 to 564 and had played himself in again after eight interruptions, lunch or tea intervals and overnight stops. In all he had batted for 10 hours and 42 minutes. English fieldsmen heard him say: "I can't stick it any longer," as he hit a catch to Ikin off Bedser. A reader later wrote to the Sydney *Daily Telegraph* commending Barnes for not taking the Australian Test record for the SCG away from Bradman but sharing the 234 with Bradman.

Only two batsmen had ever batted longer than Barnes in first-class matches to that time: Vijay Merchant, who took ten and three-quarter hours for 359 not out at Bombay in 1943, and Len Hutton, who took 13 hours and 17 minutes for his Test record 364 in 1938 at The Oval. The pity of it was that Barnes' amazing marathon hid a batsman who could score more freely and excitingly than most.

SLOWEST HUNDREDS

Mins	Batsman	Runs	Opponent	Venue	Series
384	Border, AR	115	England	Perth	1979-80
377	Border, AR	123*	England	Manchester	1981
374	Hughes, KJ	129	England	Brisbane2	1978-79
370	Wood, GM	100	Pakistan	Melbourne	1981-82
350	Lawry, WM	135	England	The Oval	1968
346	Hassett, AL	115	England	Nottingham	1953
344	Hassett, AL	128	England	Brisbane2	1946-47
337	Hughes, KJ	129	West Indies	Brisbane2	1979-80
330	Simpson, RB	311	England	Manchester	1964

SLOWEST DOUBLE HUNDREDS

Mins	Batsman	Runs	Opponent	Venue	Series
608	Simpson, RB	311	England	Manchester	1964
570	Barnes, SG	234	England	Sydney	1946-47

SLOWEST TRIPLE HUNDREDS

Mins	Batsman	Runs	Opponent	Venue	Series
753	Simpson, RB	311	England	Manchester	1964

SLOWEST INNINGS

Runs	Mins	Batsman	Opponent	Venue	Series
28*	250	Burke, JW	England	Brisbane2	1958-59
31	264	Mackay, KD	England	Lord's	1956
40	289	Collins, HL	England	Manchester	1921
2	63	Alderman, TM	West Indies	Bridgetown	1983-84
4	61	Border, AR	West Indies	Melbourne	1981-82

FEWEST BOUNDARIES IN AN INNINGS

Runs	4s	Batsman	Opponent	Venue	Series
84	0	Lawry, WM	England	Brisbane2	1970-71
102	3	Woodfull, WM	England	Melbourne	1928-29
161	5	Woodfull, WM	South Africa	Melbourne	1931-32

AN HOUR BEFORE SCORING FIRST RUN

Mins	Batsman	Runs	Opponent	Venue	Series
70	Murdoch, WL	17	England	Sydney	1882-83
69	Hogg, RM	7*	West Indies	Adelaide	1984-85

AN HOUR WITHOUT ADDING TO SCORE

Mins	Batsman	Runs	Opponent	Venue	Series
60	Border, AR	9	Pakistan	Faisalabad	1982-83

DISMISSED FIRST BALL OF A TEST

Batsman	Bowler	Opponent	Venue	Series
Bardsley, W	Tate, MW	England	Leeds	1926
Stackpole, KR	Hadlee, RJ	New Zealand	Auckland	1973-74

DISMISSED FOR A PAIR

Batsman	Opponent	Venue	Series
Three times:			
Hurst, AG	England	Brisbane2	1978-79
	England	Sydney	1978-79
	Pakistan	Melbourne	1978-79

Batsman	Opponent	Venue	Series
Twice:			
Mackay, KD	England	Manchester	1956
	India	Kanpur	1959-60
McKenzie, GD	South Africa	Sydney	1963-64
	England	Manchester	1968
Gleeson, JW	South Africa	Johannesburg3	1969-70
	England	Sydney	1970-71
Clark, WM	West Indies	Port-of-Spain	1977-78
	West Indies	Bridgetown	1977-78
Hogg, RM	India	Delhi	1979-80
	West Indies	Perth	1984-85
Holland, RG	England	Birmingham	1985
	New Zealand	Brisbane2	1985-86
Once:			
McDonnell, PS	England	Sydney	1882-83
Garrett, TW	England	Sydney	1882-83
Evans, E	England	Sydney	1886
McShane, PG	England	Sydney	1887-88
Bannerman, AC	England	Lord's	1888
Noble, MA	England	Leeds	1899
Gregory, SE	England	Leeds	1899
McLeod, CE	England	Sydney	1901-02
Darling, J	England	Sheffield	1902
Kelly, JJ	England	Sheffield	1902
Trumble, H	England	Sydney	1903-04
Trumper, VT	England	Melbourne	1907-08
Saunders, JV	England	Sydney	1907-08
Grimmett, CV	England	Nottingham	1930
Oldfield, WAS	South Africa	Melbourne	1931-32
Fingleton, JHW	England	Adelaide	1932-33
Richardson, VY	England	Sydney	1932-33
Badcock, CL	England	Lord's	1938
Johnson, IW	England	Melbourne	1946-47
Moroney, J	England	Brisbane2	1950-51
Iverson, JB	England	Melbourne	1950-51
Maddocks, LV	England	Leeds	1956
Harvey, RN	England	Manchester	1956

Batsman	Opponent	Venue	Series
Grout, AWT	West Indies	Sydney	1960-61
Benaud, R	England	Leeds	1961
Connolly, AN	West Indies	Brisbane2	1968-69
Edwards, R	England	Leeds	1972
Stackpole, KR	New Zealand	Auckland	1973-74
Dymock, G	England	Melbourne	1974-75
Marsh, RW	England	Nottingham	1977
Thomson, JR	England	Leeds	1977
Serjeant, CS	India	Brisbane2	1977-78
Mann, AL	India	Sydney	1977-78
Hookes, DW	Pakistan	Karachi	1979-80
Wood, GM	New Zealand	Perth	1980-81
Whitney, MR	England	Manchester	1981
Yardley, B	Pakistan	Karachi	1982-83
Bright, RJ	Pakistan	Faisalabad	1982-83
Rackemann, CG	West Indies	Perth	1984-85
Hughes, KJ	West Indies	Melbourne	1984-85
Hughes, KJ	England	Brisbane2	1986-87

DISMISSED FOR A DUCK BY SAME COMBINATION IN EACH INNINGS OF A TEST

Batsman	Dismissed by	Opponent	Venue	Series
Darling, J	ct Braund b Barnes	England	Sheffield	1902
Mackay, KD	ct Oakman b Laker	England	Manchester	1956
Benaud, R	b Trueman	England	Leeds	1961

MOST CONSECUTIVE DUCKS

Batsman	Scores	Opponent	Venue	Series
Five:				
Holland, RG	0 & 0	England	Birmingham	1985
	0 & 0	New Zealand	Brisbane2	1985-86
	0 & 4	New Zealand	Sydney	1985-86

Batsman	Scores	Opponent	Venue	Series
Four:				
Clark, WM	0 & 0	West Indies	Port-of-Spain	1977-78
	0 & 0	West Indies	Bridgetown	1977-78
Three:				
McShane, PG	0 & –	England	Sydney	1886-87
	0 & 0	England	Sydney	1887-88
Trumper, VT	4 & 0	England	Adelaide	1907-08
	0 & 0	England	Melbourne	1907-08
Massie, RAL	0 & –	England	Lord's	1972
	0 & –	England	Nottingham	1972
	0 & 18	England	Leeds	1972
Thomson, JR	21 & 0	England	Nottingham	1977
	0 & 0	England	Leeds	1977
Hogg, RM	0 & 0	India	Delhi	1979-80
	0 & –	India	Calcutta	1979-80
Wood, GM	0 & 0	New Zealand	Perth	1980-81
	0 & 21	New Zealand	Melbourne	1980-81
Rackemann, CG	12 & 0	West Indies	St. John's	1983-84
	0 & 0	West Indies	Perth	1984-85
Hughes, MG	0 & –	India	Adelaide	1985-86
	0 & 0	England	Brisbane2	1986-87

Massie & Hughes were on debut.

MOST DUCKS IN A SERIES

Batsman	Inns	N.O	Opponent	Venue	Series
Six:					
Hurst, AG	12	2	England	Australia	1978-79
Five:					
Clark, WM	7	1	West Indies	West Indies	1977-78
Four:					
Trumble, H	8	–	England	Australia	1903-04
Saunders, JV	9	2	England	Australia	1907-08
Hogg, RM	12	–	England	Australia	1978-79

Batsman	Inns	N.O	Opponent	Venue	Series
Three:					
Garrett, TW	5	–	England	Australia	1882-83
Bannerman, AC	6	–	England	England	1888
Edwards, JD	6	1	England	England	1888
Turner, CTB	5	–	England	England	1893
Howell, WP	7	2	England	England	1899
Kelly, JJ	7	3	England	England	1902
Oldfield, WAS	8	1	England	England	1934
Badcock, CL	8	1	England	England	1938
Johnson, IW	8	2	England	Australia	1950-51
Harvey, RN	10	–	England	England	1956
Grout, ATW	9	–	West Indies	Australia	1960-61
McKenzie, GD	8	1	England	England	1968
Chappell, IM	8	–	South Africa	South Africa	1969-70
Gleeson, JW	8	1	South Africa	South Africa	1969-70
Gleeson, JW	7	–	England	Australia	1970-71
Massie, RAL	5	–	England	England	1972
Thomson, JR	7	–	West Indies	Australia	1975-76
Thomson, JR	8	1	England	England	1977
Hogg, RM	10	2	India	India	1979-80
Lillee, DK	5	–	West Indies	Australia	1979-80
Wood, GM	5	–	New Zealand	Australia	1980-81
Whitney, MR	4	–	England	England	1981
Hughes, KJ	8	–	West Indies	Australia	1984-85
Wessels, KC	9	–	West Indies	Australia	1984-85
Holland, RG	5	1	England	England	1985
Holland, RG	5	1	England	New Zealand	1985-86

MOST INNINGS BEFORE FIRST DUCK

Inns	Batsman	Series
51	Davidson, AK	1953 to 1961
41	Harvey, RN	1947-48 to 1952-53
40	Duff, RA	1901-02 to 1905
40	Ponsford, WH	1924-25 to 1932-33
40	Burke, JW	1950-51 to 1958-59

MOST CONSECUTIVE INNINGS WITHOUT A DUCK

Inns	Batsman	Series
73	Border, AR	1982-83 to 1986-87
68	Walters, KD	1969-70 to 1976-77
54	Simpson, RB	1963-64 to 1977-78
54	Marsh, RW	1972-73 to 1977
51	Davidson, AK	1953 to 1961
51	Lawry, WM	1962-63 to 1965-66
50	Redpath, IR	1969-70 to 1975-76
41	Harvey, RN	1947-48 to 1952-53
40	Ponsford, WH	1924-25 to 1932-33

FEWEST DUCKS IN A CAREER

Ducks	Inns	N.O	Batsman	Series
0	44	7	Burke, JW	1950-51 to 1958-59
0	40	3	Duff, RA	1901-02 to 1905
0	31	1	Collins, HL	1920-21 to 1926
0	23	1	Andrews, TJE	1921 to 1926
1	69	3	Hassett, AL	1938 to 1953
1	61	7	Davidson, AK	1953 to 1962-63
1	60	2	Darling, WM	1977-78 to 1979-80
1	55	4	Macartney, CG	1907-08 to 1926
1	53	5	Ritchie, GM	1982-83 to 1986-87
1	48	2	Phillips, WB	1982-83 to 1985-86
1	48	4	Ponsford, WH	1924-25 to 1934
1	42	4	Kelleway, C	1910-11 to 1928-29
2	83	4	McDonald, CC	1951-52 to 1961
3	70	3	Yallop, GN	1975-76 to 1984-85
4	157	26	Border, AR	1978-79 to 1986-87
4	125	14	Walters, KD	1965-66 to 1980-81

MOST DUCKS IN A CAREER

Ducks	Inns	N.O	Batsman	Series
10	20	3	Hurst, AG	1973-74 to 1979-80
10	45	20	Connolly, AN	1963-64 to 1970-71
11	46	8	Gleeson, JW	1967-68 to 1972
10	50	13	Mallett, AA	1968 to 1980
14	58	13	Hogg, RM	1978-79 to 1984-85
10	66	12	Johnson, IW	1945-46 to 1956-57
11	67	8	Grout, ATW	1957-58 to 1965-66
14	73	20	Thomson, JR	1972-73 to 1985
14	89	12	McKenzie, GD	1961 to 1970-71
10	90	24	Lillee, DK	1970-71 to 1983-84
12	100	7	Gregory, SE	1890 to 1912
10	124	6	Hughes, KJ	1977 to 1984-85
11	136	10	Chappell, IM	1964-65 to 1979-80
12	150	13	Marsh, RW	1970-71 to 1983-84
12	151	19	Chappell, GS	1970-71 to 1983-84

DUCKS ON DEBUTS

Batsman	2nd inns	Opponent	Venue	Series
Gregory, EJ	11	England	Melbourne	1876-77
Hodges, JH	8	England	Melbourne	1876-77
Spofforth, FR	17	England	Melbourne	1876-77
Pope, RJ	3	England	Melbourne	1884-85
Marr, AP	5	England	Melbourne	1884-85
Robertson, WR	2	England	Melbourne	1884-85
Trott, GHS	3	England	Lord's	1888
Gregory, SE	9	England	Lord's	1890
Darling, J	53	England	Sydney	1894-95
Kelly, JJ	24	England	Lord's	1896
Trumper, VT	11	England	Nottingham	1899
Burn, KE	19	England	Lord's	1899
Saunders, JV	–	England	Sydney	1901-02
Cotter, A	34	England	Sydney	1903-04
Park, RL	–	England	Melbourne	1920-21

Batsman	2nd inns	Opponent	Venue	Series
Hurwood, A	–	West Indies	Adelaide	1930-31
Lee, PK	–	South Africa	Sydney	1931-32
Hunt, WA	–	South Africa	Adelaide	1931-32
Thurlow, HM	–	South Africa	Adelaide	1931-32
Nagel, LE	21*	England	Sydney	1932-33
Ward, FA	1	England	Brisbane2	1936-37
Meuleman, KD	–	New Zealand	Wellington	1945-46
Lindwall, RR	–	New Zealand	Wellington	1945-46
Moroney, J	–	South Africa	Johannesburg2	1949-50
Langley, GRA	–	West Indies	Brisbane2	1951-52
Hill, JC	4	England	Nottingham	1953
Sellers, RHD	–	India	Calcutta	1964-65
Jenner, TJ	2	England	Brisbane2	1970-71
Massie, RAL	–	England	Lord's	1972
Carlson, PH	21	England	Adelaide	1978-79
Whitney, MR	0	England	Manchester	1981
McDermott, CJ	–	West Indies	Melbourne	1984-85
O'Donnell, SP	24	England	Leeds	1985
Hughes, MG	–	India	Adelaide	1985-86
Davis, SP	–	New Zealand	Wellington	1985-86

DISMISSAL STATISTICS

I reviewed the number of times Australian batsmen have been dismissed on each score in all 473 Test matches from 1877 until the recently completed Test series against England. The following statistics emerged.

1. Australian batsmen have ventured to the crease on 8410 occasions, of which 1079 have resulted in their being not out or retired hurt.

2. In all those innings, on ten occasions only have batsmen been dismissed for a score of 87, the so-called hoodoo score, (0.14%).

3. The only Australian batsmen to have been dismissed for 87 and the year in which it was scored were

1. Bonnor, GJ.................1883
2. Jones, SP..................1886
3. Hill, C.....................1902
4. Hill, C.....................1907
5. Trumper, VT..............1911
6. Ryder, J...................1929
7. Moroney, J...............1949
8. Booth, BC................1964
9. Stackpole, KR.............1971
10. Dyson, J..................1982

4. W.M. Lawry is the only Australian batsman who has been left on 87 not out. It happened in 1963 in Brisbane when Australia's captain, R. Benaud, declared closed the 2nd innings against South Africa.

5. The most common scores at which Australian batsmen have been dismissed in all Tests are

Score	Frequency of Score	% of dismissals
0	860	11.73
1	348	4.75
2	306	4.17
4	301	4.11
5	261	3.56
3	235	3.21
6	211	2.88
7	187	2.55
8	185	2.52
10	160	2.18
9	156	2.13

Innings completed for scores 0-10 inclusive account for 43.79% of all dismissals.

6. If batsmen were dismissed for more than 19 the most frequent scores made were

Range of scores	Most frequent score	Times made	%
20–29	20	91	1.24
30–39	30	82	1.12
40–49	41	49	0.67
50–59	50	38	0.52
60–69	62,65,66,67	22	0.30
70–79	74	21	0.29
80–89	80,83,85	16	0.22
90–99	92	12	0.16

7. Eleven (0.15%) Australian batsmen have been dismissed on 99.

8. The scores below 100 that have yielded least dismissals are 86,95 & 96, which have all had four dismissals.

9. The score of 187 has been obtained on two occasions, but only D.G. Bradman has been dismissed on that total. S.J. McCabe was left 187 not out in 1932-33.

10. 139,148,150,174,175,177,180,184,186,193,194,195,197,198 & 199 are the only scores below 200 on which Australian batsmen have not been dismissed.

Score	No. dis	% dis	No. N.O	% N.O	Total no.	%
0	860	11.73	133	1.58	993	11.81
1	348	4.75	64	0.76	412	4.90
2	306	4.17	52	0.62	358	4.26
3	235	3.21	40	0.48	275	3.27
4	301	4.11	35	0.42	336	4.00
5	261	3.56	31	0.37	292	3.47
6	211	2.88	35	0.42	246	2.93
7	187	2.55	33	0.39	220	2.62
8	185	2.52	29	0.34	214	2.54
9	156	2.13	16	0.19	172	2.05
10	160	2.18	23	0.27	183	2.18
11	144	1.96	21	0.25	165	1.96
12	140	1.91	27	0.32	167	1.99
13	134	1.83	20	0.24	154	1.83
14	149	2.03	16	0.19	165	1.96
15	125	1.71	19	0.23	144	1.71
16	130	1.77	17	0.20	147	1.75
17	129	1.76	16	0.19	145	1.72
18	100	1.36	17	0.20	117	1.39

Score	No. dis	% dis	No. N.O	% N.O	Total no.	%
19	115	1.57	8	0.10	123	1.46
20	91	1.24	14	0.17	105	1.25
21	78	1.06	17	0.20	95	1.13
22	80	1.09	18	0.21	98	1.17
23	75	1.02	11	0.13	86	1.02
24	76	1.04	11	0.13	87	1.03
25	83	1.13	15	0.18	98	1.17
26	63	0.86	15	0.18	78	0.93
27	69	0.94	11	0.13	80	0.95
28	71	0.97	11	0.13	82	0.98
29	64	0.87	1	0.01	65	0.77
30	83	1.13	9	0.11	92	1.09
31	61	0.83	10	0.12	71	0.84
32	71	0.97	9	0.11	80	0.95
33	62	0.85	10	0.12	72	0.86
34	70	0.95	7	0.08	77	0.92
35	48	0.65	6	0.07	54	0.64
36	48	0.65	8	0.10	56	0.67
37	48	0.65	10	0.12	58	0.69
38	42	0.57	11	0.13	53	0.63
39	47	0.64	10	0.12	57	0.68
40	41	0.56	5	0.06	46	0.55
41	49	0.67	8	0.10	57	0.68
42	42	0.57	3	0.04	45	0.54
43	46	0.63	5	0.06	51	0.61
44	40	0.55	2	0.02	42	0.50
45	31	0.42	6	0.07	37	0.44
46	35	0.48	5	0.06	40	0.48
47	42	0.57	4	0.05	46	0.55
48	38	0.52	3	0.04	41	0.49
49	32	0.44	4	0.05	36	0.43
50	38	0.52	2	0.02	40	0.48
51	33	0.45	3	0.04	36	0.43
52	31	0.42	5	0.06	36	0.43
53	35	0.48	4	0.05	39	0.46
54	33	0.45	3	0.04	36	0.43
55	26	0.35	3	0.04	29	0.34
56	34	0.46	8	0.10	42	0.50

Score	No. dis	% dis	No. N.O	% N.O	Total no.	%
57	26	0.35	6	0.07	32	0.38
58	26	0.35	6	0.07	32	0.38
59	20	0.27	–	–	20	0.24
60	19	0.26	5	0.06	24	0.29
61	19	0.26	2	0.02	21	0.25
62	22	0.30	7	0.08	29	0.34
63	20	0.27	1	0.01	21	0.25
64	19	0.26	7	0.08	26	0.31
65	22	0.30	2	0.02	24	0.29
66	22	0.30	4	0.05	26	0.31
67	22	0.30	2	0.02	24	0.29
68	17	0.23	–	–	17	0.20
69	14	0.19	2	0.02	16	0.19
70	20	0.27	1	0.01	21	0.25
71	20	0.27	3	0.04	23	0.27
72	14	0.19	1	0.01	15	0.18
73	16	0.22	5	0.06	21	0.25
74	21	0.29	4	0.05	25	0.30
75	14	0.19	–	–	14	0.17
76	14	0.19	2	0.02	16	0.19
77	15	0.20	3	0.04	18	0.21
78	15	0.20	3	0.04	18	0.21
79	15	0.20	1	0.01	16	0.19
80	16	0.22	–	–	16	0.19
81	14	0.19	1	0.01	15	0.18
82	9	0.12	1	0.01	10	0.12
83	16	0.22	1	0.01	17	0.20
84	14	0.19	–	–	14	0.17
85	16	0.22	1	0.01	17	0.20
86	4	0.05	1	0.01	5	0.06
87	10	0.14	1	0.01	11	0.13
88	14	0.19	–	–	14	0.17
89	14	0.19	–	–	14	0.17
90	8	0.11	–	–	8	0.10
91	8	0.11	1	0.01	9	0.11
92	12	0.16	3	0.04	15	0.18
93	7	0.10	–	–	7	0.08
94	8	0.11	1	0.01	9	0.11

Score	No. dis	% dis	No. N.O	% N.O	Total no.	%
95	4	0.05	1	0.01	5	0.06
96	4	0.05	–	–	4	0.05
97	6	0.08	–	–	6	0.07
98	10	0.14	2	0.02	12	0.14
99	11	0.15	–	–	11	0.13
100	15	0.20	5	0.06	20	0.24
101	6	0.08	2	0.02	8	0.10
102	12	0.16	3	0.04	15	0.18
103	12	0.16	1	0.01	13	0.15
104	6	0.08	2	0.02	8	0.10
105	9	0.12	–	–	9	0.11
106	5	0.07	3	0.04	8	0.10
107	5	0.07	–	–	5	0.06
108	6	0.08	–	–	6	0.07
109	9	0.12	2	0.02	11	0.13
110	5	0.07	1	0.01	6	0.07
111	5	0.07	–	–	5	0.06
112	16	0.22	–	–	16	0.19
113	5	0.07	–	–	5	0.06
114	8	0.11	1	0.01	9	0.11
115	8	0.11	–	–	8	0.10
116	5	0.07	1	0.01	6	0.07
117	7	0.10	1	0.01	8	0.10
118	9	0.12	–	–	9	0.11
119	4	0.05	–	–	4	0.05
120	2	0.03	–	–	2	0.02
121	8	0.11	–	–	8	0.10
122	6	0.08	–	–	6	0.07
123	3	0.04	2	0.02	5	0.06
124	5	0.07	1	0.01	6	0.07
125	2	0.03	–	–	2	0.02
126	2	0.03	–	–	2	0.02
127	4	0.05	2	0.02	6	0.07
128	5	0.07	–	–	5	0.06
129	2	0.03	–	–	2	0.02
130	3	0.04	1	0.01	4	0.05
131	3	0.04	–	–	3	0.04
132	6	0.08	–	–	6	0.07

Score	No. dis	% dis	No. N.O	% N.O	Total no.	%
133	6	0.08	2	0.02	8	0.10
134	3	0.04	–	–	3	0.04
135	3	0.04	1	0.01	4	0.05
136	4	0.05	–	–	4	0.05
137	5	0.07	–	–	5	0.06
138	3	0.04	–	–	3	0.04
139	–	–	–	–	–	–
140	3	0.04	–	–	3	0.04
141	4	0.05	1	0.01	5	0.06
142	4	0.05	–	–	4	0.05
143	2	0.03	2	0.02	4	0.05
144	1	0.01	1	0.01	2	0.02
145	1	0.01	1	0.01	2	0.02
146	3	0.04	1	0.01	4	0.05
147	3	0.04	–	–	3	0.04
148	–	–	–	–	–	–
149	1	0.01	–	–	1	0.01
150	–	–	2	0.02	2	0.02
151	3	0.04	1	0.01	4	0.05
152	1	0.01	1	0.01	2	0.02
153	5	0.07	1	0.01	6	0.07
154	2	0.03	–	–	2	0.02
155	3	0.04	–	–	3	0.04
156	1	0.01	–	–	1	0.01
157	2	0.03	–	–	2	0.02
158	1	0.01	–	–	1	0.01
159	2	0.03	2	0.02	4	0.05
160	3	0.04	–	–	3	0.04
161	3	0.04	–	–	3	0.04
162	4	0.05	–	–	4	0.05
163	3	0.04	–	–	3	0.04
164	2	0.03	–	–	2	0.02
165	2	0.03	1	0.01	3	0.04
166	2	0.03	–	–	2	0.02
167	4	0.05	–	–	4	0.05
168	1	0.01	–	–	1	0.01
169	2	0.03	–	–	2	0.02
170	2	0.03	1	0.01	3	0.04

Score	No. dis	% dis	No. N.O	% N.O	Total no.	%
171	1	0.01	–	–	1	0.01
172	2	0.03	–	–	2	0.02
173	1	0.01	1	0.01	2	0.02
174	–	–	–	–	–	–
175	–	–	–	–	–	–
176	2	0.03	–	–	2	0.02
177	–	–	–	–	–	–
178	2	0.03	–	–	2	0.02
179	1	0.01	–	–	1	0.01
180	–	–	–	–	–	–
181	3	0.04	–	–	3	0.04
182	2	0.03	1	0.01	3	0.04
183	1	0.01	–	–	1	0.01
184	–	–	1	0.01	1	0.01
185	1	0.01	1	0.01	2	0.02
186	–	–	–	–	–	–
187	1	0.01	1	0.01	2	0.02
188	1	0.01	–	–	1	0.01
189	1	0.01	1	0.01	2	0.02
190	1	0.01	–	–	1	0.01
191	1	0.01	–	–	1	0.01
192	1	0.01	–	–	1	0.01
193	–	–	1	0.01	1	0.01
194	–	–	–	–	–	–
195	–	–	–	–	–	–
196	3	0.04	–	–	3	0.04
197	–	–	–	–	–	–
198	–	–	1	0.01	1	0.01
199	–	–	–	–	–	–
200	–	–	–	–	–	–
201	4	0.05	1	0.01	5	0.06
202	–	–	–	–	–	–
203	1	0.01	–	–	1	0.01
204	2	0.03	–	–	2	0.02
205	2	0.03	–	–	2	0.02
206	1	0.01	1	0.01	2	0.02
207	1	0.01	–	–	1	0.01
208	–	–	–	–	–	–

Score	No. dis	% dis	No. N.O	% N.O	Total no.	%
209	–	–	–	–	–	–
210	2	0.03	–	–	2	0.02
211	1	0.01	–	–	1	0.01
212	1	0.01	–	–	1	0.01
213	1	0.01	–	–	1	0.01
214	–	–	1	0.01	1	0.01
215	–	–	–	–	–	–
216	–	–	–	–	–	–
217	–	–	–	–	–	–
218	–	–	–	–	–	–
219	–	–	–	–	–	–
220	–	–	–	–	–	–
221	–	–	–	–	–	–
222	–	–	–	–	–	–
223	1	0.01	–	–	1	0.01
224	–	–	–	–	–	–
225	1	0.01	–	–	1	0.01
226	1	0.01	–	–	1	0.01
227	–	–	–	–	–	–
228	–	–	–	–	–	–
229	–	–	–	–	–	–
230	–	–	–	–	–	–
231	–	–	–	–	–	–
232	2	0.03	–	–	2	0.02
233	–	–	–	–	–	–
234	2	0.03	–	–	2	0.02
235	1	0.01	–	–	1	0.01
236	–	–	–	–	–	–
237	–	–	–	–	–	–
238	–	–	–	–	–	–
239	–	–	–	–	–	–
240	–	–	–	–	–	–
241	–	–	–	–	–	–
242	1	0.01	–	–	1	0.01
243	–	–	–	–	–	–
244	1	0.01	–	–	1	0.01
245	–	–	–	–	–	–
246	–	–	–	–	–	–

Score	No. dis	% dis	No. N.O	% N.O	Total no.	%
247	–	–	1	0.01	1	0.01
248	–	–	–	–	–	–
249	–	–	–	–	–	–
250	1	0.01	–	–	1	0.01
251	–	–	–	–	–	–
252	–	–	–	–	–	–
253	–	–	–	–	–	–
254	1	0.01	–	–	1	0.01
255	–	–	–	–	–	–
256	–	–	–	–	–	–
257	–	–	–	–	–	–
258	–	–	–	–	–	–
259	–	–	–	–	–	–
260	–	–	–	–	–	–
261	–	–	–	–	–	–
262	–	–	–	–	–	–
263	–	–	–	–	–	–
264	–	–	–	–	–	–
265	–	–	–	–	–	–
266	1	0.01	–	–	1	0.01
267	–	–	–	–	–	–
268	1	0.01	–	–	1	0.01
269	–	–	–	–	–	–
270	1	0.01	–	–	1	0.01
271	–	–	–	–	–	–
272	–	–	–	–	–	–
273	–	–	–	–	–	–
274	–	–	–	–	–	–
275	–	–	–	–	–	–
276	–	–	–	–	–	–
277	–	–	–	–	–	–
278	–	–	–	–	–	–
279	–	–	–	–	–	–
280	–	–	–	–	–	–
281	–	–	–	–	–	–
282	–	–	–	–	–	–
283	–	–	–	–	–	–
284	–	–	–	–	–	–

Score	No. dis	% dis	No. N.O	% N.O	Total no.	%
285	–	–	–	–	–	–
286	–	–	–	–	–	–
287	–	–	–	–	–	–
288	–	–	–	–	–	–
289	–	–	–	–	–	–
290	–	–	–	–	–	–
291	–	–	–	–	–	–
292	–	–	–	–	–	–
293	–	–	–	–	–	–
294	–	–	–	–	–	–
295	–	–	–	–	–	–
296	–	–	–	–	–	–
297	–	–	–	–	–	–
298	–	–	–	–	–	–
299	–	–	1	0.01	1	0.01
300	–	–	–	–	–	–
301	–	–	–	–	–	–
302	–	–	–	–	–	–
303	–	–	–	–	–	–
304	1	0.01	–	–	1	0.01
305	–	–	–	–	–	–
306	–	–	–	–	–	––
307	1	0.01	–	–	1	0.01
308	–	–	–	–	–	–
309	–	–	–	–	–	–
310	–	–	–	–	–	–
311	1	0.01	–	–	1	0.01
312	–	–	–	–	–	–
313	–	–	–	–	–	–
314	–	–	–	–	–	–
315	–	–	–	–	–	–
316	–	–	–	–	–	–
317	–	–	–	–	–	–
318	–	–	–	–	–	–
319	–	–	–	–	–	–
320	–	–	–	–	–	–
321	–	–	–	–	–	–
322	–	–	–	–	–	–

Score	No. dis	% dis	No. N.O	% N.O	Total no.	%
323	–	–	–	–	–	–
324	–	–	–	–	–	–
325	–	–	–	–	–	–
326	–	–	–	–	–	–
327	–	–	–	–	–	–
328	–	–	–	–	–	–
329	–	–	–	–	–	–
330	–	–	–	–	–	–
331	–	–	–	–	–	–
332	–	–	–	–	–	–
333	–	–	–	–	–	–
334	1	0.01	–	–	1	0.01
Total	**7331**	**100.00**	**1079**	**100.00**	**8410**	**100.00**

PARTNERSHIP RECORDS

AUSTRALIAN

Wkt	Runs	Opponent	Players		Venue	Series
1st	382	West Indies	Lawry, WM	& Simpson, RB	Bridgetown	1964-65
2nd	451	England	Ponsford, WH	& Bradman, DG	The Oval	1934
3rd	295	West Indies	McDonald, CC	& Harvey, RN	Kingston	1954-55
4th	388	England	Ponsford, WH	& Bradman, DG	Leeds	1934
5th	405	England	Bradman, DG	& Barnes, SG	Sydney	1946-47
6th	346	England	Bradman, DG	& Fingleton, JHW	Melbourne	1936-37
7th	217	New Zealand	Walters, KD	& Gilmour, GJ	Christchurch	1976-77
8th	243	England	Hill, C	& Hartigan, RJ	Adelaide	1907-08
9th	154	England	Blackman, JM	& Gregory, SE	Sydney	1894-95
10th	127	England	Taylor, JM	& Mailey, AA	Sydney	1924-25

IN AUSTRALIA

Wkt	Runs	Opponent	Players		Venue	Series
1st	244	England	Simpson, RB	& Lawry, WM	Adelaide	1965-66
2nd	298	West Indies	Lawry, WM	& Chappell, IM	Melbourne	1968-69
3rd	276	England	Bradman, DG	& Hassett, AL	Brisbane2	1946-47
4th	336	West Indies	Lawry, WM	& Walters, KD	Sydney	1968-69
5th	405	England	Bradman, DG	& Barnes, SG	Sydney	1946-47
6th	346	England	Bradman, DG	& Fingleton, JHW	Melbourne	1936-37
7th	185	Pakistan	Yallop, GN	& Matthews, GRJ	Melbourne	1983-84
8th	243	England	Hill, C	& Hartigan, RJ	Adelaide	1907-08
9th	154	England	Blackman, JM	& Gregory, SE	Sydney	1894-95
10th	127	England	Taylor, JM	& Mailey, AA	Sydney	1924-25

ABROAD

Wkt	Runs	Opponent	Players		Venue	Series
1st	382	West Indies	Lawry, WM	& Simpson, RB	Bridgetown	1964-65
2nd	451	England	Ponsford, WH	& Bradman, DG	The Oval	1934
3rd	295	West Indies	McDonald, CC	& Harvey, RN	Kingston	1954-55
4th	388	England	Ponsford, WH	& Bradman, DG	Leeds	1934
5th	220	West Indies	Miller, KR	& Archer, RG	Kingston	1954-55
6th	206	West Indies	Miller, KR	& Archer, RG	Bridgetown	1954-55
7th	217	New Zealand	Walters, KD	& Gilmour, GJ	Christchurch	1976-77
8th	137	West Indies	Benaud, R	& Johnson, IW	Kingston	1954-55
9th	104	England	Marsh, RW	& Gleeson, JW	Manchester	1972
10th	98	England	Davidson, AK	& McKenzie, GD	Manchester	1961

HIGHEST PARTNERSHIPS AGAINST EACH OPPONENT

Wkt	Runs	Players		Venue	Series
England:					
1st	244	Lawry, WM	& Simpson, RB	Adelaide	1965-66
2nd	451	Ponsford, WH	& Bradman, DG	The Oval	1934
3rd	276	Bradman, DG	& Hassett, AL	Brisbane2	1946-47
4th	388	Ponsford, WH	& Bradman, DG	Leeds	1934
5th	405	Bradman, DG	& Barnes, SG	Sydney	1946-47
6th	346	Bradman, DG	& Fingleton, JHW	Melbourne	1936-37
7th	165	Hill, C	& Trumble, H	Melbourne	1897-98
8th	243	Hill, C	& Hartigan, RJ	Adelaide	1907-08
9th	154	Blackhan, JM	& Gregory, SE	Sydney	1894-95
10th	127	Taylor, JM	& Mailey, AA	Sydney	1924-25
India:					
1st	217	Boon, DC	& Marsh, GR	Sydney	1985-86
2nd	236	Barnes, SG	& Bradman, DG	Adelaide	1947-48
3rd	222	Border, AR	& Hughes, KJ	Madras2	1979-80
4th	178	Jones, DM	& Border, AR	Madras2	1986-87
5th	223*	Morris, AR	& Bradman, DG	Melbourne	1947-48
6th	151	Veivers, TR	& Jarman, BN	Bombay2	1964-65
7th	64	Veivers, TR	& Martin, JW	Madras2	1964-65

Wkt	Runs	Players		Venue	Series
8th	73	Veivers, TR	& McKenzie, GD	Madras2	1964-65
9th	87	Johnson, IW	& Crawford, WPA	Madras2	1956-57
10th	7	Border, AR	& Gilbert, DR	Melbourne	1985-86

New Zealand:

Wkt	Runs	Players		Venue	Series
1st	106	Wood, GM	& Laird, BM	Auckland	1981-82
2nd	168	Marsh, GR	& Phillips, WB	Auckland	1985-86
3rd	264	Chappell, IM	& Chappell, GS	Wellington	1973-74
4th	106	Redpath, IR	& Davis, IC	Christchurch	1973-74
5th	213	Ritchie, GM	& Matthews, GRJ	Wellington	1985-86
6th	197	Border, AR	& Matthews, GRJ	Brisbane2	1985-86
7th	217	Walters, KD	& Gilmour, GJ	Christchurch	1976-77
8th	93	Gilmour, GJ	& O'Keeffe, KJ	Auckland	1976-77
9th	57	Marsh, RW	& Pascoe, LS	Perth	1980-81
10th	60	Walters, KD	& Higgs, JD	Melbourne	1980-81

Pakistan:

Wkt	Runs	Players		Venue	Series
1st	134	Davis, IC	& Turner, A	Melbourne	1976-77
2nd	259	Phillips, WB	& Yallop, GN	Perth	1983-84
3rd	203	Yallop, GN	& Hughes, KJ	Melbourne	1983-84
4th	217	Chappell, GS	& Yallop, GN	Faisalabad	1979-80
5th	171	Chappell, GS	& Cosier, GJ	Melbourne	1976-77
"	171	Border, AR	& Chappell, GS	Brisbane2	1983-84
6th	139	Cowper, RM	& Veivers, TR	Melbourne	1964-65
7th	185	Yallop, GN	& Matthews, GRJ	Melbourne	1983-84
8th	117	Cosier, GJ	& O'Keeffe, KJ	Melbourne	1976-77
9th	83	Watkins, JR	& Massie, RAL	Sydney	1972-73
10th	52	Lillee, DK	& Walker, MHN	Sydney	1972-73
"	52	Lawson, GF	& Alderman, TM	Lahore2	1982-83

South Africa:

Wkt	Runs	Players		Venue	Series
1st	233	Fingleton, JHW	& Brown, WA	Cape Town	1935-36
2nd	275	McDonald, CC	& Hassett, AL	Adelaide	1952-53
3rd	242	Kelleway, C	& Bardsley, W	Lord's	1912
4th	168	Harvey, RN	& Miller, KR	Sydney	1952-53
5th	143	Armstrong, WW	& Trumper, VT	Melbourne	1910-11
6th	107	Kelleway, C	& Ransford, VS	Melbourne	1910-11
7th	160	Benaud, R	& McKenzie, GD	Sydney	1963-64
8th	83	Chipperfield, AG	& Grimmett, CV	Durban2	1935-36

Wkt	Runs	Players		Venue	Series
9th	78	Bradman, DG	& O'Reilly, WJ	Adelaide	1931-32
"	78	Mackay, KD	& Meckiff, I	Johannesburg3	1957-58
10th	82	Ransford, VS	& Whitty, WJ	Melbourne	1910-11

Sri Lanka:

Wkt	Runs	Players		Venue	Series
1st	43	Wessels, KC	& Wood, GM	Kandy	1982-83
2nd	170	Wessels, KC	& Yallop, GN	Kandy	1982-83
3rd	77	Wessels, KC	& Chappell, GS	Kandy	1982-83
4th	69	Chappell, GS	& Hookes, DW	Kandy	1982-83
5th	155*	Hookes, DW	& Border, AR	Kandy	1982-83
6th	–				
7th	–				
8th	–				
9th	–				
10th	–				

West Indies:

Wkt	Runs	Players		Venue	Series
1st	382	Lawry, WM	& Simpson, RB	Bridgetown	1964-65
2nd	298	Lawry, WM	& Chappell, IM	Melbourne	1968-69
3rd	295	McDonald, CC	& Harvey, RN	Kingston	1954-55
4th	336	Lawry, WM	& Walters, KD	Sydney	1968-69
5th	220	Miller, KR	& Archer, RG	Kingston	1954-55
6th	206	Miller, KR	& Archer, RG	Bridgetown	1954-55
7th	134	Davidson, AK	& Benaud, R	Brisbane2	1960-61
8th	137	Benaud, R	& Johnson, IW	Kingston	1954-55
9th	97	Mackay, KD	& Martin, JW	Melbourne	1960-61
10th	97	Hogan, TG	& Hogg, RM	Georgetown	1983-84

HIGHEST PARTNERSHIPS FOR EACH GROUND

Wkt	Runs	Opponent	Players		Series
Adelaide (Aust):					
1st	244	England	Simpson, RB	& Lawry, WM	1965-66
2nd	275	South Africa	McDonald, CC	& Hassett, AL	1952-53
3rd	189	England	Morris, AR	& Hassett, AL	1946-47
4th	194	England	Kelleway, C	& Armstrong, WW	1920-21
5th	150	England	Miller, KR	& Johnson, IW	1946-47

Wkt	*Runs*	*Opponent*	*Players*		*Series*
6th	146	England	Waugh, SR	& Matthews, GRJ	1986-87
7th	168	New Zealand	Marsh, RW	& O'Keeffe, KJ	1973-74
8th	243	England	Hill, C	& Hartigan, RJ	1907-08
9th	108	England	Ryder, J	& Oldfield, WAS	1924-25
10th	81	England	Trott, AE	& Callaway, ST	1894-95

Brisbane1 (Aust):

1st	6	England	Woodfull, WM	& Ponsford, WH	1928-29
2nd	229	West Indies	Ponsford, WH	& Bradman, DG	1930-31
3rd	193	West Indies	Bradman, DG	& Kippax, AF	1930-31
4th	16	England	Hendry, HSTL	& Kelleway, CE	1928-29
5th	31	England	Hendry, HSTL	& Ryder, J	1928-29
6th	30	England	Ryder, J	& Bradman, DG	1928-29
7th	4	England	Bradman, DG	& Oldfield, WAS	1928-29
”	4	England	Woodfull, WM	& Bradman, DG	1928-29
8th	75	West Indies	Oxenham, RK	& Oldfield, WAS	1930-31
9th	8	West Indies	Oldfield, WAS	& Grimmett, CV	1930-31
10th	7	West Indies	Oldfield, WAS	& Ironmonger, H	1930-31

Brisbane2 (Aust):

1st	136	England	Lawry, WM	& Simpson, RB	1962-63
2nd	217	West Indies	Lawry, WM	& Chappell, IM	1968-69
3rd	276	England	Bradman, DG	& Hassett, AL	1946-47
4th	170	England	Yallop, GN	& Hughes, KJ	1978-79
5th	187	England	Lawry, WM	& Walters, KD	1965-66
6th	197	New Zealand	Border, AR	& Matthews, GRJ	1985-86
7th	134	West Indies	Davidson, AK	& Benaud, R	1960-61
8th	91	England	Mackay, KD	& Benaud, R	1962-63
9th	55	India	Walters, KD	& Connolly, AN	1967-68
10th	52*	India	Thomson, JR	& Hurst, AG	1977-78

Melbourne (Aust):

1st	219	South Africa	Lawry, WM	& Redpath, IR	1963-64
2nd	298	West Indies	Lawry, WM	& Chappell, IM	1968-69
3rd	249	England	Bradman, DG	& McCabe, SJ	1936-37
4th	177	Pakistan	Border, AR	& Hughes, KJ	1978-79
5th	223*	India	Morris, AR	& Bradman, DG	1947-48
6th	346	England	Fingleton, JHW	& Bradman, DG	1936-37
7th	185	Pakistan	Yallop, GN	& Matthews, GRJ	1983-84
8th	173	England	Pellew, CE	& Gregory, JM	1920-21

Wkt	Runs	Opponent	Players		Series
9th	100	England	Hartkopf, AE	& Oldfield, WAS	1924-25
10th	120	England	Duff, RA	& Armstrong, WW	1901-02

Perth (Aust):

Wkt	Runs	Opponent	Players		Series
1st	91	England	Weiner, JM	& Laird, BM	1979-80
2nd	259	Pakistan	Phillips, WB	& Yallop, GN	1983-84
3rd	139	India	Mann, AL	& Ogilvie, AD	1977-78
4th	141	England	Chappell, GS	& Hughes, KJ	1982-83
5th	170	England	Edwards, R	& Walters, KD	1974-75
6th	219	England	Redpath, IR	& Chappell, GS	1970-71
7th	67	England	Redpath, IR	& Marsh, RW	1970-71
8th	78	England	Border, AR	& Lillee, DK	1979-80
9th	57	England	Toohey, PM	& Dymock, G	1978-79
"	57	New Zealand	Marsh, RW	& Pascoe, LS	1980-81
10th	59	West Indies	Lawson, GF	& Alderman, TM	1984-85

Sydney (Aust):

Wkt	Runs	Opponent	Players		Series
1st	217	India	Boon, DC	& Marsh, GR	1985-86
2nd	224	South Africa	Bardsley, W	& Hill, C	1910-11
3rd	193	England	Darling, J	& Worrall, J	1897-98
4th	336	West Indies	Lawry, WM	& Walters, KD	1968-69
5th	405	England	Barnes, SG	& Bradman, DG	1946-47
6th	187	England	Kelleway, C	& Armstrong, WW	1920-21
7th	160	South Africa	Benaud, R	& McKenzie, GD	1963-64
8th	154	England	Bonnor, GJ	& Jones, SP	1884-85
9th	154	England	Gregory, SE	& Blackham, JM	1894-95
10th	127	England	Taylor, JM	& Mailey, AA	1924-25

Birmingham (Eng):

Wkt	Runs	Opponent	Players		Series
1st	80	England	McCosker, RB	& Turner, A	1975
2nd	111	England	Cowper, RM	& Chappell, IM	1968
3rd	146	England	Harvey, RN	& O'Neill, NC	1961
4th	58	England	Border, AR	& Yallop, GN	1981
5th	51	England	Hughes, KJ	& Yallop, GN	1981
6th	79	England	Edwards, R	& Marsh, RW	1975
7th	88	England	Simpson, RB	& Mackay, KD	1961
8th	58	England	Lawson, GF	& McDermott, CJ	1985
9th	59	England	Lawson, GF	& Thomson, JR	1985
10th	26	England	O'Connor, JDA	& Whitty, WJ	1909

Wkt	Runs	Opponent	Players		Series
Leeds (Eng):					
1st	71	England	Bardsley, W	& Andrews, TJE	1921
2nd	301	England	Morris, AR	& Bradman, DG	1948
3rd	229	England	Bradman, DG	& Kippax, AF	1930
4th	388	England	Ponsford, WH	& Bradman, DG	1934
5th	112	England	Hughes, KJ	& Yallop, GN	1981
6th	58	England	Trumper, VT	& Kelly, JJ	1899
7th	80	England	Phillips, WB	& O'Donnell, SP	1985
8th	105	England	Burge, PJP	& Hawke, NJN	1964
9th	89	England	Burge, PJP	& Grout, ATW	1964
10th	55	England	Lindwall, RR	& Toshack, ERH	1948
Lord's (Eng):					
1st	162	England	Woodfull, WM	& Ponsford, WH	1930
2nd	231	England	Woodfull, WM	& Bradman, DG	1930
3rd	242	South Africa	Kelleway, C	& Macartney, CG	1912
4th	221	England	Trott, GHS	& Gregory, SE	1896
5th	216	England	Border, AR	& Ritchie, GM	1985
6th	142	England	Gregory, SE	& Graham, H	1893
7th	117	England	Mackay, KD	& Benaud, R	1956
8th	85	England	Brown, WA	& O'Reilly, WJ	1938
9th	66	England	Edwards, R	& Lillee, DK	1975
10th	69	England	Scott, HJH	& Boyle, HF	1884
"	69	England	Lillee, DK	& Mallett, AA	1975
Manchester (Eng):					
1st	201	England	Lawry, WM	& Simpson, RB	1964
2nd	196	England	Brown, WA	& McCabe, SJ	1934
3rd	202	South Africa	Kelleway, C	& Bardsley, W	1912
4th	173	England	Harvey, RN	& Hole, GB	1953
5th	219	England	Simpson, RB	& Booth, BC	1964
6th	127*	England	Border, AR	& Phillips, WB	1985
7th	64	England	Bruce, W	& Trumble, H	1893
8th	87	England	Fairfax, AG	& Grimmett, CV	1930
9th	104	England	Marsh, RW	& Gleeson, JW	1972
10th	98	England	Davidson, AK	& McKenzie, GD	1961
Nottingham (Eng):					
1st	89	England	Fingleton, JHW	& Brown, WA	1938

Wkt	Runs	Opponent	Players		Series
2nd	170	England	Brown, WA	& Bradman, DG	1938
3rd	146	England	Edwards, R	& Chappell, GS	1972
4th	112	England	Brown, WA	& McCabe, SJ	1934
5th	120	England	Bradman, DG	& Hassett, AL	1948
6th	161	England	Wood, GM	& Ritchie, GM	1985
7th	69	England	McCabe, SJ	& Barnett, BA	1938
8th	107	England	Hassett, AL	& Lindwall, RR	1948
9th	48	England	O'Donnell, SP	& Lawson, GF	1985
10th	77	England	McCabe, SJ	& Fleetwood-Smith, LO	1938

Sheffield (Eng):

Wkt	Runs	Opponent	Players		Series
1st	20	England	Trumper, VT	& Duff, RA	1902
2nd	60	England	Trumper, VT	& Hill, C	1902
3rd	0	England	Duff, RA	& Darling, J	1902
"	0	England	Hill, C	& Darling, J	1902
4th	107	England	Hill, C	& Gregory, SE	1902
5th	27	England	Hill, C	& Noble, MA	1902
6th	54	England	Noble, MA	& Hopkins, AJY	1902
7th	52	England	Hopkins, AJY	& Armstrong, WW	1902
8th	10	England	Hopkins, AJY	& Kelly, JJ	1902
9th	57	England	Armstrong, WW	& Trumble, H	1902
10th	2	England	Hopkins, AJY	& Saunders, J	1902

The Oval (Eng):

Wkt	Runs	Opponent	Players		Series
1st	180	England	Gregory, SE	& Bardsley, W	1909
2nd	451	England	Ponsford, WH	& Bradman, DG	1934
3rd	207	England	Murdoch, WL	& Scott, HJH	1884
4th	243	England	Bradman, DG	& Jackson, A	1930
5th	185	England	Burge, PJP	& Booth, BC	1961
6th	86	England	Wellham, DW	& Marsh, RW	1981
7th	107	England	Collins, HL	& Gregory, JM	1926
8th	83	England	Gregory, SE	& McLeod, CE	1899
9th	100	England	Walker, MHN	& Malone, MF	1977
10th	88	England	Murdoch, WL	& Moule, WH	1880

Bangalore (India):

Wkt	Runs	Opponent	Players		Series
1st	21	India	Hilditch, AMJ	& Darling, WM	1979-80
2nd	69	India	Hilditch, AMJ	& Border, AR	1979-80
3rd	47	India	Hilditch, AMJ	& Hughes, KJ	1979-80

Wkt	Runs	Opponent	Players		Series
4th	32	India	Hughes, KJ	& Yallop, GN	1979-80
5th	89	India	Hughes, KJ	& Yardley, B	1979-80
6th	36	India	Hughes, KJ	& Wood, GM	1979-80
7th	0	India	Wood, GM	& Wright, KJ	1979-80
8th	38	India	Wright, KJ	& Hogg, RM	1979-80
9th	1	India	Wright, KJ	& Higgs, JD	1979-80
10th	5	India	Wright, KJ	& Hurst, AG	1979-80

Bombay2 (India):

1st	81	India	Lawry, WM	& Stackpole, KR	1969-70
2nd	204	India	Burke, JW	& Harvey, RN	1956-57
3rd	207	India	Harvey, RN	& O'Neill, NC	1959-60
4th	118	India	Stackpole, KR	& Redpath, IR	1969-70
5th	76	India	O'Neill, NC	& Grout, ATW	1959-60
6th	151	India	Burge, PJP	& Jarman, BN	1964-65
7th	10	India	Booth, BC	& Martin, JW	1964-65
8th	53*	India	Lindwall, RR	& Maddocks, L	1956-57
9th	16	India	McKenzie, GD	& Connolly, AN	1964-65
10th	8	India	Mallett, AA	& Connolly, AN	1969-70

Bombay3 (India):

1st	76	India	Marsh, GR	& Boon, DC	1986-87
2nd	75	India	Marsh, GR	& Jones, DM	1986-87
3rd	146*	India	Border, AR	& Jones, DM	1986-87
4th	11	India	Border, AR	& Ritchie, GM	1986-87
5th	43	India	Ritchie, GM	& Matthews, GRJ	1986-87
6th	17	India	Hughes, KJ	& Wright, KJ	1979-80
7th	19	India	Yallop, GN	& Wright, KJ	1979-80
8th	32	India	Zoehrer, TJ	& Bright, RJ	1986-87
9th	13	India	Wright, KJ	& Hogg, RM	1979-80
10th	5	India	Gilbert, DR	& Reid, BA	1986-87

Calcutta (India):

1st	115	India	Lawry, WM	& Simpson, RB	1964-65
2nd	97	India	Yallop, GN	& Border, AR	1979-80
3rd	206	India	Yallop, GN	& Hughes, KJ	1979-80
4th	150	India	O'Neill, NC	& Burge, PJP	1959-60
5th	72	India	Chappell, IM	& Sheahan, AP	1969-70
6th	49	India	Yallop, GN	& Yardley, B	1979-80

Wkt	Runs	Opponent	Players		Series
7th	36*	India	Hughes, KJ	& Wright, KJ	1979-80
8th	29	India	Harvey, RN	& Johnson, IW	1956-57
9th	8	India	Yardley, B	& Hogg, RM	1979-80
10th	33	India	Mallett, AA	& Connolly, AN	1969-70

Delhi (India):

1st	53	India	McDonald, CC	& Favell, LE	1959-60
2nd	127	India	Border, AR	& Hilditch, AMJ	1979-80
3rd	79	India	Harvey, RN	& O'Neill, NC	1959-60
4th	132	India	Harvey, RN	& Mackay, KD	1969-70
5th	44	India	Whatmore, DF	& Sleep, PR	1979-80
6th	118	India	Chappell, IM	& Taber, HB	1969-70
7th	45	India	Benaud, R	& Grout, ATW	1959-60
8th	51	India	Sleep, PR	& Dymock, G	1979-80
9th	41	India	Kline, LF	& Meckiff, I	1959-60
10th	52	India	Wright, KJ	& Higgs, JD	1979-80

Kanpur (India):

1st	95*	India	Stackpole, KR	& Lawry, WM	1969-70
2nd	57	India	Stevens, GB	& Harvey, RN	1959-60
3rd	37	India	Chappell, IM	& Walters, KD	1969-70
4th	93	India	Hughes, KJ	& Yallop, GN	1979-80
5th	131	India	Redpath, IR	& Sheahan, AP	1969-70
6th	19	India	Whatmore, DF	& Wright, KJ	1979-80
7th	54	India	Yallop, GN	& Darling, WM	1979-80
8th	30	India	Davidson, AK	& Kline, LF	1959-60
9th	34	India	Sheahan, AP	& Gleeson, JW	1969-70
10th	17	India	Gleeson, JW	& Connolly, AN	1969-70

Madras1 (India):

1st	60	India	Stackpole, KR	& Lawry, WM	1969-70
2nd	158	India	Boon, DC	& Jones, DM	1986-87
3rd	222	India	Border, AR	& Hughes, KJ	1979-80
4th	178	India	Jones, DM	& Border, AR	1969-70
5th	102	India	Walters, KD	& Redpath, IR	1969-70
6th	63	India	Border, AR	& Matthews, GRJ	1986-87
7th	33	India	Redpath, IR	& McKenzie, GD	1969-70
8th	50	India	Redpath, IR	& Mayne, LC	1969-70
9th	33	India	Mayne, LC	& Mallett, AA	1969-70
10th	14	India	Dymock, G	& Higgs, JD	1979-80

Wkt	Runs	Opponent	Players		Series
Madras2 (India):					
1st	91	India	Lawry, WM	& Simpson, RB	1964-65
2nd	61	India	Lawry, WM	& O'Neill, NC	1964-65
3rd	84	India	Simpson, RB	& Burge, PJP	1964-65
4th	55	India	Craig, ID	& Burge, PJP	1956-57
5th	34	India	Burge, PJP	& Mackay, KD	1956-57
6th	29	India	Martin, JW	& Redpath, IR	1964-65
7th	64	India	Veivers, TR	& Martin, JW	1964-65
8th	73	India	Veivers, TR	& McKenzie, GD	1964-65
9th	87	India	Johnson, IW	& Crawford, WPA	1956-57
10th	32	India	Johnson, IW	& Langley, GRA	1956-57
Auckland (NZ):					
1st	106	New Zealand	Laird, BM	& Wood, GM	1981-8
2nd	168	New Zealand	Marsh, GR	& Phillips, WB	1985-86
3rd	115	New Zealand	McCosker, RB	& Chappell, GS	1976-77
4th	44	New Zealand	Dyson, J	& Chappell, GS	1981-82
5th	53	New Zealand	Zoehrer, TJ	& Ritchie, GM	1985-86
6th	87	New Zealand	Redpath, RB	& Marsh, RW	1973-74
7th	85	New Zealand	Redpath, IR	& O'Keeffe, KJ	1973-74
8th	93	New Zealand	Gilmour, GJ	& O'Keeffe, KJ	1976-77
9th	29	New Zealand	Walters, KD	& Walker, MHN	1973-74
10th	32	New Zealand	Boon, DC	& Reid, BA	1985-86
Christchurch (NZ):					
1st	57	New Zealand	Marsh, GR	& Boon, DC	1985-86
2nd	67	New Zealand	Davis, IC	& McCosker, RB	1976-77
3rd	56	New Zealand	Redpath, IR	& Chappell, GS	1973-74
4th	106	New Zealand	Redpath, IR	& Davis, IC	1973-74
5th	93	New Zealand	Chappell, GS	& Walters, KD	1973-74
6th	117	New Zealand	Border, AR	& Waugh, SR	1985-86
7th	217	New Zealand	Walters, KD	& Gilmour, GJ	1976-77
8th	84	New Zealand	Chappell, GS	& Thomson, JR	1981-82
9th	50	New Zealand	Walters, KD	& Lillee, DK	1973-74
10th	48	New Zealand	Walters, KD	& Walker, MHN	1976-77
Wellington (NZ):					
1st	104	New Zealand	Boon, DC	& Marsh, GR	1985-86
2nd	141	New Zealand	Redpath, IR	& Chappell, IM	1973-74
3rd	264	New Zealand	Chappell, IM	& Chappell, GS	1973-74

Wkt	Runs	Opponent	Players		Series
4th	40	New Zealand	Chappell, GS	& Davis, IC	1973-74
5th	213	New Zealand	Ritchie, GM	& Matthews, GRJ	1985-86
6th	80	New Zealand	Chappell, GS	& Marsh, RW	1973-74
7th	19	New Zealand	Chappell, GS	& O'Keeffe, KJ	1973-74
8th	17	New Zealand	Zoehrer, TJ	& McDermott, CJ	1985-86
9th	0	New Zealand	McDermott, CJ	& Reid, BA	1985-86
10th	0	New Zealand	Reid, BA	& Davis, SP	1985-86

Dacca (Pak):

1st	12	Pakistan	McDonald, CC	& Favell, LE	1959-60
2nd	53	Pakistan	McDonald, CC	& Harvey, RN	1959-60
3rd	47*	Pakistan	McDonald, CC	& O'Neill, NC	1959-60
4th	0	Pakistan	Harvey, RN	& Burge, PJP	1959-60
5th	59	Pakistan	Harvey, RN	& Benaud, R	1959-60
6th	22	Pakistan	Harvey, RN	& Mackay, KD	1959-60
7th	9	Pakistan	Harvey, RN	& Davidson, AK	1959-60
8th	8	Pakistan	Harvey, RN	& Grout, ATW	1959-60
9th	38	Pakistan	Grout, ATW	& Lindwall, RR	1959-60
10th	36	Pakistan	Grout, ATW	& Meckiff, I	1959-60

Faisalabad (Pak):

1st	73	Pakistan	Laird, BM	& Dyson, J	1982-83
2nd	62	Pakistan	Wood, GM	& Dyson, J	1982-83
3rd	179	Pakistan	Hughes, KJ	& Chappell, GS	1982-83
4th	217	Pakistan	Chappell, GS	& Yallop, GN	1979-80
5th	56	Pakistan	Ritchie, GM	& Sleep, PR	1982-83
6th	127	Pakistan	Yallop, GN	& Marsh, RW	1979-80
7th	24	Pakistan	Yallop, GN	& Beard, GR	1979-80
8th	7	Pakistan	Yallop, GN	& Bright, RJ	1979-80
9th	20	Pakistan	Yallop, GN	& Lillee, DK	1979-80
10th	20	Pakistan	Ritchie, GM	& Thomson, JR	1982-83

Karachi (Pak):

1st	54	Pakistan	McDonald, CC	& Stevens, GB	1959-60
"	54	Pakistan	Lawry, WM	& Simpson, RB	1964-65
2nd	119	Pakistan	Simpson, RB	& Redpath, IR	1964-65
3rd	116	Pakistan	Simpson, RB	& Burge, PJP	1964-65
4th	34	Pakistan	Simpson, RB	& Booth, BC	1964-65
5th	68	Pakistan	Hughes, KJ	& Border, AR	1979-80
6th	64	Pakistan	Benaud, R	& Archer, RG	1956-57

Wkt	Runs	Opponent	Players		Series
7th	29	Pakistan	Harvey, RN	& Burge, PJP	1959-60
8th	64	Pakistan	Marsh, RW	& Bright, RJ	1982-83
9th	31	Pakistan	Border, AR	& Lillee, DK	1979-80
10th	50	Pakistan	Davidson, AK	& Lindwall, RR	1959-60

Lahore2 (Pak):

1st	85	Pakistan	Wood, GM	& Laird, BM	1982-83
2nd	56	Pakistan	McDonald, CC	& Harvey, RN	1959-60
3rd	108	Pakistan	Laird, BM	& Chappell, GS	1979-80
4th	99	Pakistan	O'Neill, NC	& Favell, LE	1959-60
5th	57	Pakistan	Hughes, KJ	& Ritchie, GM	1982-83
6th	63	Pakistan	Harvey, RN	& Benaud, R	1959-60
7th	132	Pakistan	Border, AR	& Beard, GR	1979-80
8th	109*	Pakistan	Border, AR	& Bright, RJ	1979-80
9th	11	Pakistan	Lawson, GF	& Thomson, JR	1982-83
10th	52	Pakistan	Lawson, GF	& Alderman, TM	1982-83

Cape Town (SA):

1st	233	South Africa	Fingleton, JHW	& Brown, WA	1935-36
2nd	117	South Africa	Simpson, RB	& Redpath, IR	1966-67
3rd	78	South Africa	Simpson, RB	& Cowper, RM	1966-67
4th	130	South Africa	Burke, JW	& Mackay, KD	1957-58
5th	140	South Africa	Harvey, RN	& Loxton, SJE	1949-50
6th	86	South Africa	Harvey, RN	& McCool, CL	1949-50
7th	128	South Africa	Stackpole, KR	& Watson, GD	1966-67
8th	48	South Africa	Grimmett, CV	& O'Reilly, WJ	1935-36
9th	30	South Africa	Mallett, AA	& Gleeson, JW	1969-70
10th	41	South Africa	Redpath, IR	& Connolly, AN	1969-70

Durban1 (SA):

1st	85	South Africa	Collins, HL	& Gregory, JM	1921-22
2nd	74	South Africa	Collins, HL	& Macartney, CG	1921-22
3rd	26	South Africa	Macartney, CG	& Gregory, JM	1921-22
4th	106	South Africa	Macartney, CG	& Ryder, J	1921-22
5th	47	South Africa	Macartney, CG	& Ryder, J	1921-22
6th	39	South Africa	Ryder, J	& Taylor, JM	1921-22
7th	62	South Africa	Ryder, J	& Hendry, HSTL	1921-22
8th	15	South Africa	Ryder, J	& Carter, H	1921-22
9th	5	South Africa	Ryder, J	& McDonald, EA	1921-22
10th	3	South Africa	Ryder, J	& Mailey, AA	1921-22

Wkt	Runs	Opponent	Players		Series
Durban2 (SA):					
1st	162	South Africa	Fingleton, JHW	& Brown, WA	1935-36
2nd	161	South Africa	Brown, WA	& McCabe, SJ	1935-36
3rd	96	South Africa	McCabe, SJ	& Darling, J	1935-36
4th	76	South Africa	O'Brien, LPJ	& Darling, J	1935-36
5th	135	South Africa	Harvey, RN	& Loxton, SJE	1949-50
6th	106*	South Africa	Harvey, RN	& McCool, CL	1949-50
7th	62	South Africa	Chipperfield, AG	& Richardson, VY	1935-36
8th	83	South Africa	Chipperfield, AG	& Grimmett, CV	1935-36
9th	68	South Africa	Redpath, IR	& Gleeson, JW	1969-70
10th	18	South Africa	Redpath, IR	& Connolly, AN	1969-70
Johannesburg1 (SA):					
1st	105	South Africa	Fingleton, JHW	& Brown, WA	1935-36
2nd	177	South Africa	Fingleton, JHW	& McCabe, SJ	1935-36
3rd	209	South Africa	Collins, HL	& Gregory, JM	1921-22
4th	76	South Africa	O'Brien, LPJ	& Oldfield, WAS	1935-36
5th	35	South Africa	Collins, HL	& Taylor, JM	1921-22
6th	51	South Africa	Chipperfield, AG	& O'Brien, LPJ	1935-36
7th	57	South Africa	Noble, MA	& Hopkins, AJY	1902-03
8th	32	South Africa	Hopkins, AJY	& Kelly, JJ	1902-03
9th	54	South Africa	Duff, RA	& Kelly, JJ	1902-03
10th	69	South Africa	O'Reilly, WJ	& McCormick, EL	1935-36
Johannesburg2 (SA):					
1st	214	South Africa	Morris, AR	& Moroney, JR	1949-50
2nd	170	South Africa	Moroney, JR	& Harvey, RN	1949-50
3rd	69	South Africa	Miller, KR	& Hassett, AL	1949-50
4th	109	South Africa	Miller, KR	& Hassett, AL	1949-50
5th	37	South Africa	Hassett, AL	& Loxton, SJE	1949-50
6th	83	South Africa	Loxton, SJE	& McCool, CL	1949-50
7th	37	South Africa	Loxton, SJE	& Johnson, IW	1949-50
8th	52	South Africa	Johnson, IW	& Saggers, RA	1949-50
9th	36	South Africa	Johnson, IW	& Lindwall, RR	1949-50
10th	5	South Africa	Johnson, IW	& Johnston, WA	1949-50
Johannesburg3 (SA):					
1st	118	South Africa	Simpson, RB	& Lawry, WM	1966-67
2nd	86	South Africa	Lawry, WM	& Redpath, IR	1966-67

Wkt	Runs	Opponent	Players		Series
3rd	158	South Africa	Burke, JW	& Benaud, R	1957-58
4th	44*	South Africa	Mackay, KD	& Simpson, RB	1957-58
5th	90	South Africa	McDonald, CC	& Simpson, RB	1957-58
6th	71	South Africa	Chappell, IM	& Veivers, TR	1966-67
7th	67	South Africa	Benaud, R	& Davidson, AK	1957-58
8th	81	South Africa	Mackay, KD	& Davidson, AK	1957-58
9th	78	South Africa	Mackay, KD	& Meckiff, I	1957-58
10th	52	South Africa	Taber, HB	& Connolly, AN	1969-70

Port Elizabeth (SA):

Wkt	Runs	Opponent	Players		Series
1st	50	South Africa	Simpson, RB	& Lawry, WM	1966-67
2nd	76	South Africa	Lawry, WM	& Redpath, IR	1969-70
3rd	187	South Africa	Morris, AR	& Harvey, RN	1949-50
4th	114	South Africa	Morris, AR	& Hassett, AL	1949-50
5th	99	South Africa	Hassett, AL	& Loxton, SJE	1949-50
6th	41	South Africa	Cowper, RM	& Martin, JW	1966-67
7th	60	South Africa	Hassett, AL	& Johnson, IW	1949-50
8th	26	South Africa	Mackay, KD	& Grout, ATW	1957-58
9th	39	South Africa	McKenzie, GD	& Taber, HB	1966-67
10th	13	South Africa	Mackay, KD	& Kline, LF	1957-58

Kandy (SL):

Wkt	Runs	Opponent	Players		Series
1st	43	Sri Lanka	Wessels, KC	& Wood, GM	1982-83
2nd	170	Sri Lanka	Wessels, KC	& Yallop, GN	1982-83
3rd	77	Sri Lanka	Wessels, KC	& Chappell, GS	1982-83
4th	69	Sri Lanka	Chappell, GS	& Hookes, DW	1982-83
5th	155*	Sri Lanka	Hookes, DW	& Border, AR	1982-83
6th	—				
7th	—				
8th	—				
9th	—				
10th	—				

Bridgetown (WI):

Wkt	Runs	Opponent	Players		Series
1st	382	West Indies	Lawry, WM	& Simpson, RB	1964-65
2nd	140	West Indies	Lawry, WM	& Cowper, RM	1964-65
3rd	192*	West Indies	Chappell, IM	& Walters, KD	1972-73
4th	41	West Indies	Chappell, GS	& Edwards, R	1972-73
5th	24	West Indies	Border, AR	& Hookes, DW	1983-84

Wkt	Runs	Opponent	Players		Series
6th	206	West Indies	Miller, KR	& Archer, RG	1954-55
7th	55	West Indies	Simpson, RB	& Yardley, B	1977-78
8th	79	West Indies	Lindwall, RR	& Johnson, IW	1954-55
9th	64	West Indies	Johnson, IW	& Langley, GRA	1954-55
10th	63	West Indies	Phillips, WB	& Alderman, TM	1983-84

Georgetown (WI):

Wkt	Runs	Opponent	Players		Series
1st	135*	West Indies	Stackpole, KR	& Redpath, IR	1972-73
2nd	64	West Indies	McDonald, CC	& Harvey, RN	1954-55
3rd	121	West Indies	Chappell, IM	& Chappell, GS	1972-73
4th	251	West Indies	Wood, GM	& Serjeant, CS	1977-78
5th	76	West Indies	Ritchie, GM	& Hookes, DW	1983-84
6th	125	West Indies	Border, AR	& Phillips, WB	1983-84
7th	95	West Indies	Simpson, RB	& Rixon, SJ	1977-78
8th	40	West Indies	Booth, BC	& Grout, ATW	1964-65
"	40	West Indies	Lawson, GF	& Hogg, RM	1983-84
9th	19	West Indies	Benaud, R	& Langley, GRA	1954-55
10th	97	West Indies	Hogan, TG	& Hogg, RM	1983-84

Kingston (WI):

Wkt	Runs	Opponent	Players		Series
1st	161	West Indies	Stackpole, KR	& Redpath, IR	1972-73
2nd	180	West Indies	Wood, GM	& Toohey, PM	1977-78
3rd	295	West Indies	McDonald, CC	& Harvey, RN	1954-55
4th	71	West Indies	Harvey, RN	& Miller, KR	1954-55
5th	220	West Indies	Miller, KR	& Archer, RG	1954-55
6th	94	West Indies	Edwards, R	& Marsh, RW	1972-73
7th	63	West Indies	Marsh, RW	& O'Keeffe, KJ	1972-73
8th	137	West Indies	Benaud, R	& Johnson, IW	1954-55
9th	31	West Indies	Archer, RG	& Johnson, IW	1954-55
10th	24	West Indies	Hawke, NJN	& Mayne, LC	1954-55
"	24	West Indies	McKenzie, GD	& Mayne, LC	1954-55

Port-of-Spain (WI):

Wkt	Runs	Opponent	Players		Series
1st	191	West Indies	McDonald, CC	& Morris, AR	1954-55
2nd	138	West Indies	Simpson, RB	& Cowper, RM	1964-65
3rd	225	West Indies	Cowper, RM	& Booth, BC	1964-65
4th	111	West Indies	Chappell, GS	& Walters, KD	1972-73
5th	66	West Indies	Booth, BC	& Thomas, G	1964-65
6th	100	West Indies	Border, AR	& Jones, DM	1983-84

Wkt	Runs	Opponent	Players		Series
7th	90	West Indies	Archer, RG	& Johnson, IW	1954-55
8th	58	West Indies	Hawke, NJN	& Grout, ATW	1964-65
9th	42	West Indies	Border, AR	& Lawson, GF	1983-84
10th	61*	West Indies	Border, AR	& Alderman, TM	1983-84

St. John's (WI):

Wkt	Runs	Opponent	Players		Series
1st	50	West Indies	Phillips, WB	& Ritchie, GM	1983-84
2nd	7	West Indies	Phillips, WB	& Border, AR	1983-84
3rd	53	West Indies	Border, AR	& Hughes, KJ	1983-84
4th	19	West Indies	Hughes, KJ	& Jones, DM	1983-84
5th	123	West Indies	Border, AR	& Hookes, DW	1983-84
6th	17	West Indies	Hookes, DW	& Woolley, RD	1983-84
7th	9	West Indies	Woolley, RD	& Lawson, GF	1983-84
"	9	West Indies	Woolley, RD	& Hogan, TG	1983-84
8th	9	West Indies	Woolley, RD	& Lawson, GF	1983-84
9th	22	West Indies	Hogan, TG	& Maguire, JN	1983-84
10th	16	West Indies	Maguire, JN	& Rackemann, CG	1983-84

100 WICKET PARTNERSHIPS

Opponent	1st	2nd	3rd	4th	5th	6th	7th	8th	9th	10th	Total
England	28	48	32	39	31	14	9	9	5	2	217
India	5	5	15	12	7	3	–	–	–	–	47
New Zealand	2	5	2	2	1	3	2	–	–	–	17
Pakistan	2	8	4	7	5	2	4	2	–	–	34
South Africa	9	16	14	10	5	3	2	–	–	–	59
Sri Lanka	–	1	–	–	1	–	–	–	–	–	2
West Indies	10	14	17	12	8	4	1	1	–	–	67
Total	**56**	**97**	**84**	**82**	**58**	**29**	**18**	**12**	**5**	**2**	**443**

Players	Venue	Series	ENG	IND	NZ	Opponents PAK	SA	SL	WI
1st wicket:									
Lawry, WM & Simpson, RB	Bridgetown	1964-65	–	–	–	–	–	–	382
Simpson, RB & Lawry, WM	Adelaide	1865-66	244	–	–	–	–	–	–
Fingleton, JHW & Brown, WA	Cape Town	1935-36	–	–	–	–	233	–	–
Lawry, WM & Redpath, IR	Melbourne	1963-64	–	–	–	–	219	–	–
Boon, DC & Marsh, GR	Sydney	1985-86	–	217	–	–	–	–	–
Morris, AR & Moroney, JR	Johannesburg2	1949-50	–	–	–	–	214	–	–
Lawry, WM & Simpson, RB	Manchester	1964	201	–	–	–	–	–	–
McDonald, CC & Morris, AR	Port-of-Spain	1954-55	–	–	–	–	–	–	191
Simpson, RB & Lawry, WM	Melbourne	1967-68	–	191	–	–	–	–	–
McDonald, CC & Burke, JW	Cape Town	1957-58	–	–	–	–	190	–	–
Bardsley, W & Gregory, SE	The Oval	1909	180	–	–	–	–	–	–
Ponsford, WH & Jackson, A	Adelaide	1930-31	–	–	–	–	–	–	172*
McDonald, CC & Burke, JW	Adelaide	1958-59	171	–	–	–	–	–	–
Woodfull, WM & Ponsford, WH	Lord's	1930	162	–	–	–	–	–	–
Fingleton, JHW & Brown, WA	Durban2	1935-36	–	–	–	–	162	–	–
Stackpole, KR & Redpath, IR	Kingston	1972-73	–	–	–	–	–	–	161
Woodfull, WM & Ponsford, WH	The Oval	1930	159	–	–	–	–	–	–
Redpath, IR & Turner, A	Adelaide	1975-76	–	–	–	–	–	–	148
McDonald, CC & Simpson, RB	Melbourne	1960-61	–	–	–	–	–	–	146
McDonald, CC & Burke, JW	Lord's	1956	137	–	–	–	–	–	–
Lawry, WM & Simpson, RB	Brisbane2	1962-63	136	–	–	–	–	–	–

		Venue	Season						
Stackpole, KR	& Redpath, IR	Georgetown	1972-73	–	–	–	–	–	135*
Trumper, VT	& Duff, RA	Manchester	1902	135	–	–	–	–	–
Davis, IC	& Turner, A	Melbourne	1976-77	–	–	134	–	–	–
Woodfull, WM	& Richardson, VY	Brisbane2	1932-33	133	–	–	–	–	–
Trumper, VT	& Duff, RA	Adelaide	1903-04	129	–	–	–	–	–
Trumper, VT	& Noble, MA	Melbourne	1907-08	126	–	–	–	–	–
Barnes, SG	& Morris, AR	Sydney	1946-47	126	–	–	–	–	–
Collins, HL	& Bardsley, W	Sydney	1920-21	123	–	–	–	–	–
Barnes, SG	& Morris, AR	Lord's	1948	122	–	–	–	–	–
McDonald, CC	& Morris, AR	Melbourne	1952-53	–	–	–	122	–	–
Simpson, RB	& Lawry, WM	Melbourne	1965-66	120	–	–	–	–	–
Wood, GM	& Kent, MF	The Oval	1981	120	–	–	–	–	–
Simpson, RB	& Lawry, WM	Johannesburg3	1966-67	–	–	–	118	–	–
Collins, HL	& Bardsley, W	Melbourne	1920-21	117	–	–	–	–	–
Barnes, SG	& Morris, AR	The Oval	1948	117	–	–	–	–	–
McLeod, CE	& Worrall, J	The Oval	1899	116	–	–	–	–	–
Collins, HL	& Bardsley, W	Melbourne	1920-21	116	–	–	–	–	–
Morris, AR	& Harvey, MR	Adelaide	1946-47	116	–	–	–	–	–
Lawry, WM	& Redpath, IR	Brisbane2	1967-68	–	116	–	–	–	–
Lawry, WM	& Simpson, RB	Calcutta	1964-65	–	115	–	–	–	–
Lawry, WM	& Simpson, RB	Manchester	1961	113	–	–	–	–	–
Marsh, GR	& Boon, DC	Adelaide	1986-87	113	–	–	–	–	–
Lawry, WM	& Cowper, RM	Sydney	1967-68	–	111	–	–	–	–
Redpath, IR	& McCosker, RB	Melbourne	1974-75	111	–	–	–	–	–

Players		Venue	Series	ENG	IND	Opponents NZ	PAK	SA	SL	WI
Bannerman, AC	& Murdoch, WL	Melbourne	1881-82	110	–	–	–	–	–	–
Laird, BM	& Wood, GM	Brisbane2	1981-82	–	–	–	109	–	–	–
McDonald, CC	& Favell, LE	Bridgetown	1954-55	–	–	–	–	–	–	108
Woodfull, WM	& Ponsford, WH	Manchester	1930	106	–	–	–	–	–	–
Laird, BM	& Wood, GM	Auckland	1981-82	–	–	106	–	–	–	–
Fingleton, JHW	& Brown, WA	Johannesburg1	1935-36	–	–	–	–	105	–	–
Laird, BM	& Dyson, J	Sydney	1981-82	–	–	–	–	–	–	104
Boon, DC	& Marsh, GR	Wellington	1985-86	–	–	104	–	–	–	–
Bardsley, W	& Andrews, TJE	Lord's	1921	103	–	–	–	–	–	–
McDonald, CC	& Morris, AR	Kingston	1954-55	–	–	–	–	–	–	102
Trumper, VT	& Duff, RA	Cape Town	1902-03	–	–	–	–	100	–	–
			Total	**28**	**5**	**2**	**2**	**9**	**—**	**10**

2nd wicket:

Players		Venue	Series	ENG	IND	NZ	PAK	SA	SL	WI
Ponsford, WH	& Bradman, DG	The Oval	1934	451	–	–	–	–	–	–
Morris, AR	& Bradman, DG	Leeds	1948	301	–	–	–	–	–	–
Lawry, WM	& Chappell, IM	Melbourne	1968-69	–	–	–	–	–	–	298
McCosker, RB	& Chappell, IM	The Oval	1975	277	–	–	–	–	–	–
McDonald, CC	& Hassett, AL	Adelaide	1952-53	–	–	–	–	275	–	–
Woodfull, WM	& Bradman, DG	Melbourne	1931-32	–	–	–	–	274	–	–
Phillips, WB	& Yallop, GN	Perth	1983-84	–	–	–	259	–	–	–
Barnes, SG	& Bradman, DG	Adelaide	1947-48	–	236	–	–	–	–	–

Woodfull, WM	& Macartney, CG	Leeds	1926	235	–	–	–	–	–
Sheahan, AP	& Benaud, J	Melbourne	1972-73	–	–	–	233	–	–
Woodfull, WM	& Bradman, DG	Lord's	1930	231	–	–	–	–	–
Ponsford, WH	& Bradman, DG	Brisbane1	1930-31	–	–	–	–	–	229
Bardsley, W	& Hill, C	Sydney	1910-11	–	–	–	–	224	–
Redpath, IR	& Chappell, GS	Sydney	1974-75	220	–	–	–	–	–
Lawry, WM	& Chappell, IM	Brisbane2	1968-69	–	–	–	–	–	217
Woodfull, WM	& Hendry, HSTL	Sydney	1928-29	215	–	–	–	–	–
Burke, JW	& Harvey, RN	Bombay2	1956-57	–	204	–	–	–	–
Stackpole, KR	& Chappell, IM	Adelaide	1970-71	202	–	–	–	–	–
Brown, WA	& McCabe, SJ	Manchester	1934	196	–	–	–	–	–
Woodfull, WM	& Macartney, CG	Manchester	1926	192	–	–	–	–	–
Woodfull, WM	& Bradman, DG	Leeds	1930	192	–	–	–	–	–
Collins, HL	& Ponsford, WH	Sydney	1924-25	190	–	–	–	–	–
Redpath, IR	& Chappell, IM	Melbourne	1970-71	180	–	–	–	–	–
Wood, GM	& Toohey, PM	Kingston	1977-78	–	–	–	–	–	180
Fingleton, JHW	& McCabe, SJ	Johannesburg1	1935-36	–	–	–	–	177	–
Woodfull, WM	& Bradman, DG	Adelaide	1931-32	–	–	–	176	–	–
Davis, IC	& McCosker, RB	Melbourne	1976-77	–	–	176	–	–	–
Bannerman, AC	& Lyons, JJ	Sydney	1891-92	174	–	–	–	–	–
Barnes, SG	& Bradman, DG	Lord's	1948	174	–	–	–	–	–
Brown, WA	& Bradman, DG	Nottingham	1938	170	–	–	–	–	–
Moroney, JR	& Harvey, RN	Johannesburg2	1949-50	–	–	–	–	170	–

Players	&	Venue	Series	ENG	IND	NZ	Opponents PAK	SA	SL	WI
Wessels, KC	& Yallop, GN	Kandy	1982-83	–	–	–	–	–	170	–
Marsh, GR	& Phillips, WB	Auckland	1985-86	–	–	168	–	–	–	–
Morris, AR	& Miller, KR	Lord's	1953	165	–	–	–	–	–	–
Woodfull, WM	& Bradman, DG	Brisbane2	1931-32	–	–	–	–	163	–	–
Brown, WA	& McCabe, SJ	Durban2	1935-36	–	–	–	–	161	–	–
Simpson, RB	& Harvey, RN	Sydney	1962-63	160	–	–	–	–	–	–
Boon, DC	& Jones, DM	Madras2	1986-87	–	158	–	–	–	–	–
Morris, AR	& Harvey, RN	Adelaide	1952-53	–	–	–	–	157	–	–
Woodfull, WM	& Bradman, DG	Melbourne	1930-31	–	–	–	–	–	–	156
Stackpole, KR	& Chappell, IM	Brisbane2	1970-71	151	–	–	–	–	–	–
Darling, WM	& Hill, C	Adelaide	1897-98	148	–	–	–	–	–	–
Kelleway, C	& Macartney, CG	Lord's	1912	146	–	–	–	–	–	–
McDonnell, PS	& Murdoch, WL	The Oval	1884	143	–	–	–	–	–	–
Trumper, VT	& Hill, C	Adelaide	1903-04	143	–	–	–	–	–	–
Wessels, KC	& Yallop, GN	Adelaide	1983-84	–	–	–	142	–	–	–
Redpath, IR	& Chappell, IM	Wellington	1973-74	–	–	141	–	–	–	–
Lawry, WM	& O'Neill, NC	Sydney	1963-64	–	–	–	–	140	–	–
Lawry, WM	& Cowper, RM	Bridgetown	1964-65	–	–	–	–	–	–	140
Hilditch, AMJ	& Wessels, KC	Leeds	1985	139	–	–	–	–	–	–
Simpson, RB	& Cowper, RM	Port-of-Spain	1964-65	–	–	–	–	–	–	138
Woodfull, WM	& Rigg, KE	Sydney	1931-32	–	–	–	–	137	–	–
Trumper, VT	& Hill, C	Adelaide	1901-02	136	–	–	–	–	–	–

Batsmen		Venue	Season						
Hilditch, AMJ	& Wessels, KC	Leeds	1985	–	–	–	–	–	132
Iredale, FA	& Giffen, G	Manchester	1896	–	–	–	–	–	131
Lawry, WM	& Redpath, IR	The Oval	1968	–	–	–	–	–	129
Stackpole, KR	& Chappell, IM	Melbourne	1973-74	–	–	–	128	–	–
Redpath, IR	& Yallop, GN	Adelaide	1975-76	128	–	–	–	–	–
Hilditch, AMJ	& Border, AR	Delhi	1979-80	–	–	–	–	127	–
Laird, BM	& Chappell, IM	Melbourne	1979-80	–	–	–	–	–	127
McDonald, CC	& Harvey, RN	Melbourne	1958-59	–	–	–	–	–	126
Marsh, GR	& Jones, DM	Perth	1986-87	–	–	–	–	–	126
Hassett, AL	& Harvey, RN	Lord's	1953	–	–	–	–	–	125
Davis, IC	& McCosker, RB	Adelaide	1976-77	–	–	125	–	–	–
Darling, WM	& Hughes, KJ	Sydney	1978-79	–	–	–	–	–	125
McLeod, CE	& Hill, C	Melbourne	1897-98	–	–	–	–	–	124
Macartney, CG	& Hordern, H	Sydney	1910-11	–	124	–	–	–	–
Fingleton, JHW	& Bradman, DG	Sydney	1936-37	–	–	–	–	–	124
Edwards, R	& Chappell, IM	Nottingham	1972	–	–	–	–	–	124
Collins, HL	& Macartney, CG	Lord's	1926	–	–	–	–	–	123
Redpath, IR	& Chappell, IM	Melbourne	1972-73	–	–	123	–	–	–
Hilditch, AMJ	& Wessels, KC	Melbourne	1984-85	123	–	–	–	–	–
Morris, AR	& Hassett, AL	Nottingham	1953	–	–	–	–	–	122
Kelleway, C	& Hill, C	Sydney	1911-12	–	–	–	–	–	121
Archer, KA	& Hassett, AL	Sydney	1950-51	–	–	–	–	–	121
Simpson, RB	& Redpath, IR	Karachi	1964-65	–	–	119	–	–	–

Players		Venue	Series	Opponents						
				ENG	IND	NZ	PAK	SA	SL	WI
McCosker, RB	& Chappell, IM	Lord's	1975	119	–	–	–	–	–	–
Simpson, RB	& Redpath, IR	Cape Town	1966-67	–	–	–	–	117	–	–
Stackpole, KR	& Chappell, IM	The Oval	1972	116	–	–	–	–	–	–
Woodfull, WM	& Bradman, DG	Sydney	1932-33	115	–	–	–	–	–	–
Wood, GM	& Wessels, KC	Sydney	1984-85	–	–	–	–	–	–	114
Collins, HL	& Ryder, J	Johannesburg1	1921-22	–	–	–	–	113	–	–
Collins, HL	& Macartney, CG	Sydney	1920-21	111	–	–	–	–	–	–
Cowper, RM	& Chappell, IM	Birmingham	1968	111	–	–	–	–	–	–
Brown, WA	& Barnes, SG	Wellington	1945-46	–	–	109	–	–	–	–
Edwards, R	& Chappell, IM	Port-of-Spain	1972-73	–	–	–	–	–	–	109
Redpath, IR	& Chappell, GS	Port-of-Spain	1972-73	–	–	–	–	–	–	107
Noble, MA	& Hill, C	Nottingham	1905	106	–	–	–	–	–	–
McCosker, RB	& Chappell, IM	Leeds	1975	106	–	–	–	–	–	–
Turner, A	& Yallop, GN	Adelaide	1975-76	–	–	–	–	–	–	105
Phillips, WB	& Boon, DC	Sydney	1985-86	–	–	105	–	–	–	–
Moroney, JR	& Miller, KR	Cape Town	1949-50	–	–	–	–	104	–	–
Redpath, IR	& Chappell, IM	Melbourne	1974-75	104	–	–	–	–	–	–
Wood, GM	& Ritchie, GM	Bridgetown	1983-84	–	–	–	–	–	–	103
Bardsley, W	& Hill, C	Melbourne	1910-11	–	–	–	–	101	–	–
Hilditch, AMJ	& Border, AR	Madras1	1979-80	–	101	–	–	–	–	–
Sheahan, AP	& Chappell, IM	Adelaide	1972-73	–	–	–	100	–	–	–
			Total	48	5	5	8	16	1	14

3rd Wicket:

Batsmen		Venue	Season	Score
McDonald, CC	& Harvey, RN	Kingston	1954-55	295
Bradman, DG	& Hassett, AL	Brisbane2	1946-47	276
Chappell, IM	& Chappell, GS	Wellington	1973-74	264
Bradman, DG	& McCabe, SJ	Melbourne	1936-37	249
Kelleway, C	& Bardsley, W	Lord's	1912	242
Bradman, DG	& Kippax, AF	Leeds	1930	229
Cowper, RM	& Booth, BC	Port-of-Spain	1964-65	225
Harvey, RN	& Miller, KR	Kingston	1954-55	224
Border, AR	& Hughes, KJ	Madras1	1979-80	222
Lawry, WM	& Cowper, RM	Melbourne	1965-66	212
Collins, HL	& Gregory, JM	Johannesburg1	1921-22	209
Stackpole, KR	& Walters, KD	Brisbane2	1970-71	209
Murdoch, WL	& Scott, HJH	The Oval	1884	207
Harvey, RN	& O'Neill, NC	Bombay2	1959-60	207
Yallop, GN	& Hughes, KJ	Calcutta	1979-80	206
Yallop, GN	& Hughes, KJ	Melbourne	1983-84	203
Kelleway, C	& Bardsley, W	Manchester	1912	202
Morris, AR	& Harvey, RN	Brisbane2	1954-55	202
Chappell, IM	& Chappell, GS	The Oval	1972	201
Darling, J	& Worrall, J	Sydney	1897-98	193
Bradman, DG	& Kippax, AF	Brisbane1	1930-31	193
Chappell, IM	& Walters, KD	Bridgetown	1972-73	192*

Players		Venue	Series	Opponents						
				ENG	IND	NZ	PAK	SA	SL	WI
Bradman, DG	& Kippax, AF	Lord's	1930	192	–	–	–	–	–	–
Morris, AR	& Hassett, AL	Adelaide	1946-47	189	–	–	–	–	–	–
Morris, AR	& Harvey, RN	Port Elizabeth	1949-50	–	–	–	–	187	–	–
Hughes, KJ	& Chappell, GS	Faisalabad	1979-80	–	–	–	179	–	–	–
Simpson, RB	& Cowper, RM	Adelaide	1967-68	–	172	–	–	–	–	–
Bradman, DG	& Hassett, AL	Melbourne	1947-48	–	169	–	–	–	–	–
Laird, BM	& Border, AR	Adelaide	1981-82	–	–	–	–	–	–	166
Armstrong, WW	& Hill, C	Johannesburg1	1902-03	–	–	–	–	164	–	–
Chappell, IM	& Chappell, GS	Brisbane2	1975-76	–	–	–	–	–	–	159*
Burke, JW	& Benaud, R	Johannesburg3	1957-58	–	–	–	–	158	–	–
Carter, H	& Hill, C	Adelaide	1911-12	157	–	–	–	–	–	–
Harvey, RN	& Hassett, AL	Brisbane2	1952-53	–	–	–	–	155	–	–
Bradman, DG	& McCabe, SJ	The Oval	1934	150	–	–	–	–	–	–
Jones, DM	& Border, AR	Bombay3	1986-87	–	146	–	–	–	–	–
Harvey, RN	& O'Neill, NC	Birmingham	1961	146	–	–	–	–	–	–
Edwards, R	& Chappell, GS	Nottingham	1972	146	–	–	–	–	–	–
Macartney, CG	& Bardsley, W	Sydney	1910-11	–	–	–	–	145	–	–
Hill, C	& Gehrs, DRA	Sydney	1910-11	–	–	–	–	144	–	–
Lawry, WM	& Walters, KD	Manchester	1968	144	–	–	–	–	–	–
Wessels, KC	& Border, AR	Sydney	1984-85	–	–	–	–	–	–	144
Mann, AL	& Ogilvie, AD	Perth	1977-78	–	139	–	–	–	–	–
Burke, JW	& Burge, PJP	Bombay2	1956-57	–	137	–	–	–	–	–

Simpson, RB	& Booth, BC	Adelaide	1962-63	133	–	–	–	–	–	–	–	–	–
Toohey, PM	& Yallop, GN	Kingston	1977-78	–	–	–	–	–	–	–	–	–	133
Border, AR	& Hughes, KJ	Bombay[3]	1979-80	132	–	–	–	–	–	–	–	–	–
Ryder, J &	Gregory, JM	Melbourne	1920-21	130	–	–	–	–	–	–	–	–	–
Laird, BM	& Chappell, GS	Brisbane[2]	1979-80	–	–	–	–	–	–	–	–	–	130
Chappell, IM	& Chappell, GS	Bridgetown	1972-73	–	–	–	–	–	–	–	–	–	129
Lawry, WM	& O'Neill, NC	Bridgetown	1964-65	–	–	–	–	–	–	–	–	–	126*
Chappell, GS	& Hughes, KJ	Adelaide	1982-83	126	–	–	–	–	–	–	–	–	–
Jones, DM	& Border, AR	Adelaide	1986-87	126	–	–	–	–	–	–	–	–	–
Laird, BM	& Chappell, GS	Brisbane[2]	1979-80	–	–	–	–	–	–	–	–	–	124
Lawry, WM	& Walters, KD	Melbourne	1968-69	–	–	–	–	–	–	–	–	–	123
Chappell, IM	& Chappell, GS	Georgetown	1972-73	–	–	–	–	–	–	–	–	–	121
Yallop, GN	& Toohey, PM	Adelaide	1977-78	–	–	–	–	120	–	–	–	–	–
Harvey, RN	& O'Neill, NC	Melbourne	1958-59	118	–	–	–	–	–	–	–	–	–
Sheahan, AP	& Cowper, RM	Adelaide	1967-68	–	–	–	–	118	–	–	–	–	–
Simpson, RB	& Burge, PJP	Karachi	1964-65	–	–	–	–	–	116	–	–	–	–
Duff, RA	& Noble, MA	The Oval	1905	115	–	–	–	–	–	–	–	–	–
McCosker, RB	& Chappell, GS	Auckland	1976-77	–	–	–	–	–	–	115	–	–	–
Trumper, VT	& Gregory, SE	Sydney	1907-08	114	–	–	–	–	–	–	–	–	–
McDonald, CC	& Harvey, RN	Sydney	1952-53	–	–	–	–	–	–	–	113	–	–
Rigg, KE	& Bradman, DG	Sydney	1931-32	–	–	–	–	–	–	–	111	–	–
Chappell, GS	& Hughes, KJ	Lord's	1980	111	–	–	–	–	–	–	–	–	–
Morris, AR	& Harvey, RN	Adelaide	1950-51	110	–	–	–	–	–	–	–	–	–

Players		Venue	Series	ENG	IND	NZ	PAK	SA	SL	WI
							Opponents			
Wood, GM	& Hughes, KJ	Lord's	1980	110	–	–	–	–	–	–
Bradman, DG	& McCabe, SJ	Adelaide	1936-37	109	–	–	–	–	–	–
Morris, AR	& Hassett, AL	The Oval	1948	109	–	–	–	–	–	–
Macartney, CG	& Andrews, TJE	The Oval	1921	108	–	–	–	–	–	–
Harvey, RN	& O'Neill, NC	Sydney	1960-61	–	–	–	–	–	–	108
Laird, BM	& Chappell, GS	Lahore2	1979-80	–	–	–	108	–	–	–
Bradman, DG	& Hassett, AL	Adelaide	1947-48	–	105	–	–	–	–	–
Simpson, RB	& Burge, PJP	Adelaide	1963-64	–	–	–	–	104	–	–
Cosier, GJ	& Serjeant, CS	Melbourne	1977-78	–	104	–	–	–	–	–
Harvey, RN	& Hassett, AL	Melbourne	1952-53	–	–	–	–	103	–	–
Bardsley, W	& Armstrong, WW	Melbourne	1910-11	–	–	–	–	102	–	–
Macartney, CG	& Pellew, CE	Leeds	1921	101	–	–	–	–	–	–
Bradman, DG	& Hassett, AL	Brisbane2	1947-48	–	101	–	–	–	–	–
Chappell, IM	& Walters, KD	Calcutta	1969-70	–	101	–	–	–	–	–
Redpath, IR	& Chappell, GS	Melbourne	1974-75	101	–	–	–	–	–	–
Harvey, RN	& Watson, WJ	Bridgetown	1954-55	–	–	–	–	–	–	100
Chappell, IM	& Chappell, GS	Brisbane2	1974-75	100	–	–	–	–	–	–
			Total	**32**	**15**	**2**	**4**	**14**	**—**	**17**

4th wicket:

Players		Venue	Series	ENG	IND	NZ	PAK	SA	SL	WI
Ponsford, WH	& Bradman, DG	Leeds	1934	388	–	–	–	–	–	–
Lawry, WM	& Walters, KD	Sydney	1968-69	–	336	–	–	–	–	–

Batsmen	Partner	Venue	Season						
Wood, GM	& Serjeant, CS	Georgetown	1977-78	–	–	–	–	–	251
Bradman, DG	& Jackson, A	The Oval	1930	243	–	–	–	–	–
Hassett, AL	& Miller, KR	Sydney	1951-52	–	–	–	–	–	235
Trott, GHS	& Gregory, SE	Lord's	1896	221	–	–	–	–	–
Chappell, GS	& Yallop, GN	Faisalabad	1979-80	–	–	–	–	217	–
Redpath, IR	& Walters, KD	Sydney	1968-69	–	–	–	–	–	210
Bannerman, AC	& McDonnell, PS	Sydney	1881-82	199	–	–	–	–	–
Macartney, CG	& Gregory, JM	Sydney	1920-21	198	–	–	–	–	–
Kelleway, C	& Armstrong, WW	Adelaide	1920-21	194	–	–	–	–	–
Harvey, RN	& O'Neill, NC	Adelaide	1962-63	194	–	–	–	–	–
Kippax, AF	& McCabe, SJ	Adelaide	1930-31	–	–	–	–	–	182
Jones, DM	& Border, AR	Madras2	1986-87	–	178	–	–	–	–
Border, AR	& Hughes, KJ	Melbourne	1978-79	–	–	177	–	–	–
Harvey, RN	& Hole, GB	Manchester	1953	173	–	–	–	–	–
Cowper, RM	& Walters, KD	Melbourne	1965-66	172	–	–	–	–	–
Chappell, IM	& Edwards, R	Adelaide	1972-73	–	–	172	–	–	–
Giffen, G	& Iredale, FA	Sydney	1894-95	171	–	–	–	–	–
Chappell, GS	& Hughes, KJ	Sydney	1983-84	–	–	171	–	–	–
Yallop, GN	& Hughes, KJ	Brisbane2	1978-79	170	–	–	–	–	–
Harvey, RN	& Miller, KR	Sydney	1952-53	–	–	–	168	–	–
Noble, MA	& Gregory, SE	Adelaide	1903-04	162	–	–	–	–	–
Ponsford, WH	& Taylor, JM	Melbourne	1924-25	161	–	–	–	–	–
Kippax, AF	& Ryder, J	Melbourne	1928-29	161	–	–	–	–	–

Players		Venue	Series	ENG	IND	NZ	Opponents PAK	SA	SL	WI
Harvey, RN	& Loxton, SJE	Melbourne	1947-48	–	159	–	–	–	–	–
Armstrong, WW	& Hill, C	Melbourne	1910-11	–	–	–	–	154	–	–
O'Neill, NC	& Burge, PJP	Calcutta	1959-60	–	150	–	–	–	–	–
Harvey, RN	& Craig, ID	Melbourne	1952-53	–	–	–	–	148	–	–
Hassett, AL	& Miller, KR	Adelaide	1947-48	–	142	–	–	–	–	–
Chappell, GS	& Hughes, KJ	Perth	1982-83	141	–	–	–	–	–	–
Kippax, AF	& Ryder, J	Adelaide	1928-29	137	–	–	–	–	–	–
Wessels, KC	& Border, AR	Adelaide	1983-84	–	–	–	134	–	–	–
Harvey, RN	& Mackay, KD	Delhi	1959-60	–	–	132	–	–	–	–
Harvey, RN	& Hole, GB	Brisbane2	1954-55	131	–	–	–	–	–	–
Hill, C	& Noble, MA	Lord's	1899	130	–	–	–	–	–	–
Burke, JW	& Mackay, KD	Cape Town	1957-58	–	–	–	–	130	–	–
Woodfull, WM	& Richardson, AJ	Leeds	1926	129	–	–	–	–	–	–
Hughes, KJ	& Border, AR	Adelaide	1980-81	–	129	–	–	–	–	–
Jackson, A	& Ryder, J	Adelaide	1928-29	126	–	–	–	–	–	–
Cowper, RM	& Booth, BC	Bombay2	1964-65	–	125	–	–	–	–	–
Border, AR	& Ritchie, GM	Adelaide	1986-87	124*	–	–	–	–	–	–
Brown, WA	& Hassett, AL	Lord's	1938	124	–	–	–	–	–	–
Harvey, RN	& Miller, KR	Melbourne	1951-52	–	–	–	–	–	–	124
Redpath, IR	& Chappell, GS	Melbourne	1975-76	–	–	–	–	–	–	124
O'Neill, NC	& Burge, PJP	The Oval	1961	123	–	–	–	–	–	–
Miller, KR	& Harvey, RN	Leeds	1948	121	–	–	–	–	–	–

Batsman	Partner	Venue	Season					
Bradman, DG	& Miller, KR	Brisbane2	1947-48	–	–	120	–	–
O'Neill, NC	& Booth, BC	Brisbane2	1963-64	–	–	–	120	–
Bardsley, W	& Trumper, VT	Adelaide	1910-11	–	–	–	118	–
Walters, KD	& Redpath, IR	Bombay2	1969-70	–	–	118	–	–
Chappell, GS	& Hughes, KJ	Brisbane2	1979-80	–	–	–	–	118
Boon, DC	& Ritchie, GM	Adelaide	1985-86	–	–	117	–	–
Morris, AR	& Hassett, AL	Port Elizabeth	1949-50	–	–	–	114	–
Chappell, GS	& Edwards, R	Brisbane2	1974-75	114	–	–	–	–
Brown, WA	& McCabe, SJ	Nottingham	1934	112	–	–	–	–
Kippax, AF	& McCabe, SJ	Melbourne	1931-32	–	–	–	111	–
Chappell, GS	& Walters, KD	Port-of-Spain	1972-73	–	–	–	–	111
Hilditch, AMJ	& Border, AR	Melbourne	1984-85	–	–	–	–	111
McCosker, RB	& Chappell, GS	Melbourne	1975-76	–	–	–	–	110*
O'Neill, NC	& Favell, LE	Sydney	1958-59	110	–	–	–	–
Macartney, CG	& Taylor, JM	Leeds	1921	109	–	–	–	–
Miller, KR	& Hassett, AL	Johannesburg2	1949-50	–	–	–	109	–
Hassett, AL	& Miller, KR	Nottingham	1953	109	–	–	–	–
O'Neill, NC	& Burge, PJP	Sydney	1962-63	109	–	–	–	–
Chappell, GS	& Border, AR	Melbourne	1980-81	–	–	108	–	–
Hughes, KJ	& Border, AR	Brisbane2	1983-84	–	108	–	–	–
Chappell, GS	& Edwards, R	Lord's	1975	107*	–	–	–	–
Hughes, KJ	& Hookes, DW	Brisbane2	1982-83	107*	–	–	–	–
Hill, C	& Gregory, SE	Sheffield	1902	107	–	–	–	–

Players		Venue	Series	ENG	IND	NZ	Opponents PAK	SA	SL	WI
Noble, MA	& Armstrong, WW	Sydney	1903-04	106	–	–	–	–	–	–
Macartney, CG	& Ryder, J	Durban1	1921-22	–	–	–	–	106	–	–
Hassett, AL	& Miller, KR	Brisbane2	1946-47	106	–	–	–	–	–	–
Lawry, WM	& Booth, BC	The Oval	1964	106	–	–	–	–	–	–
Redpath, IR	& Davis, IC	Christchurch	1973-74	–	–	106	–	–	–	–
Chappell, GS	& Hughes, KJ	Sydney	1979-80	105	–	–	–	–	–	–
Yallop, GN	& Simpson, RB	Adelaide	1977-78	–	104	–	–	–	–	–
Serjeant, CS	& Walters, KD	Lord's	1977	103	–	–	–	–	–	–
Chappell, GS	& Walters, KD	Adelaide	1976-77	–	–	–	101	–	–	–
Yallop, GN	& Serjeant, CS	Port-of-Spain	1977-78	–	–	–	–	–	–	101
Chappell, GS	& Walters, KD	Adelaide	1973-74	–	–	100	–	–	–	–
Hughes, KJ	& Hookes, DW	Melbourne	1982-83	100	–	–	–	–	–	–
			Total	39	12	2	7	10	—	12

5th Wicket:

Players		Venue	Series	ENG	IND	NZ	PAK	SA	SL	WI
Barnes, SG	& Bradman, DG	Sydney	1946-47	405	–	–	–	–	–	–
Morris, AR	& Bradman, DG	Melbourne	1947-48	–	223*	–	–	–	–	–
Miller, KR	& Archer, RG	Kingston	1954-55	–	–	–	–	–	–	220
Simpson, RB	& Booth, BC	Manchester	1964	219	–	–	–	–	–	–
Border, AR	& Ritchie, GM	Lord's	1985	216	–	–	–	–	–	–
Ritchie, GM	& Matthews, GRJ	Wellington	1985-86	–	–	213	–	–	–	–
Burge, PJP	& Walters, KD	Melbourne	1965-66	198	–	–	–	–	–	–

Player	Partner	Venue	Year						
Lawry, WM	& Walters, KD	Brisbane2	1965-66	187	–	–	–	–	–
Burge, PJP	& Booth, BC	The Oval	1961	185	–	–	–	–	–
Bradman, DG	& Fairfax, AG	Melbourne	1928-29	183	–	–	–	–	–
Ponsford, WH	& Woodfull, WM	Sydney	1930-31	–	–	–	–	–	183
Chappell, GS	& Walters, KD	Sydney	1980-81	–	172	–	–	–	–
Chappell, GS	& Cosier, GJ	Melbourne	1976-77	–	–	171	–	–	–
Border, AR	& Chappell, GS	Brisbane2	1983-84	–	–	171	–	–	–
Edwards, R	& Walters, KD	Perth	1974-75	170	–	–	–	–	–
Badcock, CL	& Gregory, RG	Melbourne	1936-37	161	–	–	–	–	–
Hookes, DW	& Border, AR	Kandy	1982-83	–	–	–	–	155*	–
Chappell, GS	& Border, AR	Sydney	1983-84	–	–	153	–	–	–
Sheahan, AP	& Chappell, IM	Manchester	1968	152	–	–	–	–	–
Miller, KR	& Johnson, IW	Adelaide	1946-47	150	–	–	–	–	–
Hughes, KJ	& Border, AR	Sydney	1982-83	149	–	–	–	–	–
Chappell, GS	& Marsh, RW	Melbourne	1972-73	–	–	146	–	–	–
Armstrong, WW	& Trumper, VT	Melbourne	1910-11	–	–	–	143	–	–
Gregory, SE	& Darling, J	Melbourne	1894-95	142	–	–	–	–	–
Harvey, RN	& Loxton, SJE	Cape Town	1949-50	–	–	–	140	–	–
Giffen, G	& Gregory, SE	Sydney	1894-95	139	–	–	–	–	–
Bradman, DG	& Gregory, RG	Adelaide	1936-37	135	–	–	–	–	–
Harvey, RN	& Loxton, SJE	Durban2	1949-50	–	–	–	135	–	–
Redpath, IR	& Sheahan, AP	Kanpur	1969-70	131	–	–	–	–	–
Border, AR	& Walters, KD	Melbourne	1980-81	131	–	–	–	–	–

Players		Venue	Series	ENG	IND	NZ	Opponents PAK	SA	SL	WI
Chappell, GS	& Wellham, DM	Brisbane2	1981-82	–	–	–	131	–	–	–
McCabe, SJ	& Richardson, VY	Sydney	1932-33	129	–	–	–	–	–	–
Border, AR	& Chappell, GS	Melbourne	1979-80	126	–	–	–	–	–	–
Iredale, FA	& Trott, GHS	Melbourne	1897-98	124	–	–	–	–	–	–
Border, AR	& Hookes, DW	St. John's	1983-84	–	–	–	–	–	–	124
Chappell, GS	& Marsh, RW	Brisbane2	1975-76	–	–	–	–	–	–	122
Bradman, DG	& Hassett, AL	Nottingham	1948	120	–	–	–	–	–	–
Bardsley, W	& Trumper, VT	The Oval	1909	118	–	–	–	–	–	–
Bradman, DG	& Rigg, KE	Adelaide	1931-32	–	–	–	–	114	–	–
Chappell, GS	& Cosier, GJ	Melbourne	1975-76	–	–	–	–	–	–	114
Walters, KD	& Marsh, RW	Adelaide	1974-75	112	–	–	–	–	–	–
Hughes, KJ	& Yallop, GN	Leeds	1981	112	–	–	–	–	–	–
Walters, KD	& Sheahan, AP	Sydney	1968-69	–	–	–	–	–	–	110
Trumper, VT	& Hill, C	Sydney	1907-08	108	–	–	–	–	–	–
Horan, TP	& Giffen, G	Melbourne	1881-82	107	–	–	–	–	–	–
Trott, GHS	& Graham, H	The Oval	1893	106	–	–	–	–	–	–
Armstrong, WW	& Macartney, CG	Melbourne	1907-08	106	–	–	–	–	–	–
Chappell, GS	& Edwards, R	Lord's	1972	106	–	–	–	–	–	–
Harvey, RN	& Loxton, SJE	Leeds	1948	105	–	–	–	–	–	–
Chappell, GS	& Border, AR	Adelaide	1981-82	–	–	–	–	–	–	105
O'Neill, NC	& Mackay, KD	Brisbane2	1960-61	–	–	–	–	–	–	103
Booth, BC	& Benaud, R	Brisbane2	1963-64	–	–	–	–	102	–	–

Walters, KD	& Redpath, IR	Madras1	1969-70	–	102	–	–	–	–	–
Ryder, J	& Nothling, OE	Sydney	1928-29	101	–	–	–	–	–	–
Simpson, RB	& Rixon, SJ	Perth	1977-78	–	101	–	–	–	–	–
Border, AR	& Wellham, DM	The Oval	1981	101	–	–	–	–	–	–
Darling, J	& Gregory, SE	The Oval	1899	100	–	–	–	–	–	–
Toohey, PM	& Simpson, RB	Perth	1977-78	–	100	–	–	–	–	–
			Total	**31**	**7**	**1**	**5**	**1**	**1**	**8**
6th Wicket:										
Fingleton, JHW	& Bradman, DG	Melbourne	1936-37	346	–	–	–	–	–	–
Redpath, IR	& Chappell, GS	Perth	1970-71	219	–	–	–	–	–	–
Miller, KR	& Archer, RG	Bridgetown	1954-55	–	–	–	–	–	–	206
Border, AR	& Matthews, GRJ	Brisbane2	1985-86	–	–	197	–	–	–	–
Kelleway, C	& Armstrong, WW	Sydney	1920-21	187	–	–	–	–	–	–
Border, AR	& Waugh, SR	Christchurch	1985-86	–	–	177	–	–	–	–
Wood, GM	& Ritchie, GM	Nottingham	1985	161	–	–	–	–	–	–
Veivers, TR	& Jarman, BN	Bombay2	1964-65	–	151	–	–	–	–	–
Matthews, GRJ	& Waugh, SR	Adelaide	1986-87	146*	–	–	–	–	–	–
Gregory, JM	& Armstrong, WW	Melbourne	1920-21	145	–	–	–	–	–	–
Gregory, SE	& Graham, H	Lord's	1893	142	–	–	–	–	–	–
Cowper, RM	& Veivers, TR	Melbourne	1964-65	–	–	–	139	–	–	–
Chappell, IM	& Jarman, BN	Melbourne	1967-68	–	134	–	–	–	–	–
McCool, CL	& Johnson, IW	Brisbane2	1946-47	131	–	–	–	–	–	–

Players		Venue	Series	ENG	IND	NZ	Opponents PAK	SA	SL	WI
Border, AR	& Phillips, WB	Manchester	1985	127*	–	–	–	–	–	–
Yallop, GN	& Marsh, RW	Faisalabad	1979-80	–	–	–	127	–	–	–
Kelleway, C	& Pellew, CE	Adelaide	1920-21	126	–	–	–	–	–	–
Border, AR	& Phillips, WB	Georgetown	1983-84	–	–	–	–	–	–	125
Richardson, VY	& Kelleway, C	Melbourne	1924-25	123	–	–	–	–	–	–
Walters, KD	& Veivers, TR	Brisbane2	1965-66	119	–	–	–	–	–	–
Chappell, IM	& Taber HB	Delhi	1969-70	–	118	–	–	–	–	–
Chappell, GS	& Marsh, RW	Sydney	1975-76	–	–	–	–	–	–	117
Ritchie, GM	& Matthews, GRJ	Sydney	1985-86	–	–	115	–	–	–	–
Trumper, VT	& Minnett, RB	Sydney	1911-12	109	–	–	–	–	–	–
Kelleway, C	& Ransford, VS	Melbourne	1910-11	–	–	–	–	107	–	–
Harvey, RN	& McCool, CL	Durban2	1949-50	–	–	–	–	106*	–	–
Ponsford, WH	& Kippax, AF	Sydney	1924-25	105	–	–	–	–	–	–
Booth, BC	& Benaud, R	Sydney	1963-64	–	–	–	–	100	–	–
Border, AR	& Jones, DM	Port-of-Spain	1983-84	–	–	–	–	–	–	100
			Total	**14**	**3**	**3**	**2**	**3**	**—**	**4**

7th wicket:

Players		Venue	Series	ENG	IND	NZ	PAK	SA	SL	WI
Walters, KD	& Gilmour, GJ	Christchurch	1976-77	–	–	217	–	–	–	–
Yallop, GN	& Matthews, GRJ	Melbourne	1983-84	–	–	–	185	–	–	–
Marsh, RW	& O'Keeffe, KJ	Adelaide	1973-74	–	–	168	–	–	–	–
Hill, C	& Trumble, H	Melbourne	1897-98	165	–	–	–	–	–	–

Benaud, R	& McKenzie, GD	Sydney	1963-64	—	—	160	—	—	—	—
Miller, KR	& Johnson, IW	Sydney	1950-51	150	—	—	—	—	—	—
Ryder, J	& Andrews, TJE	Adelaide	1924-25	134	—	—	—	—	—	—
Davidson, AK	& Benaud, R	Brisbane2	1960-61	—	—	—	—	134	—	—
Border, AR	& Beard, GR	Lahore2	1979-80	—	—	—	134	—	—	—
Stackpole, KR	& Watson, GD	Cape Town	1966-67	—	—	128	—	—	—	—
Marsh, RW	& O'Keeffe, KJ	Adelaide	1972-73	—	—	—	120	—	—	—
Mackay, KD	& Benaud, R	Lord's	1956	117	—	—	—	—	—	—
Mackay, KD	& Davidson, AK	Sydney	1958-59	115	—	—	—	—	—	—
Benaud, R	& Grout, ATW	Melbourne	1958-59	115	—	—	—	—	—	—
Collins, HL	& Gregory, JM	The Oval	1926	107	—	—	—	—	—	—
Booth, BC	& Mackay, KD	Brisbane2	1962-63	103	—	—	—	—	—	—
Chappell, GS	& Lawson, GF	Brisbane2	1983-84	—	—	—	103	—	—	—
Wessels, KC	& Yardley, B	Brisbane2	1982-83	100	—	—	—	—	—	—
			Total	9	—	2	4	2	—	1

8th wicket:

Hartigan, RJ	& Hill, C	Adelaide	1907-08	243	—	—	—	—	—	—
Pellew, CE	& Gregory, JM	Melbourne	1920-21	173	—	—	—	—	—	—
Bonnor, GJ	& Jones, SP	Sydney	1884-85	154	—	—	—	—	—	—
Tallon, D	& Lindwall, RR	Melbourne	1946-47	154	—	—	—	—	—	—
Benaud, R	& Johnson, IW	Kingston	1954-55	—	—	—	—	137	—	—
Cosier, GJ	& O'Keeffe, KJ	Melbourne	1976-77	—	—	—	117	—	—	—

Players	Venue	Series	ENG	IND	NZ	Opponents PAK	SA	SL	WI
Kelleway, C & Oldfield, WAS	Sydney	1924-25	116	–	–	–	–	–	–
Graham, H & Trott, AE	Sydney	1894-95	112	–	–	–	–	–	–
Armstrong, WW & Carter, H	Melbourne	1907-08	112	–	–	–	–	–	–
Border, AR & Bright, RJ	Lahore2	1979-80	–	–	–	109*	–	–	–
Hassett, AL & Lindwall, RR	Nottingham	1948	107	–	–	–	–	–	–
Burge, PJP & Hawke, NJN	Leeds	1964	105	–	–	–	–	–	–
Total			**9**	–	–	**2**	–	–	**1**

9th wicket:

Players	Venue	Series	ENG	IND	NZ	Opponents PAK	SA	SL	WI
Gregory, SE & Blackham, JM	Sydney	1894-95	154	–	–	–	–	–	–
Ryder, J & Oldfield, WAS	Adelaide	1924-25	108	–	–	–	–	–	–
Marsh, RW & Gleeson, JW	Manchester	1972	104	–	–	–	–	–	–
Hartkopf, AEV & Oldfield, WAS	Melbourne	1924-25	100	–	–	–	–	–	–
Walker, MHN & Malone, MF	The Oval	1977	100	–	–	–	–	–	–
Total			**5**	–	–	–	–	–	–

10th wicket:

Players	Venue	Series	ENG	IND	NZ	Opponents PAK	SA	SL	WI
Taylor, JM & Mailey, AA	Sydney	1924-25	127	–	–	–	–	–	–
Duff, RA & Armstrong, WW	Melbourne	1901-02	120	–	–	–	–	–	–
Total			**2**	–	–	–	–	–	–

HIGHEST WICKET PARTNERSHIPS

Wkt	Runs	Opponent	Players		Venue	Series
2nd	451	England	Ponsford, WH	& Bradman, DG	The Oval	1934
5th	405	England	Barnes, SG	& Bradman, DG	Sydney	1946-47
4th	388	England	Ponsford, WH	& Bradman, DG	Leeds	1934
1st	382	West Indies	Lawry, WM	& Simpson, RB	Bridgetown	1964-65
6th	346	England	Fingleton, JHW	& Bradman, DG	Melbourne	1936-37
4th	336	West Indies	Lawry, WM	& Walters, KD	Sydney	1968-69
2nd	301	England	Morris, AR	& Bradman, DG	Leeds	1948
2nd	298	West Indies	Lawry, WM	& Chappell, IM	Melbourne	1968-69
3rd	295	West Indies	McDonald, CC	& Harvey, RN	Kingston	1954-55
2nd	277	England	McCosker, RB	& Chappell, IM	The Oval	1975
3rd	276	England	Bradman, DG	& Hassett, AL	Brisbane2	1946-47
2nd	275	West Indies	McDonald, CC	& Hassett, AL	Adelaide	1952-53
2nd	274	South Africa	Woodfull, WM	& Bradman, DG	Melbourne	1931-32
3rd	264	New Zealand	Chappell, IM	& Chappell, GS	Wellington	1973-74
2nd	259	Pakistan	Phillips, WB	& Yallop, GN	Perth	1983-84
4th	251	West Indies	Wood, GM	& Serjeant, CS	Georgetown	1977-78
3rd	249	England	Bradman, DG	& McCabe, SJ	Melbourne	1936-37
1st	244	England	Simpson, RB	& Lawry, WM	Adelaide	1965-66
4th	243	England	Bradman, DG	& Jackson, A	The Oval	1930
8th	243	England	Hartigan, RJ	& Hill, C	Adelaide	1907-08

Wkt	Runs	Players		Opponent	Venue	Series
3rd	242	Kelleway, C	& Bardsley, W	South Africa	Lord's	1912
2nd	236	Barnes, SG	& Bradman, DG	India	Adelaide	1947-48
2nd	235	Woodfull, WM	& Macartney, CG	England	Leeds	1926
4th	235	Hassett, AL	& Miller, KR	West Indies	Sydney	1951-52
1st	233	Fingleton, JHW	& Brown, WA	South Africa	Cape Town	1935-36
2nd	233	Sheahan, AP	& Benaud, J	Pakistan	Melbourne	1972-73
2nd	231	Woodfull, WM	& Bradman, DG	England	Lord's	1930
3rd	229	Bradman, DG	& Kippax, AF	England	Leeds	1930
2nd	229	Ponsford, WH	& Bradman, DG	West Indies	Brisbane1	1930-31
3rd	225	Cowper, RM	& Booth, BC	West Indies	Port-of-Spain	1964-65
2nd	224	Bardsley, W	& Hill, C	South Africa	Sydney	1910-11
3rd	224	Harvey, RN	& Miller, KR	West Indies	Kingston	1954-55
5th	223*	Morris, AR	& Bradman, DG	India	Melbourne	1947-48
3rd	222	Border, AR	& Hughes, KJ	India	Madras1	1979-80
4th	221	Trott, GHS	& Gregory, SE	England	Lord's	1896
5th	220	Miller, KR	& Archer, RG	West Indies	Kingston	1954-55
2nd	220	Redpath, IR	& Chappell, GS	England	Sydney	1974-75
1st	219	Lawry, WM	& Redpath, IR	South Africa	Melbourne	1963-64
5th	219	Simpson, RB	& Booth, BC	England	Manchester	1964
6th	219	Redpath, IR	& Chappell, GS	England	Perth	1970-71
2nd	217	Lawry, WM	& Chappell, IM	West Indies	Brisbane2	1968-69
7th	217	Walters, KD	& Gilmour, GJ	New Zealand	Christchurch	1976-77

4th	217	Pakistan	Chappell, GS	& Yallop, GN	Faisalabad	1979-80
1st	217	India	Boon, DC	& Marsh, GR	Sydney	1985-86
5th	216	England	Border, AR	& Ritchie, GM	Lord's	1985
2nd	215	England	Woodfull, WM	& Hendry, HSTL	Sydney	1928-29
1st	214	South Africa	Morris, AR	& Moroney, JR	Johannesburg2	1949-50
5th	213	New Zealand	Ritchie, GM	& Matthews, GRJ	Wellington	1985-86
3rd	212	England	Lawry, WM	& Cowper, RM	Melbourne	1965-66
4th	210	West Indies	Redpath, IR	& Walters, KD	Sydney	1968-69
3rd	209	South Africa	Collins, HL	& Gregory, JM	Johannesburg1	1921-22
3rd	209	England	Stackpole, KR	& Walters, KD	Brisbane2	1970-71
3rd	207	England	Murdoch, WL	& Scott, HJH	The Oval	1884
3rd	207	India	Harvey, RN	& O'Neill, NC	Bombay?	1959-60
6th	206	West Indies	Miller, KR	& Archer, RG	Bridgetown	1954-55
3rd	206	India	Yallop, GN	& Hughes, KJ	Calcutta	1979-80
2nd	204	India	Burke, JW	& Harvey, RN	Bombay?	1956-57
3rd	203	Pakistan	Yallop, GN	& Hughes, KJ	Melbourne	1983-84
3rd	202	South Africa	Kelleway, C	& Bardsley, W	Manchester	1912
3rd	202	England	Morris, AR	& Harvey, RN	Brisbane2	1954-55
2nd	202	England	Stackpole, KR	& Chappell, IM	Adelaide	1970-71
1st	201	England	Lawry, WM	& Simpson, RB	Manchester	1964
3rd	201	England	Chappell, IM	& Chappell, GS	The Oval	1972

Reggie Duff, North Sydney opening batsman.

REGGIE DUFF

The Second Test at Melbourne in 1901-2 between England and Australia was one of the most exciting ever played, with fortunes fluctuating from the second ball bowled. On an uncovered pitch heavy rain fell before and during play without favouring one side or the other. In the end Australia emerged the winner because of a last-wicket stand by two players appearing in their first Test.

England had won the First Test in Sydney by an innings and 124 runs, a defeat that caused the electors to drop Charlie McLeod and Frank Laver and bring in North Sydney opening batsman Reggie Duff and lanky Melbourne Cricket Club allrounder Warwick Armstrong for their Test debuts.

Rain had saturated the pitch before Archie MacLaren won the toss for England, and he had no hesitation sending Australia in to bat under an overcast sky.

MacLaren threw Sydney Barnes, whom he had plucked from League cricket in England to make the tour, to open the bowling. Morose, uncommunicative, Barnes was one of cricket's most controversial figures, a master bowler who considered the game's administrators a bunch of fools and often said so.

With the second ball of the morning, Barnes had Victor Trumper caught for a duck by Dick Tyldesley, a dismissal the Australians immediately attributed to the pitch. With little respect for technique, all the Australians who followed hit out recklessly. Barnes and Colin Blythe bowled unchanged in an innings of 112, Barnes taking 6 for 42, Blythe 4 for 64 in two hours.

Sun made the pitch spiteful when England batted, and this time Hugh Trumble and Monty Noble bowled unchanged. England lost her first wicket at 5, her second and third at 16 and only a whirlwind 27 by Gilbert Jessop, who followed the Australian example by swinging mightily at every ball, allowed the total to reach 61 in 68 minutes. Noble took 7 for 17.

Joe Darling drastically reshuffled his batting order in an attempt to save some of the best batsmen for the second day, opening Australia's second innings himself with Trumble. The tactics worked to an extent, for Australia were 5 for 48 at stumps, a lead of 99, with fine weather

Reggie Duff was also a competent bowler.

forecast and Syd Gregory not out. Clem Hill, Trumper, Noble, Duff and Armstrong were still to come. Twenty-five wickets had fallen on the first day, a record for Tests in Australia.

The pitch rolled out well on the second morning, and all the Australian batsmen who had been held back contributed useful scores. Gregory was sixth out with the score on 98, but England missed a wonderful chance when Clem Hill was dropped at cover off Blythe just before lunch. Trumper was out first ball after the break but Hill stayed for more than three hours until 105 more had been added.

Armstrong strode to the crease to join Duff, batting at number 10, with Australia on 233, a lead of 294. At that stage England could still have won, for the pitch was playing easily, but Duff and Armstrong stayed while another 120 runs were scored. Duff batted for three hours and 26 minutes to make 104, a record for a number 10 batsman in Tests against England and an innings that enabled him to join the select few to make a century on debut. Armstrong did not offer a chance and was 45 not out when Australia's innings ended at 353.

MacLaren showed his dependence on Barnes by not relieving him until he had bowled 42 overs and taken 6 for 76. Barnes' rest was short-lived as the scoring became so fast MacLaren had to bring him back. When Len Braund clean bowled Duff with a leg-break to end one of the epic last-wicket stands, Barnes had taken 7 for 121 from 64 overs and his match figures stood at 13 for 163.

Requiring 405 to win, England began disastrously when MacLaren was out with the score on two and at stumps they were 5 for 147, 258 short of a win but with a full day to get them. Heavy rain overnight made the Australian victory a formality, and England lasted only a further 134 minutes. Trumble, the 193-centimetre (6 feet 4 inches) off-spinner "Plum" Warner called "that great camel", finished off a remarkable match with a hat-trick, Arthur Jones, John Gunn and Barnes all falling to catches as the ball spun viciously. Australia had won by 229 runs, Monty Noble taking 13 wickets for 77 in the match.

MOST 100 WICKET PARTNERSHIPS BY A BATSMAN

Player	No.	Wicket 1st	2nd	3rd	4th	5th	6th	7th	8th	9th	10th	Opponents ENG	IND	NZ	PAK	SA	SL	WI
Chappell, GS	38	–	2	9	13	11	2	1	–	–	–	12	2	2	11	–	–	11
Chappell, IM	36	–	18	8	1	1	2	–	–	–	–	14	3	3	3	–	–	7
Bradman, DG	35	–	14	11	3	6	1	–	–	–	–	21	6	–	–	5	–	3
Border, AR	33	–	2	6	8	10	5	1	1	–	–	7	9	2	7	–	1	7
Harvey, RN	32	–	6	13	9	3	1	–	–	–	–	12	4	–	–	11	–	5
Lawry, WM	24	12	5	4	2	1	–	–	–	–	–	10	4	–	–	3	–	7
Redpath, IR	24	6	10	1	4	2	1	–	–	–	–	7	4	2	2	2	–	7
Walters, KD	23	–	–	5	8	8	1	1	–	–	–	9	5	2	1	–	–	6
Simpson, RB	22	10	4	4	1	3	–	–	–	–	–	8	6	–	2	3	–	3
Hassett, AL	21	–	4	8	7	1	–	–	1	–	–	11	4	–	–	5	–	1
Hughes, KJ	21	–	1	8	10	2	–	–	–	–	–	11	4	–	5	–	–	1
Morris, AR	19	8	4	5	1	1	–	–	–	–	–	11	1	–	–	5	–	2
Hill, C	17	–	8	3	3	1	–	1	1	–	–	12	–	–	–	5	–	–
Woodfull, WM	17	4	11	–	1	1	–	–	–	–	–	11	–	–	–	4	–	2
Miller, KR	16	–	2	1	9	2	1	1	–	–	–	6	2	–	–	3	–	5
Yallop, GN	16	–	5	4	4	1	1	1	–	–	–	2	3	–	6	–	1	4
Bardsley, W	13	5	2	4	1	1	–	–	–	–	–	6	–	–	–	7	–	–
Macartney, CG	13	–	6	3	3	1	–	–	–	–	–	10	–	–	–	3	–	–
O'Neill, NC	13	–	1	5	6	1	–	–	–	–	–	6	2	–	–	2	–	–

Trumper, VT	12	4	2	1	1	3	1	–	–	–	–	9	–	–	3	–	–
McDonald, CC	12	8	2	2	–	–	–	–	–	–	–	3	–	–	4	–	–
Armstrong, WW	11	–	2	3	2	2	–	1	–	1	–	7	–	–	4	–	–
Cowper, RM	11	1	3	4	2	–	1	–	–	–	–	3	4	1	–	–	3
Ponsford, WH	11	4	3	–	2	1	1	–	–	–	–	8	–	–	–	–	3
Gregory, SE	10	1	–	1	3	3	1	–	1	–	–	10	–	–	–	–	–
Kelleway, C	10	–	2	2	1	–	4	1	–	1	–	7	–	–	3	–	–
McCabe, SJ	10	–	3	3	3	1	–	–	–	–	–	6	–	–	3	–	–
Brown, WA	10	3	5	–	2	–	–	–	–	–	–	5	–	1	4	–	–
Booth, BC	10	–	–	2	3	3	1	–	–	–	1	5	1	–	3	–	1

MOST HUNDRED WICKET PARTNERSHIPS AS A PAIR

Players		No.	ENG	IND	NZ	PAK	SA	SL	WI
Chappell, IM	& Chappell, GS	12	4	–	2	–	–	–	6
Lawry, WM	& Simpson, RB	9	5	2	–	–	1	–	1
Bradman, DG	& Woodfull, WM	7	3	–	–	–	3	–	1
Chappell, GS	& Hughes, KJ	7	4	–	–	2	–	–	1
Border, AR	& Hughes, KJ	6	1	3	–	2	–	–	–
Bradman, DG	& Hassett, AL	5	2	3	–	–	–	–	–
Hassett, AL	& Miller, KR	5	2	1	–	–	1	–	1
Harvey, RN	& O'Neill, NC	5	3	1	–	–	–	–	1
Redpath, IR	& Chappell, GS	5	3	–	–	–	–	–	2
Chappell, GS	& Border, AR	5	1	1	–	2	–	–	1
Ponsford, WH	& Woodfull, WM	4	3	–	–	–	–	–	1
Morris, AR	& Hassett, AL	4	3	–	–	–	1	–	–
Morris, AR	& Harvey, RN	4	2	–	–	–	2	–	–
Harvey, RN	& Loxton, SJE	4	1	1	–	–	2	–	–
Harvey, RN	& Miller, KR	4	1	–	–	–	2	–	1
Lawry, WM	& Walters, KD	4	2	–	–	–	–	–	2
Redpath, IR	& Chappell, IM	4	2	–	1	1	–	–	–
Stackpole, KR	& Chappell, IM	4	3	–	1	–	–	–	–
Chappell, GS	& Edwards, R	4	4	–	–	–	–	–	–
Chappell, GS	& Walters, KD	4	–	1	1	1	–	–	1
Border, AR	& Jones, DM	4	1	2	–	–	–	–	1

THREE 100 WICKET PARTNERSHIPS IN AN INNINGS

Opponent	Venue	Series	Wkt	Runs	Players	
England	Sydney	1894-95	4th	171	Giffen, G	& Iredale, FA
			5th	139	Giffen, G	& Gregory, SE
			9th	154	Gregory, SE	& Blackham, JM
England	Sydney	1920-21	1st	123	Collins, HL	& Bardsley, W
			2nd	111	Collins, HL	& Macartney, CG
			6th	187	Kelleway, C	& Armstrong, WW
England	Melbourne	1924-25	9th	100	Hartkopf, AEV	& Oldfield, WAS
			6th	123	Richardson, VY	& Kelleway, C
			4th	161	Ponsford, WH	& Taylor, JM
England	Lord's	1930	1st	162	Woodfull, WM	& Ponsford, WH
			2nd	231	Woodfull, WM	& Bradman, DG
			3rd	192	Bradman, DG	& Kippax, AF
England	Brisbane2	1946-47	3rd	276	Bradman, DG	& Hassett, AL
			4th	106	Hassett, AL	& Miller, KR
			6th	131	McCool, CL	& Johnson, IW
India	Adelaide	1947-48	2nd	236	Barnes, SG	& Bradman, DG
			3rd	105	Bradman, DG	& Hassett, AL
			4th	142	Hassett, AL	& Miller, KR
South Africa	Melbourne	1952-53	1st	122	McDonald, CC	& Morris, AR
			3rd	103	Harvey, RN	& Hassett, AL
			4th	148	Harvey, RN	& Craig, ID
West Indies	Bridgetown	1954-55	1st	108	McDonald, CC	& Favell, LE
			3rd	100	Harvey, RN	& Watson, WJ
			6th	206	Miller, KR	& Archer, RG
West Indies	Kingston	1954-55	3rd	295	McDonald, CC	& Harvey, RN
			5th	220	Miller, KR	& Archer, RG
			8th	137	Benaud, R	& Johnson, IW
Pakistan	Adelaide	1972-73	2nd	100	Sheahan, AP	& Chappell, IM
			4th	172	Chappell, IM	& Edwards, R
			7th	120	Marsh, RW	& O'Keeffe, KJ
Pakistan	Melbourne	1976-77	1st	134	Davis, IC	& Turner, A
			5th	171	Chappell, GS	& Cosier, GJ
			8th	117	Cosier, GJ	& O'Keeffe, KJ

Opponent	Venue	Series	Wkt	Runs	Players	
Pakistan	Faisalabad	1979-80	3rd	179	Hughes, KJ	& Chappell, GS
			4th	217	Chappell, GS	& Yallop, GN
			6th	127	Yallop, GN	& Marsh, RW
Pakistan	Brisbane2	1983-84	4th	108	Hughes, KJ	& Border, AR
			5th	171	Border, AR	& Chappell, GS
			7th	103	Chappell, GS	& Lawson, GF
England	Adelaide	1986-87	1st	113	Marsh, GR	& Boon, DC
			3rd	126	Jones, DM	& Border, AR
			6th	146*Matthews, GRJ		& Waugh, SR

FOUR 100 WICKET PARTNERSHIPS IN A MATCH

Opponent	Venue	Series	Inns	Wkt	Runs	Players	
South Africa	Melbourne	1910-11	1	3rd	102	Bardsley, W	& Armstrong, WW
				6th	107	Kelleway, C	& Ransford, VS
			2	4th	154	Armstrong, WW	& Hill, C
				5th	143	Armstrong, WW	& Trumper, VT
Pakistan	Melbourne	1976-77	1	1st	134	Davis, IC	& Turner, A
				5th	171	Chappell, GS	& Cosier, GJ
				8th	117	Cosier, GJ	& O'Keeffe, KJ
			2	2nd	176	Davis, IC	& McCosker, RB
England	Adelaide	1986-87	1	1st	113	Marsh, GR	& Boon, DC
				3rd	126	Jones, DM	& Border, AR
				6th	146*Matthews, GRJ		& Waugh, SR
			2	4th	124*Border, AR		& Ritchie, GM

PARTNERSHIPS OF NINETY-NINE

Wkt	Players		Opponent	Venue	Series
1st	Simpson, RB	& Lawry, WM	India	Adelaide	1967-68
2nd	Morris, AR	& Bradman, DG	England	Adelaide	1946-47
4th	Harvey, RN	& Miller, KR	England	Melbourne	1950-51
"	O'Neill, NC	& Favell, LE	Pakistan	Lahore2	1959-60
5th	Hassett, AL	& Loxton, SJE	South Africa	Port Elizabeth	1949-50
"	Chappell, GS	& Cosier, GJ	West Indies	Sydney	1975-76
"	Yardley, B	& Hughes, KJ	India	Bangalore	1979-80

PARTNERSHIPS DOMINATING TEST INNINGS

Wkt	%	Runs	Inns total	Players	Opponent	Venue	Series
4th	76.54	199	260	Bannerman, AC & McDonnell, PS	England	Sydney	1881-82
2nd	76.41	217	284	Lawry, WM & Chappell, IM	West Indies	Brisbane2	1968-69
2nd	70.77	46	65	Jennings, CB & Macartney, CG	England	The Oval	1912
7th	68.57	48	70	Turner, CTB & Lyons, JJ	England	Manchester	1888
3rd	66.67	132	9-198	Border, AR & Hughes, KJ	India	Bombay	1979-80
4th	66.44	388	584	Ponsford, WL & Bradman, DG	England	Leeds	1934
2nd	64.34	451	701	Ponsford, WL & Bradman, DG	England	The Oval	1934
3rd	63.96	71	111	Kelleway, C & Bardsley, W	England	The Oval	1912
4th	63.69	221	347	Trott, GHS & Gregory, SE	England	Lord's	1896
2nd	63.19	115	182	Woodfull, WM & Bradman, DG	England	Sydney	1932-33
1st	63.03	75	119	Darling, J & Ireland, FA	England	The Oval	1896
4th	62.79	54	86	Darling, J & Gregory, SE	England	Manchester	1902
3rd	62.05	242	390	Kelleway, C & Bardsley, W	South Africa	Lord's	1912
6th	61.35	346	564	Bradman, DG & Fingleton, JHW	England	Melbourne	1936-37
5th	60.16	74	8-123	Barnes, SG & Barnett, BA	England	The Oval	1938

ARTHUR MAILEY

The 1924-25 rubber between the English team captained by Arthur
Gilligan and the Australian side led by Herbie Collins saw the start
of the celebrated opening pairing of Jack Hobbs and Herbert Sutcliffe.
It also saw eight-ball overs used in Tests for the first time, and the
start of Bill Ponsford's outstanding Test career.

Hobbs, then 42 years old, and Sutcliffe, 30, began with opening
stands of 157 and 110 in the First Test at Sydney, but despite these
splendid beginnings England was thwarted in the end by an unexpected
last-wicket partnership of 127 by Arthur Mailey and Johnnie Taylor.
Mailey made 46 not out, his highest Test score, going in at number
11, and having achieved the record for England—Australia Tests, never
again took his batting seriously.

Australia began with a first innings of 450, a total that was largely
due to Herbie Collins, who not only made 114 himself but cleverly
shepherded Ponsford through a shaky start against Maurice Tate. When
Ponsford went in at the fall of Warren Bardsley's wicket with the score
on 46, Tate beat him comprehensively for most of the first over. Collins
then took control of the strike.

In the Australian dressing-room, after he had scored 110 on debut,
Ponsford was congratulated by team-mates. "I owe it all to Herbie,"
he said in grateful tribute to his captain. Former Test captain Clem
Hill said he had never seen such a hostile opening spell as Tate had
provided, and added that he was amazed Australia was not all out for
under 100.

Hobbs and Sutcliffe then began their long association, but after
Mailey had Sutcliffe caught for 59, Hobbs found support only in the
batting of "Patsy" Hendren (74 not out) and England was dismissed
for 298. Leading by 152, Australia scored freely in its second innings,
with Collins (60) again in form and Arthur Richardson (98) narrowly
missing a century in his maiden Test.

The final flourish of the Australian innings came with the stand
between Mailey and Taylor. Running between wickets with superb
judgment, Taylor protected Mailey from the strike for long periods,
picking up boundaries and twos. When he was compelled to face the
bowling, Mailey was particularly impressive against the leg-spin of

"Tich" Freeman.

Taylor's stroke-play blossomed after an uncertain start, and he punished all the bowling as the partnership built up. England had appeared to have a slim chance of victory before this stand began, but its hopes dwindled with every run added.

Tate finally ended it by clean bowling Taylor, but the 127 runs added had taken the match out of England's grasp on a wicket that was still ideal for batting. Faced with scoring 605 to win, England batted for six hours and 51 minutes for 411.

Hobbs and Sutcliffe began with another century stand, and Sutcliffe and Frank Woolley both made centuries. Despite compiling a record fourth-wicket total, however, England never appeared to have a chance of reaching the target and was beaten by 193 runs. Of these, 189 had come in Australia's two last-wicket partnerships.

Collins' clever protection of Ponsford until Ponsford had settled down, the uncanny manner in which he shuffled Australia's batting line-up and the shrewd use he made of his bowlers enabled Australia to win that series 4-1. At Adelaide in the Third Test, when England needed 27 runs to win, with two wickets in hand on the final morning, Collins pulled a typical surprise when he opened the bowling with Mailey and Jack Gregory.

Mailey could scarcely believe it when Collins told him he was to open. "A couple of full tosses from me and they'll have got half the runs they need," said Mailey. "Why not open with Kelleway? He'll at least keep the runs down."

"Don't talk back to your captain," said Collins. "You are going on first."

Mailey took the ball, and with England only 11 runs from victory took the last England wicket when he had Freeman caught by Bert Oldfield. Collins' gamble had given Australia a narrow win and sealed the rubber.

BOWLING

CLARRIE GRIMMETT

Clarence Victor Grimmett entered Test cricket at an age when many cricketers have retired. He was 34 when he took the field for Australia against England in 1924-25, and behind him lay years of frustration as he struggled to gain recognition for his highly individual style of leg-spin.

Grimmett was born in New Zealand in 1891 and lived his early life with his parents in a house near the Basin Reserve in Wellington. He went to Mount Cook High School and after school played cricket with three neighbours who all wanted to become spin bowlers. Grimmett initially wanted to be a fast bowler, but his schoolmasters persuaded him to follow his neighbours and bowl spin.

Probably no cricketer in the history of the game has made such a close study of the cause of a cricket ball spinning. Grimmett talked about top spin and side spin the way mathematics masters talk of calculus. He did not waste energy with a long approach run, just a few skips and then an easy swing of his arm, usually at 45 degrees from the body, as he curled the ball up to the batsman.

Adult cricketers, fooled by the teenage Grimmett's over-spinner or top-spinner, often thought them flukes until they discussed the delivery with Grimmett and discovered he knew perfectly well why the ball did not turn but simply rushed off the pitch. He played for the East Wellington Club and then for Wellington Province in Plunket Shield matches, but at a time when New Zealand was isolated from international cricket; he soon became irritated by the lack of opportunity.

When he completed his apprenticeship as a signwriter he migrated to Australia, aged 23, and in 1914 joined the Sydney Club. Despite captains who were apprehensive about spinners, he played his way from third grade to first grade in his first season by taking 76 wickets. His 28 wickets in first grade cost only 10 runs apiece.

He settled in Melbourne in 1917 and played for the South Melbourne Club, where he received plenty of coaching from the former Test bowler Jack Saunders. He alternated between the States seconds and the senior side but in 1920-21 he had his first taste of international cricket, playing for Victoria against Johnny Douglas' England side. He had four good seasons with the Prahran Club but in 1924 moved to South Australia, convinced that Victorian selectors would continue to limit his opportunities.

Bowling in a cap, he made his debut for South Australia in 1924-25, and that same season was picked to play in the Fifth Test at Sydney for Australia against England. The Australian selectors were mindful of the manner in which Arthur Gilligan's batsmen had struggled against spin throughout their Australian tour and gambled by including both Grimmett and Arthur Mailey in the attack.

Jack Gregory, Charles Kelleway, Mailey and Jack Ryder all used the ball before Grimmett had a turn in the first innings, but once he took the ball England's batting collapsed. From 11.7 overs, two of them maidens, Grimmett took 5 for 45 in a performance that gave Australia an unexpected first innings lead of 128 runs. He clean bowled Frank Woolley to take his first Test wicket, had Jack Hearne and Frank Whysall LBW, and then had both Ray Kilner and Arthur Gilligan stumped by Bert Oldfield when they tried to move down the pitch and knock him off his length.

Set to score 454 to win in the final innings, England were never likely to get the runs after Jack Gregory bowled Herbert Sutcliffe for a duck, but Grimmett forestalled any attempt to force a draw by having Hobbs stumped, Andy Sandham LBW and Patsy Hendren caught behind. There were few loose balls in Grimmett's mixture of leg spinners, top-spinners and the odd googly, and he bowled splendidly to his field.

Oldfield's great skill as a 'keeper was never more emphatically shown than when he stood up on the stumps to Grimmett. Oldfield brilliantly stumped Whysall for his fourth stumping of the match off Grimmett, who eventually wound up the match by having Herbert Strudwick caught by Mailey. Grimmett's second innings figures of 6 for 37 off 19.4 overs gave him a match bag of 11 for 82.

Over the next 11 years Grimmett took his total of Test wickets to 216 at 24.21 apiece and over the next 15 years he took 668 wickets for South Australia, more than double that of any other South Australian bowler.

Clarrie Grimmett, leg-spin bowler.

LEADING WICKET TAKERS

Bowler	M	Balls	Mdns	Runs	Wkts	Avrge	5WI	10WM	Best	Opponent						
										ENG	IND	NZ	PAK	SA	SL	WI
Lillee, DK	70	18467	652	8493	355	23.92	23	7	7/83	167	21	38	71	–	3	55
Benaud, R	63	19108	805	6704	248	27.03	16	1	7/72	83	52	–	19	52	–	42
McKenzie, GD	61	17684	547	7328	246	29.79	16	3	8/71	96	47	–	15	41	–	47
Lindwall, RR	61	13642	419	5251	228	23.03	12	–	7/38	114	36	2	4	31	–	41
Grimmett, CV	37	14513	736	5231	216	24.22	21	7	7/40	106	–	–	–	77	–	33
Thomson, JR	51	10535	300	5602	200	28.01	8	–	6/46	100	22	6	10	–	–	62
Davidson, AK	44	11587	431	3819	186	20.53	14	2	7/93	84	30	–	14	25	–	33
Miller, KR	55	10474	337	3905	170	22.97	7	1	7/60	87	9	2	2	30	–	40
Johnston, WA	40	11048	372	3826	160	23.91	7	–	6/44	75	16	–	–	44	–	25
Lawson, GF	37	8705	284	4420	145	30.48	10	2	8/112	68	–	8	33	–	–	36
O'Reilly, WJ	27	10024	585	3254	144	22.60	11	3	7/54	102	–	8	–	34	–	–
Trumble, H	32	8099	452	3072	141	21.79	9	3	8/65	141	–	–	–	–	–	–
Walker, MHN	34	10094	380	3792	138	27.48	6	–	8/143	56	–	28	17	–	–	37
Mallett, AA	39	9990	419	3940	132	29.85	6	1	8/59	50	28	19	13	6	–	16
Yardley, B	33	8909	379	3986	126	31.63	6	1	7/98	29	21	13	21	–	7	35
Hogg, RM	38	7633	230	3503	123	28.48	6	2	6/74	56	15	10	19	–	1	22
Noble, MA	42	7109	361	3027	121	25.02	9	2	7/17	115	–	–	–	6	–	–
Johnson, IW	45	8780	330	3182	109	29.19	3	–	7/44	42	19	–	4	22	–	22
Giffen, G	31	6325	434	2791	103	27.10	7	1	7/117	103	–	–	–	–	–	–
Connolly, AN	30	7818	289	2981	102	29.23	4	–	6/47	25	31	–	–	26	–	20
Turner, CTB	17	5195	457	1670	101	16.53	11	2	7/43	101	–	–	–	–	–	–

Mailey, AA	21	6119	115	3358	99	33.92	6	2	9/121	86	–	–	–	–	13	–	–
Spofforth, FR	18	4185	416	1731	94	18.41	7	4	7/44	94	–	–	–	–	–	–	–
Gleeson, JW	30	8857	378	3367	93	36.20	3	–	5/61	29	19	–	–	19	–	26
Hawke, NJN	27	6974	238	2677	91	29.42	6	1	7/105	37	4	–	8	18	–	24
Cotter, A	21	4633	86	2549	89	28.64	7	–	7/148	67	–	–	–	22	–	–
Armstrong, WW	50	8022	407	2923	87	33.60	3	–	6/35	74	–	–	–	13	–	–
Gregory, JM	24	5582	138	2648	85	31.15	4	–	7/69	70	–	–	–	15	–	–
Alderman, TM	22	5373	217	2597	79	32.87	5	–	6/128	43	–	8	10	–	–	18
Saunders, JV	14	3565	116	1796	79	22.73	6	–	7/34	64	–	–	–	15	–	–
Dymock, G	21	5545	179	2116	78	27.13	5	1	7/67	25	24	13	5	–	–	11
Palmer, GE	17	4519	452	1678	78	21.51	6	2	7/65	78	–	–	–	–	–	–
Ironmonger, H	14	4695	328	1330	74	17.97	4	2	7/23	21	–	–	–	31	–	22
Simpson, RB	62	6881	253	3001	71	42.27	2	–	5/57	16	23	–	1	13	–	18
Higgs, JD	22	4752	176	2057	66	31.17	2	–	7/143	19	18	11	–	13	–	18
Whitty, WJ	14	3357	163	1373	65	21.12	3	–	6/17	15	–	–	–	50	–	–
Jones, E	19	3748	160	1857	64	29.02	3	1	7/88	60	–	–	–	4	–	–
Pascoe, LS	14	3403	112	1668	64	26.06	1	–	5/59	29	16	12	–	–	–	7
Wall, TW	18	4812	154	2010	56	35.89	3	–	5/14	43	–	–	–	13	–	–
Gilmour, GJ	15	2661	51	1406	54	26.04	3	–	6/85	9	–	17	8	–	–	20
O'Keeffe, KJ	24	5384	189	2018	53	38.08	1	–	5/101	12	–	21	14	–	–	6
Bright, RJ	25	5541	298	2180	53	41.13	4	1	7/87	18	9	7	18	–	–	1
McDermott, CJ	17	3352	79	1935	53	36.51	2	–	8/141	34	3	6	–	–	–	10
Kelleway, C	26	4363	146	1683	52	32.37	1	–	5/33	37	–	–	–	15	–	–
Mackay, KD	37	5792	267	1721	50	34.42	2	–	6/42	24	7	–	10	3	–	6

MOST WICKETS IN A SERIES

Bowler	Opponent	Venue	Series	M	Overs	Mdns	Runs	Wkts	Avrge	5WI	10WM	Best
Grimmett, CV	South Africa	South Africa	1935-36	5	346.1	140	642	44	14.59	5	3	7/40
Alderman, TM	England	England	1981	6	325.0	76	893	42	21.26	4	–	6/135
Hogg, RM	England	Australia	1978-79	6	217.4	60	527	41	12.85	5	2	6/74
Lillee, DK	England	England	1981	6	311.4	81	870	39	22.31	2	1	7/89
Whitty, WJ	South Africa	Australia	1910-11	5	232.3	55	632	37	17.08	2	–	6/17
Mailey, AA	England	Australia	1920-21	5	244.1	27	946	36	26.28	4	2	9/121
Lawson, GF	England	Australia	1982-83	5	230.4	51	687	34	20.21	4	1	6/47
Giffen, G	England	Australia	1894-95	5	343.2	111	820	34	24.12	3	–	6/155
Grimmett, CV	South Africa	Australia	1931-32	5	306.0	108	557	33	16.88	3	1	7/83
Thomson, JR	England	Australia	1974-75	5	175.1	34	592	33	17.94	2	–	6/46
Grimmett, CV	West Indies	Australia	1930-31	5	239.2	61	593	33	17.97	2	1	7/87
Davidson, AK	West Indies	Australia	1960-61	4	173.7	25	612	33	18.55	5	1	6/53
Noble, MA	England	Australia	1901-02	5	230.0	68	608	32	19.00	4	1	7/17
Hordern, HV	England	Australia	1911-12	5	277.3	43	780	32	24.38	4	2	7/90
Ironmonger, H	South Africa	South Africa	1931-32	4	221.5	112	296	31	9.55	3	1	6/18
Lillee, DK	England	England	1972	5	249.5	83	548	31	17.68	3	1	6/66
Benaud, R	England	Australia	1958-59	5	233.2	65	584	31	18.84	2	–	5/83
Saunders, JV	England	Australia	1907-08	5	267.1	52	716	31	23.10	3	–	5/28
Benaud, R	South Africa	South Africa	1957-58	5	242.1	56	658	30	21.93	4	–	5/49
McKenzie, GD	West Indies	Australia	1968-69	5	206.1	27	758	30	25.27	1	1	8/71
McDermott, CJ	England	England	1985	6	234.2	21	901	30	30.03	2	–	8/141

Name			Season									
Davidson, AK	India	India	1959-60	5	244.5	85	431	29	14.86	2	1	7/93
Benaud, R	India	India	1959-60	5	322.2	146	568	29	19.59	2	–	5/43
McKenzie, GD	England	England	1964	5	256.0	61	654	29	22.55	2	–	7/153
Thomson, JR	West Indies	Australia	1975-76	6	150.5	15	831	29	28.67	2	–	6/50
Grimmett, CV	England	England	1930	5	349.4	78	925	29	31.90	4	1	6/167
Mallett, AA	India	India	1969-70	5	298.4	129	535	28	19.11	3	1	6/64
Trumble, H	Australia	Australia	1901-02	5	267.2	93	561	28	20.04	2	–	6/74
O'Reilly, WJ	England	England	1934	5	334.4	128	698	28	24.93	2	1	7/54
Clark, WM	India	Australia	1977-78	5	198.1	27	701	28	25.04	–	–	4/46
O'Reilly, WJ	South Africa	South Africa	1935-36	5	250.2	112	460	27	17.04	2	–	5/20
Lindwall, RR	England	England	1948	5	222.5	57	530	27	19.63	2	–	6/20
Johnston, WA	England	England	1948	5	309.2	92	630	27	23.33	1	–	5/36
McDonald, EA	England	England	1921	5	205.5	32	668	27	24.74	1	–	5/32
Lillee, DK	West Indies	Australia	1975-76	5	129.3	7	712	27	26.37	1	–	5/63
O'Reilly, WJ	England	Australia	1932-33	5	383.4	144	724	27	26.81	2	1	5/63
Trumble, H	England	England	1902	3	172.4	55	371	26	14.27	2	2	8/65
Lindwall, RR	England	England	1953	5	240.4	62	490	26	18.85	3	–	5/54
Walker, MHN	West Indies	West Indies	1972-73	5	271.1	83	539	26	20.73	3	–	6/114
Jones, E	England	England	1899	5	255.1	73	657	26	25.27	2	1	7/88
Gleeson, JW	West Indies	Australia	1968-69	5	250.6	57	844	26	42.20	2	–	5/61
Davidson, AK	South Africa	South Africa	1957-58	5	201.5	47	425	25	17.00	2	–	6/34
O'Reilly, WJ	England	Australia	1936-37	5	247.6	89	555	25	22.20	2	–	5/51
Hurst, AG	England	Australia	1978-79	6	204.2	44	577	25	23.08	1	–	5/28
Lillee, DK	Australia	Australia	1974-75	6	182.6	36	596	25	23.84	–	–	4/49
Grimmett, CV	England	England	1934	5	396.3	148	668	25	26.72	2	–	7/83

LEADING BOWLING AVERAGES

Bowler	M	Balls	Mdns	Runs	Wkts	Avrge	5WI	10WM	Best
Benaud, J	3	24	1	12	2	6.00	–	–	2/12
Moule, WH	1	51	4	23	3	7.67	–	–	3/23
Charlton, PC	2	45	1	24	3	8.00	–	–	3/18
Johnson, LJ	1	282	10	74	6	12.33	–	–	3/08
Nash, LJ	2	311	12	126	10	12.60	–	–	4/18
Malone, MF	1	342	24	77	6	12.83	1	–	5/63
Horan, TP	15	373	45	143	11	13.00	1	–	6/40
Travers, JPF	1	48	2	14	1	14.00	–	–	1/14
Hodges, JH	2	136	9	84	6	14.00	–	–	2/07
Ferris, JJ	8	2030	224	684	48	14.25	4	–	5/26
Rutherford, JW	1	36	2	15	1	15.00	–	–	1/11
Iverson, JB	5	1108	29	320	21	15.24	1	–	6/27
Crawford, WPA	4	437	27	107	7	15.29	–	–	3/28
Kendall, T	2	563	56	215	14	15.36	1	–	7/55
Hurwood, A	2	517	28	170	11	15.45	–	–	4/22
Eady, CJ	2	223	14	112	7	16.00	–	–	3/30
Turner, CTB	17	5195	457	1670	101	16.53	11	2	7/43
Sievers, MW	3	602	25	161	9	17.89	1	–	5/21
Ironmonger, H	14	4695	328	1330	74	17.97	4	2	7/23
Spofforth, FR	18	4185	416	1731	94	18.41	7	4	7/44
Jones, SP	12	262	26	112	6	18.67	–	–	4/47
Taylor, PL	1	330	17	154	8	19.25	1	–	6/78

LEADING STRIKE RATE BOWLERS

Bowler	M	Balls	Mdns	Runs	Wkts	Avrge	5WI	10WM	Best	Stk/rt
Benaud, J	3	24	1	12	2	6.00	–	–	2/12	12.00
Charlton, PC	2	45	1	24	3	8.00	–	–	3/18	15.00
Moule, WH	1	51	4	23	3	7.67	–	–	3/23	17.00
Hodges, JH	2	136	9	84	6	14.00	–	–	2/07	22.67
Nash, LJ	2	311	12	126	10	12.60	–	–	4/18	31.10
Eady, CJ	2	223	14	112	7	16.00	–	–	3/30	31.86
Horan, TP	15	373	45	143	11	13.00	1	–	6/40	33.91
Rutherford, JW	1	36	2	15	1	15.00	–	–	1/11	36.00
Eastwood, KH	1	40	–	21	1	21.00	–	–	1/21	40.00

Bowler	M	Balls	Mdns	Runs	Wkts	Avrge	5WI	10WM	Best	Stk/rt
Kendall, T	2	563	56	215	14	15.36	1	–	7/55	40.21
Rackemann, CG	5	936	31	540	23	23.48	3	1	6/86	40.70
Taylor, PL	1	330	17	154	8	19.25	1	–	6/78	41.25
Ferris, JJ	8	2030	224	684	48	14.25	4	–	5/26	42.29
Ransford, VS	20	43	3	28	1	28.00	–	–	1/09	43.00
Woods, SMH	3	217	18	121	5	24.20	–	–	2/35	43.40
Jones, SP	12	262	26	112	6	18.67	–	–	4/47	43.67
Spofforth, FR	18	4185	416	1731	94	18.41	7	4	7/44	44.52
Allan, FE	1	180	15	80	4	20.00	–	–	2/30	45.00
Duff, RA	22	180	8	85	4	21.25	–	–	2/43	45.00
Saunders, JV	14	3565	116	1796	79	22.73	6	–	7/34	45.13
Hordern, HV	7	2148	50	1075	46	23.37	5	2	7/90	46.70
Hurwood, A	2	517	28	170	11	15.45	–	–	4/22	47.00
Johnson, LJ	1	282	10	74	6	12.33	–	–	3/08	47.00
Travers, JPF	1	48	2	14	1	14.00	–	–	1/14	48.00
Gilmour, GJ	15	2661	50	1406	54	26.04	3	–	6/85	49.28

FIVE WICKETS IN AN INNINGS

Bowler	No.	Wkts	Inns	Opponent	Venue	Series
Alderman, TM	5	5/62	d	England	Nottingham	1981
		6/135		England	Leeds	1981
		5/42		England	Birmingham	1981
		5/109		England	Manchester	1981
		6/128		West Indies	Perth	1984-85
Archer, RG		5/53		England	The Oval	1956
Armstrong, WW	3	5/122		England	Headingley	1905
		5/27		England	Birmingham	1909
		6/35		England	Lord's	1909
Benaud, R	16	7/72		India	Madras1	1956-57
		6/52	1	India	Calcutta	1956-57
		5/53	2			
		5/49		South Africa	Cape Town	1957-58
		5/114		South Africa	Durban2	1957-58
		5/84		South Africa	Johannesburg3	1957-58
		5/82		South Africa	Port Elizabeth	1957-58
		5/83		England	Sydney	1958-59

Bowler	No.	Wkts	Inns	Opponent	Venue	Series
		5/91		England	Adelaide	1958-59
		5/93		Pakistan	Karachi	1959-60
		5/76		India	Delhi	1959-60
		5/43		India	Madras1	1959-60
		5/96		West Indies	Adelaide	1960-61
		6/70		England	Manchester	1961
		6/115		England	Brisbane2	1962-63
		5/68		South Africa	Brisbane2	1963-64
Blackie, DD		6/94		England	Melbourne	1928-29
Boyle, HF		6/42		England	Manchester	1884-85
Bright, RJ	4	7/87		Pakistan	Karachi	1979-80
		5/172		Pakistan	Lahore2	1979-80
		5/68		England	Birmingham	1981
		5/94		India	Madras2	1986-87
Callaway, ST		5/37		England	Adelaide	1894-95
Chappell, GS		5/61		Pakistan	Sydney	1972-73
Connolly, AN	4	5/72		England	Leeds	1968
		5/122		West Indies	Adelaide	1968-69
		5/47		South Africa	Cape Town	1969-70
		6/47		South Africa	Port Elizabeth	1969-70
Cooper, WH		6/120	d	England	Melbourne	1881-82
Cotter, A	7	6/40		England	Melbourne	1903-04
		7/148		England	The Oval	1905
		6/101		England	Sydney	1907-08
		5/142		England	Melbourne	1907-08
		5/38		England	Leeds	1909
		6/95		England	The Oval	1909
		6/69		South Africa	Sydney	1910-11
Davidson, AK	14	6/34		South Africa	Johannesburg3	1957-58
		5/38		South Africa	Port Elizabeth	1957-58
		6/64		England	Melbourne	1958-59
		5/31	1	India	Kanpur	1959-60
		7/93	2			
		5/135	1	West Indies	Brisbane2	1960-61
		6/87	2			
		6/53		West Indies	Melbourne	1960-61
		5/80		West Indies	Sydney	1960-61
		5/84		West Indies	Melbourne	1960-61
		5/42		England	Lord's	1961
		5/63		England	Leeds	1961

Bowler	No.	Wkts	Inns	Opponent	Venue	Series
		6/75		England	Melbourne	1962-63
		5/25		England	Sydney	1962-63
Dymock, G	5	5/58	d	New Zealand	Adelaide	1973-74
		5/99	1	India	Kanpur	1979-80
		7/67	2			
		6/34		England	Perth	1979-80
		5/104		West Indies	Adelaide	1979-80
Ferris, JJ	4	5/76	d	England	Sydney	1886-87
		5/71		England	Sydney	1886-87
		5/26		England	Lord's	1888
		5/49		England	The Oval	1890
Fleetwood-Smith, LO	2	5/124		England	Melbourne	1936-37
		6/110		England	Adelaide	1936-37
Garrett, TW	2	6/78		England	Sydney	1881-82
		5/80		England	Melbourne	1881-82
Giffen, G	7	7/117		England	Sydney	1884-85
		6/72		England	Sydney	1891-92
		5/43		England	Lord's	1893
		7/128		England	The Oval	1893
		6/155		England	Melbourne	1894-95
		5/76		England	Adelaide	1894-95
		5/26		England	Sydney	1894-95
Gilmour, GJ	3	5/64		New Zealand	Auckland	1973-74
		6/85		England	Leeds	1975
		5/34		West Indies	Melbourne	1975-76
Gleeson, JW	3	5/122		West Indies	Brisbane2	1968-69
		5/61		West Indies	Melbourne	1968-69
		5/125		South Africa	Johannesburg3	1969-70
Gregory, JM	4	7/69		England	Melbourne	1920-21
		6/58		England	Nottingham	1921
		6/77		South Africa	Durban1	1921
		5/111		England	Sydney	1924-25
Grimmett, CV	21	5/45	d 1	England	Sydney	1924-25
		6/37	2			
		5/88		England	Leeds	1926
		6/131		England	Brisbane1	1928-29
		5/102		England	Adelaide	1928-29
		5/107	1	England	Nottingham	1930
		5/94	2			
		6/167		England	Lord's	1930

Bowler	No.	Wkts	Inns	Opponent	Venue	Series
		5/135		England	Leeds	1930
		7/87		West Indies	Adelaide	1930-31
		5/49		West Indies	Brisbane1	1930-31
		6/92		South Africa	Melbourne	1931-32
		7/116	1	South Africa	Adelaide	1931-32
		7/83	2			
		5/81		England	Nottingham	1934
		5/64		England	The Oval	1934
		5/32	1	South Africa	Cape Town	1935-36
		5/36	2			
		7/40		South Africa	Johannesburg1	1935-36
		7/100	1	South Africa	Durban2	1935-36
		6/73	2			
Hawke, NJN	6	6/139		South Africa	Adelaide	1963-64
		5/75		England	Leeds	1964
		6/47		England	The Oval	1964
		6/72		West Indies	Georgetown	1964-65
		7/105		England	Sydney	1965-66
		5/54		England	Adelaide	1965-66
Hazlitt, GR		7/25		England	The Oval	1912
Higgs, JD	2	5/148		England	Sydney	1978-79
		7/143		India	Madras2	1979-80
Hogan, TG		5/66	d	Sri Lanka	Kandy	1982-83
Hogg, RM	6	6/74	d	England	Brisbane2	1978-79
		5/65	1	England	Perth	1978-79
		5/57	2			
		5/30	1	England	Melbourne	1978-79
		5/36	2			
		6/77		West Indies	Bridgetown	1983-84
Holland, RG	3	6/54		West Indies	Sydney	1984-85
		5/68		England	Lord's	1985
		6/106		New Zealand	Sydney	1985-86
Horan, TP		6/40		England	Sydney	1884-85
Hordern, HV	5	5/66	d	South Africa	Melbourne	1910-11
		5/85	1	England	Sydney	1911-12
		7/90	2			
		5/95	1	England	Sydney	1911-12
		5/66	2			
Hornibrook, PM		7/92		England	The Oval	1930
Howell, WP		5/81		South Africa	Cape Town	1902-03

Bowler	No.	Wkts	Inns	Opponent	Venue	Series
Hurst, AG	2	5/28		England	Sydney	1978-79
		5/94		Pakistan	Perth	1978-79
Ironmonger, H	4	7/23		West Indies	Melbourne	1930-31
		5/42		South Africa	Brisbane2	1931-32
		5/6 6/18	1 2	South Africa	Melbourne	1931-32
Iverson, JB		6/27		England	Sydney	1950-51
Jenner, TJ		5/90		West Indies	Port-of-Spain	1972-73
Johnson, IW	3	6/42		England	Sydney	1946-47
		5/34		South Africa	Durban2	1949-50
		7/44		West Indies	Georgetown	1954-55
Johnston, WA	7	5/36		England	Nottingham	1948
		6/44		South Africa	Johannesburg2	1949-50
		5/35		England	Brisbane2	1950-51
		6/62		West Indies	Adelaide	1951-52
		5/110		South Africa	Adelaide	1952-53
		6/152		South Africa	Melbourne	1952-53
		5/85		England	Melbourne	1954-55
Jones, E	3	6/82		England	Sydney	1897-98
		5/88		England	Nottingham	1899
		7/88		England	Lord's	1899
Kelleway, C		5/33		South Africa	Manchester	1912
Kendall, T		7/55	d	England	Melbourne	1876-77
Kline, LF		7/75		Pakistan	Lahore2	1959-60
Laughlin, TJ		5/101		West Indies	Kingston	1977-78
Laver, F	2	7/64		England	Nottingham	1905
		8/31		England	Manchester	1909
Lawson, GF	10	7/81		England	Lord's	1981
		5/108		England	Perth	1982-83
		6/47 5/87	1 2	England	Brisbane2	1982-83
		5/66		England	Adelaide	1982-83
		5/49		Pakistan	Brisbane2	1983-84
		5/59		Pakistan	Sydney	1983-84
		5/116		West Indies	Brisbane2	1984-85
		8/112		West Indies	Adelaide	1984-85
		5/103		England	Nottingham	1985
Lillee, DK	23	5/84	d	England	Adelaide	1970-71
		6/66		England	Nottingham	1972

Bowler	No.	Wkts	Inns	Opponent	Venue	Series
		5/58 5/123	1 2	England	The Oval	1972
		5/15		England	Birmingham	1975
		5/63		England	Melbourne	1975-76
		5/163		Pakistan	Adelaide	1976-77
		6/82		Pakistan	Melbourne	1976-77
		5/51 6/72	1 2	New Zealand	Auckland	1976-77
		6/26 5/139	1 2	England	Melbourne	1976-77
		5/78		West Indies	Adelaide	1979-80
		6/60 5/78	1 2	England	Melbourne	1979-80
		6/53		New Zealand	Brisbane2	1980-81
		5/63		New Zealand	Perth	1980-81
		5/46		England	Nottingham	1981
		7/89		England	The Oval	1981
		5/18		Pakistan	Perth	1981-82
		5/81		Pakistan	Brisbane2	1981-82
		7/83		West Indies	Melbourne	1981-82
		6/171		Pakistan	Adelaide	1983-84
Lindwall, RR	12	7/63		England	Sydney	1946-47
		7/38		India	Adelaide	1947-48
		5/70		England	Lord's	1948
		6/20		England	The Oval	1948
		5/32		South Africa	Cape Town	1949-50
		5/52		West Indies	Sydney	1951-52
		5/60		South Africa	Brisbane2	1952-53
		5/57		England	Nottingham	1953
		5/66		England	Lord's	1953
		5/54		England	Leeds	1953
		6/95		West Indies	Port-of-Spain	1954-55
		7/43		India	Madras1	1956-57
Lyons, JJ		5/30		England	Lord's	1890
Macartney, CG	2	7/58		England	Leeds	1909
		5/44		South Africa	Cape Town	1921-22
Mackay, KD	2	6/42		Pakistan	Dacca	1959-60
		5/121		England	The Oval	1961
Mailey, AA	6	5/160 5/142	1 2	England	Adelaide	1920-21

Bowler	No.	Wkts	Inns	Opponent	Venue	Series
		9/121		England	Melbourne	1920-21
		5/119		England	Sydney	1920-21
		5/92		England	Melbourne	1924-25
		6/138		England	The Oval	1926
Mallett, AA	6	6/64		India	Delhi	1969-70
		5/91	1	India	Madras1	1969-70
		5/53	2			
		5/126		South Africa	Cape Town	1969-70
		5/114		England	Leeds	1972
		8/59		Pakistan	Adelaide	1972-73
Malone, MF		5/63	d	England	The Oval	1977
Massie, RAL	2	8/84	d 1	England	Lord's	1972
		8/53	2			
Matthews, GRJ	2	5/103	1	India	Madras2	1986-87
		5/148	2			
McCool, CL	3	5/109		England	Sydney	1946-47
		5/44		England	Sydney	1946-47
		5/41		South Africa	Cape Town	1949-50
McDermott, CJ	2	6/70		England	Lord's	1985
		8/141		England	Manchester	1985
McDonald, EA	2	5/32		England	Nottingham	1921
		5/143		England	The Oval	1921
McKenzie, GD	16	5/37	d	England	Lord's	1961
		5/89		England	Adelaide	1962-63
		5/53		England	Nottingham	1964
		7/153		England	Manchester	1964
		6/58		India	Madras1	1964-65
		6/69		Pakistan	Karachi	1964-65
		5/33		West Indies	Port-of-Spain	1964-65
		5/134		England	Melbourne	1965-66
		6/48		England	Adelaide	1965-66
		5/46		South Africa	Johannesburg3	1966-67
		5/65		South Africa	Cape Town	1966-67
		5/65		South Africa	Port Elizabeth	1966-67
		7/66		India	Melbourne	1967-68
		8/71		West Indies	Melbourne	1968-69
		5/69		India	Bombay2	1969-70
		6/67		India	Calcutta	1969-70
McLeod, CE	2	5/65		England	Adelaide	1897-98
		5/125		England	Nottingham	1905

Bowler	No.	Wkts	Inns	Opponent	Venue	Series
McLeod, RW		5/55	d	England	Melbourne	1891-92
Meckiff, I	2	5/125	d	South Africa	Johannesburg3	1957-58
		6/38		England	Melbourne	1958-59
Midwinter, WE		5/78		England	Melbourne	1876-77
Miller, KR	7	7/60		England	Brisbane2	1946-47
		5/40		South Africa	Johannesburg2	1949-50
		5/60		West Indies	Melbourne	1950-51
		5/26		West Indies	Sydney	1950-51
		6/107		West Indies	Kingston	1954-55
		5/72 5/80	1 2	England	Lord's	1956
Noble, MA	9	6/49	d	England	Melbourne	1897-98
		5/84		England	Adelaide	1897-98
		7/17 6/60	1 2	England	Melbourne	1901-02
		5/54		England	Sydney	1901-02
		6/98		England	Melbourne	1901-02
		5/51 6/52	1 2	England	Birmingham	1902
		7/100		England	Sydney	1903-04
O'Connor, JDA		5/40	d	England	Adelaide	1907-06
O'Keeffe, KJ		5/101		New Zealand	Christchurch	1976-77
O'Reilly, WJ	11	5/63 5/66	1 2	England	Melbourne	1932-33
		7/54		England	Nottingham	1934
		7/189		England	Manchester	1934
		5/49		South Africa	Durban2	1935-36
		5/20		South Africa	Johannesburg1	1935-36
		5/102		England	Brisbane2	1936-37
		5/51		England	Melbourne	1936-37
		5/66 5/56	1 2	England	Leeds	1938
		5/14		New Zealand	Wellington	1945-46
Palmer, GE	6	7/68		England	Sydney	1881-82
		5/46		England	Sydney	1881-82
		7/65		England	Melbourne	1882-83
		5/103		England	Melbourne	1882-83
		6/111		England	Lord's	1884
		5/81		England	Adelaide	1884-85
Pascoe, LS		5/59		England	Lord's	1980

Bowler	No.	Wkts	Inns	Opponent	Venue	Series
Philpott, PI		5/90		England	Brisbane2	1965-66
Rackemann, CG	3	5/32	1	Pakistan	Perth	1983-84
		6/86	2			
		5/161		West Indies	St John's	1983-84
Renneberg, DA	2	5/97		South Africa	Johannesburg3	1966-67
		5/39		India	Adelaide	1967-68
Ring, DT	2	6/80		West Indies	Brisbane2	1951-52
		6/72		South Africa	Brisbane2	1952-53
Saunders, JV	6	5/43	d	England	Sydney	1901-02
		5/50		England	Sheffield	1902
		7/34		South Africa	Johannesburg1	1902-03
		5/65		England	Adelaide	1907-08
		5/28		England	Melbourne	1907-08
		5/82		England	Sydney	1907-08
Sievers, MW		5/21		England	Melbourne	1936-37
Simpson, RB	2	5/57		England	Sydney	1962-63
		5/59		India	Sydney	1967-68
Sleep, PR		5/72		England	Sydney	1986-87
Spofforth, FR	7	6/48	1	England	Melbourne	1878-79
		7/62	2			
		7/46	1	England	The Oval	1882
		7/44	2			
		7/44		England	Sydney	1882-83
		6/90		England	Sydney	1884-85
		5/30		England	Sydney	1884-85
Taylor, PL		6/78	d	England	Sydney	1986-87
Thomson, JR	8	6/46		England	Brisbane2	1974-75
		5/93		England	Perth	1974-75
		5/38		England	Birmingham	1975
		5/62		West Indies	Perth	1975-76
		6/50		West Indies	Sydney	1975-76
		6/77		West Indies	Bridgetown	1977-78
		5/73		England	Brisbane2	1982-83
		5/50		England	Sydney	1982-83
Toshack, ERH	4	6/82		England	Brisbane2	1946-47
		5/2	1	India	Brisbane2	1947-48
		6/29	2			
		5/40		England	Lord's	1948
Trott, AE		8/43	d	England	Adelaide	1894-95

Bowler	No.	Wkts	Inns	Opponent	Venue	Series
Trumble, H	9	6/59 6/30	1 2	England	The Oval	1896
		5/60		England	Leeds	1899
		6/74		England	Adelaide	1901-02
		5/62		England	Melbourne	1901-02
		6/53		England	Manchester	1902
		8/65		England	The Oval	1902
		5/34		England	Melbourne	1903-04
		7/28		England	Melbourne	1903-04
Turner, CTB	11	6/15	d	England	Sydney	1886-87
		5/41		England	Sydney	1886-87
		5/44 7/43	1 2	England	Sydney	1887-88
		5/27 5/36	1 2	England	Lord's	1888
		6/112 5/86	1 2	England	The Oval	1888
		5/51		England	Melbourne	1891-92
		6/67		England	Lord's	1893
		5/32		England	Melbourne	1894-95
Walker, MHN	6	6/15		Pakistan	Sydney	1972-73
		6/114		West Indies	Kingston	1972-73
		5/97		West Indies	Bridgetown	1972-73
		5/75		West Indies	Port-of-Spain	1972-73
		8/143		England	Melbourne	1974-75
		5/48		England	Birmingham	1975
Wall, TW	3	5/66	d	England	Melbourne	1928-29
		5/14		South Africa	Brisbane2	1931-32
		5/72		England	Adelaide	1932-33
Walters, KD		5/66		West Indies	Georgetown	1972-73
Ward, FA		6/102	d	England	Brisbane2	1936-37
Waugh, SR		5/69		England	Perth	1986-87
Whitty, WJ	3	6/17		South Africa	Melbourne	1910-11
		6/104		South Africa	Adelaide	1910-11
		5/55		South Africa	Manchester	1912
Yardley, B	6	6/84		Pakistan	Perth	1981-82
		7/187		Pakistan	Melbourne	1981-82
		7/98		West Indies	Sydney	1981-82
		5/132		West Indies	Adelaide	1981-82
		5/107		England	Perth	1982-83
		5/88		Sri Lanka	Kandy	1982-83

'd' denotes debut

MOST WICKETS IN A MATCH

Bowler	Venue	Series	Opponents ENG	IND	NZ	PAK	SA	SL	WI
Massie, RAL	Lord's	1972	16/137	–	–	–	–	–	–
Spofforth, FR	The Oval	1882	14/90	–	–	–	–	–	–
Grimmett, CV	Adelaide	1931-32	–	–	–	–	14/199	–	–
Noble, MA	Melbourne	1901-02	13/77	–	–	–	–	–	–
Spofforth, FR	Melbourne	1878-79	13/110	–	–	–	–	–	–
Grimmett, CV	Durban2	1935-36	–	–	–	–	13/173	–	–
Mailey, AA	Melbourne	1920-21	13/236	–	–	–	–	–	–
Turner, CTB	Sydney	1887-88	12/87	–	–	–	–	–	–
Trumble, H	The Oval	1896	12/89	–	–	–	–	–	–
Davidson, AK	Kanpur	1959-60	–	12/124	–	–	–	–	–
Dymock, G	Kanpur	1979-80	–	12/166	–	–	–	–	–
Trumble, H	The Oval	1902	12/173	–	–	–	–	–	–
Hordern, HV	Sydney	1911-12	12/175	–	–	–	–	–	–
Ironmonger, H	Melbourne	1931-32	–	–	–	–	11/24	–	–
Toshack, ERH	Brisbane2	1947-48	–	11/31	–	–	–	–	–
Ironmonger, H	Melbourne	1930-31	–	–	–	–	–	–	11/79
Grimmett, CV	Sydney	1924-25	11/82	–	–	–	–	–	–
Macartney, CG	Leeds	1909	11/85	–	–	–	–	–	–
Noble, MA	Sheffield	1902	11/103	–	–	–	–	–	–

Bowler	Venue	Series	Opponents ENG	IND	NZ	PAK	SA	SL	WI
Benaud, J	Calcutta	1956-57	–	11/105	–	–	–	–	–
Spofforth, FR	Sydney	1882-83	11/117	–	–	–	–	–	–
Rackemann, CG	Perth	1983-84	–	–	–	11/118	–	–	–
Lillee, DK	Auckland	1976-77	–	–	11/123	–	–	–	–
O'Reilly, WJ	Nottingham	1934	11/129	–	–	–	–	–	–
Lawson, GF	Brisbane2	1982-83	11/134	–	–	–	–	–	–
Lillee, DK	Melbourne	1979-80	11/138	–	–	–	–	–	–
Lillee, DK	The Oval	1981	11/159	–	–	–	–	–	–
Palmer, GE	Sydney	1881-82	11/165	–	–	–	–	–	–
Lillee, DK	Melbourne	1976-77	11/165	–	–	–	–	–	–
Lawson, GF	Adelaide	1984-85	–	–	–	–	–	–	11/181
Grimmett, CV	Adelaide	1930-31	–	–	–	–	–	–	11/183
Davidson, AK	Brisbane2	1960-61	–	–	–	–	–	–	11/222
Turner, CTB	Lord's	1888	10/63	–	–	–	–	–	–
Hogg, RM	Melbourne	1978-79	10/66	–	–	–	–	–	–
Grimmett, CV	Cape Town	1935-36	–	–	–	–	10/88	–	–
McKenzie, GD	Madras2	1964-65	–	10/91	–	–	–	–	–
Grimmett, CV	Johannesburg1	1935-36	–	–	–	–	10/110	–	–
Bright, RJ	Karachi	1979-80	–	–	–	10/111	–	–	–
Hawke, NJN	Georgetown	1964-65	–	–	–	–	–	–	10/115
O'Reilly, WJ	Leeds	1938	10/122	–	–	–	–	–	–
Hogg, RM	Perth	1978-79	10/122	–	–	–	–	–	–

Palmer, GE	Melbourne	1882-83	10/126	–	–	–	–	–	–
Lillee, DK	Melbourne	1981-82	–	–	–	–	–	–	10/127
Trumble, H	Manchester	1902	10/128	–	–	–	–	–	–
O'Reilly, WJ	Melbourne	1932-33	10/129	–	–	–	–	–	–
Lillee, DK	Melbourne	1976-77	–	–	–	10/135	–	–	–
Spofforth, FR	Sydney	1884-85	10/144	–	–	–	–	–	–
Mallett, AA	Madras1	1969-70	–	10/144	–	–	–	–	–
Holland, RG	Sydney	1984-85	–	–	–	–	–	–	10/144
McKenzie, GD	Melbourne	1967-68	–	10/151	–	–	–	–	–
Miller, KR	Lord's	1956	10/152	–	–	–	–	–	–
McKenzie, GD	Melbourne	1968-69	–	–	–	–	–	–	10/159
Giffen, G	Sydney	1891-92	10/160	–	–	–	–	–	–
Hordern, HV	Sydney	1911-12	10/161	–	–	–	–	–	–
Jones, E	Lord's	1899	10/164	–	–	–	–	–	–
Holland, RG	Sydney	1985-86	–	–	10/174	–	–	–	–
Lillee, DK	The Oval	1972	10/181	–	–	–	–	–	–
Yardley, B	Sydney	1981-82	–	–	10/185	–	–	–	–
Grimmett, CV	Nottingham	1930	10/201	–	–	–	–	–	–
Fleetwood-Smith, LO	Adelaide	1936-37	10/239	–	–	–	–	–	–
Matthews, GRJ	Madras2	1986-87	–	10/249	–	–	–	–	–
Mailey, AA	Adelaide	1920-21	10/302	–	–	–	–	–	–

MOST WICKETS IN AN INNINGS

Bowler	Venue	Series	Opponents ENG	IND	NZ	PAK	SA	SL	WI
Mailey, AA	Melbourne	1920-21	9/121	–	–	–	–	–	–
Laver, F	Manchester	1909	8/31	–	–	–	–	–	–
Trott, AE	Adelaide	1894-95	8/43	–	–	–	–	–	–
Massie, RAL	Lord's	1972	8/53	–	–	–	–	–	–
Mallett, AA	Adelaide	1972-73	–	–	–	8/59	–	–	–
Trumble, H	The Oval	1902	8/65	–	–	–	–	–	–
McKenzie, GD	Melbourne	1968-69	–	–	–	–	–	–	8/71
Massie, RAL	Lord's	1972	8/84	–	–	–	–	–	–
Lawson, GF	Adelaide	1984-85	–	–	–	–	–	–	8/112
McDermott, CJ	Manchester	1985	8/141	–	–	–	–	–	–
Walker, MHN	Melbourne	1974-75	8/143	–	–	–	–	–	–
Noble, MA	Melbourne	1901-02	7/17	–	–	–	–	–	–
Ironmonger, H	Melbourne	1930-31	–	–	–	–	–	–	7/23
Hazlitt, GR	The Oval	1912	7/25	–	–	–	–	–	–
Trumble, H	Melbourne	1903-04	–	–	–	–	7/28	–	–
Saunders, JV	Johannesburg1	1902-03	–	–	–	–	7/34	–	–
Lindwall, RR	Adelaide	1947-48	–	7/38	–	–	–	–	–
Grimmett, CV	Johannesburg1	1936-37	–	–	–	–	7/40	–	–
Turner, CTB	Sydney	1887-88	7/43	–	–	–	–	–	–
Lindwall, RR	Madras2	1956-57	–	7/43	–	–	–	–	–

Player	Ground	Season						
Spofforth, FR	The Oval	1882	7/44	—	—	—	—	—
Spofforth, FR	Sydney	1882-83	7/44	—	—	—	—	—
Johnson, IW	Georgetown	1954-55	—	—	—	—	—	7/44
Spofforth, FR	The Oval	1882	7/46	—	—	—	—	—
O'Reilly, WJ	Nottingham	1934	7/54	—	—	—	—	—
Kendall, T	Melbourne	1876-77	7/55	—	—	—	—	—
Macartney, CG	Leeds	1909	7/58	—	—	—	—	—
Miller, KR	Brisbane2	1946-47	7/60	—	—	—	—	—
Spofforth, FR	Melbourne	1878-79	7/62	—	—	—	—	—
Lindwall, RR	Sydney	1946-47	7/63	—	—	—	—	—
Laver, F	Nottingham	1905	7/64	—	—	—	—	—
Palmer, GE	Melbourne	1884	7/65	—	—	—	—	—
McKenzie, GD	Melbourne	1967-68	—	7/66	—	—	—	—
Dymock, G	Adelaide	1973-74	—	—	7/67	—	—	—
Palmer, GE	Sydney	1881-82	7/68	—	—	—	—	—
Gregory, JM	Melbourne	1920-21	7/69	—	—	—	—	—
Benaud, R	Madras1	1956-57	—	7/72	—	—	—	—
Kline, LF	Lahore2	1959-60	—	—	—	7/75	—	—
Lawson, GF	Lord's	1981	7/81	—	—	—	—	—
Grimmett, CV	Adelaide	1931-32	—	—	—	—	7/83	—
Lillee, DK	Melbourne	1981-82	—	—	—	—	7/83	—
Grimmett, CV	Adelaide	1930-31	—	7/87	—	—	—	—
Bright, RJ	Karachi	1979-80	—	7/87	—	—	—	—

Bowler	Venue	Series	Opponents ENG	IND	NZ	PAK	SA	SL	WI
Jones, E	Lord's	1899	7/88	–	–	–	–	–	–
Lillee, DK	The Oval	1981	7/89	–	–	–	–	–	–
Hordern, HV	Sydney	1911-12	7/90	–	–	–	–	–	–
Hornibrook, PM	The Oval	1930	7/92	–	–	–	–	–	–
Davidson, AK	Kanpur	1959-60	–	7/93	–	–	–	–	–
Yardley, B	Sydney	1981-82	–	–	–	–	–	–	7/98
Noble, MA	Sydney	1903-04	7/100	–	–	–	–	–	–
Grimmett, CV	Durban2	1936-37	–	–	–	–	7/100	–	–
Hawke, NJN	Sydney	1965-66	7/105	–	–	–	–	–	–
Grimmett, CV	Adelaide	1931-32	–	–	–	–	7/116	–	–
Giffen, G	Sydney	1884-85	7/117	–	–	–	–	–	–
Giffen, G	The Oval	1893	7/128	–	–	–	–	–	–
Higgs, JD	Madras2	1979-80	–	7/143	–	–	–	–	–
Cotter, A	The Oval	1905	7/148	–	–	–	–	–	–
McKenzie, GD	Nottingham	1964	7/153	–	–	–	–	–	–
Yardley, B	Melbourne	1981-82	–	–	–	7/187	–	–	–
O'Reilly, WJ	Manchester	1934	7/189	–	–	–	–	–	–

BEST BOWLING IN AN INNINGS FOR EACH GROUND

Venue	Wkts	Bowler	Opponent	Series
Australia:				
Adelaide	8/43	Trott, AE	England	1894-95
Brisbane1	6/131	Grimmett, CV	England	1928-29
Brisbane2	7/60	Miller, KR	England	1946-47
Melbourne	9/121	Mailey, AA	England	1920-21
Perth	6/34	Dymock, G	England	1979-80
Sydney	7/43	Turner, CTB	England	1887-88
England:				
Birmingham	5/15	Lillee, DK	England	1975
Leeds	7/58	Macartney, CG	England	1909
Lord's	8/53	Massie, RAL	England	1972
Manchester	8/31	Laver, F	England	1909
Nottingham	7/54	O'Reilly, WJ	England	1934
Sheffield	6/52	Noble, MA	England	1902
The Oval	8/65	Trumble, H	England	1902
India:				
Bangalore	4/107	Yardley, B	India	1979-80
Bombay2	5/69	McKenzie, GD	India	1959-60
Bombay3	4/158	Matthews, GRJ	India	1986-87
Calcutta	6/52	Benaud, R	India	1956-57
Delhi	6/64	Mallett, AA	India	1969-70
Kanpur	7/67	Dymock, G	India	1979-80
Madras1	7/143	Higgs, JD	India	1979-80
Madras2	7/43	Lindwall, RR	India	1956-57
New Zealand:				
Auckland	6/72	Lillee, DK	New Zealand	1976-77
Christchurch	5/101	O'Keeffe, KJ	New Zealand	1976-77
Wellington	5/14	O'Reilly, WJ	New Zealand	1945-46
Pakistan:				
Dacca	6/42	Mackay, KD	Pakistan	1959-60
Faisalabad	4/96	Lawson, GF	Pakistan	1982-83

Venue	Wkts	Bowler	Opponent	Series
Karachi	7/87	Bright, RJ	Pakistan	1979-80
Lahore2	7/75	Kline, LF	Pakistan	1959-60
South Africa:				
Cape Town	5/32	Grimmett, CV	South Africa	1935-36
"	5/32	Lindwall, RR	South Africa	1949-50
Durban1	6/77	Gregory, JM	South Africa	1921-22
Durban2	7/100	Grimmett, CV	South Africa	1935-36
Johannesburg1	7/34	Saunders, JV	South Africa	1902-03
Johannesburg2	6/44	Johnston, WA	South Africa	1949-50
Johannesburg3	6/34	Davidson, AK	South Africa	1957-58
Port Elizabeth	6/47	Connolly, AN	South Africa	1969-70
Sri Lanka:				
Kandy	5/66	Hogan, TG	Sri Lanka	1982-83
West Indies:				
Bridgetown	6/77	Thomson, JR	West Indies	1977-78
Georgetown	7/44	Johnson, IW	West Indies	1954-55
Kingston	6/107	Miller, KR	West Indies	1954-55
Port-of-Spain	6/95	Lindwall, RR	West Indies	1954-55
St. John's	5/161	Rackemann, CG	West Indies	1983-84

BEST BOWLING IN A MATCH FOR EACH GROUND

Venue	Wkts	Bowler	Opponent	Series
Australia:				
Adelaide	14/199	Grimmett, CV	South Africa	1931-32
Brisbane1	9/144	Grimmett, CV	West Indies	1930-31
Brisbane2	11/131	Toshack, ERH	England	1946-47
Melbourne	13/77	Noble, MA	England	1901-02
Perth	11/118	Rackemann, CG	Pakistan	1983-84
Sydney	12/87	Turner, CTB	England	1887-88

Venue	*Wkts*	*Bowler*	*Opponent*	*Series*
England:				
Birmingham	7/60	Lillee, DK	England	1975
Leeds	11/85	Macartney, CG	England	1909
Lord's	16/137	Massie, RAL	England	1972
Manchester	10/128	Trumble, H	England	1902
Nottingham	11/129	O'Reilly, WJ	England	1934
Sheffield	11/103	Noble, MA	England	1902
The Oval	14/90	Spofforth, FR	England	1882
India:				
Bangalore	4/107	Yardley, B	India	1979-80
Bombay2	7/108	Gleeson, JW	India	1969-70
Bombay3	4/158	Matthews, GRJ	India	1986-87
Calcutta	11/105	Benaud, R	India	1956-57
Delhi	8/76	Benaud, R	India	1959-60
Kanpur	12/124	Davidson, AK	India	1959-60
Madras1	10/144	Mallett, AA	India	1969-70
Madras2	10/91	McKenzie, GD	India	1964-65
New Zealand:				
Auckland	11/123	Lillee, DK	New Zealand	1976-77
Christchurch	7/131	O'Keeffe, KJ	New Zealand	1976-77
Wellington	8/33	O'Reilly, WJ	New Zealand	1945-46
Pakistan:				
Dacca	8/111	Benaud, R	Pakistan	1959-60
Faisalabad	4/96	Lawson, GF	Pakistan	1982-83
Karachi	10/111	Bright, RJ	Pakistan	1979-80
Lahore2	8/90	Kline, LF	Pakistan	1959-60
South Africa:				
Cape Town	10/88	Grimmett, CV	South Africa	1935-36
Durban1	8/105	Gregory, JM	South Africa	1921-22
Durban2	13/173	Grimmett, CV	South Africa	1935-36
Johannesburg1	10/110	Grimmett, CV	South Africa	1935-36
Johannesburg2	8/65	Johnston, WA	South Africa	1949-50
Johannesburg3	9/154	Benaud, R	South Africa	1957-58
Port Elizabeth	9/82	Davidson, AK	South Africa	1957-58

Venue	Wkts	Bowler	Opponent	Series
Sri Lanka:				
Kandy	7/166	Yardley, B	Sri Lanka	1982-83
West Indies:				
Bridgetown	6/77	Thomson, JR	West Indies	1977-78
Georgetown	10/115	Hawke, NJN	West Indies	1964-65
Kingston	8/99	Mayne, LC	West Indies	1964-65
Port-of-Spain	6/73	Hawke, NJN	West Indies	1964-65
St. John's	5/161	Rackemann, CG	West Indies	1983-84

YOUNGEST TO TAKE FIVE WICKETS IN AN INNINGS

Years	Days	Bowler	Wkts	Opponent	Venue	Series
19	269	Ferris, JJ	5/76	England	Sydney	1886-87
20	2	McKenzie, GD	5/37	England	Lord's	1961
20	75	McDermott, CJ	6/70	England	Lord's	1985
20	95	Cotter, A	6/40	England	Melbourne	1903-04
21	183	Waugh, SR	5/69	England	Perth	1986-87
21	196	Lillee, DK	5/84	England	Adelaide	1970-71
21	347	Trott, AE	8/43	England	Adelaide	1894-95
21	353	Meckiff, I	5/125	South Africa	Johannesburg3	1957-58
21	361	Palmer, GE	7/68	England	Sydney	1881-82
22	6	Macartney, CG	7/58	England	Leeds	1909
22	151	Archer, RG	5/53	England	The Oval	1956
22	270	Gilmour, GJ	5/64	New Zealand	Auckland	1973-74
23	33	Kelleway, C	5/33	South Africa	Manchester	1912
23	160	Rackemann, CG	5/32	Pakistan	Perth	1983-84
23	208	Lawson, GF	7/81	England	Lord's	1981
23	223	Garrett, TW	6/78	England	Sydney	1881-82
23	351	McLeod, RW	5/55	England	Melbourne	1891-92
23	352	Hazlitt, GR	7/25	England	The Oval	1912
24	74	Turner, CTB	6/15	England	Sydney	1886-87
24	110	Thomson, JR	6/46	England	Brisbane2	1974-75

YOUNGEST TO TAKE TEN WICKETS IN A MATCH

Years	Days	Bowler	Wkts	Opponent	Venue	Series
23	28	Lillee, DK	5/58 & 5/123	England	The Oval	1972
23	161	Rackemann, CG	5/32 & 6/86	Pakistan	Perth	1983-84
24	168	Mallett, AA	5/91 & 5/53	India	Madras2	1969-70
24	358	Lawson, GF	5/87 & 6/47	England	Brisbane2	1982-83
25	73	Massie, RAL	8/53 & 8/84	England	Lord's	1972
25	90	Turner, CTB	7/43 & 5/44	England	Sydney	1887-88
25	117	Spofforth, FR	6/48 & 7/62	England	Melbourne	1878-79
26	31	Benaud, R	5/53 & 6/62	India	Calcutta	1956-57
27	14	O'Reilly, WJ	5/66 & 5/63	England	Melbourne	1931-32
27	290	Hogg, RM	5/57 & 5/65	England	Perth	1978-79

OLDEST TO TAKE FIVE WICKETS IN AN INNINGS

Years	Days	Bowler	Wkts	Opponent	Venue	Series
49	317	Ironmonger, H	6/18	South Africa	Melbourne	1931-32
46	270	Blackie, DD	6/94	England	Melbourne	1928-29
44	69	Grimmett, CV	6/73	South Africa	Durban1	1935-36
40	223	Mailey, AA	6/138	England	The Oval	1926
40	99	O'Reilly, WJ	5/14	New Zealand	Wellington	1945-46
39	231	Laver, FA	8/31	England	Manchester	1909
39	35	Holland, RG	6/106	New Zealand	Sydney	1985-86
36	301	Trumble, H	7/28	England	Melbourne	1903-04
36	214	Boyle, HF	6/42	England	Manchester	1884
36	211	Miller, KR	5/80	England	Lord's	1956
36	142	Johnson, IW	7/44	West Indies	Georgetown	1954-55
35	314	Giffen, G	5/26	England	Sydney	1894-95
35	302	Mackay, KD	5/121	England	The Oval	1961
35	274	McLeod, CE	5/125	England	Manchester	1905
35	231	Yardley, B	5/88	Sri Lanka	Kandy	1982-83
35	166	Iverson, JB	6/27	England	Sydney	1950-51
35	155	Macartney, CG	5/44	South Africa	Cape Town	1921-22
35	20	Lindwall, RR	7/43	India	Madras1	1956-57

Years	Days	Bowler	Wkts	Opponent	Venue	Series
34	147	Lillee, DK	6/171	Pakistan	Adelaide	1983-84
34	55	Ring, DT	6/72	South Africa	Brisbane2	1952-53
34	24	McCool, CL	5/41	South Africa	Cape Town	1949-50
34	25	Mackay, KD	6/42	Pakistan	Dacca	1959-60
33	215	Davidson, AK	5/25	England	Sydney	1962-63
33	197	Toshack, ERH	5/40	England	Lord's	1948

OLDEST TO TAKE TEN WICKETS IN A MATCH

Years	Days	Bowler	Wkts	Opponent	Venue	Series
49	317	Ironmonger, H	5/6 & 6/18	South Africa	Melbourne	1931-32
44	69	Grimmett, CV	7/100 & 6/73	South Africa	Durban1	1935-36
36	211	Miller, KR	5/72 & 5/80	England	Lord's	1956
35	17	Mailey, AA	5/142 & 5/106	England	Adelaide	1920-21
33	78	Dymock, G	7/67 & 5/99	India	Kanpur	1979-80
32	354	Toshack, ERH	6/29 & 5/2	India	Brisbane2	1947-48
32	217	O'Reilly, WJ	5/56 & 5/66	England	Leeds	1938
31	183	Davidson, AK	6/87 & 5/135	West Indies	Brisbane2	1960-61
30	230	Lillee, DK	5/78 & 6/60	England	Melbourne	1979-80
29	158	Noble, MA	6/52 & 5/51	England	Sheffield	1902

BEST MATCH BOWLING PERFORMANCE ON DEBUT

Bowler	Wkts	1st inns	2nd inns	Opponent	Venue	Series
Massie, RAL	16/137	8/84	8/53	England	Lord's	1972
Grimmett, CV	11/82	5/45	6/37	England	Sydney	1924-25
Ferris, JJ	9/103	4/27	4/27	England	Sydney	1886-87
Alderman, TM	9/130	4/68	5/62	England	Nottingham	1981
Saunders, JV	9/162	4/119	5/43	England	Sydney	1901-02
Cooper, WH	9/200	3/80	6/120	England	Melbourne	1881-82
O'Connor, JDA	8/50	3/10	5/40	England	Adelaide	1907-08
Trott, AE	8/52	-/9	8/43	England	Adelaide	1894-95

Bowler	Wkts	1st inns	2nd inns	Opponent	Venue	Series
Turner, CTB	8/68	6/15	2/53	England	Sydney	1886-87
Mayne, LC	8/99	4/43	4/56	West Indies	Kingston	1964-65
Hordern, HV	8/105	3/39	5/66	South Africa	Melbourne	1910-11
Kendall, T	8/109	1/54	7/55	England	Melbourne	1876-77
Clark, WM	8/147	4/46	4/101	India	Brisbane2	1977-78
Taylor, PL	8/154	6/78	2/76	England	Sydney	1986-87
Meckiff, I	8/177	5/125	3/52	South Africa	Johannesburg3	1957-58
Wall, TW	8/189	3/123	5/66	England	Melbourne	1928-29
Ward, FA	8/240	2/138	6/102	England	Brisbane2	1936-37

BEST INNINGS BOWLING PERFORMANCE ON DEBUT

Bowler	Wkts	2nd inns	Opponent	Venue	Series
1st Innings:					
Massie, RAL	8/84	8/53	England	Lord's	1972
Turner, CTB	6/15	2/53	England	Sydney	1886-87
Hogg, RM	6/74	1/35	England	Brisbane2	1978-79
Taylor, PL	6/78	2/76	England	Sydney	1976-77
Grimmett, CV	5/45 –	6/37	England	Sydney	1924-25
McLeod, RW	5/55	1/39	England	Melbourne	1891-92
Malone, MF	5/63	1/14	England	The Oval	1977
Midwinter, WE	5/78	1/23	England	Melbourne	1876-77
Lillee, DK	5/84	0/40	England	Adelaide	1970-71
Meckiff, I	5/125	3/52	South Africa	Johannesburg3	1957-58

Johnson took 6/42 v England, Sydney 1946-47 after not bowling in his debut v New Zealand, Wellington 1945-46.

Bowler	Wkts	1st inns	Opponent	Venue	Series
2nd Innings:					
Trott, AE	8/43	0/9	England	Adelaide	1894-95
Massie, RAL	8/53	8/84	England	Lord's	1972
Kendall, T	7/55	1/54	England	Melbourne	1876-77
Grimmett, CV	6/37	5/45	England	Sydney	1924-25
Noble, MA	6/49	1/31	England	Melbourne	1897-98

Bowler	Wkts	2nd inns	Opponent	Venue	Series
Ward, FA	6/102	2/138	England	Brisbane2	1936-37
Cooper, WH	6/120	3/80	England	Melbourne	1881-82
McKenzie, GD	5/37	1/81	England	Lord's	1961
O'Connor, JDA	5/40	3/10	England	Adelaide	1907-08
Saunders, JV	5/43	4/119	England	Sydney	1901-02
Dymock, G	5/58	2/44	New Zealand	Adelaide	1973-74
Hogan, TG	5/60	1/50	Sri Lanka	Kandy	1982-83
Alderman, TM	5/62	4/68	England	Nottingham	1981
Hordern, HV	5/66	3/39	South Africa	Melbourne	1910-11
Wall, TW	5/66	3/123	England	Melbourne	1928-29
Ferris, JJ	5/76	4/27	England	Sydney	1886-87

BOWLERS UNCHANGED IN A COMPLETED INNINGS

Bowler	Overs	Mdns	Runs	Wkts	Opponent	Inns total	Venue	Series
Palmer, GE	58	36	68	7	England	133	Sydney	1881-82
Evans, E	57	32	64	3				
Spofforth, FR	19.1	7	32	4	England	269	Sydney	1884-85
Palmer, GE	20	8	30	5				
Turner, CTB	18	11	15	6	England	45	Sydney	1886-87
Ferris, JJ	17.3	7	27	4				
Turner, CTB	24	8	36	5	England	53	Lord's	1888
Ferris, JJ	23	11	26	5				
Giffen, G	15	7	26	5	England	9-72	Sydney	1894-95
Turner, CTB	14.1	6	33	4				
Trumble, H	8	1	38	3	England	61	Melbourne	1901-02
Noble, MA	7.4	2	17	7				
Noble, MA	24	7	54	5	England	99	Sydney	1901-02
Saunders, JV	24.1	8	43	5				

DISMISSED ALL ELEVEN BATSMEN IN A MATCH

Bowler	Opponent	Venue	Series
Dymock, G	India	Kanpur	1979-80

HAT-TRICKS

Bowler	Batsman	Howout	Opponent	Venue	Series
Spofforth, FR	Royle, VPFA	b	England	Melbourne	1878-79
	MacKinnon, FA	b			
	Emmett, T	ct Horan, TP			
Trumble, H	Jones, AO	ct Darling, J	England	Melbourne	1901-02
	Gunn, JR	ct Jones, E			
	Barnes, SF	c&b			
Trumble, H	Bosanquet, BJT	ct Gehrs, DRA	England	Melbourne	1903-04
	Warner, PF	c&b			
	Lilley, AFA	lbw			
Matthews, TJ	Beaumont, R	b	South Africa	Manchester	1912
	Pegler, SJ	lbw			
	Ward, TA	lbw			
Matthews, TJ	Taylor, HW	b	South Africa	Manchester	1912
	Schwarz, RO	c&b			
	Ward, TA	lbw			
Kline, LF	Fuller, ERH	ct Benaud, R	South Africa	Cape Town	1957-58
	Tayfield, HJ	lbw			
	Adcock, NAT	ct Simpson, RB			

THREE WICKETS IN FOUR BALLS

Bowler	No.	Opponent	Venue	Series
Spofforth, FR	2	England	The Oval	1882
		England	Sydney	1884-85
Howell, WH		South Africa	Cape Town	1902-03
Gregory, JM		England	Nottingham	1921
O'Reilly, WJ		England	Manchester	1934
Lindwall, RR		England	Adelaide	1946-47
Benaud, R		West Indies	Georgetown	1954-55
Martin, JW		West Indies	Melbourne	1960-61
Mackay, KD		England	Birmingham	1961
McKenzie, GD		West Indies	Port-of-Spain	1964-65
Lillee, DK	2	England	Manchester	1972
		England	The Oval	1972

"JIMMY" MATTHEWS

Thomas James ("Jimmy') Matthews was a gnarled, sun-dried bantamweight who bowled top-spinners and leg-breaks to a tight length and sometimes contributed useful runs as a late order right-handed batsman. He spent most of his days in the open, working as a groundsman or playing cricket, and won a special place in cricket history in a few hours at Manchester in 1912.

On hard Australian pitches he seldom turned the ball much, bowling what Warwick Armstrong called "straight breaks", but he always achieved plenty of bounce and frequently surprised batsmen by making the ball hurry on to them. He was a useful, resourceful cricketer without any show of brilliance.

Matthews was born at Williamstown, Victoria, in 1884 and spent his teens playing for the local club before moving to the Essendon Club in Melbourne. Later he switched to the St Kilda and East Melbourne clubs as his reputation as a groundsman grew.

He played his initial first-class games for Victoria against Tasmania in 1906-7, when he had match figures of 5 for 93 and made 20-odd in each innings. Critics believed he had a bigger future as a batsman than as a bowler, probably because he had made 200 for Williamstown against South Melbourne's second team.

There were plenty of outstanding spinners in first-class cricket at the time; the wily Warwick Armstrong who wheeled his leg-breaks down for hours on end without the slightest hint of a loose delivery; Gervys Hazlitt, the brilliant off-spinner who played Test cricket despite heart disease; and Jack Saunders, the dandy with the heavily waxed moustache whose left-arm spinners turned so far people said he just had to be a chucker. But the flavour of the decade when Matthews arrived in big cricket was "Ranji" Hordern, the New South Wales dentist who had perfected a new delivery called the "bosey" or "googly".

Matthews' chance came when the Australian Board of Control moved to assert its authority by appointing its own manager for the 1912 visit to England of the Australian team. Several leading players, including Armstrong, dropped out of the tour because the Board deprived them of their traditional right to appoint the manager. Clem Hill was so disgusted with the Board he refused the tour. Jack Saunders went off to end his career in New Zealand, and Hordern thought it best to retire and concentrate on his dental practice.

The feud between the Board and leading players left several vacancies in the Australian side, and what was accepted as the worst Australian side ever to tour went to England, Matthews among them. At Manchester, in the First Test of the triangular tournament against South Africa, he made 49 not out in Australia's first innings of 448. On the second day South Africa were on 7 for 265 when Matthews was given the ball.

He took a hat-trick by bowling Rolland Beaumont with his first delivery, trapping Sidney Pegler LBW with his second and Thomas Ward LBW with his third, both his LBW victims falling to his top-spinner or the leg-break that did not turn.

Following on, South Africa could not handle the bowling of the crafty Charles Kelleway. At 5 for 70, Matthews went on and bowled Taylor, caught and bowled Reginald Schwarz with his next delivery and then caught and bowled Ward with his third for his second hat-trick in the match. Ward had been the third victim in both hat-tricks. Matthews' two hat-tricks were the only wickets he took in the match, in which his figures were 3 for 16 and 3 for 38.

Although he never again showed such sensational form, Matthews remained a hostile leg-spinner in dry weather, securing unpredictable bounce that worried the best batsmen, but he lost this penetration on damp pitches. He completed his sole English tour with 35 wickets at 19.37 and 584 runs at 18.25, with 93 against Sussex at Brighton his highest score.

Matthews, who played in eight Tests, finished his first-class career with four hat-tricks to his credit. Apart from the two at Manchester, he took one on the way home at Germanstown, Pennsylvania. The other one came in a match for Victoria against Tasmania in 1908-9 when he had match figures of 12 for 91. In all first-class matches he took five wickets in an innings eight times, best figures 7 for 49 in that match against Tasmania. His career ended with World War I. When peace returned he went back to his old job as groundsman for the Williamstown club, a modest, softly spoken man with a unique place in cricket's record books.

BOB MASSIE

Two years before he took the field to bowl for Australia in the Lord's Test of 1972, Perth right-arm medium-pacer Bob Massie had a trial with Northamptonshire. Massie was playing for Kilmarnock in the Scottish League at the time but wanted to break into county cricket. The Northants selectors were unimpressed and rejected him.

The reaction of the Northants administration when Massie turned in one of cricket's all-time great bowling performances has not been recorded, but there was no denying the enthusiasm with which Massie's team-mates greeted his display.

Robert Arnold Lockyer Massie made his Test debut in the 1972 Lord's Test along with fellow Western Australian Ross Edwards, who was five years younger than 27-year-old Massie. Massie, son of a chiropodist, was born in the Perth suburb of Subiaco, and had entered first-class cricket from the Bassendean-Bayswater Club. Edwards, born in the Perth suburb of Cottesloe, was the son of E.K. Edwards who played for Western Australia in 1948-49. Ross Edwards made his debut for Western Australia as a wicket-keeper from the Fremantle Club, batting at number 10, but played his way into the Australian team as a batsman and brilliant cover fieldsman.

Of the two, Massie was to enjoy the more spectacular debut. England won the toss and in humid conditions, absolutely ideal for swing bowling, Massie made the ball dart about so alarmingly in the air that he took 8 for 84 and was responsible for England scoring only 272 on a firm pitch. At the other end Dennis Lillee and David Colley, established as bowlers who could swing the ball when conditions helped, looked comparatively innocuous.

A masterly 131 from Greg Chappell and outstanding batting by Ian Chappell (56) and Rodney Marsh (50) enabled Australia to take a first innings lead of 36 runs despite a spirited display by John Snow (5 for 57). With Australia to bat last on a pitch that looked helpful to pace, the matches appeared evenly poised.

Massie quickly changed that balance in England's second innings with an exhibition that was even more dramatic than his first innings effort. He made renowned players of swing bowling, like Geoffrey Boycott and John Edrich, look novices as he repeatedly deceived them with movement of the ball in the air. Indeed, Massie's wizardry was so complete that some critics refused to believe his methods were fair and complained about the shape of the ball.

All the Australians who played in what became known as "Massie's match" agreed conditions were absolutely ideal for swing bowling. There was a heavy cloud cover over Lord's, the humidity was high, and Massie bowled with the right speed and arm action required to exploit the conditions. He swung the ball so much that he repeatedly beat the batsmen without hitting the stumps or finding an edge.

Lillee again toiled for his two wickets, moving the ball more from the pitch than in the air, while Massie bowled as if he had the ball on a string. Massie finished with second innings figures that were even better than those of the first. His 8 for 53 off 27.2 overs, which he bowled unchanged, gave him the amazing match analysis of 16 for 137 in his first Test.

His performance remains unmatched by any bowler in his first Test and for any Test at Lord's. Only Jim Laker (19 for 90 for England v. Australia at Old Trafford in 1956) and Sydney Barnes (17 for 159 for England v. South Africa at Johannesburg in 1913-14) have taken more wickets in a Test. Only two other bowlers, Australian Albert Trott (8 for 43 for Australia v. England at Adelaide in 1894-95) and West Indian Alf Valentine (8 for 104 for West Indies v. England at Manchester in 1950) have taken eight wickets in their Test debuts.

Massie's 16 wickets destroyed the confidence England's leading batsmen had built up when facing Australian bowlers, creating an uncertainty that Lillee, Jeff Thomson, Mick Malone and others were to exploit in the seasons that followed.

But Massie never repeated his display. He never again took five wickets in a Test innings, and within two years could not find a place in the Western Australian side. When he went without wickets on Australia's 1972-73 tour of the West Indies, his failures were blamed on the thin atmosphere. He had lost control of swing and in his frustration tried to bowl too fast, digging the ball into the pitch, trying to replace swing with lift and in the process changing the action that had given him his historic coup at Lord's. To the end of his career he remained a puzzle, a bowler who never once took five wickets in an innings for Western Australia, though he did it six times for Australia. His five other Tests brought him only 15 wickets to go with the 16 he took at Lord's.

THREE WICKETS IN AN OVER

Bowler	Opponent	Venue	Series
Sievers, MW	England	Melbourne	1936-37
O'Reilly, WJ	New Zealand	Wellington	1945-46
Toshack, ERH	India	Brisbane2	1947-48
Davidson, AK	England	Melbourne	1958-59

WICKET IN FIRST OVER IN TEST CRICKET

Ball	Bowler	Batsman	Howout	Opp	Venue	Series
1	Conningham, A	MacLaren, AC	ct Trott, GHS	ENG	Melbourne	1894-95
2	McCool, CL	McRae, DAN	ct Meuleman, K	NZ	Wellington	1945-46
2	Misson, FM	Hunte, CC	ct Simpson, RB	WI	Melbourne	1960-61
2	Philpott, PI	Hunte, CC	ct Grout, ATW	WI	Kingston	1964-65
2	Dymock, G	Parker, JM	ct Marsh, RW	NZ	Adelaide	1973-74
3	Johnson, IW	Hutton, L	ct Tallon, D	ENG	Sydney	1946-47
3	Freeman, EW	Abid Ali, S	ct Redpath, IR	IND	Brisbane	1967-68
4	Freer, FW	Washbrook, C	b	ENG	Sydney	1946-47
5	Mallett, AA	Cowdrey, MC	lbw	ENG	The Oval	1968
7	Gaunt, RA	Westcott, RJ	b	SA	Durban2	1957-58
7	Mann, AL	Viswanath, GR	ct Hurst, AG	IND	Brisbane2	1977-78

McCool & Johnson were in the same innings.

FIVE WICKETS IN CONSECUTIVE INNINGS

Bowler	Wickets	Opponent	Venue	Series
Six times:				
Turner, CTB	5/44 & 7/43	England	Sydney	1887-88
	5/27 & 5/36	England	Lord's	1888
	6/112 & 5/86	England	Manchester	1888
Four times:				
Lillee, DK	5/51 & 6/72	New Zealand	Auckland	1976-77
	6/26 & 5/139	England	Melbourne	1976-77
Hogg, RM	5/65 & 5/57	England	Perth	1978-79
	5/30 & 5/36	England	Melbourne	1978-79

Bowler	Wickets	Opponent	Venue	Series
Three times:				
Grimmett, CV	5/45 & 6/37	England	Sydney	1924-25
	5/88 & 2/59	England	Leeds	1926
Grimmett, CV	2/100 & 6/92	South Africa	Melbourne	1931-32
	7/116 & 7/83	South Africa	Adelaide	1931-32
Davidson, AK	5/135 & 6/87	West Indies	Brisbane2	1960-61
	6/53 & 2/51	West Indies	Melbourne	1960-61
Mallett, AA	5/91 & 5/53	India	Madras2	1969-70
	5/126 & 1/79	South Africa	Cape Town	1969-70
Lawson, GF	1/89 & 5/108	England	Perth	1982-83
	6/47 & 5/87	England	Brisbane	1982-83

400 BALLS IN AN INNINGS

Balls	Bowler	Overs	Mdns	Runs	Wkts	Opponent	Venue	Series
571	Veivers, TR	95.1	36	155	3	England	Manchester	1964
522	Fleetwood-Smith, LO	87	11	298	1	England	The Oval	1938
510	O'Reilly, WJ	85	26	178	3	England	The Oval	1938
478	Higgs, JD	59.6	15	148	5	England	Sydney	1978-79
470	Giffen, G	78.2	21	155	6	England	Melbourne	1894-95
450	Giffen, G	75	25	164	4	England	Sydney	1894-95
432	Waite, MG	72	16	150	1	England	The Oval	1938
424	O'Keeffe, KJ	53	12	166	3	Pakistan	Adelaide	1976-77
408	Ironmonger, H	68	21	142	2	England	Sydney	1928-29
408	Mackay, KD	68	21	121	5	England	The Oval	1961
407	Benaud, R	50.7	13	114	5	South Africa	Durban2	1957-58
406	O'Reilly, WJ	67.4	27	120	4	England	Brisbane2	1932-33
402	O'Reilly, WJ	67	32	117	3	England	Sydney	1931-32

BERT "DAINTY" IRONMONGER

The Australians had already had four one-sided victories when they went to Melbourne to play South Africa in the Fifth Test in 1931-32. The South African attack had been humbled by a Bradman in superlative form, and the Springbok batsmen had been unable to cope with the spin and guile of Bert Ironmonger and Clarrie Grimmett.

Bradman began the Melbourne Test with a record of having scored 226, 127, 2 and 167, and 299 not out when he ran out of partners. The South Africans' vulnerability to spin had been emphasised in the State matches as well as the Tests. Indeed, Norm O'Reilly, Clarrie Grimmett, Hugh Thurlow, Bert Ironmonger, Bill Hunt and a newcomer named Leslie O'Brien Fleetwood-Smith did so well against them that the selectors were embarrassed only by the problem of which bowlers to pick.

For Melbourne, they chose Ironmonger and O'Reilly, although Grimmett had already taken 33 wickets at 16.68, and brought in batsman Jack Fingleton and pace bowler Laurie Nash (their first Tests). South African hopes of a reversal of form increased when their side won the toss, but that was all they were to win in a remarkable match.

The MCG produced a vicious sticky wicket on which the South African batsmen were powerless. Their first innings lasted only 90 minutes, and they were all out for 36. Nash took 4 for 18 and Ironmonger 5 for 6, while O'Reilly did not even get a bowl. Only one South African batsman, captain Bert Cameron, reached double figures, with sundries comprising the second highest contributor at 8 runs to Cameron's 11.

Ironmonger was one of the most fascinating cricketers ever to take the field for Australia. He was born at Ipswich, Queensland, in 1882, where he worked for a time in a timber mill. He lost the top of one of the fingers on his bowling hand by getting too close to a cross-cut saw. After a period in hospital he returned to work, and in the process of showing the foreman how his accident had occurred, he lost the top of another finger! He rested the ball on the stubs of those two fingers as he moved in to bowl, and perhaps because of his peculiar grip some batsmen considered him a chucker.

He moved south because of the limited opportunities in

Queensland, playing first for the Balmain Club in Sydney and later for the Melbourne and St Kilda clubs. Perhaps because of his "nomadic" background, officials lost track of how old he was, and when he made his Test debut in 1928-29 he said he was 41 when he was in fact 46. He was an abysmal fieldsman and a lamentable batsman known to one and all as "Dainty".

Ironmonger's wife was reported to have telephoned him at the MCG, only to be told when she got through to the dressing-room that "Dainty" had just gone out to bat. "Oh, then I'd better hold on," she said. The old horse that pulled the roller at the MCG went round and stood between the shafts when "Dainty" went in to bat, according to another legend. The late Johnnie Moyes wrote: "Ironmonger went out to bat mainly to satisfy convention." Dainty, in fact, batted 21 times in his 14 Tests for an average of 2.62, most of them off the edge.

Now, in his moment of triumph, Ironmonger followed his first innings' bowling coup with a hard-earned innings of nought not out. Only Alan Kippax (42) and Fingleton (40) handled the sticky wicket conditions with any aplomb, and with Bradman unable to bat because of injury Australia made only 153.

Trailing by 117 on the first innings, South Africa fared no better against Ironmonger in their second innings. This time they made 45, and their two innings' aggregate of 81 runs remains the lowest by any side, losing all 20 wickets, in a Test match. Ironmonger bowled 15.3 overs for his 6 for 18 and ended with the amazing figures of 11 for 24. As he had earlier taken 9 for 86 in the First Test of the series he could be well satisfied with his international season. O'Reilly took 3 for 19 to complete South Africa's humiliation; Australia won by an innings and 72 runs.

Given that the conditions were all in his favour, this was still a remarkable display by Ironmonger. He showed it was no fluke the following season when he took 15 wickets against England in four Tests, playing a vital role in winning the Second Test. But he was denied a tour of England, which his talents deserved. Many believed he would have been a sensation on English wickets.

600 BALLS IN A MATCH

Balls	Bowler	1st innings O	M	R	W	2nd innings O	M	R	W	Opponent	Venue	Series
708	Giffen, G	43	17	75	4	75	25	164	4	England	Sydney	1894-95
672	Johnston, WA	46	8	152	6	38	7	114	1	South Africa	Melbourne	1952-53
656	Grimmett, CV	66.2	18	135	4	43	12	90	1	England	The Oval	1930
656	Ward, FA	36	3	138	2	46	16	102	6	England	Brisbane2	1936-37
654	Trumble, H	65	25	124	3	44	18	74	6	England	Adelaide	1901-02
654	Grimmett, CV	63	23	100	2	46	14	92	6	South Africa	Melbourne	1931-32
642	Mackay, KD	39	14	75	2	68	21	121	5	England	The Oval	1961
633	Grimmett, CV	58.3	24	81	5	47	28	39	3	England	Nottingham	1934
625	Grimmett, CV	52.1	12	102	5	52	15	117	1	England	Adelaide	1928-29
622	Higgs, JD	18	4	42	3	59.6	15	148	5	England	Sydney	1978-79
606	O'Reilly, WJ	40.6	13	102	5	35	15	59	–	England	Brisbane2	1936-37
603	O'Reilly, WJ	50	19	82	2	50.3	21	79	4	England	Adelaide	1932-33

CONCEDING 150 RUNS IN AN INNINGS

Bowler	Overs	Mdns	Runs	Wkts	Opponent	Venue	Series
Fleetwood-Smith, LO	87	11	298	1	England	The Oval	1938
Grimmett, CV	64	14	191	2	England	Sydney	1928-29
O'Reilly, WJ	59	9	189	7	England	Manchester	1934
Mailey, AA	43.6	2	186	4	England	Melbourne	1924-25
Mailey, AA	32	–	179	3	England	Sydney	1924-25
O'Reilly, WJ	85	26	178	3	England	The Oval	1938
Gleeson, JW	35	2	176	1	West Indies	Adelaide	1968-69
Bright, RJ	56	14	172	5	Pakistan	Lahore2	1979-80
Lillee, DK	50.2	8	171	6	Pakistan	Adelaide	1983-84
Grimmett, CV	40	2	167	3	England	Brisbane1	1928-29
Grimmett, CV	53	13	167	6	England	Lord's	1930
O'Keeffe, KJ	53	13	166	3	Pakistan	Adelaide	1976-77
Thomson, JR	34	3	166	2	England	Leeds	1985
Giffen, G	75	25	164	4	England	Sydney	1894-95
Jones, E	53	12	164	4	England	The Oval	1899
O'Reilly, WJ	56	11	164	3	England	Nottingham	1938
Lillee, DK	47.4	10	163	5	Pakistan	Adelaide	1976-77
Mailey, AA	32.1	3	160	5	England	Adelaide	1920-21
Gleeson, JW	51	9	160	3	South Africa	Durban2	1969-70
Sleep, PR	36	2	159	1	Pakistan	Faisalabad	1982-83

Bowler	Overs	Mdns	Runs	Wkts	Opponent	Venue	Series
Cotter, A	43	5	158	2	South Africa	Melbourne	1910-11
Matthews, GRJ	52	8	158	4	India	Bombay3	1986-87
McKenzie, GD	30.1	2	156	1	South Africa	Adelaide	1963-64
Giffen, G	78.2	21	155	6	England	Melbourne	1894-95
Veivers, TR	95.1	36	155	3	England	Leeds	1964
McDermott, CJ	31	2	155	2	England	Birmingham	1985
Giffen, G	51.1	17	154	2	England	Adelaide	1891-92
Fleetwood-Smith, LO	49	9	153	4	England	Nottingham	1938
McKenzie, GD	60	15	153	7	England	Manchester	1964
Johnston, WA	46	8	152	6	South Africa	Melbourne	1952-53
Alderman, TM	42.4	6	152	1	West Indies	Bridgetown	1983-84
Johnson, IW	47	10	151	4	England	Manchester	1956
Waite, MG	72	16	150	1	England	The Oval	1938
Higgs, JD	47	11	150	3	India	Delhi	1979-80
Lawson, GF	33.2	4	150	2	West Indies	Bridgetown	1983-84

Ward conceded in consecutive innings 138, 102, 132, 60 & 142.
Gregory conceded in consecutive innings 111, 115 & 124 v England 1924-25

CONCEDING 200 RUNS IN A MATCH

Balls	Bowler	1st innings				2nd innings				Opponent	Venue	Series
		O	M	R	W	O	M	R	W			
308	Mailey, AA	31	2	129	4	32	–	179	3	England	Sydney	1924-25
302	Mailey, AA	32.1	3	160	5	29.2	3	142	5	England	Adelaide	1920-21
298	Fleetwood-Smith, LO	87	11	298	1	–	–	–	–	England	The Oval	1938
298	Grimmett, CV	40	2	167	3	44.1	9	131	6	England	Brisbane1	1928-29
272	Grimmett, CV	33	4	105	2	53	13	167	6	England	Lord's	1930
267	Gleeson, JW	25	5	91	3	35	2	176	1	West Indies	Adelaide	1968-69
267	Lillee, DK	19	1	104	1	47.7	10	163	5	Pakistan	Adelaide	1976-77
266	Mailey, AA	33.5	3	138	6	42.5	6	128	3	England	The Oval	1926
266	Johnston, WA	46	8	152	6	38	7	114	1	South Africa	Melbourne	1952-53
259	Mailey, AA	44	5	133	3	30.2	4	126	3	England	Adelaide	1924-25
249	Matthews, GRJ	28.2	3	103	5	39.5	7	146	5	India	Madras2	1986-87
240	Ward, FA	36	3	138	2	46	14	102	6	England	Brisbane2	1936-37
239	Giffen, G	43	17	75	4	75	25	164	4	England	Sydney	1894-95
239	Fleetwood-Smith, LO	41.4	10	129	4	30	1	110	6	England	Adelaide	1936-37
236	Giffen, G	45	13	130	4	31	4	106	4	England	Melbourne	1894-95
236	Mailey, AA	29.2	1	115	4	47	8	121	9	England	Melbourne	1920-21
233	Mailey, AA	34	5	141	2	24	2	92	5	England	Melbourne	1924-25
232	Gleeson, JW	32	9	90	2	30.2	5	142	1	South Africa	Pt Elizabeth	1969-70
226	Gregory, JM	28.7	2	111	5	28	2	115	2	England	Sydney	1924-25

Balls	Bowler	1st innings				2nd innings				Opponent	Venue	Series
		O	M	R	W	O	M	R	W			
225	Grimmett, CV	66.2	18	135	4	43	12	90	1	England	The Oval	1930
222	Davidson, AK	30	2	135	5	24.6	4	87	6	West Indies	Brisbane2	1960-61
221	Cotter, A	40	4	148	7	21	2	73	2	England	The Oval	1909
219	Grimmett, CV	52.1	12	102	5	52	15	117	1	England	Adelaide	1928-29
218	Whitty, WJ	34	7	114	2	39.2	5	104	6	South Africa	Adelaide	1910-11
214	O'Reilly, WJ	59	9	189	7	13	4	25	–	England	Manchester	1934
211	Gregory, JM	34	4	124	5	27.3	6	87	4	England	Melbourne	1924-25
211	Mallett, AA	27	5	77	2	38	7	134	2	West Indies	Adelaide	1979-80
210	Grimmett, CV	55	14	114	2	42	12	96	2	England	Melbourne	1928-29
208	Mailey, AA	23	1	89	2	36.2	5	119	5	England	Sydney	1920-21
208	O'Keeffe, KJ	19	5	42	3	53	12	166	3	Pakistan	Adelaide	1976-77
208	Yardley, B	42.4	15	107	5	41	10	101	3	England	Perth	1982-83
205	Mallett, AA	55.1	16	126	5	32	10	79	1	South Africa	Cape Town	1969-70
205	Cotter, A	43	5	158	2	15	3	47	4	South Africa	Melbourne	1910-11
203	Benaud, R	27	5	96	5	27	3	107	2	West Indies	Adelaide	1960-61
202	Cotter, A	21.5	–	101	6	26	1	101	2	England	Sydney	1907-08
201	Grimmett, CV	32	6	107	5	30	4	94	5	England	Nottingham	1930
200	Cooper, WH	32.2	8	80	3	75.2	45	63	–	England	Melbourne	1881-82
200	Mailey, AA	23	4	95	3	24	2	105	3	England	Sydney	1920-21
200	Yardley, B	40.5	10	132	5	16	–	68	–	West Indies	Adelaide	1981-82

WICKET-KEEPING

AUSTRALIAN WICKET-KEEPERS

Keeper	M	Inns kept	Dis	Ct	St	Opponent ENG	IND	NZ	PAK	SA	SL	WI
Marsh, RW	97	181	355	343	12	148	16	58	68	–	–	65
Grout, ATW	51	97	187	163	24	76	20	–	17	–	–	41
Oldfield, WAS	54	96	130	78	52	90	–	–	–	30	–	13
Langley, GRA	26	50	98	83	15	37	3	–	3	14	–	41
Carter, H	28	58	65	44	21	52	–	–	–	13	–	–
Kelly, JJ	36	67	63	43	20	55	–	–	–	8	–	–
Taber, HB	16	29	60	56	4	2	14	–	–	38	–	6
Blackham, JM	35	56	60	36	24	60	–	–	–	–	–	–
Tallon, D	21	41	58	50	8	42	14	2	–	–	–	–
Jarman, BN	19	35	54	50	4	18	19	–	4	–	–	13
Rixon, SJ	13	23	47	42	5	–	22	–	–	–	–	25
Phillips, WB	27	27	43	43	–	11	8	7	–	–	–	17
Wright, KJ	10	15	35	31	4	8	13	–	14	–	–	–
Saggers, RA	6	10	24	16	8	3	–	–	–	21	–	–
Zoehrer, TF	10	17	19	18	1	10	4	5	–	–	–	–
Maddocks, LV	7	10	19	18	1	13	4	–	–	–	–	2
Jarvis, AH	11	15	17	9	8	17	–	–	–	–	–	–
Maclean, JA	4	7	18	18	–	18	–	–	–	–	–	–
Woolley, RD	2	2	7	7	–	–	–	–	–	–	5	2
Carkeek, W	6	8	6	6	–	2	–	–	–	6	–	–
Barnett, BA	4	6	5	3	2	5	–	–	–	–	–	–
Love, HSB	1	1	3	3	–	3	–	–	–	–	–	–
Murdoch, WL	18	1	2	1	1	2	–	–	–	–	–	–
Burton, FJ	2	1	2	1	1	2	–	–	–	–	–	–

Jarvis took 1 catch when not wicket-keeping, Murdoch took 12 catches when not wicket-keeping and Phillips took 9 catches when not wicket-keeping.

MOST DISMISSALS IN A SERIES

Keeper	Venue	Series	Tests	Ct/St	Opponent ENG	IND	NZ	PAK	SA	SL	WI
Marsh, RW	Australia	1982-83	5	28/-	28	–	–	–	–	–	–
Marsh, RW	Australia	1975-76	6	26/-	–	–	–	–	–	–	26
Grout, ATW	Australia	1960-61	5	20/3	–	–	–	–	–	–	23
Marsh, RW	England	1972	5	21/2	23	–	–	–	–	–	–
Marsh, RW	England	1981	6	23/-	–	–	–	–	–	–	–
Rixon, SJ	Australia	1977-78	5	22/-	–	22	–	–	–	–	–
Saggers, RA	South Africa	1949-50	5	13/8	–	–	–	–	21	–	–
Langley, GRA	Australia	1951-52	5	16/5	–	–	–	–	–	–	21
Grout, ATW	England	1961	5	20/1	21	–	–	–	–	–	–
Marsh, RW	Australia	1983-84	5	21/-	–	–	–	21	–	–	–
Tallon, D	Australia	1946-47	5	16/4	20	–	–	–	–	–	–
Langley, GRA	West Indies	1954-55	4	16/4	–	–	–	–	–	–	20
Grout, ATW	Australia	1958-59	5	17/3	20	–	–	–	–	–	–
Taber, HB*	South Africa	1966-67	5	19/1	–	–	–	–	20	–	–

Taber was on debut.

MOST DISMISSALS IN A MATCH

Keeper	Venue	Series	Ct/St	Opponent ENG	IND	NZ	PAK	SA	SL	WI
Langley, GRA	Lord's	1956	8/1	9	–	–	–	–	–	–
Marsh, RW	Brisbane2	1982-83	9/-	9	–	–	–	–	–	–
Kelly, JJ	Sydney	1901-02	8/-	8	–	–	–	–	–	–
Langley, GRA	Kingston	1954-55	8/-	–	–	–	–	–	–	8
Grout, ATW	Lahore	1959-60	6/2	–	–	–	8	–	–	–
Grout, ATW	Lord's	1961	8/-	8	–	–	–	–	–	–
Taber, HB*	Johannesburg3	1966-67	7/1	–	–	–	–	8	–	–
Marsh, RW	Melbourne	1975-76	8/-	–	–	–	–	–	–	8
Marsh, RW	Christchurch	1976-77	8/-	–	–	8	–	–	–	–
Marsh, RW	Sydney	1980-81	7/1	–	8	–	–	–	–	–
Marsh, RW	Adelaide	1982-83	8/-	8	–	–	–	–	–	–
Saggers, RA	Cape Town	1949-50	4/3	–	–	–	–	7	–	–
Langley, GRA	Brisbane2	1951-52	3/4	–	–	–	–	–	–	7
Grout, ATW	Brisbane2	1960-61	6/1	–	–	–	–	–	–	7
Jarman, BN	Brisbane2	1968-69	7/-	–	–	–	–	–	–	7

Keeper	Venue	Series	Ct/St	Opponent ENG	IND	NZ	PAK	SA	SL	WI
Taber, HB	Johannesburg3	1969-70	6/1	–	–	–	–	7	–	–
Marsh, RW	Melbourne	1973-74	6/1	–	–	7	–	–	–	–
Marsh, RW	Christchurch	1973-74	7/-	–	–	7	–	–	–	–
Wright, KJ	Melbourne	1978-79	7/-	–	–	–	7	–	–	–
Wright, KJ	Perth	1978-79	7/-	–	–	–	7	–	–	–
Marsh, RW	Birmingham	1981	7/-	7	–	–	–	–	–	–
Marsh, RW	Perth	1981-82	7/-	–	–	–	7	–	–	–
Rixon, SJ	Adelaide	1984-85	7/-	–	–	–	–	–	–	7

Taber's 8 dismissals were on debut.

MOST DISMISSALS IN AN INNINGS

Keeper	Venue	Series	Ct/St	Opponent ENG	IND	NZ	PAK	SA	SL	WI
Grout, ATW	Johannesburg3	1957-58	6/-	–	–	–	–	6	–	–
Marsh, RW	Brisbane2	1982-83	6/-	6	–	–	–	–	–	–
Oldfield, WAS	Melbourne	1924-25	4/1	5	–	–	–	–	–	–
Langley, GRA	Georgetown	1954-55	2/3	–	–	–	–	–	–	5
Langley, GRA	Kingston	1954-55	5/-	–	–	–	–	–	–	5
Langley, GRA	Lord's	1956	5/-	5	–	–	–	–	–	–
Grout, ATW	Durban2	1957-58	4/1	–	–	–	–	5	–	–
Grout, ATW	Lahore2	1959-60	5/-	–	–	–	5	–	–	–
Grout, ATW	Brisbane2	1960-61	4/1	–	–	–	–	–	–	5
Grout, ATW	Lord's	1961	5/-	5	–	–	–	–	–	–
Grout, ATW	Sydney	1965-66	5/-	5	–	–	–	–	–	–
Taber, HB *	Johannesburg3	1966-67	5/-	–	–	–	–	5	–	–
Taber, HB	Sydney	1968-69	5/-	–	–	–	–	–	–	5
Taber, HB	Port Elizabeth	1969-70	5/-	–	–	–	–	5	–	–
Marsh, RW	Manchester	1972	5/-	5	–	–	–	–	–	–
Marsh, RW	Nottingham	1972	5/-	5	–	–	–	–	–	–
Marsh, RW	Sydney	1973-74	5/-	–	–	5	–	–	–	–
Marsh, RW	Christchurch	1973-74	5/-	–	–	5	–	–	–	–
Marsh, RW	Melbourne	1975-76	5/-	–	–	–	–	–	–	5
Marsh, RW	Christchurch	1976-77	5/-	–	–	5	–	–	–	–
Maclean, JA	Brisbane2	1978-79	5/-	5	–	–	–	–	–	–
Wright, KJ	Melbourne	1978-79	5/-	–	–	–	5	–	–	–
Marsh, RW	Brisbane2	1979-80	5/-	–	–	–	–	–	–	5
Marsh, RW	Sydney	1980-81	5/-	–	5	–	–	–	–	–

Keeper	Venue	Series	Ct/St	Opponent ENG	IND	NZ	PAK	SA	SL	WI
Marsh, RW	Perth	1981-82	5/-	–	–	–	5	–	–	–
Marsh, RW	Perth	1983-84	5/-	–	–	–	5	–	–	–
Marsh, RW	Sydney	1983-84	5/-	–	–	–	5	–	–	–
Phillips, WB	Kingston	1983-84	5/-	–	–	–	–	–	–	5

* Taber was on debut.

NO BYES CONCEDED IN TOTAL OF 400 RUNS

Runs	Keeper	Opponent	Venue	Series
521	Oldfield, WAS	England	Brisbane1	1928-29
509	Phillips, WB	West Indies	Bridgetown	1983-84
8d-470	Taber, HB	South Africa	Port Elizabeth	1969-70
470	Marsh, RW	Pakistan	Melbourne	1983-84
456	Phillips, WB	England	Nottingham	1985
453	Grout, ATW	West Indies	Brisbane2	1960-61
440	Oldfield, WAS	England	Lord's	1934
7d-436	Marsh, RW	England	Lord's	1975
9d-420	Marsh, RW	Pakistan	Lahore2	1979-80
408	Taber, HB	South Africa	Johannesburg3	1969-70
405	Oldfield, WAS	England	The Oval	1930
405	Rixon, SJ	West Indies	Port-of-Spain	1977-78
8d-403	Carter, H	England	The Oval	1921
4-401	Grout, ATW	England	Birmingham	1961

MOST BYES CONCEDED IN AN INNINGS

Byes	Runs	Keeper	Opponent	Venue	Series
31	366	Grout, ATW	Pakistan	Lahore2	1959-60
30	329	Carkeek, W	South Africa	Nottingham	1912
24	353	Jarvis, AH	England	Lord's	1886
23	9-251	Oldfield, WAS	England	Melbourne	1920-21
22	188	Blackham, JM	England	Sydney	1881-82
22	9d-903	Barnett, BA	England	The Oval	1938
21	196	Kelly, JJ	England	Nottingham	1905
20	282	Kelly, JJ	England	Lord's	1905
20	373	Grout, ATW	West Indies	Kingston	1964-65

BYES ALLOWED PER RUNS SCORED

Keeper	Tests	Inns kept	Byes	Runs	Byes per 100 runs
Rixon, SJ	13	23	50	7092	0.71
Taber, HB	16	29	73	8649	0.84
Phillips, WB	27	27	98	9000	1.09
Maddocks, LV	7	10	33	2907	1.14
Love, HSB	1	1	2	162	1.23
Murdoch, WL	18	1	3	232	1.29
Marsh, RW	97	181	639	47607	1.34
Barnett, BA	4	6	36	2643	1.36
Jarman, BN	19	35	139	10121	1.37
Wright, KJ	10	15	68	4793	1.42
Carter, H	28	58	221	14344	1.54
Grout, ATW	51	97	416	25653	1.62
Oldfield, WAS	54	96	433	26065	1.66
Langley, GRA	26	50	205	11994	1.71
Zoehrer, TJ	10	17	84	4847	1.73
Saggers, RA	6	10	41	2356	1.74
Kelly, JJ	36	67	287	15648	1.83
Maclean, JA	4	7	40	1507	2.65
Woolley, RD	2	2	19	703	2.70
Jarvis, AH	11	15	96	3053	3.14
Tallon, D	21	41	289	8710	3.32
Blackham, JM	35	56	402	11804	3.41
Carkeek, W	6	8	97	1793	5.41
Burton, FJ	2	1	12	154	7.79

BYES ALLOWED PER BALLS BOWLED

Keeper	Tests	Inns kept	Byes	Runs	Byes per 100 runs
Taber, HB	16	29	73	19664	0.37
Rixon, SJ	13	23	50	13641	0.37
Love, HSB	1	1	2	478	0.42
Maddocks, LV	7	10	33	7497	0.44
Murdoch, WL	18	1	3	613	0.49
Jarman, BN	19	35	139	24957	0.56

Keeper	Tests	Inns kept	Byes	Runs	Byes per 100 runs
Phillips, WB	27	27	98	16709	0.59
Marsh, RW	97	181	639	102315	0.62
Grout, ATW	51	97	416	65972	0.63
Wright, KJ	10	15	68	10262	0.66
Oldfield, WAS	54	96	433	65346	0.66
Barnett, BA	4	6	36	5291	0.68
Saggers, RA	6	10	41	6044	0.68
Langley, GRA	26	50	205	30339	0.68
Carter, H	28	58	221	30814	0.72
Kelly, JJ	36	67	287	34828	0.82
Maclean, JA	4	7	40	4543	0.88
Zoehrer, TJ	10	17	84	9366	0.90
Tallon, D	21	41	289	23501	1.23
Jarvis, AH	11	15	96	7545	1.27
Blackham, JM	35	56	402	27933	1.44
Woolley, RD	2	2	19	1266	1.50
Burton, FJ	2	1	12	561	2.14
Carkeek, W	6	8	97	4122	2.35

FIELDING

MOST CATCHES

Player	Tests	Catches	Opponent ENG	IND	NZ	PAK	SA	SL	WI
Chappell, GS	88	122	61	5	18	22	–	–	16
Simpson, RB	62	110	30	21	–	3	27	–	29
Chappell, IM	76	105	31	17	16	6	11	–	24
Border, AR	89	94	39	9	15	17	–	3	11
Redpath, IR	67	83	29	17	1	8	6	–	22
Benaud, R	63	65	32	5	–	2	15	–	11
Harvey, RN	79	64	25	17	–	6	6	–	10
Hughes, KJ	70	50	12	10	9	10	–	–	9

MOST CATCHES IN A SERIES

Player	Venue	Series	Tests	Ct	Opponent ENG	IND	NZ	PAK	SA	SL	WI
Gregory, JM	Australia	1920-21	5	15	15	–	–	–	–	–	–
Chappell, GS	Australia	1974-75	6	14	14	–	–	–	–	–	–
Simpson, RB	South Africa	1957-58	5	13	–	–	–	–	13	–	–
Simpson, RB	Australia	1960-61	5	13	–	–	–	–	–	–	13
Whatmore, DF	India	1979-80	5	12	–	12	–	–	–	–	–
Border, AR	England	1981	6	12	12	–	–	–	–	–	–
Simpson, RB	Australia	1964-65	5	11	–	–	–	–	–	–	11
Chappell, IM	Australia	1974-75	6	11	11	–	–	–	–	–	–
Redpath, IR	Australia	1974-75	6	11	11	–	–	–	–	–	–
Border, AR	England	1985	6	11	11	–	–	–	–	–	–
Trumble, H	Australia	1901-02	5	10	10	–	–	–	–	–	–
Hill, C	Australia	1911-12	5	10	10	–	–	–	–	–	–
McCabe, SJ	Australia	1930-31	5	10	–	–	–	–	–	–	10
McCabe, SJ	Australia	1931-32	5	10	–	–	–	–	10	–	–

Player	Venue	Series	Tests	Ct	ENG	IND	NZ	PAK	SA	SL	WI
Harvey, RN	India	1956-57	3	10	–	10	–	–	–	–	–
Simpson, RB	England	1964	5	10	10	–	–	–	–	–	–
Chappell, IM	Australia	1968-69	5	10	–	–	–	–	–	–	10
Chappell, IM	India	1969-70	5	10	–	10	–	–	–	–	–
Chappell, IM	Australia	1973-74	3	10	–	–	10	–	–	–	–
Chappell, GS	Australia	1979-80	3	10	10	–	–	–	–	–	–

MOST CATCHES IN A MATCH

Player	Venue	Series	ENG	IND	NZ	PAK	SA	SL	WI
Chappell, GS	Perth	1974-75	7	–	–	–	–	–	–
Gregory, JM	Sydney	1920-21	6	–	–	–	–	–	–
Richardson, VY	Durban2	1935-36	–	–	–	–	6	–	–
Harvey, RN	Sydney	1962-63	6	–	–	–	–	–	–
Chappell, IM	Adelaide	1973-74	–	–	6	–	–	–	–
Whatmore, DF	Kanpur	1979-80	–	6	–	–	–	–	–
Gregory, JM	Durban1	1921-22	–	–	–	–	5	–	–
Fairfax, AG	Melbourne	1928-29	5	–	–	–	–	–	–
Richardson, VY	Durban2	1935-36	–	–	–	–	5	–	–
Loxton, SJE	Brisbane2	1950-51	5	–	–	–	–	–	–
Hole, GB	Lord's	1953	5	–	–	–	–	–	–
Harvey, RN	Kanpur	1959-60	–	5	–	–	–	–	–
Simpson, RB	Sydney	1960-61	–	–	–	–	–	–	5
Simpson, RB	Sydney	1967-68	–	5	–	–	–	–	–
Bonnor, GJ	Sydney	1882-83	4	–	–	–	–	–	–
Murdoch, WL	Sydney	1882-83	4	–	–	–	–	–	–
Giffen, G	Sydney	1891-92	4	–	–	–	–	–	–
Jones, E	Adelaide	1897-98	4	–	–	–	–	–	–
Trumble, H	Lord's	1899	4	–	–	–	–	–	–
Iredale, FA	Manchester	1899	4	–	–	–	–	–	–
Darling, J	Melbourne	1901-02	4	–	–	–	–	–	–
McAlister, PA	Sydney	1903-04	4	–	–	–	–	–	–
Trumper, VT	Sydney	1911-12	4	–	–	–	–	–	–
Hill, C	Melbourne	1911-12	4	–	–	–	–	–	–
Jennings, JB	The Oval	1212	4	–	–	–	–	–	–
Ponsford, WH	Brisbane1	1928-29	4	–	–	–	–	–	–
Jackson, A	Melbourne	1928-29	–	–	–	–	–	–	4
Ryder, J	Adelaide	1928-29	4	–	–	–	–	–	–

Player	Venue	Series	Opponent ENG	IND	NZ	PAK	SA	SL	WI
Chipperfield, AG	Nottingham	1934	4	–	–	–	–	– –	–
Barnes, SG	Brisbane2	1946-47	4	–	–	–	–	–	–
Hole, GB	Sydney	1952-53	–	–	–	–	4	–	–
Hole, GB	Adelaide	1952-53	–	–	–	–	4	–	–
Benaud, R	Kingston	1954-55	–	–	–	–	–	–	4
Archer, RG	Georgetown	1954-55	–	–	–	–	–	–	4
Harvey, RN	Madras2	1956-57	–	4	–	–	–	–	–
Harvey, RN	Calcutta	1956-57	–	4	–	–	–	–	–
Benaud, R	Cape Town	1957-58	–	–	–	–	4	–	–
Davidson, AK	Melbourne	1958-59	4	–	–	–	–	–	–
Harvey, RN	Karachi	1959-60	–	–	–	4	–	–	–
Davidson, AK	Delhi	1959-60	–	4	–	–	–	–	–
Simpson, RB	Melbourne	1960-61	–	–	–	–	–	–	4
Simpson, RB	Manchester	1961	4	–	–	–	–	–	–
Redpath, IR	Leeds	1964	4	–	–	–	–	–	–
Simpson, RB	Bombay2	1964-65	–	4	–	–	–	–	–
Chappell, IM	Melbourne	1964-65	–	–	–	4	–	–	–
Simpson, RB	Bridgetown	1964-65	–	–	–	–	–	–	4
Redpath, IR	Adelaide	1968-69	–	–	–	–	–	–	4
Chappell, IM	Adelaide	1968-69	–	–	–	–	–	–	4
Stackpole, KR	Calcutta	1969-70	–	4	–	–	–	–	–
Chappell, IM	Madras2	1969-70	–	4	–	–	–	–	–
Mallett, AA	Perth	1970-71	4	–	–	–	–	–	–
Chappell, GS	Adelaide	1972-73	–	–	–	4	–	–	–
Chappell, GS	Port-of-Spain	1972-73	–	–	–	–	–	–	4
Redpath, IR	Perth	1974-75	4	–	–	–	–	–	–
Chappell, GS	Leeds	1975	4	–	–	–	–	–	–
Turner, A	Sydney	1976-77	–	–	–	4	–	–	–
Wood, GM	Port-of-Spain	1977-78	–	–	–	–	–	–	4
Wood, GM	Sydney	1977-78	4	–	–	–	–	–	–
Chappell, GS	Sydney	1979-80	4	–	–	–	–	–	–
Border, AR	Karachi	1979-80	–	–	–	4	–	–	–
Hughes, KJ	Brisbane2	1980-81	–	–	4	–	–	–	–
Border, AR	Perth	1980-81	–	–	4	–	–	–	–
Hughes, KJ	Perth	1980-81	–	–	4	–	–	–	–
Kent, MF	The Oval	1981	4	–	–	–	–	–	–
Chappell, GS	Perth	1983-84	–	–	–	4	–	–	–
Border, AR	Lord's	1985	4	–	–	–	–	–	–

MOST CATCHES IN AN INNINGS

Player	Venue	Series	Opponent ENG	IND	NZ	PAK	SA	SL	WI
Richardson, VY	Durban2	1935-36	–	–	–	–	5	–	–
Trumble, H	Lord's	1899	4	–	–	–	–	–	–
Loxton, SJE	Brisbane2	1950-51	4	–	–	–	–	–	–
Hole, GB	Sydney	1952-53	–	–	–	–	4	–	–
Archer, RG	Georgetown	1954-55	–	–	–	–	–	–	4
Davidson, AK	Delhi	1959-60	–	4	–	–	–	–	–
Simpson, RB	Sydney	1960-61	–	–	–	–	–	–	4
Harvey, RN	Sydney	1962-63	4	–	–	–	–	–	–
Simpson, RB	Bridgetown	1964-65	–	–	–	–	–	–	4
Chappell, IM	Adelaide	1973-74	–	–	4	–	–	–	–
Turner, A	Sydney	1976-77	–	–	–	4	–	–	–
Whatmore, DF	Kanpur	1979-80	–	4	–	–	–	–	–
Border, AR	Karachi	1979-80	–	–	–	4	–	–	–
Hughes, KJ	Perth	1980-81	–	–	4	–	–	–	–
Bonnor, GJ	Sydney	1882-83	3	–	–	–	–	–	–
Murdoch, WL	Sydney	1882-83	3	–	–	–	–	–	–
Bonnor, GJ	Lord's	1884	3	–	–	–	–	–	–
Giffen, G	Sydney	1891-92	3	–	–	–	–	–	–
Giffen, G	The Oval	1893	3	–	–	–	–	–	–
Trott, AE	Adelaide	1894-95	3	–	–	–	–	–	–
Worrall, J	Adelaide	1894-95	3	–	–	–	–	–	–
Bruce, W	Sydney	1894-95	3	–	–	–	–	–	–
Trumble, H	Manchester	1896	3	–	–	–	–	–	–
Iredale, FA	Manchester	1899	3	–	–	–	–	–	–
Darling, J	Melbourne	1901-02	3	–	–	–	–	–	–
Trumble, H	Melbourne	1901-02	3	–	–	–	–	–	–
Hill, C	Melbourne	1901-02	3	–	–	–	–	–	–
Noble, MA	Sydney	1907-08	3	–	–	–	–	–	–
Kelleway, C	Melbourne	1910-11	–	–	–	–	3	–	–
Gregory, JM	Sydney	1920-21	3	–	–	–	–	–	–
Gregory, JM	Durban1	1921-22	–	–	–	–	3	–	–
Hendry, HSTL	Durban1	1921-22	–	–	–	–	3	–	–
Fairfax, AG	Melbourne	1928-29	3	–	–	–	–	–	–
Ryder, J	Adelaide	1928-29	3	–	–	–	–	–	–
McCabe, SJ	Sydney	1930-31	–	–	–	–	–	–	3

Player	Venue	Series	Opponent ENG	IND	NZ	PAK	SA	SL	WI
McCabe, SJ	Melbourne	1931-32	–	–	–	–	3	–	–
Chipperfield, AG	Nottingham	1934	3	–	–	–	–	–	–
Darling, LS	Melbourne	1936-37	3	–	–	–	–	–	–
McCabe, SJ	Lord's	1938	3	–	–	–	–	–	–
Barnes, SG	Brisbane2	1946-47	3	–	–	–	–	–	–
Johnson, IW	Melbourne	1950-51	3	–	–	–	–	–	–
Johnson, IW	Sydney	1951-52	–	–	–	–	–	–	3
Hole, GB	Lord's	1953	3	–	–	–	–	–	–
Harvey, RN	Madras2	1956-57	–	3	–	–	–	–	–
Harvey, RN	Calcutta	1956-57	–	3	–	–	–	–	–
Simpson, RB	Johannesburg3	1957-58	–	–	–	–	3	–	–
Davidson, AK	Melbourne	1958-59	3	–	–	–	–	–	–
Harvey, RN	Sydney	1958-59	3	–	–	–	–	–	–
Benaud, J	Melbourne	1958-59	3	–	–	–	–	–	–
Harvey, RN	Kanpur	1959-60	–	3	–	–	–	–	–
Benaud, R	The Oval	1961	3	–	–	–	–	–	–
Simpson, RB	Sydney	1962-63	3	–	–	–	–	–	–
Martin, JW	Melbourne	1963-64	–	–	–	–	3	–	–
Chappell, IM	Melbourne	1964-65	–	–	–	3	–	–	–
Simpson, RB	Johannesburg3	1966-67	–	–	–	–	3	–	–
Simpson, RB	Sydney	1967-68	–	3	–	–	–	–	–
Redpath, IR	Melbourne	1968-69	–	–	–	–	–	–	3
Redpath, IR	Madras2	1969-70	–	3	–	–	–	–	–
Chappell, IM	Cape Town	1969-70	–	–	–	–	3	–	–
Chappell, IM	Sydney	1970-71	3	–	–	–	–	–	–
Chappell, GS	Lord's	1972	3	–	–	–	–	–	–
Redpath, IR	Perth	1974-75	3	–	–	–	–	–	–
Chappell, IM	Melbourne	1974-75	3	–	–	–	–	–	–
Serjeant, CS	Bridgetown	1977-78	–	–	–	–	–	–	3
Whatmore, DF	Bombay2	1979-80	–	3	–	–	–	–	–
Hughes, KJ	Brisbane2	1980-81	–	–	3	–	–	–	–
Hughes, KJ	Melbourne	1980-81	–	3	–	–	–	–	–
Border, AR	Manchester	1981	3	–	–	–	–	–	–
Kent, MF	The Oval	1981	3	–	–	–	–	–	–
Phillips, WB	Perth	1983-84	–	–	–	3	–	–	–
Chappell, GS	Perth	1983-84	–	–	–	3	–	–	–
Waugh, SR	Perth	1986-87	3	–	–	–	–	–	–

CATCHES BY SUBSTITUTES

Player	Venue	Series	Opponent ENG	IND	NZ	PAK	SA	SL	WI
Gregory, SE	Melbourne	1891-92	1	–	–	–	–	–	–
Iredale, FA	Lord's	1896	2	–	–	–	–	–	–
Gehrs, DRA	The Oval	1905	1	–	–	–	–	–	–
Hartigan, RJ	The Oval	1909	1	–	–	–	–	–	–
Darling, LS	Melbourne	1911-12	–	–	–	–	1	–	–
Macartney, CG	Adelaide	1911-12	1	–	–	–	–	–	–
McLaren, JW	Manchester	1912	1	–	–	–	–	–	–
Pellew, CE	Johannesburg1	1921-22	–	–	–	–	1	–	–
Andrews, TJE	Sydney	1924-25	2	–	–	–	–	–	–
Bradman, DG	Sydney	1928-29	1	–	–	–	–	–	–
Oxenham, RK	Brisbane1	1928-29	1	–	–	–	–	–	–
Thompson, FC	Brisbane1	1928-29	1	–	–	–	–	–	–
A'Beckett, EL	Melbourne	1928-29	1	–	–	–	–	–	–
Rigg, KE	Brisbane2	1931-32	–	–	–	–	2	–	–
O'Brien, LPJ	Adelaide	1932-33	1	–	–	–	–	–	–
Barnett, BA	Manchester	1934	1	–	–	–	–	–	–
Brown, WA	Brisbane2	1936-37	1	–	–	–	–	–	–
Robinson, RH	Sydney	1936-37	1	–	–	–	–	–	–
Waite, MG	Lord's	1938	1	–	–	–	–	–	–
Barnett, BA	Manchester	1938	1	–	–	–	–	–	–
Loxton, SJE	Adelaide	1950-51	2	–	–	–	–	–	–
De Courcy, JH	Sydney	1952-53	–	–	–	–	2	–	–
Davidson, AK	Kingston	1954-55	–	–	–	–	–	–	1
Favell, LE	Georgetown	1954-55	–	–	–	–	–	–	1
McDonald, CC	Bombay2	1956-57	–	1	–	–	–	–	–
Simpson, RB	Sydney	1958-59	1	–	–	–	–	–	–
Connolly, AN	Sydney	1963-64	–	–	–	–	1	–	–
Redpath, IR	Bombay3	1964-65	–	1	–	–	–	–	–
Sellers, RHD	Karachi	1964-65	–	–	–	1	–	–	–
Sincock, DJ	Bridgetown	1964-65	–	–	–	–	–	–	1
Jenner, TJ	Melbourne	1974-75	1	–	–	–	–	–	–
Gilmour, GJ	Birmingham	1975	1	–	–	–	–	–	–
Turner, A	Leeds	1975	1	–	–	–	–	–	–
Walker, MHN	Adelaide	1975-76	–	–	–	–	–	–	1
Hughes, KJ	Melbourne	1976-77	–	–	–	1	–	–	–
Hughes, KJ	Adelaide	1977-78	–	2	–	–	–	–	–

Player	Venue	Series	Opponent ENG	IND	NZ	PAK	SA	SL	WI
Laughlin, TJ	Port-of-Spain	1977-78	–	–	–	–	–	–	1
Higgs, JD	Melbourne	1978-79	–	–	–	1	–	–	–
Laughlin, TJ	Perth	1978-79	–	–	–	1	–	–	–
Sleep, PR	Kanpur	1979-80	–	2	–	–	–	–	–
Porter, GD	Bombay3	1979-80	–	1	–	–	–	–	–
Lawson, GF	Karachi	1979-80	–	–	–	1	–	–	–
Graf, SF	Sydney	1980-81	–	1	–	–	–	–	–
Kent, MF	Nottingham	1981	1	–	–	–	–	–	–
Hookes, DW	Adelaide	1981-82	–	–	–	–	–	–	1
Bright, RJ	Wellington	1985-86	–	–	1	–	–	–	–
Total		**(53)**	**26**	**8**	**1**	**5**	**7**	**—**	**6**

MOST CATCHES BY SUBSTITUTES IN AN INNINGS

Catches	Player	Opponent	Venue	Series
2	Andrews, TJE	England	Sydney	1924-25
2	Oxenham, RK	England	Brisbane2	1928-29
	Thompson, NC	England	Brisbane2	1928-29
2	Loxton, SJE	England	Adelaide	1950-51
2	De Courcy, JH	South Africa	Sydney	1952-53

Murdoch, WL v England, Lord's, 1884, Jarvis, AH v England, Melbourne, 1884-85 and Turner, CTB v England, Sydney, 1886-87 took catches while substituting for the opposing teams.

MOST CATCHES BY SUBSTITUTES IN A MATCH

Catches	Player	Opponent	Venue	Series
2	Iredale, FA	England	Lord's	1896
2	Andrews, TJE	England	Sydney	1924-25
2	Oxenham, RK	England	Brisbane2	1928-29
	Thompson, NC	England	Brisbane2	1928-29
2	Loxton, SJE	England	Adelaide	1950-51
2	De Courcy, JH	South Africa	Sydney	1952-53
2	Hughes, KJ	India	Adelaide	1977-78
2	Sleep, PR	India	Kanpur	1979-80

MOST CATCHES BY SUBSTITUTES IN A SERIES

Catches	Opponent	Series
4	England	1928-29
3	India	1979-80
2	England	1896
2	England	1911-12
2	South Africa	1931-32
2	England	1936-37
2	England	1938
2	England	1950-51
2	South Africa	1952-53
2	England	1975
2	India	1977-78

ALL-ROUNDERS

BEST ALL-ROUND PERFORMANCE ON DEBUT

Player	Runs	Wkts	Opponent	Venue	Series
McLeod, RW	45	6	England	Melbourne	1891-92
Trott, AE	110	8	England	Adelaide	1894-95
Hornibrook, PM	44	4	England	Melbourne	1928-29
Mallett, AA	43	5	England	The Oval	1968
Gilmour, GJ	52	4	New Zealand	Melbourne	1973-74
Malone, MF	46	6	England	The Oval	1977
Yardley, B	48	4	India	Adelaide	1977-78
Hogg, RM	52	7	England	Brisbane2	1978-79
Matthews, GRJ	75	4	Pakistan	Melbourne	1983-84
Taylor, PL	53	8	England	Sydney	1986-87

MOST RUNS IN A SERIES BY A WICKET-KEEPER

Player	Tests	Runs	Avrge	Opponent	Venue	Series
Phillips, WB	6	350	35.00	England	England	1985
Marsh, RW	6	313	34.78	England	Australia	1974-75
Carter, H	5	300	42.85	England	Australia	1907-08
Marsh, RW	5	297	49.50	West Indies	West Indies	1972-73
Oldfield, WAS	5	291	41.57	England	Australia	1924-25
Phillips, WB	5	258	25.80	West Indies	West Indies	1983-84
Marsh, RW	5	242	34.57	England	England	1972
Marsh, RW	6	236	29.50	West Indies	Australia	1975-76
Carter, H	5	231	25.66	England	Australia	1911-12
Marsh, RW	6	216	19.64	England	England	1981
Marsh, RW	7	215	26.87	England	Australia	1970-71
Marsh, RW	3	210	42.00	Pakistan	Australia	1972-73

Phillips, WB in 1983-84 kept in 4 of the 5 Tests.

ALAN "DAVO" DAVIDSON

Alan Keith Davidson gave many outstanding performances with both
bat and ball in a career that took him from a rough, lopsided hillside
pitch at Lisarow, near Gosford, New South Wales, to the centre of
the world's most prestigious grounds.

He began a first-class career that was to include 193 first-class
matches and 33 Tests when he made his debut for New South Wales
in the 1949-50 season. He was heavily built, as befitted a splendid
rugby league player, determined, and ready to work hard at the nets.
These qualities won him his first overseas trip that summer in the
Australian team, led by Billy Brown, which played 14 matches in New
Zealand.

At Masterton, against Wairarapa, Davidson demonstrated his
potential by taking 10 for 29 off 81 deliveries followed by an innings
of 157 not out. But this match was not regarded as first-class because
it was played over two days and Wairarapa, defeated by an innings
and 466 runs, was not a first-class team.

Davidson returned to Australia classified as a promising cricketer
and for a period had to undertake a supporting role to the great
Australian pace trio of Ray Lindwall, Keith Miller and Bill Johnston.
When his time came to take over, Davidson quickly proved himself
to be the best new ball bowler in cricket. He took 24 wickets in the
Tests against England in Australia in 1958-59, and 23 Test wickets
against England in England in 1961. His batting, too, improved as
he developed a defence to match his natural powers as a big-hitter.

At Sydney, in the match between New South Wales and England
in 1954-55, Davidson won a reputation for big-hitting when he hit
a full toss from part-time bowler Colin Cowdrey on to the roof of the
Brewongle Stand and straight drove the next ball into the wall at the
back of The Hill, with this ball still rising on impact. The first blow
hit an ornament a metre over the top of the Brewongle roof, which
prevented the ball from falling into the street.

Davidson's notoriety as a hitter went with him to Brisbane for
the First Test of the 1960-61 series against the West Indies. But at
the critical point of one of the most exciting matches in history, it
was Davidson's clever stealing of singles on his way to his highest Test

score that remained memorable.

The West Indians began by scoring 7 for 359 on the first day, with Garfield Sobers contributing a classic 132, and took their total to 453 on the second morning. Australia accepted the challenge and rattled up 505 in good time, Norman O'Neill scoring 181. The West Indies then made 284 in their second innings, and on the last day Australia were set 232 to win.

At tea Australia's cause seemed hopeless with six batsmen out for 92. Davidson was on 16, Richie Benaud on 6. The Australians decided to keep the score moving by picking up singles, knowing occasional boundaries would come along on such a small ground.

Davidson's skill in dabbing the ball into open spaces flourished as the Australian score mounted. He still clubbed the ball to the fence periodically, but it was the singles he and his captain took that frustrated the West Indies.

With eight minutes left, Australia wanted seven runs for victory. Then Benaud hit the ball straight at Joe Solomon at square leg and bolted off for a suicidal single. Davidson had no alternative but to attempt the run and Solomon ran him out by two metres. "For the one and only time in his career, I thought Richie became flustered in a crisis," Davidson wrote in his book *Fifteen Paces*. It was the closest Davidson ever got to a Test century, though he made 77 not out in the Manchester Test against England in 1961.

Davidson's match figures of 11 for 222 (5 for 135 and 6 for 87) and his total of 124 runs with innings of 44 and 80 made him the first Australian to take 10 wickets and score 100 runs in a Test match. In a game that featured many spectacular sixes he did not once lift the ball over the fence and hit only 12 fours, far below his usual percentage when he got among the runs.

1000 RUNS AND 100 WICKETS

Player	Tests	Runs	Wkts	Tests for double
Benaud, R	63	2201	248	32
Davidson, AK	44	1328	186	34
Giffen, G	31	1238	103	30
Johnson, IW	45	1000	109	45
Lindwall, RR	61	1502	228	38
Miller, KR	55	2958	170	33
Noble, MA	42	1997	121	27

1000 RUNS AND 100 WICKET-KEEPING DISMISSALS

Player	Tests	Runs	Dis	Tests for double
Marsh, RW	97	3633	355	25
Oldfield, WAS	54	1427	130	41

1000 RUNS, 50 WICKETS AND 50 CATCHES

Player	Tests	Runs	Wkts	Catches
Benaud, R	63	2201	248	65
Simpson, RB	62	4869	71	110

200 RUNS AND 20 WICKET-KEEPING DISMISSALS IN A SERIES

Player	Tests	Runs	Dis	Opponent	Venue	Series
Marsh, RW	5	242	23	England	England	1972
Marsh, RW	6	236	26	West Indies	Australia	1975-76
Marsh, RW	6	216	23	England	England	1981

200 RUNS AND 20 WICKETS IN A SERIES

Player	Tests	Runs	Wkts	Opponent	Venue	Series
Giffen, G	5	475	34	England	Australia	1894-95
Gregory, JM	5	442	23	England	Australia	1920-21
Miller, KR	5	362	20	England	Australia	1951-52
Miller, KR	5	439	20	West Indies	West Indies	1954-55
Benaud, R	5	329	30	South Africa	South Africa	1957-58
Davidson, AK	5	212	33	West Indies	Australia	1960-61
Gregory, JM	5	224	22	England	Australia	1924-25
Lindwall, RR	5	211	21	West Indies	Australia	1951-52
Miller, KR	5	203	21	England	England	1956

100 RUNS AND 10 WICKETS IN A MATCH

Player	Runs	Wkts	Opponent	Venue	Series
Davidson, AK	44	5-135	West Indies	Brisbane2	1960-61
	80	6-87			

100 RUNS AND 5 WICKETS IN AN INNINGS

Player	Runs	Wkts	Opponent	Venue	Series
Kelleway, C	114	5-33	South Africa	Manchester	1912
Gregory, JM	100	7-69	England	Melbourne	1920-21
Miller, KR	109	6-107	West Indies	Kingston	1954-55
Benaud, R	100	5-84	South Africa	Johannesburg3	1957-58

CAPTAINS

MOST CONSECUTIVE TESTS AS CAPTAIN

Captain	Tests	Series
Chappell, IM	30	1970-71 to 1975
Lawry, WM	27	1967-68 to 1970-71
Border, AR	26	1984-85 to 1986-87
Woodfull, WM	25	1930 to 1934
Benaud, R	19	1958-59 to 1961
Simpson, RB	19	1963-64 to 1964-65
Chappell, GS	17	1975-76 to 1977
Chappell, GS	16	1979-80 to 1980-81
Johnson, IW	15	1954-55 to 1956-57

CAPTAINS WHO ELECTED TO FIELD FIRST

Captain	Opponent	Venue	Series	Result
McDonnell, PS	England	Sydney	1886-87	Lost by 13 runs
McDonnell, PS	England	Sydney	1887-88	Lost by 126 runs
Giffen, G	England	Melbourne	1894-95	Lost by 94 runs
Noble, MA	England	Lord's	1909	Won by 9 wkts
Hassett, AL	West Indies	Sydney	1951-52	Won by 7 wkts
Hassett, AL	England	Leeds	1953	Drawn
Morris, AR	England	Sydney	1954-55	Lost by 38 runs
Johnson, IW	England	Sydney	1954-55	Drawn
Benaud, R	England	Melbourne	1958-59	Won by 9 wkts
Benaud, R	Pakistan	Dacca	1959-60	Won by 8 wkts
Benaud, R	West Indies	Melbourne	1960-61	Won by 2 wkts
Simpson, RB	South Africa	Melbourne	1963-64	Won by 8 wkts
Simpson, RB	Pakistan	Melbourne	1964-65	Drawn

Captain	Opponent	Venue	Series	Result
Simpson, RB	West Indies	Port-of-Spain	1964-65	Drawn
Simpson, RB	South Africa	Durban2	1966-67	Lost by 8 wkts
Lawry, WM	West Indies	Melbourne	1968-69	Won by an Inns & 30 runs
Lawry, WM	India	Calcutta	1969-70	Won by 10 wkts
Lawry, WM	England	Perth	1970-71	Drawn
Chappell, IM	England	Sydney	1970-71	Lost by 62 runs
Chappell, IM	New Zealand	Sydney	1973-74	Drawn
Chappell, IM	England	Perth	1974-75	Won by 9 wkts
Chappell, IM	England	Melbourne	1974-75	Drawn
Chappell, GS	West Indies	Melbourne	1975-76	Won by 8 wkts
Chappell, GS	West Indies	Sydney	1975-76	Won by 7 wkts
Chappell, GS	New Zealand	Auckland	1976-77	Won by 10 wkts
Chappell, GS	England	The Oval	1977	Drawn
Simpson, RB	West Indies	Port-of-Spain	1977-78	Lost by 198 runs
Yallop, GN	England	Perth	1978-79	Lost by 166 runs
Yallop, GN	England	Adelaide	1978-79	Lost by 205 runs
Yallop, GN	Pakistan	Melbourne	1978-79	Lost by 71 runs
Hughes, KJ	Pakistan	Perth	1978-79	Won by 7 wkts
Chappell, GS	England	Sydney	1979-80	Won by 6 wkts
Chappell, GS	West Indies	Adelaide	1979-80	Lost by 408 runs
Chappell, GS	New Zealand	Brisbane2	1980-81	Won by 10 wkts
Chappell, GS	New Zealand	Perth	1980-81	Won by 8 wkts
Chappell, GS	India	Melbourne	1980-81	Lost by 59 runs
Hughes, KJ	England	Nottingham	1981	Won by 4 wkts
Hughes, KJ	England	Lord's	1981	Drawn
Chappell, GS	Pakistan	Brisbane2	1981-82	Won by 10 wkts
Chappell, GS	New Zealand	Wellington	1981-82	Drawn
Chappell, GS	England	Perth	1982-83	Drawn
Chappell, GS	England	Brisbane2	1982-83	Won by 7 wkts
Chappell, GS	England	Melbourne	1982-83	Lost by 3 runs
Hughes, KJ	Pakistan	Sydney	1983-84	Won by 10 wkts
Hughes, KJ	West Indies	Perth	1983-84	Lost by an Inns & 112 runs
Border, AR	West Indies	Melbourne	1984-85	Drawn
Border, AR	England	Lord's	1985	Won by 4 wkts
Border, AR	New Zealand	Sydney	1985-86	Won by 4 wkts
Border, AR	England	Brisbane2	1986-87	Lost by 7 wkts

MOST CONSECUTIVE LOSS
OF THE TOSS

Wins	Captain		Venue	Series	Venue	Series
6	Murdoch, WL	(5)	Melbourne	1878-89	to Melbourne	1881-82
	Gregory, SE	(1)				
6	Darling, J	(5)	Manchester	1899	to Sydney	1901-02
	Trumble, H	(1)				
6	Darling, J		Nottingham	1905	to Sydney	1907-08
5	Gregory, SE		Lord's	1912	to The Oval	1912
5	Bradman, DG	(4)	Nottingham	1938	to Wellington	1945-46
	Brown, WA	(1)				
5	Craig, ID	(1)	Port Elizabeth	1957-58	to Adelaide	1958-59
	Benaud, R	(4)				
5	Benaud, R		Lahore2	1959-60	to Madras2	1959-60
5	Lawry, WM		Sydney	1968-69	to Kanpur	1969-70
5	Border, AR		Nottingham	1985	to Brisbane2	1985-86

MOST CONSECUTIVE WINS
OF THE TOSS

Wins	Captain	Venue	Series	Venue	Series
7	Noble, MA	Birmingham	1909	to Melbourne	1910-11
7	Hassett, AL	Adelaide	1952-53	to The Oval	1953
6	Chappell, GS	Karachi	1979-70	to Perth	1980-81
5	Chappell, IM	Port-of-Spain	1972-73	to Wellington	1973-74
5	Chappell, GS	Perth	1975-76	to Melbourne	1975-76
5	Simpson, RB	Port-of-Spain	1977-78	to Melbourne	1978-79
5	Border, AR	Auckland	1985-86	to Brisbane2	1986-87

AUSTRALIAN CAPTAINCY RECORDS

Captain	Tests as captain	Opponent ENG	IND	NZ	PAK	SA	SL	WI	Results Won	Lost	Drawn	Tie	Won toss
Gregory, DW	3	3	–	–	–	–	–	–	2	1	–	–	2
Murdoch, WL	16	16	–	–	–	–	–	–	5	7	4	–	7
Horan, TP	2	2	–	–	–	–	–	–	–	2	–	–	1
Massie, HH	1	1	–	–	–	–	–	–	1	–	–	–	1
Blackham, JM	8	8	–	–	–	–	–	–	3	3	2	–	4
Scott, HJH	3	3	–	–	–	–	–	–	–	3	–	–	1
McDonnell, PS	6	6	–	–	–	–	–	–	2	5	–	–	4
Giffen, G	4	4	–	–	–	–	–	–	2	2	–	–	3
Trott, GHS	8	8	–	–	–	–	–	–	5	3	–	–	5
Darling, J	21	18	–	–	–	3	–	–	7	4	10	–	7
Trumble, H	2	2	–	–	–	–	–	–	2	–	–	–	1
Noble, MA	15	15	–	–	–	–	–	–	8	5	2	–	11
Hill, C	10	5	–	–	–	5	–	–	5	5	–	–	–
Gregory, SE	6	3	–	–	–	3	–	–	2	1	3	–	1
Armstrong, WW	10	10	–	–	–	–	–	–	8	2	–	–	4
Collins, HL	11	8	–	–	–	3	–	–	5	2	4	–	7
Bardsley, W	2	2	–	–	–	–	–	–	–	–	2	–	1
Ryder, J	5	5	–	–	–	–	–	–	1	4	–	–	2
Woodfull, WM	25	15	–	–	–	5	–	5	14	7	4	–	12
Richardson, VY	5	–	–	–	–	5	–	–	4	–	1	–	1

Bradman, DG	24	19	5	–	–	–	–	15	3	6	–	10
Brown, WA	1	–	–	1	–	–	–	1	–	–	–	–
Hassett, AL	24	10	–	–	–	10	4	14	4	6	–	18
Morris, AR	2	1	–	–	–	1	1	–	2	–	–	2
Johnson, IW	17	9	2	1	–	5	5	7	5	5	–	6
Lindwall, RR	1	–	1	–	–	–	–	–	–	1	–	–
Craig, ID	5	–	–	–	5	–	–	3	–	2	–	3
Benaud, R	28	14	5	3	1	5	5	12	4	11	1	11
Harvey, RN	1	1	–	–	–	–	–	1	–	–	–	–
Simpson, RB	39	8	10	2	–	10	–	12	12	15	–	19
Booth, BC	2	2	–	–	–	–	–	–	1	1	–	1
Lawry, WM	26	10	7	–	4	5	5	9	8	9	–	8
Jarman, BN	1	1	–	–	–	–	–	–	–	1	–	1
Chappell, IM	30	16	–	6	3	5	5	15	5	10	1	17
Chappell, GS	48	15	3	8	9	12	12	21	13	14	–	29
Yallop, GN	7	6	–	–	1	–	1	1	6	–	–	6
Hughes, KJ	28	6	6	–	9	7	7	4	13	11	–	13
Border, AR	26	11	6	6	–	3	3	4	9	12	1	13
Total	**473**	**263**	**45**	**21**	**28**	**53**	**62**	**194**	**139**	**138**	**2**	**237**

CAPTAINS WINNING ALL TOSSES IN A SERIES

Captain	Tests	Opponent	Venue	Series
Noble, MA	5	England	England	1909
Hassett, AL	5	England	England	1953
Chappell, IM	3	New Zealand	Australia	1973-74
Chappell, GS	3	Pakistan	Australia	1979-80

Chappell, IM won 5 tosses in a 6 Test series v England 1974-75.
Chappell, GS won 5 tosses in a 6 Test series v West Indies 1975-76.
Yallop, GN won 5 tosses in a 6 Test series v England 1978-79.

CAPTAINS LOSING ALL TOSSES IN A SERIES

Captain	Tests	Opponent	Venue	Series
Murdoch, WL	4	England	Australia	1881-82
Darling, J	5	England	England	1905
Bradman, DG	4	England	England	1938
Johnson, IW (2)	3	India	India	1956-57
Lindwall, RR (1)				
Lawry, WM	4	South Africa	South Africa	1969-70

THE PLAYERS

OVERALL TEST MATCH REPRESENTATION
(Minimum Fifty Tests)

Player	Tests	Opponent							State					
		ENG	IND	NZ	PAK	SA	SL	WI	NSW	QLD	SA	TAS	VIC	WA
Marsh, RW	97	43	3	14	20	–	–	17	–	–	–	–	–	97
Border, AR	89	29	15	12	16	–	1	16	21	68	–	–	–	–
Chappell, GS	88	36	3	14	17	–	1	17	–	70	18	–	–	–
Harvey, RN	79	37	14	4	10	14	–	14	27	–	–	–	52	–
Chappell, IM	76	31	9	6	4	9	–	17	–	–	76	–	–	–
Walters, KD	75	37	10	11	4	4	–	9	75	–	–	–	–	–
Lillee, DK	70	29	3	8	17	–	1	12	–	–	–	–	–	70
Hughes, KJ	69	22	11	5	16	–	–	15	–	–	–	–	–	69
Lawry, WM	68	30	12	–	2	14	–	10	–	–	–	–	68	–
Redpath, IR	67	24	10	3	4	10	–	16	–	–	–	–	67	–
Benaud, R	63	27	8	–	4	13	–	11	63	–	–	–	–	–
Simpson, RB	62	19	11	–	2	15	–	15	46	–	–	–	–	16
Lindwall, RR	61	29	10	1	3	8	–	10	47	14	–	–	–	–
McKenzie, GD	61	26	10	–	2	13	–	10	–	–	–	–	–	61
Gregory, SE	58	52	–	–	–	6	–	–	58	–	–	–	–	–
Miller, KR	55	29	5	1	1	9	–	10	49	–	–	–	6	–
Oldfield, WAS	54	38	–	–	–	11	–	5	54	–	–	–	–	–
Wood, GM	53	19	6	6	7	–	1	14	–	–	–	–	–	53
Bradman, DG	52	37	5	–	–	5	–	5	28	–	24	–	–	–
Thomson, JR	51	21	5	3	8	–	–	14	1	50	–	–	–	–
Grout, ATW	51	22	5	–	4	10	–	10	–	51	–	–	–	–
Armstrong, WW	50	42	–	–	–	8	–	–	–	–	–	–	50	–

Ian, Greg and Trevor Chappell, with their parents.

THE CHAPPELLS

In 1899 Reginald Erskine Foster and Wilfrid Lionel Foster, two of the six brothers who played for Worcestershire and caused it to be renamed "Fostershire", both scored centuries in each innings of a match against Hampshire at Worcester.

This remained one of those unlikely records cricket throws up only occasionally, and perhaps the one least likely to be challenged, until Australia met New Zealand at the Basin Reserve, Wellington, from 1 to 6 March 1974.

The New Zealanders entered the match confident of doing well, after a hard tour of Australia earlier in the summer in which they lost five of their first-class matches, including the three Tests. They had gone to Australia lacking match practice and with an unbalanced attack, but now that the brilliant Glenn Turner had cast aside injury problems they looked a fitter, tougher side.

New Zealand's optimism seemed justified when they had Keith Stackpole out for 10 and Ian Redpath for 19, which brought the Chappell brothers, Ian and Greg, together with the score on 55. A howling wind helped the pace-bowlers, but from the first balls they faced neither Chappell was in difficulty.

They were not separated until Australia's score reached 319, when Ian Chappell was out to a wonderful running catch by wicket-keeper Ken Wadsworth. Ian had taken four hours to reach his century, which took 207 balls, and was out for 145. Greg made his century in two hours, from 160 balls, and was left unbeaten at stumps. The next morning Greg took his score on to 247 not out in just under six hours, with one six and 30 fours. Between them the Chappells accounted for 392 of Australia's 6 for 511 declared.

New Zealand made a spirited reply. Glenn Turner and John Morrison put on 108 for the second wicket, and in a third day interrupted by rain Bevan Congdon (132) and Brian Hastings (101) produced a New Zealand record stand of 229 for the fourth wicket. Australia took the last six wickets for 86 to have New Zealand out for 484 and lead by 27 runs. They increased this to 113 by taking Australia's second innings score to 1 for 86 by stumps.

On a pitch that remained brimful of runs Australia made no effort to win on the last day. Redpath and Ian Chappell added 141 for the second wicket to extend Australia's lead to 240 at lunch, but after the interval the Australians kept batting. Ian Chappell reached his second century of the match in just over three hours. This time he batted for only 44 minutes with his brother Greg, but during that period they put on 86.

Ian made 121, Greg 133 and between them they contributed 646, for three times out, of the match total of 1455 runs, a New Zealand Test record. Australia was on 8 for 460 before play was abandoned half an hour before the scheduled time for stumps.

In matching the Foster brothers' 75-year-old record the Chappell brothers had produced champagne batting, timing the ball superbly, placing the ball between fieldsmen with consummate ease. Hooks, pulls, all the drives, and some slashing square cuts flowed, and they did not make a single error of judgement in their running between wickets.

Ian grafted for his runs and took longer over them, but even when he was beaten by a fine delivery he faced up to the next with the matchless temperament that allows great players to forget their mistakes and concentrate on the next delivery. Greg was more elegant, almost imperious in his stroke play, with his leg-side shots in a class of their own.

Not only did the Chappell brothers match the Fosters, they went one better. They scored their four centuries in a Test match.

Strangely, they could not again produce the same form, and as the New Zealand tour progressed their batting deteriorated. Only a week after the Chappells' epic feats at Wellington, New Zealand defeated Australia for the first time in Tests (after six attempts) at Christchurch. This time Turner made a century in each innings (101 and 110 not out) and the Chappells contributed only 52 runs in their four innings.

Australia levelled the series at one win apiece in the Third Test at Auckland, with Doug Walters (104) and Redpath (150 not out) hitting centuries.

Greg Chappell hits a four.

CONSECUTIVE TESTS

Player	Tests	Venue	Series	Venue	Series
Border, AR	86	Melbourne	1978-79 to	Sydney	1986-87
Chappell, IM	72	Adelaide	1965-66 to	Melbourne	1975-76
Harvey, RN	66	Leeds	1948 to	Sydney	1960-61
Marsh, RW	53	Brisbane2	1970-71 to	The Oval	1977
Hughes, KJ	53	Brisbane2	1978-79 to	Sydney	1982-83
Chappell, GS	52	Perth	1970-71 to	The Oval	1977
Trumper, VT	48	Nottingham	1899 to	Sydney	1911-12
Lawry, WM	47	Birmingham	1961 to	Birmingham	1968
Benaud, R	44	Leeds	1953 to	Birmingham	1961
Noble, MA	42	Melbourne	1897-98 to	The Oval	1909
Gregory, SE	39	Adelaide	1891-92 to	Sydney	1903-04
McCabe, SJ	39	Nottingham	1930 to	The Oval	1938
Marsh, RW	39	Brisbane2	1979-80 to	Sydney	1982-83
Hill, C	38	Sydney	1901-02 to	Sydney	1911-12
Kelly, JJ	36	Lord's	1896 to	The Oval	1905
Woodfull, WM	35	Nottingham	1926 to	The Oval	1934
Miller, KR	35	Wellington	1945-46 to	Adelaide	1952-53
Simpson, RB	35	Brisbane2	1960-61 to	Port-of-Spain	1964-65
Redpath, IR	34	Manchester	1968 to	Port-of-Spain	1972-73
Oldfield, WAS	33	Sydney	1924-25 to	Adelaide	1932-33
Walters, KD	32	Sydney	1972-73 to	The Oval	1977
Lillee, DK	32	Brisbane2	1979-80 to	Perth	1982-83
O'Neill, NC	29	Brisbane2	1958-59 to	Brisbane2	1963-64
Johnston, WA	28	Melbourne	1947-48 to	Lord's	1953
Bradman, DG	27	Melbourne	1928-29 to	The Oval	1934
O'Reilly, WJ	27	Adelaide	1931-32 to	Wellington	1945-46
McDonald, CC	27	Calcutta	1956-57 to	Leeds	1961
Stackpole, KR	26	Brisbane2	1968-69 to	The Oval	1972
Wood, GM	26	Lord's	1980 to	Perth	1982-83
Armstrong, WW	25	Nottingham	1905 to	Sydney	1911-12
McKenzie, GD	25	Brisbane2	1962-63 to	Port-of-Spain	1964-65
Trott, GHS	24	Lord's	1888 to	Sydney	1897-98
Gregory, JM	24	Sydney	1920-21 to	Brisbane1	1928-29
Walters, KD	23	Sydney	1968-69 to	Leeds	1972
Duff, RA	22	Melbourne	1901-02 to	The Oval	1905
Darling, J	21	Sydney	1894-95 to	Adelaide	1901-02
Bardsley, W	21	Manchester	1912 to	Melbourne	1924-25

Player	Tests	Venue	Series	Venue	Series
Davidson, AK	21	Johannesburg3	1957-58 to Sydney		1960-61
Booth, BC	21	Sydney	1963-64 to Sydney		1965-66
Lawry, WM	21	The Oval	1968 to Adelaide		1970-71
Ranford, VS	20	Sydney	1907-08 to Sydney		1911-12
Carter, H	20	Sydney	1907-08 to Sydney		1911-12

PLAYERS WHO HAVE REPRESENTED TWO COUNTRIES

Player	Total tests	Country	Tests	Series	Country	Tests	Series
Ferris, JJ	9	Australia	8	1886-87 to 1890	England	1	1891-92
Midwinter, WE	12	Australia	8	1876-77 to 1886-87	England	4	1881-82
Murdoch, WL	19	Australia	18	1876-77 to 1890	England	1	1891-92
Trott, AE	5	Australia	3	1894-95	England	2	1898-99
Woods, SMJ	6	Australia	3	1888	England	3	1895-96

RELATED TEST PLAYERS

Players	Relationship
Gregory, DW & Gregory, SE	Father & son
Chappel, IM, Chappell, GS & Chappell, TM	Brothers
Archer, KA & Archer, RG	Brothers
Bannerman, AC & Bannerman, C	Brothers
Benaud, R & Benaud, J	Brothers
Giffen, G & Giffen, WF	Brothers
Gregory, DW & Gregory, EJ	Brothers
Harvey, MR & Harvey, RN	Brothers
McLeod, CE & McLeod, RW	Brothers
Trott, AE & Trott, GHS	Brothers
Trumble, H & Trumble, JW	Brothers
Richardson, VY & Chappell, IM, Chappell, GS & Chappell, TM	Grandfather & grandsons
Cooper, WH & Sheahan, AP	Great-grandfather & great-grandson
Park, Dr RL & Johnson, IW	Father-in-law & son-in-law
Simpson, RB & Hilditch, AMJ	Father-in-law & son-in-law

Syd Gregory at the crease.

THE GREGORYS

Since Australian cricket began in Sydney's Hyde Park in 1803, a remarkable collection of families has supported the game: clans like the Hills in South Australia, who produced six first-class players; the Bryants in Western Australia, who had three brothers in the same first-class match; the Harveys, who were represented by three brothers in a Shield match for Victoria; and the Chappells, who produced three brothers who achieved Test status.

Family traditions have been one of the continuing strengths of Australian cricket. In many country districts the names of uncles and cousins and even a few grandfathers are sprinkled liberally through scorecards. The Davidsons from the Gosford district north of Sydney fielded an entire team, and in the mid-1980s Mark and Steve Waugh became the first twins to play for their State.

The family that began all this were the Gregorys: four were Test players, two were Australian cricket captains, and seven played for New South Wales. The Gregorys also excelled at rugby, athletics, swimming, and built up admirable records for gallantry on war service.

The Gregory family stems from a man and wife who came to Australia in the *Broxbourneberry* in July 1814. The family comprised Edward William Gregory, who came free, his sons, Charles, aged 20, Edward, aged 23, and George, aged 16, and his wife Henrietta, who was a convict. Henrietta died in August 1819, aged 45, and her husband returned to England, leaving his sons in the care of Sydney's Male Orphanage. Edward was apprenticed as a shoemaker, Charles as a tailor, and George was discharged to a Mr Bogg, of Sydney.

Thus the riddle of the Gregorys' early history: why did a father who had accompanied his family to Australia and endured all the hardships involved desert them so callously by returning to England? If only he had known what honours his offspring would win!

One son, Edward, became a schoolteacher and played cricket in Hyde Park. He married Mary Ann Smith, the daughter of a politician and one-time Mayor of Melbourne, and they had 13 children, including seven sons, five of whom played for New South Wales. Twenty of E.W. Gregory's grandsons represented New South Wales at rugby, sailing, athletics or cricket.

Charles Gregory, David Gregory and Edward Gregory.

Two of E.W. Gregory's cricketing sons, Ned and Dave, graduated from the New South Wales team to Test cricket. A third wrote cricket articles for the *Sydney Morning Herald* as "Short Slip", and as Arthur Gregory played rugby for New South Wales. Ned's son, Syd, played for Australia in 58 Tests. Another of Ned's sons, Charles William, scored a triple century for New South Wales against Queensland.

Ned became the groundsman at Sydney Cricket Ground, where he lived in a brick cottage. When Phil Sheridan, who turned the SCG into a major ground, asked Ned to produce a new scoreboard, Ned did so within a fortnight. His design provided information on a scale unknown overseas and served until the electronic era.

Both Edward James and David William Gregory played in the first of all Test matches at Melbourne in March 1877, and Dave had the honour of being elected by his team-mates to captain the side. Dave also won an election among the players to captain the first Australian team on a tour of England in 1878. Dave was regarded as quite "a character". He fathered 16 children, 13 by his first wife, and three by his second wife. He was Paymaster to the New South Wales Treasury, and after Federation he rejected a knighthood and a job in Canberra running the new Federal Treasury.

Sydney Edward Gregory, son of Ned, was born to play Test cricket in a cottage at Sydney Cricket Ground. He played in 58 Tests, which was the Australian record until Neil Harvey extended it to 79 Tests in 1963. Syd was recalled to the Australian side at the age of 42 to lead the side on a 37-match tour of England in 1912.

Jack Morrison Gregory, son of Charles Smith Gregory who played for New South Wales in the early 1870s, was a nephew of Dave Gregory and a cousin of Sydney Gregory. He had not progressed beyond North Sydney third grade when he joined the First AIF, but he returned as the star fast bowler for the First Services XI and an automatic Test selection from the 1920-21 to the 1928-29 seasons. Jack still holds the record for the fastest Test century (70 minutes), gained in 1921 when Australia played South Africa. He scored more than 5000 runs (5661 at 36.52) and took over 500 wickets (504 at 20.99) in first-class cricket.

YOUNGEST TEST PLAYERS ON DEBUT

Player	Date of birth	Test Debut	Opponent	Venue	Age Years	Days
Craig, ID	12 Jun 1935	6 Feb 1953	South Africa	Sydney	17	239
Garrett, TW	26 Jly 1858	15 Mar 1877	England	Melbourne	18	232
Hill, C	18 Mar 1877	22 Jun 1896	England	Lord's	19	96
Hazlitt, GR	4 Sep 1888	13 Dec 1907	England	Sydney	19	100
Archer, RG	25 Oct 1933	6 Feb 1953	South Africa	Melbourne	19	104
Harvey, RN	8 Oct 1928	23 Jan 1948	India	Adelaide	19	107
Jackson, A	5 Sep 1909	1 Feb 1929	England	Adelaide	19	149
Cottam, JT	5 Sep 1867	25 Feb 1887	England	Sydney	19	173
Ferris, JJ	21 May 1867	28 Jan 1887	England	Sydney	19	248
McDermott, CJ	14 Apr 1965	22 Dec 1984	West Indies	Melbourne	19	253
McCabe, SJ	16 Jly 1910	13 Jun 1930	England	Nottingham	19	332
Walters, KD	21 Dec 1945	10 Dec 1965	England	Brisbane2	19	354
McKenzie, GD	24 Jun 1941	22 Jun 1961	England	Lord's	19	363
Joslin, LJ	13 Dec 1947	26 Jan 1968	India	Sydney	20	44
Hole, GB	6 Jan 1931	23 Feb 1951	England	Sydney	20	48
Cotter, A	3 Dec 1883	26 Jan 1904	England	Sydney	20	54
Bradman, DG	27 Aug 1908	30 Nov 1928	England	Brisbane2	20	96
Gregory, SE	14 Apr 1870	21 Jly 1890	England	Lord's	20	98
Bromley, EH	2 Sep 1912	10 Feb 1933	England	Brisbane2	20	161
Davis, IC	25 Jun 1953	29 Dec 1973	New Zealand	Melbourne	20	187

OLDEST TEST PLAYERS ON DEBUT

Player	Date of birth	Test Debut	Opponent	Venue	Age Years	Days
Blackie, DD	5 Apr 1882	14 Dec 1928	England	Sydney	46	254
Ironmonger, H	7 Apr 1882	30 Nov 1928	England	Brisbane1	46	238
Thomson, NC	21 Apr 1838	15 Mar 1877	England	Melbourne	38	328
Holland, RG	19 Oct 1946	23 Nov 1984	West Indies	Brisbane2	38	35
Gregory, EJ	29 May 1839	15 Mar 1877	England	Melbourne	37	290
Love, HSB	10 Aug 1895	10 Feb 1933	England	Brisbane2	37	184
Harry, J	1 Aug 1857	11 Jan 1895	England	Adelaide	37	163
Oxenham, RE	28 Jly 1891	29 Dec 1928	England	Melbourne	37	155
Richardson, AJ	24 Jly 1888	19 Dec 1924	England	Sydney	36	149
Iverson, JB	27 Jly 1915	1 Dec 1950	England	Brisbane2	35	127

Player	Date of birth	Test Debut	Opponent	Venue	Age Years	Days
Eastwood, KH	23 Nov 1935	12 Feb 1971	England	Sydney	35	81
Wilson, JW	20 Aug 1921	26 Oct 1956	India	Bombay2	35	68
Hartkopf, AEV	28 Dec 1889	1 Jan 1925	England	Melbourne	35	4
Mailey, AA	3 Jan 1886	17 Dec 1920	England	Sydney	34	349
McAlister, PA	11 Jly 1869	26 Jan 1904	England	Sydney	34	199
Carkeek, W	17 Oct 1878	27 May 1912	England	Manchester	33	223
Noblet, G	14 Sep 1916	3 Mar 1950	South Africa	Pt Elizabeth	33	170
Grimmett, CV	25 Dec 1891	27 Feb 1925	England	Sydney	33	64
Cooper, BB	15 Mar 1844	15 Mar 1877	England	Melbourne	33	0
Kelly, TJD	3 May 1844	31 Mar 1877	England	Melbourne	32	332

OLDEST TEST PLAYERS
(On last day of final test)

Player	Date of birth	Test Debut	Opponent	Venue	Age Years	Days
Ironmonger, H	7 Apr 1882	28 Feb 1933	England	Sydney	50	327
Blackie, DD	5 Apr 1882	8 Feb 1929	England	Adelaide	46	309
Grimmett, CV	25 Dec 1891	28 Feb 1936	South Africa	Durban2	44	66
Carter, H	15 Mar 1878	29 Nov 1921	South Africa	Cape Town	43	259
Bardsley, W	7 Dec 1882	18 Aug 1926	England	The Oval	43	255
Oldfield, WAS	8 Sep 1894	3 Mar 1937	England	Melbourne	42	176
Gregory, SE	14 Apr 1870	22 Aug 1912	England	The Oval	42	131
Simpson, RB	3 Feb 1936	3 May 1978	West Indies	Kingston	42	90
Armstrong, WW	22 May 1879	16 Aug 1921	England	The Oval	42	86
Richardson, VY	7 Sep 1894	3 Mar 1936	South Africa	Durban2	41	178
Mailey, AA	3 Jan 1886	18 Aug 1926	England	The Oval	40	227
Blackham, JM	11 May 1854	20 Dec 1894	England	Sydney	40	223
Oxenham, RE	28 Jly 1891	3 Dec 1931	South Africa	Brisbane2	40	128
Macartney, CG	27 Jun 1886	18 Aug 1926	England	The Oval	40	52
McAlister, PA	11 Jly 1869	3 Jly 1909	England	Leeds	39	357
Bradman, DG	27 Aug 1908	18 Aug 1948	England	The Oval	39	357
Hassett, AL	28 Aug 1913	19 Aug 1953	England	The Oval	39	356
Laver, F	7 Dec 1869	11 Aug 1909	England	The Oval	39	247
Kelleway, C	25 Apr 1889	5 Dec 1928	England	Brisbane1	39	225
Ryder, J	8 Aug 1889	16 Mar 1929	England	Melbourne	39	220

LONGEST TEST CAREER

Player	Series	Test Debut Opponent	Venue	Series	Final Test Opponent	Venue	Years	Days
Gregory, SE	1890	ENG	Lord's	1912	ENG	The Oval	22	32
Simpson, RB	1957-58	SA	Johannesburg3	1977-78	WI	Kingston	20	131
Bradman, DG	1928-29	ENG	Brisbane1	1948	ENG	The Oval	19	262
Armstrong, WW	1901-02	ENG	Melbourne	1921	ENG	The Oval	19	227
Macartney, CG	1907-08	ENG	Sydney	1926	ENG	The Oval	18	248
Kelleway, C	1910-11	SA	Sydney	1928-29	ENG	Brisbane1	17	362
Blackham, JM	1876-77	ENG	Melbourne	1894-95	ENG	Sydney	17	280
Bardsley, W	1909	ENG	Birmingham	1926	ENG	The Oval	17	83
Oldfield, WAS	1920-21	ENG	Sydney	1936-37	ENG	Melbourne	16	76
Hill, C	1896	ENG	Lord's	1911-12	ENG	Sydney	15	253
Hassett, AL	1938	ENG	Nottingham	1953	ENG	The Oval	15	70
Chappell, IM	1964-65	PAK	Melbourne	1979-80	ENG	Melbourne	15	64
Walters, KD	1965-66	ENG	Brisbane2	1980-81	IND	Melbourne	15	63
Harvey, RN	1947-48	ENG	Adelaide	1962-63	ENG	Sydney	15	29
Bannerman, AC	1878-79	ENG	Melbourne	1893	ENG	Manchester	14	234
Worrall, J	1884-85	ENG	Melbourne	1899	ENG	The Oval	14	227
Giffen, G	1881-82	ENG	Melbourne	1896	ENG	The Oval	14	225
Brown, WA	1934	ENG	Nottingham	1948	ENG	Lord's	14	21
Carter, H	1907-08	ENG	Sydney	1920-21	SA	Cape Town	13	351
Lindwall, RR	1945-46	NZ	Wellington	1959-60	IND	Calcutta	13	305

LONGEST BREAK BETWEEN TESTS

Player	Test before break			Test after break			Years	Days
	Series	Opponent	Venue	Series	Opponent	Venue		
Simpson, RB	1967-68	IND	Sydney	1977-78	IND	Brisbane2	9	313
Carter, H	1911-12	ENG	Sydney	1920-21	ENG	Melbourne	8	356
Armstrong, WW	1911-12	ENG	Sydney	1920-21	ENG	Sydney	8	300
Kelleway, C	1912	ENG	The Oval	1920-21	ENG	Sydney	8	122
Bardsley, W	1912	ENG	The Oval	1920-21	ENG	Sydney	8	122
Macartney, CG	1912	ENG	The Oval	1920-21	ENG	Sydney	8	122
Rixon, SJ	1977-78	WI	Kingston	1984-85	WI	Adelaide	6	225
Jarvis, AH	1888	ENG	The Oval	1894-95	ENG	Melbourne	6	139
Worrall, J	1888	ENG	Manchester	1894-95	ENG	Adelaide	6	135
Midwinter, WE	1876-77	ENG	Melbourne	1882-83	ENG	Sydney	5	324
Eady, CJ	1896	ENG	Lord's	1901-02	ENG	Melbourne	5	251
Hassett, AL	1938	ENG	The Oval	1945-46	NZ	Wellington	5	223
O'Reilly, WJ	1938	ENG	The Oval	1945-46	NZ	Wellington	5	223
Barnes, SG	1938	ENG	The Oval	1945-46	NZ	Wellington	5	223
Brown, WA	1938	ENG	The Oval	1945-46	NZ	Wellington	5	223
Murdoch, WL	1884-85	ENG	Adelaide	1890	ENG	Lord's	5	222

AUSTRALIAN DEBUTANTS

Player	Opponent	Venue	Series	Player No.	Place of birth NSW	QLD	SA	TAS	VIC	WA	OVERSEAS
Bannerman, AC	England	Melbourne	1876-77	1	–	–	–	–	–	–	1
Blackham, JM	England	Melbourne	1876-77	2	–	–	–	–	1	–	–
Cooper, BB	England	Melbourne	1876-77	3	–	–	–	–	–	–	2
Garrett, TW	England	Melbourne	1876-77	4	1	–	–	–	–	–	–
Gregory, DW	England	Melbourne	1876-77	5	2	–	–	–	–	–	–
Gregory, EJ	England	Melbourne	1876-77	6	3	–	–	–	–	–	–
Hodges, JH	England	Melbourne	1876-77	7	–	–	–	–	2	–	–
Horan, TP	England	Melbourne	1876-77	8	–	–	–	–	–	–	3
Kendall, T	England	Melbourne	1876-77	9	–	–	–	–	–	–	4
Midwinter, WE	England	Melbourne	1876-77	10	–	–	–	–	–	–	5
Thompson, N	England	Melbourne	1876-77	11	–	–	–	–	–	–	6
Kelly, TJD	England	Melbourne	1876-77	12	–	–	–	–	–	–	7
Murdoch, WL	England	Melbourne	1876-77	13	–	–	–	–	3	–	–
Spofforth, FR	England	Melbourne	1876-77	14	4	–	–	–	–	–	–
Allan, FE	England	Melbourne	1878-79	15	5	–	–	–	–	–	–
Bannerman, AC	England	Melbourne	1878-79	16	6	–	–	–	–	–	–
Boyle, HF	England	Melbourne	1878-79	17	7	–	–	–	–	–	–
Alexander, G	England	The Oval	1880	18	–	–	–	–	4	–	–
Bonnor, GJ	England	The Oval	1880	19	8	–	–	–	–	–	–
Groube, TU	England	The Oval	1880	20	–	–	–	–	–	–	8

Name	Country	Venue	Year							
McDonnell, PS	England	The Oval	1880	21	–	–	–	–	–	9
Moule, WH	England	The Oval	1880	22	–	–	–	–	5	–
Palmer, GE	England	The Oval	1880	23	9	–	–	–	–	–
Slight, J	England	The Oval	1880	24	–	–	–	–	6	–
Cooper, WH	England	Melbourne	1881-82	25	–	–	–	–	–	10
Evans, E	England	Melbourne	1881-82	26	10	–	–	–	–	–
Giffen, G	England	Melbourne	1881-82	27	–	1	–	–	–	–
Massie, HH	England	Melbourne	1881-82	28	–	–	–	–	7	–
Couthard, G	England	Sydney	1881-82	29	11	–	–	–	–	–
Jones, SP	England	Sydney	1881-82	30	–	–	–	–	8	–
Scott, HJH	England	Manchester	1884	31	–	–	–	–	9	–
Bruce, W	England	Melbourne	1884-85	32	–	–	–	–	10	–
Jarvis, AH	England	Melbourne	1884-85	33	–	2	–	–	–	–
Marr, AP	England	Melbourne	1884-85	34	12	–	–	–	–	–
Morris, S	England	Melbourne	1884-85	35	–	–	1	–	–	–
Musgrove, H	England	Melbourne	1884-85	36	–	–	–	–	–	11
Pope, RJ	England	Melbourne	1884-85	37	13	–	–	–	–	–
Robinson, WR	England	Melbourne	1884-85	38	14	–	–	–	–	–
Trumble, JW	England	Melbourne	1884-85	39	–	–	–	–	11	–
Worrall, J	England	Melbourne	1884-85	40	–	–	–	–	12	–
McShane, PG	England	Melbourne	1884-85	41	–	–	–	–	13	–
Walters, FH	England	Melbourne	1884-85	42	–	–	–	–	14	–
McIlwraith, J	England	The Oval	1886	43	–	–	–	–	15	–

Player	Opponent	Venue	Series	Player No.	Place of birth NSW	QLD	SA	TAS	VIC	WA	OVERSEAS
Ferris, JJ	England	Sydney	1886-87	44	15	-	-	-	-	-	-
Moses, H	England	Sydney	1886-87	45	16	-	-	-	-	-	-
Turner, CTB	England	Sydney	1886-87	46	17	-	-	-	-	-	-
Allen, RC	England	Sydney	1886-87	47	18	-	-	-	-	-	-
Burton, FJ	England	Sydney	1886-87	48	19	-	-	-	-	-	-
Cottam, JT	England	Sydney	1886-87	49	-	-	-	-	-	1	-
Giffen, WF	England	Sydney	1886-87	50	-	-	3	-	-	-	-
Lyons, JJ	England	Sydney	1886-87	51	-	-	4	-	-	-	-
Edwards, JD	England	Lord's	1888	52	-	-	-	-	16	-	-
Trott, GHS	England	Lord's	1888	53	-	-	-	-	17	-	-
Woods, SMJ	England	Lord's	1888	54	20	-	-	-	-	-	-
Barrett, JE	England	Lord's	1890	55	-	-	-	-	18	-	-
Burn, EJK	England	Lord's	1890	56	-	-	-	2	-	-	-
Charlton, PC	England	Lord's	1890	57	21	-	-	-	-	-	-
Gregory, PC	England	Lord's	1890	58	22	-	-	-	-	-	-
Trumble, H	England	Lord's	1890	59	-	-	-	-	19	-	-
Callaway, ST	England	Melbourne	1891-92	60	23	-	-	-	-	-	-
Donnan, H	England	Melbourne	1891-92	61	24	-	-	-	-	-	-
McLeod, RW	England	Melbourne	1891-92	62	-	-	-	-	20	-	-
Graham, H	England	Lord's	1893	63	-	-	-	-	21	-	-
Darling, J	England	Sydney	1894-95	64	-	-	5	-	-	-	-
Iredale, FA	England	Sydney	1894-95	65	25	-	-	-	-	-	-

Player	Country	Venue	Season	No.					
Jones, E	England	Sydney	1894-95	66	–	6	–	–	–
McLeod, CE	England	Sydney	1894-95	67	–	7	–	22	–
Reedman, JC	England	Sydney	1894-95	68	–	–	–	–	–
Coningham, A	England	Sydney	1894-95	69	–	–	–	23	–
Harry, J	England	Adelaide	1894-95	70	–	–	–	24	–
Trott, AE	England	Adelaide	1894-95	71	–	–	–	25	–
McKibbin, TR	England	Melbourne	1894-95	72	26	–	–	–	–
Eady, CJ	England	Lord's	1896	73	–	–	3	–	–
Hill, C	England	Lord's	1896	74	–	8	–	–	–
Kelly, JJ	England	Lord's	1896	75	–	–	–	26	–
Noble, MA	England	Melbourne	1897-98	76	27	–	–	–	–
Howell, WP	England	Adelaide	1897-98	77	28	–	–	–	–
Laver, F	England	Nottingham	1899	78	–	–	–	27	–
Trumper, VT	England	Nottingham	1899	79	29	–	–	–	–
Armstrong, WW	England	Melbourne	1901-02	80	–	–	–	28	–
Duff, RA	England	Melbourne	1901-02	81	30	–	–	–	–
Hopkins, AJY	England	Sydney	1901-02	82	31	–	–	–	–
Saunders, JV	England	Sydney	1901-02	83	–	–	–	29	–
Travers, JPF	England	Melbourne	1901-02	84	–	9	–	–	–
Cotter, A	England	Sydney	1903-04	85	32	–	–	–	–
McAlister, PA	England	Sydney	1903-04	86	–	–	–	30	–
Gehrs, DRA	England	Melbourne	1903-04	87	–	10	–	–	–
Carter, H	England	Sydney	1907-08	88	–	–	–	–	12

Player	Opponent	Venue	Series	Player No.	Place of birth NSW	QLD	SA	TAS	VIC	WA	OVERSEAS
Hazlitt, GR	England	Sydney	1907-08	89	33	-	-	-	-	-	-
Macartney, CG	England	Sydney	1907-08	90	34	-	-	-	-	-	-
Ransford, VS	England	Sydney	1907-08	91	-	-	-	-	31	-	-
Hartigan, RJ	England	Adelaide	1907-08	92	35	-	-	-	-	-	-
O'Connor, JDA	England	Adelaide	1907-08	93	36	-	-	-	-	-	-
Bardsley, W	England	Birmingham	1909	94	37	-	-	-	-	-	-
Whitty, WJ	England	Birmingham	1909	95	38	-	-	-	-	-	-
Kelleway, C	South Africa	Sydney	1910-11	96	39	-	-	-	-	-	-
Hordern, HV	South Africa	Melbourne	1910-11	97	40	-	-	-	-	-	-
Minnett, RB	England	Sydney	1911-12	98	41	-	-	-	-	-	-
Matthews, TJ	England	Adelaide	1911-12	99	-	-	-	-	32	-	-
McLaren, JW	England	Sydney	1911-12	100	-	1	-	-	-	-	-
Carkeek, W	South Africa	Manchester	1912	101	-	-	-	-	33	-	-
Emery, SH	South Africa	Manchester	1912	102	42	-	-	-	-	-	-
Jennings, CB	South Africa	Manchester	1912	103	-	-	-	-	34	-	-
Smith, DBM	England	Lord's	1912	104	-	-	-	-	35	-	-
Mayne, ER	South Africa	Lord's	1912	105	-	-	11	-	-	-	-
Collins, HL	England	Sydney	1920-21	106	43	-	-	-	-	-	-
Gregory, JM	England	Sydney	1920-21	107	44	-	-	-	-	-	-
Mailey, AA	England	Sydney	1920-21	108	45	-	-	-	-	-	-
Oldfield, WAS	England	Sydney	1920-21	109	46	-	-	-	-	-	-
Pellew, CE	England	Sydney	1920-21	110	-	-	12	-	-	-	-

Name				No.							
Ryder, J	England	Sydney	1920-21	111	—	—	—	—	36	—	—
Taylor, JM	England	Sydney	1920-21	112	47	—	—	—	—	—	—
Park, RL	England	Melbourne	1920-21	113	—	—	—	—	37	—	—
McDonald, EA	England	Adelaide	1920-21	114	—	—	—	4	—	—	—
Andrews, TJE	England	Nottingham	1921	115	48	—	—	—	—	—	—
Hendry, HSTL	England	Nottingham	1921	116	49	—	—	—	—	—	—
Ponsford, WH	England	Sydney	1924-25	117	—	—	—	—	38	—	—
Richardson, AJ	England	Sydney	1924-25	118	—	—	13	—	—	—	—
Richardson, VY	England	Sydney	1924-25	119	—	—	14	—	—	—	—
Hartkopf, AEV	England	Melbourne	1924-25	120	—	—	—	—	39	—	—
Grimmett, CV	England	Sydney	1924-25	121	—	—	—	—	—	—	13
Kippax, AF	England	Sydney	1924-25	122	50	—	—	—	—	—	—
Woodfull, WM	England	Nottingham	1926	123	—	—	—	—	40	—	—
Bradman, DG	England	Brisbane1	1928-29	124	51	—	—	—	—	—	—
Ironmonger, H	England	Brisbane1	1928-29	125	—	2	—	—	—	—	—
Blackie, DD	England	Sydney	1928-29	126	—	—	—	—	41	—	—
Nothling, OE	England	Sydney	1928-29	127	—	3	—	—	—	—	—
A'Beckett, EL	England	Melbourne	1928-29	128	—	—	—	—	42	—	—
Oxenham, RK	England	Melbourne	1928-29	129	—	4	—	—	—	—	—
Jackson, A	England	Adelaide	1928-29	130	—	—	—	—	—	—	14
Fairfax, AG	England	Melbourne	1928-29	131	52	—	—	—	—	—	—
Hornibrook, PM	England	Melbourne	1928-29	132	—	5	—	—	—	—	—
Wall, TW	England	Melbourne	1928-29	133	—	—	15	—	—	—	—

Player	Opponent	Venue	Series	Player No.	Place of birth						
					NSW	QLD	SA	TAS	VIC	WA	OVERSEAS
McCabe, SJ	England	Nottingham	1930	134	53	–	–	–	–	–	–
Hurwood, A	West Indies	Adelaide	1930-31	135	–	6	–	–	–	–	–
Rigg, KE	West Indies	Sydney	1930-31	136	–	–	–	–	43	–	–
Nitschke, HC	South Africa	Brisbane2	1931-32	137	–	–	16	–	–	–	–
Lee, PK	South Africa	Sydney	1931-32	138	–	7	–	–	–	–	–
Hunt, WA	South Africa	Adelaide	1931-32	139	54	–	–	–	–	–	–
O'Reilly, WJ	South Africa	Adelaide	1931-32	140	55	–	–	–	–	–	–
Thurlow, HM	South Africa	Adelaide	1931-32	141	–	8	–	–	–	–	–
Fingleton, JHW	South Africa	Melbourne	1931-32	142	56	–	–	–	–	–	–
Nash, LJ	South Africa	Melbourne	1931-32	143	–	–	–	–	44	–	–
Nagel, LE	England	Sydney	1932-33	144	–	–	–	–	45	–	–
O'Brien, LPJ	England	Melbourne	1932-33	145	–	–	–	–	46	–	–
Bromley, EH	England	Brisbane2	1932-33	146	–	–	–	–	–	2	–
Darling, LS	England	Brisbane2	1932-33	147	–	–	–	–	47	–	–
Love, HSB	England	Brisbane2	1932-33	148	57	–	–	–	–	–	–
Alexander, H	England	Sydney	1932-33	149	–	–	–	–	48	–	–
Brown, WA	England	Nottingham	1934	150	–	9	–	–	–	–	–
Chipperfield, AG	England	Nottingham	1934	151	58	–	–	–	–	–	–
Ebeling, HI	England	The Oval	1934	152	–	–	–	–	49	–	–
Fleetwood-Smith, LO	South Africa	Durban2	1935-36	153	–	–	–	–	50	–	–
McCormick, EL	South Africa	Durban2	1935-36	154	–	–	–	–	51	–	–
Badcock, CL	England	Brisbane2	1936-37	155	–	–	–	5	–	–	–

Name	Country	Venue	No.	Year								
Robinson, RH	England	Brisbane2	156	1936-37	59	–	–	–	–	–	–	–
Sievers, MW	England	Brisbane2	157	1936-37	–	–	–	–	52	–	–	–
Ward, FA	England	Brisbane2	158	1936-37	60	–	–	–	–	–	–	–
Gregory, RG	England	Adelaide	159	1936-37	–	–	–	–	53	–	–	–
Barnett, BA	England	Nottingham	160	1938	–	–	–	–	54	–	–	–
Hassett, AL	England	Nottingham	161	1938	–	–	–	–	55	–	–	–
Waite, MG	England	Leeds	162	1938	–	–	17	–	–	–	–	–
Barnes, SG	England	The Oval	163	1938	–	10	–	–	–	–	–	–
Johnson, IW	New Zealand	Wellington	164	1945-46	–	–	–	–	56	–	–	–
Lindwall, RR	New Zealand	Wellington	165	1945-46	61	–	–	–	–	–	–	–
McCool, CL	New Zealand	Wellington	166	1945-46	62	–	–	–	–	–	–	–
Meuleman, KD	New Zealand	Wellington	167	1945-46	–	–	–	–	57	–	–	–
Miller, KR	New Zealand	Wellington	168	1945-46	–	–	–	–	58	–	–	–
Tallon, D	New Zealand	Wellington	169	1945-46	–	11	–	–	–	–	–	–
Toshack, ERH	New Zealand	Wellington	170	1945-46	63	–	–	–	–	–	–	–
Morris, AR	England	Brisbane2	171	1946-47	64	–	–	–	–	–	–	–
Tribe, GE	England	Brisbane2	172	1946-47	–	–	–	–	59	–	–	–
Freer, FW	England	Sydney	173	1946-47	–	–	–	–	60	–	–	–
Dooland, B	England	Melbourne	174	1946-47	–	–	18	–	–	–	–	–
Harvey, MR	England	Adelaide	175	1946-47	65	–	–	–	–	–	–	–
Hamence, RA	England	Sydney	176	1946-47	–	–	19	–	–	–	–	–
Johnston, WA	India	Brisbane2	177	1947-48	–	–	–	–	61	–	–	–
Harvey, RN	India	Adelaide	178	1947-48	–	–	–	–	62	–	–	–

Player	Opponent	Venue	Series	Player No.	Place of birth						
					NSW	QLD	SA	TAS	VIC	WA	OVERSEAS
Johnson, LJ	India	Melbourne	1947-48	179	–	12	–	–	–	–	–
Loxton, SJE	India	Melbourne	1947-48	180	–	–	–	–	63	–	–
Ring, DT	India	Melbourne	1947-48	181	–	–	–	6	–	–	–
Saggers, RA	England	Leeds	1948	182	66	–	–	–	–	–	–
Moroney, J	South Africa	Johannesburg2	1949-50	183	67	–	–	–	–	–	–
Noblet, G	South Africa	Port Elizabeth	1949-50	184	–	–	20	–	–	–	–
Iverson, JB	England	Brisbane2	1950-51	185	–	–	–	–	64	–	–
Archer, KA	England	Melbourne	1950-51	186	–	13	–	–	–	–	–
Burke, JW	England	Adelaide	1950-51	187	68	–	–	–	–	–	–
Hole, GB	England	Melbourne	1950-51	188	69	–	–	–	–	–	–
Langley, GRA	West Indies	Brisbane2	1951-52	189	–	–	21	–	–	–	–
Benaud, R	West Indies	Sydney	1951-52	190	70	–	–	–	–	–	–
McDonald, CC	West Indies	Sydney	1951-52	191	–	–	–	–	65	–	–
Thoms, GR	West Indies	Sydney	1951-52	192	–	–	–	–	66	–	–
Archer, RG	South Africa	Melbourne	1952-53	193	–	14	–	–	–	–	–
Craig, ID	South Africa	Melbourne	1952-53	194	71	–	–	–	–	–	–
Davidson, AK	England	Nottingham	1953	195	72	–	–	–	–	–	–
Hill, JC	England	Nottingham	1953	196	–	–	–	–	67	–	–
De Courcy, JH	England	Manchester	1953	197	73	–	–	–	–	–	–
Favell, LE	England	Brisbane2	1954-55	198	74	–	–	–	–	–	–
Maddocks, LV	England	Melbourne	1954-55	199	–	–	–	–	68	–	–
Burge, PJP	England	Sydney	1954-55	200	–	15	–	–	–	–	–

Player	Country	Venue	Season	No.						
Watson, WJ	England	Sydney	1954-55	201	75	–	–	–	–	–
Crawford, WPA	England	Lord's	1956	202	76	–	–	–	–	–
Mackay, KD	England	Lord's	1956	203	–	16	–	–	–	–
Rutherford, JW	India	Bombay2	1956-57	204	–	–	–	–	3	–
Wilson, JW	India	Bombay2	1956-57	205	–	17	–	–	–	–
Grout, ATW	South Africa	Johannesburg3	1957-58	206	–	–	–	69	–	–
Kline, LF	South Africa	Johannesburg3	1957-58	207	–	–	–	70	–	–
Meckiff, I	South Africa	Johannesburg3	1957-58	208	–	–	–	71	–	–
Simpson, RB	South Africa	Johannesburg3	1957-58	209	77	–	–	–	–	–
Gaunt, RA	South Africa	Durban2	1957-58	210	–	–	–	–	–	4
O'Neill, NC	England	Brisbane2	1958-59	211	78	–	–	–	–	–
Slater, KN	England	Sydney	1958-59	212	–	–	–	–	5	–
Rorke, GR	England	Adelaide	1958-59	213	79	–	–	–	–	–
Stevens, GB	Pakistan	Lahore2	1959-60	214	–	–	22	–	–	–
Jarman, BN	India	Kanpur	1959-60	215	–	–	23	–	–	–
Martin, JW	West Indies	Melbourne	1960-61	216	80	–	–	–	–	–
Misson, FM	West Indies	Melbourne	1960-61	217	81	–	–	–	–	–
Hoare, DE	West Indies	Adelaide	1960-61	218	–	–	–	–	6	–
Lawry, WM	England	Birmingham	1961	219	–	–	–	72	–	–
McKenzie, GD	England	Lord's	1961	220	–	–	–	–	7	–
Booth, BC	England	Manchester	1961	221	82	–	–	–	–	–
Guest, CEJ	England	Sydney	1962-63	222	–	–	–	73	–	–
Shepherd, BK	England	Sydney	1962-63	223	–	–	–	–	8	–

Player	Opponent	Venue	Series	Player No.	Place of birth NSW	QLD	SA	TAS	VIC	WA	OVERSEAS
Hawke, NJN	England	Sydney	1962-63	224	–	–	24	–	–	–	–
Connolly, AN	South Africa	Brisbane2	1963-64	225	–	–	–	–	74	–	–
Veivers, TR	South Africa	Brisbane2	1963-64	226	–	18	–	–	–	–	–
Redpath, IR	South Africa	Melbourne	1963-64	227	–	–	–	–	75	–	–
Corling, GE	England	Nottingham	1964	228	83	–	–	–	–	–	–
Cowper, RM	England	Leeds	1964	229	–	–	–	–	76	–	–
Sellers, RHD	India	Calcutta	1964-65	230	–	–	–	–	–	–	15
Chappell, IM	Pakistan	Melbourne	1964-65	231	–	–	25	–	–	–	–
Sincock, DJ	Pakistan	Melbourne	1964-65	232	–	–	26	–	–	–	–
Mayne, LC	West Indies	Kingston	1964-65	233	–	–	–	–	–	9	–
Philpott, PI	West Indies	Kingston	1964-65	234	84	–	–	–	–	–	–
Thomas, G	West Indies	Kingston	1964-65	235	85	–	–	–	–	–	–
Allan, PJ	England	Brisbane2	1965-66	236	–	19	–	–	–	–	–
Walters, KD	England	Brisbane2	1965-66	237	86	–	–	–	–	–	–
Stackpole, KR	England	Adelaide	1965-66	238	–	–	–	–	77	–	–
Renneberg, DA	South Africa	Johannesburg3	1966-67	239	87	–	–	–	–	–	–
Taber, HB	South Africa	Johannesburg3	1966-67	240	88	–	–	–	–	–	–
Watson, GD	South Africa	Cape Town	1966-67	241	–	–	–	–	78	–	–
Gleeson, JW	India	Adelaide	1967-68	242	89	–	–	–	–	–	–
Sheahan, AP	India	Adelaide	1967-68	243	–	–	–	–	79	–	–
Freeman, EW	India	Brisbane2	1967-68	244	–	–	27	–	–	–	–
Joslin, LR	India	Sydney	1967-68	245	–	–	–	–	80	–	–

Name	For	Venue	Season	No.								
Inverarity, RJ	England	Leeds	1968	246	–	–	–	–	–	–	–	10
Mallett, AA	England	The Oval	1968	247	90	–	–	–	–	–	–	–
Jenner, TJ	England	Brisbane2	1970-71	248	–	–	–	–	–	–	–	11
Marsh, RW	England	Brisbane2	1970-71	249	–	–	–	–	–	–	–	12
Thomson, AL	England	Brisbane2	1970-71	250	–	–	–	–	81	–	–	–
Chappell, GS	England	Perth	1970-71	251	–	–	28	–	–	–	–	–
Duncan, JRF	England	Melbourne	1970-71	252	–	20	–	–	–	–	–	–
O'Keeffe, KJ	England	Melbourne	1970-71	253	91	–	–	–	–	–	–	–
Lillee, DK	England	Adelaide	1970-71	254	–	–	–	–	–	–	–	13
Dell, AR	England	Sydney	1970-71	255	–	–	–	–	–	–	–	16
Eastwood, KH	England	Sydney	1970-71	256	92	–	–	–	–	–	–	–
Colley, DJ	England	Manchester	1972	257	93	–	–	–	–	–	–	–
Francis, BC	England	Manchester	1972	258	94	–	–	–	–	–	–	–
Edwards, R	England	Lord's	1972	259	–	–	–	–	–	–	–	14
Massie, RAL	England	Lord's	1972	260	–	–	–	–	–	–	–	15
Benaud, J	Pakistan	Adelaide	1972-73	261	95	–	–	–	–	–	–	–
Thomson, JR	Pakistan	Melbourne	1972-73	262	96	–	–	–	–	–	–	–
Walker, MHN	Pakistan	Melbourne	1972-73	263	–	–	–	7	–	–	–	–
Watkins, JR	Pakistan	Sydney	1972-73	264	97	–	–	–	–	–	–	–
Hammond, JR	West Indies	Kingston	1972-73	265	–	–	29	–	–	–	–	–
Davis, IC	New Zealand	Melbourne	1973-74	266	98	–	–	–	–	–	–	–
Gilmour, GJ	New Zealand	Melbourne	1973-74	267	99	–	–	–	–	–	–	–
Dymock, G	New Zealand	Adelaide	1973-74	268	21	–	–	–	–	–	–	–

Player	Opponent	Venue	Series	Player No.	Place of birth						
					NSW	QLD	SA	TAS	VIC	WA	OVERSEAS
Hurst, AG	New Zealand	Adelaide	1973-74	269	–	–	–	–	82	–	–
Woodcock, AJ	New Zealand	Adelaide	1973-74	270	–	–	30	–	–	–	–
Edwards, WJ	England	Brisbane2	1974-75	271	–	–	–	–	–	16	–
McCosker, RB	England	Sydney	1974-75	272	100	–	–	–	–	–	–
Turner, A	England	Birmingham	1975	273	101	–	–	–	–	–	–
Cosier, GJ	West Indies	Melbourne	1975-76	274	–	–	–	–	83	–	–
Yallop, GN	West Indies	Sydney	1975-76	275	–	–	–	–	84	–	–
Hookes, DW	England	Melbourne	1976-77	276	–	–	31	–	–	–	–
Pascoe, LS	England	Lord's	1977	277	–	–	–	–	–	17	–
Robinson, RD	England	Lord's	1977	278	–	–	–	–	85	–	–
Serjeant, CS	England	Lord's	1977	279	–	–	–	–	–	18	–
Bright, RJ	England	Manchester	1977	280	–	–	–	–	86	–	–
Hughes, KJ	England	The Oval	1977	281	–	–	–	–	–	19	–
Malone, MF	England	The Oval	1977	282	–	–	–	–	–	20	–
Clark, WM	India	Brisbane2	1977-78	283	–	–	–	–	–	21	–
Hibbert, PA	India	Brisbane2	1977-78	284	–	–	–	–	87	–	–
Mann, AL	India	Brisbane2	1977-78	285	–	–	–	–	–	22	–
Ogilvie, AD	India	Brisbane2	1977-78	286	–	22	–	–	–	–	–
Rixon, SJ	India	Brisbane2	1977-78	287	102	–	–	–	–	–	–
Toohey, PM	India	Brisbane2	1977-78	288	103	–	–	–	–	–	–
Dyson, J	India	Perth	1977-78	289	104	–	–	–	–	–	–
Gannon, JB	India	Perth	1977-78	290	–	–	–	–	–	23	–

Name	Country	Venue	Season	No.							
Callen, IW	India	Adelaide	1977-78	291	—	—	—	—	88	—	—
Darling, WM	India	Adelaide	1977-78	292	—	—	32	—	—	—	—
Wood, GM	India	Adelaide	1977-78	293	—	—	—	—	—	24	—
Yardley, B	India	Adelaide	1977-78	294	—	—	—	—	—	25	—
Higgs, JD	West Indies	Port-of-Spain	1977-78	295	—	—	—	—	89	—	—
Laughlin, TJ	West Indies	Georgetown	1977-78	296	—	—	—	—	90	—	—
Hogg, RM	England	Brisbane2	1978-79	297	—	—	—	—	91	—	—
Maclean, JA	England	Brisbane2	1978-79	298	—	23	—	—	—	—	—
Border, AR	England	Melbourne	1978-79	299	105	—	—	—	—	—	—
Carlson, PH	England	Adelaide	1978-79	300	—	24	—	—	—	—	—
Wright, KJ	England	Adelaide	1978-79	301	—	—	—	—	—	26	—
Hilditch, AMJ	England	Sydney	1978-79	302	—	—	33	—	—	—	—
Sleep, PR	Pakistan	Melbourne	1978-79	303	—	—	34	—	—	—	—
Whatmore, DF	Pakistan	Melbourne	1978-79	304	—	—	—	—	—	—	17
Moss, JK	Pakistan	Perth	1978-79	305	—	—	—	—	92	—	—
Laird, BM	West Indies	Brisbane2	1979-80	306	—	—	—	—	—	27	—
Wiener, JM	England	Perth	1979-80	307	—	—	—	—	93	—	—
Beard, GR	Pakistan	Karachi	1979-80	308	106	—	—	—	—	—	—
Lawson, GF	New Zealand	Brisbane2	1980-81	309	107	—	—	—	—	—	—
Alderman, TM	England	Nottingham	1981	310	—	—	—	—	—	28	—
Chappell, TM	England	Nottingham	1981	311	—	—	35	—	—	—	—
Kent, MF	England	Birmingham	1981	312	—	25	—	—	—	—	—
Whitney, MR	England	Manchester	1981	313	108	—	—	—	—	—	—

Player	Opponent	Venue	Series	Player No.	Place of birth NSW	QLD	SA	TAS	VIC	WA	OVERSEAS
Wellham, DM	England	The Oval	1981	314	109	-	-	-	-	-	-
Ritchie, GM	Pakistan	Karachi	1982-83	315	-	26	-	-	-	-	-
Rackemann, CG	England	Brisbane2	1982-83	316	-	27	-	-	-	-	-
Wessels, KC	England	Brisbane2	1982-83	317	-	-	-	-	-	-	18
Hogan, TG	Sri Lanka	Kandy	1982-83	318	-	-	-	-	-	29	-
Woolley, RD	Sri Lanka	Kandy	1982-83	319	-	-	-	8	-	-	-
Phillips, WB	Pakistan	Perth	1983-84	320	-	-	36	-	-	-	-
Maguire, JN	Pakistan	Melbourne	1983-84	321	110	-	-	-	-	-	-
Matthews, GRJ	Pakistan	Melbourne	1983-84	322	111	-	-	-	-	-	-
Smith, SB	West Indies	Georgetown	1983-84	323	112	-	-	-	-	-	-
Jones, DM	West Indies	Port-of-Spain	1983-84	324	-	-	-	-	94	-	-
Boon, DC	West Indies	Brisbane2	1984-85	325	-	-	-	9	-	-	-
Holland, RG	West Indies	Brisbane2	1984-85	326	113	-	-	-	-	-	-
Bennett, MJ	West Indies	Melbourne	1984-85	327	114	-	-	-	-	-	-
McDermott, CJ	West Indies	Melbourne	1984-85	328	-	28	-	-	-	-	-
O'Donnell, SP	England	Leeds	1985	329	115	-	-	-	-	-	-
Gilbert, DR	England	The Oval	1985	330	116	-	-	-	-	-	-
Kerr, RB	New Zealand	Sydney	1985-86	331	-	29	-	-	-	-	-
Hughes, MG	India	Adelaide	1985-86	332	-	-	-	-	95	-	-
Reid, BA	India	Adelaide	1985-86	333	-	-	-	-	-	30	-
Marsh, GR	India	Melbourne	1985-86	334	-	-	-	-	-	31	-
Waugh, SR	India	Melbourne	1985-86	335	117	-	-	-	-	-	-

Name	Country	Venue	Year								
Davis, SP	New Zealand	Wellington	1985-86	336	—	—	—	—	96	—	—
Zoehrer, TJ	New Zealand	Wellington	1985-86	337	—	—	—	—	—	32	—
Matthews, CD	England	Brisbane2	1986-87	338	—	—	—	—	—	33	—
Dyer, GC	England	Adelaide	1986-87	339	—	—	—	118	—	—	—
Taylor, PL	England	Sydney	1986-87	340	—	—	—	119	—	—	—
Total				**(340)**	**29**	**36**	**9**	**119**	**96**	**33**	**18**

PLAYERS BORN OVERSEAS

Players	Place of Birth	Country	Year
Bannerman, C	Woolwich, Kent	England	1851
Carter, H	Halifax, Yorkshire	England	1878
Cooper, BB	Dacca	India	1844
Cooper, WH	Maidstone, Kent	England	1849
Dell, AR	Lymington, Hants	England	1947
Grimmett, CV	Caversham, Dunedin	New Zealand	1891
Groube, TU	Taranaki	New Zealand	1857
Horan, TP	Midleton, Co. Cork	Ireland	1854
Jackson, A	Rutherglen, Lanarkshire	Scotland	1909
Kelly, TJD	Co. Waterford	Ireland	1884
Kendall, T	Bedford	England	1851
McDonnell, PS	Kensington, London	England	1858
Midwinter, MW	St. Briavels, Gloucs.	England	1851
Musgrove, HA	Surbiton, Surrey	England	1860
Sellers, RHD	Balsar	India	1940
Thompson, N	Birmingham	England	1838
Wessels, KC	Bloemfontien	South Africa	1957
Whatmore, DF	Colombo	Sri Lanka	1954

AUSTRALIAN TEST BATTING RECORDS

Player	M	Inn	NO	Runs	H.S	50s	100s	Avrge	Ct	St
A'Beckett, EL	4	7	–	143	41	–	–	20.43	4	–
Alderman, TM	22	33	15	113	23	–	–	6.28	17	–
Alexander, G	2	4	–	52	33	–	–	13.00	2	–
Alexander, HH	1	2	1	17	17*	–	–	17.00	–	–
Allan, FE	1	1	–	5	5	–	–	5.00	–	–
Allan, PJ	1	–	–	–	–	–	–	–	–	–
Allen, RC	1	2	–	44	30	–	–	22.00	2	–
Andrews, TJE	16	23	1	592	94	4	–	26.91	12	–
Archer, KA	5	9	–	234	48	–	–	26.00	–	–
Archer, RG	19	30	1	713	128	2	1	24.59	20	–
Armstrong, WW	50	84	10	2863	159*	8	6	38.69	44	–

Player	M	Inn	NO	Runs	H.S	50s	100s	Avrge	Ct	St
Badcock, CL	7	12	1	160	118	–	1	14.55	3	–
Bannerman, AC	28	50	2	1108	94	8	–	23.08	21	–
Bannerman, C	3	6	2	239	165*	–	1	59.75	–	–
Bardsley, W	41	66	5	2469	193*	14	6	40.48	12	–
Barnes, SG	13	19	2	1072	234	5	3	63.06	14	–
Barnett, BA	4	8	1	195	57	1	–	27.86	4	2
Barrett, JE	2	4	1	80	67*	1	–	26.67	1	–
Beard, GR	3	5	–	114	49	–	–	22.80	–	–
Benaud, J	3	5	–	223	142	–	1	44.60	–	–
Benaud, R	63	97	7	2201	122	9	3	24.46	65	–
Bennett, MJ	3	5	2	71	23	–	–	23.67	5	–
Blackham, JM	35	62	11	800	74	4	–	15.69	36	24
Blackie, DD	3	6	3	24	11*	–	–	8.00	2	–
Bonnor, GJ	17	30	–	512	128	2	1	17.07	16	–
Boon, DC	23	42	2	1399	131	7	4	34.98	12	–
Booth, BC	29	48	6	1773	169	10	5	42.21	17	–
Border, AR	89	157	26	6917	196	33	21	52.80	94	–
Boyle, HF	12	16	4	153	36*	–	–	12.75	10	–
Bradman, DG	52	80	10	6996	334	13	29	99.94	31	–
Bright, RJ	25	39	8	445	33	–	–	14.35	13	–
Bromley, EH	2	4	–	38	26	–	–	9.50	2	–
Brown, WA	22	35	1	1592	206*	9	4	46.82	14	–
Bruce, W	14	26	2	702	80	5	–	29.25	12	–
Burge, PJP	42	68	8	2290	181	12	4	38.17	23	–
Burke, JW	24	44	7	1280	189	5	3	34.59	18	–
Burn, EJK	2	4	–	41	19	–	–	10.25	–	–
Burton, FJ	2	4	2	4	2*	–	–	2.00	1	1
Callaway, ST	3	6	1	87	41	–	–	17.40	–	–
Callen, IW	1	2	2	26	22*	–	–	–	1	–
Carkeek, W	6	5	2	16	6*	–	–	5.33	6	–
Carlson, PH	2	4	–	23	21	–	–	5.75	2	–
Carter, H	28	47	9	873	72	4	–	22.97	44	21
Chappell, GS	88	151	19	7110	247*	31	24	53.86	122	–
Chappell, IM	76	136	10	5345	196	26	14	42.42	105	–
Chappell, TM	3	6	1	79	27	–	–	15.80	2	–
Charlton, PC	2	4	–	29	11	–	–	7.25	–	–
Chipperfield, AG	14	20	3	552	109	2	1	32.47	15	–
Clark, WM	10	19	2	98	33	–	–	5.76	6	–
Colley, DJ	3	4	–	84	54	1	–	21.00	1	–

Player	M	Inn	NO	Runs	H.S	50s	100s	Avrge	Ct	St
Collins, HL	19	31	1	1352	203	6	4	45.07	13	–
Coningham, A	1	2	–	13	10	–	–	6.50	–	–
Connolly, AN	30	45	20	260	37	–	–	10.40	17	–
Cooper, BB	1	2	–	18	15	–	–	9.00	2	–
Cooper, WH	2	3	1	13	7	–	–	6.50	1	–
Corling, GE	5	4	1	5	3	–	–	1.67	–	–
Cosier, GJ	18	32	1	897	168	3	2	28.94	14	–
Cottam, JT	1	2	–	4	3	–	–	2.00	1	–
Cotter, A	21	37	2	457	45	–	–	13.06	8	–
Couthard, G	1	1	1	6	6*	–	–	–	–	–
Cowper, RM	27	46	2	2061	307	10	5	46.84	21	–
Craig, ID	11	18	–	358	53	2	–	19.89	2	–
Crawford, WPA	4	5	2	53	34	–	–	17.67	1	–
Darling, J	34	60	2	1657	178	8	3	28.57	27	–
Darling, LS	12	18	1	474	85	3	–	27.88	8	–
Darling, WM	14	27	1	697	91	6	–	26.81	5	–
Davidson, AK	44	61	7	1328	80	5	–	24.59	42	–
Davis, IC	15	27	1	692	105	4	1	26.62	9	–
Davis, SP	1	1	–	0	0	–	–	0.00	–	–
De Courcy, JH	3	6	1	81	41	–	–	16.20	3	–
Dell, AR	2	2	2	6	3*	–	–	–	–	–
Donnan, H	5	10	1	75	15*	–	–	8.33	1	–
Dooland, B	3	5	1	76	29	–	–	19.00	3	–
Duff, RA	22	40	3	1317	146	6	2	35.59	14	–
Duncan, JRF	1	1	–	3	3	–	–	3.00	–	–
Dyer, GC	1	–	–	–	–	–	–	–	2	–
Dymock, G	21	32	7	236	31*	–	–	9.44	1	–
Dyson, J	30	58	7	1359	127*	5	2	26.65	10	–
Eady, CJ	2	4	1	20	10*	–	–	6.67	2	–
Eastwood, KH	1	2	–	5	5	–	–	2.50	–	–
Ebeling, HI	1	2	–	43	41	–	–	21.50	–	–
Edwards, JD	3	6	1	48	26	–	–	9.60	1	–
Edwards, R	20	32	3	1171	170*	9	2	40.38	7	–
Edwards, WJ	3	6	–	68	30	–	–	11.33	–	–
Emery, SH	4	2	–	6	5	–	–	3.00	2	–
Evans, E	6	10	2	82	33	–	–	10.25	5	–
Fairfax, AG	10	12	4	410	65	4	–	51.25	15	–
Favell, LE	19	31	3	757	101	5	1	27.04	9	–
Ferris, JJ	8	16	4	98	20*	–	–	8.17	4	–

Player	M	Inn	NO	Runs	H.S	50s	100s	Avrge	Ct	St
Fingleton, JHW	18	29	1	1189	136	3	5	42.46	13	–
Fleetwood-Smith, LO	10	11	5	54	16*	–	–	9.00	–	–
Francis, BC	3	5	–	52	27	–	–	10.40	1	–
Freeman, EW	11	18	–	345	76	2	–	19.17	5	–
Freer, FW	1	1	1	28	28*	–	–	–	–	–
Gannon, JB	3	5	4	3	3*	–	–	3.00	3	–
Garrett, TW	19	33	6	339	51*	1	–	12.56	7	–
Gaunt, RA	3	4	2	6	3	–	–	3.00	1	–
Gehrs, DRA	6	11	–	221	67	2	–	20.09	6	–
Giffen, G	31	53	–	1238	161	6	1	23.36	24	–
Giffen, WF	3	6	–	11	3	–	–	1.83	1	–
Gilbert, DR	9	12	4	57	15	–	–	7.12	–	–
Gilmour, GJ	15	22	1	483	101	3	1	23.00	8	–
Gleeson, JW	30	46	8	395	45	–	–	10.39	17	–
Graham, H	6	10	–	301	107	–	2	30.10	3	–
Gregory, DW	3	5	2	60	43	–	–	20.00	–	–
Gregory, EJ	1	2	–	11	11	–	–	5.50	1	–
Gregory, JM	24	34	3	1146	119	7	2	36.97	37	–
Gregory, RG	2	3	–	153	80	2	–	51.00	1	–
Gregory, SE	58	100	7	2282	201	8	4	24.54	25	–
Grimmett, CV	37	50	10	557	50	1	–	13.93	17	–
Groube, TU	1	2	–	11	11	–	–	5.50	–	–
Grout, ATW	51	67	8	890	74	3	–	15.08	163	24
Guest, CEJ	1	1	–	11	11	–	–	11.00	–	–
Hamence, RA	3	4	1	81	30*	–	–	27.00	1	–
Hammond, JR	5	5	2	28	19	–	–	9.33	2	–
Harry, J	1	2	–	8	6	–	–	4.00	1	–
Hartigan, RJ	2	4	–	170	116	–	1	42.50	1	–
Hartkopf, AEV	1	2	–	80	80	1	–	40.00	–	–
Harvey, MR	1	2	–	43	31	–	–	21.50	–	–
Harvey, RN	79	137	10	6149	205	24	21	48.42	64	–
Hassett, AL	43	69	3	3073	198*	11	10	46.56	30	–
Hawke, NJN	27	37	15	365	45*	–	–	16.59	9	–
Hazlitt, GR	9	12	4	89	34*	–	–	11.12	4	–
Hendry, HSTL	11	18	2	335	112	–	1	20.94	10	–
Hibbert, PA	1	2	–	15	13	–	–	7.50	1	–
Higgs, JD	22	36	16	111	16	–	–	5.55	3	–
Hilditch, AMJ	18	34	–	1073	119	6	2	31.56	13	–

Player	M	Inn	NO	Runs	H.S	50s	100s	Avrge	Ct	St
Hill, C	49	89	2	3412	191	19	7	39.22	33	–
Hill, JC	3	6	3	21	8*	–	–	7.00	2	–
Hoare, DE	1	2	–	35	35	–	–	17.50	2	–
Hodges, JH	2	4	1	10	8	–	–	3.33	–	–
Hogan, TG	7	12	1	205	42*	–	–	18.64	2	–
Hogg, RM	38	58	13	439	52	1	–	9.76	7	–
Hole, GB	18	33	2	789	66	6	–	25.45	21	–
Holland, RG	11	15	4	35	10	–	–	3.18	5	–
Hookes, DW	23	41	3	1306	143*	8	1	34.37	12	–
Hopkins, AJY	20	33	2	509	43	–	–	16.42	11	–
Horan, TP	15	27	2	471	124	1	1	18.84	6	–
Hordern, HV	7	13	2	254	50	1	–	23.09	6	–
Hornibrook, PM	6	7	1	60	26	–	–	10.00	7	–
Howell, WP	18	27	6	158	35	–	–	7.52	12	–
Hughes, KJ	70	124	6	4415	213	22	9	37.42	50	–
Hughes, MG	5	7	–	31	16	–	–	4.43	3	–
Hunt, WA	1	1	–	0	0	–	–	0.00	1	–
Hurst, AG	12	20	3	102	26	–	–	6.00	3	–
Hurwood, A	2	2	–	5	5	–	–	2.50	2	–
Inverarity, RJ	6	11	1	174	56	1	–	17.40	4	–
Iredale, FA	14	23	1	807	140	4	2	36.68	16	–
Ironmonger, H	14	21	5	42	12	–	–	2.62	3	–
Iverson, JB	5	7	3	3	1*	–	–	0.75	2	–
Jackson, A	8	11	1	474	164	2	1	47.40	7	–
Jarman, BN	19	30	3	400	78	2	–	14.81	50	4
Jarvis, AH	11	21	3	303	82	1	–	16.83	9	8
Jenner, TJ	9	14	5	208	74	1	–	23.11	5	–
Jennings, CB	6	8	2	107	32	–	–	17.83	5	–
Johnson, IW	45	66	12	1000	77	6	–	18.52	30	–
Johnson, LJ	1	1	1	25	25*	–	–	–	2	–
Johnston, WA	40	49	25	273	29	–	–	11.38	16	–
Jones, DM	10	19	2	947	210	4	2	55.71	4	–
Jones, E	19	26	1	126	20	–	–	5.04	21	–
Jones, SP	12	24	4	432	87	1	–	21.60	12	–
Joslin, LR	1	2	–	9	7	–	–	4.50	–	–
Kelleway, C	26	42	4	1422	147	6	3	37.42	24	–
Kelly, JJ	36	56	17	664	46*	–	–	17.03	43	20
Kelly, TJD	2	3	–	64	35	–	–	21.33	1	–
Kendall, T	2	4	1	39	17*	–	–	13.00	2	–

Player	M	Inn	NO	Runs	H.S	50s	100s	Avrge	Ct	St
Kent, MF	3	6	–	171	54	2	–	28.50	6	–
Kerr, RB	2	4	–	31	17	–	–	7.75	1	–
Kippax, AF	22	34	1	1192	146	8	2	36.12	13	–
Kline, LF	13	16	9	58	15*	–	–	8.29	9	–
Laird, BM	21	40	2	1341	92	11	–	35.29	16	–
Langley, GRA	26	37	12	374	53	1	–	14.96	83	15
Laughlin, TJ	3	5	–	87	35	–	–	17.40	3	–
Laver, F	15	23	6	196	45	–	–	11.53	8	–
Lawry, WM	68	123	12	5234	210	27	13	47.15	30	–
Lawson, GF	37	60	10	756	57*	3	–	15.12	8	–
Lee, PK	2	3	–	57	42	–	–	19.00	1	–
Lillee, DK	70	90	24	905	73*	1	–	13.71	23	–
Lindwall, RR	61	84	13	1502	118	5	2	21.15	26	–
Love, HSB	1	2	–	8	5	–	–	4.00	3	–
Loxton, SJE	12	15	–	554	101	3	1	36.93	7	–
Lyons, JJ	14	27	–	731	134	3	1	27.07	3	–
Macartney, CG	35	55	4	2131	170	9	7	41.78	17	–
Mackay, KD	37	52	7	1507	89	13	–	33.49	15	–
Maclean, JA	4	8	1	79	33*	–	–	11.29	18	–
Maddocks, LV	7	12	2	177	69	1	–	17.70	18	1
Maguire, JN	3	5	1	28	15*	–	–	7.00	2	–
Mailey, AA	21	29	9	222	46*	–	–	11.10	14	–
Mallett, AA	39	50	13	430	43*	–	–	11.62	30	–
Malone, MF	1	1	–	46	46	–	–	46.00	–	–
Mann, AL	4	8	–	189	105	–	1	23.62	2	–
Marr, AP	1	2	–	5	5	–	–	2.50	–	–
Marsh, GR	14	26	1	974	118	3	3	38.96	8	–
Marsh, RW	97	150	13	3633	132	16	3	26.52	343	12
Martin, JW	8	13	1	214	55	1	–	17.83	5	–
Massie, HH	9	16	–	249	55	1	–	15.56	5	–
Massie, RAL	6	8	1	78	42	–	–	11.14	1	–
Matthews, CD	2	3	–	21	11	–	–	7.00	1	–
Matthews, GRJ	21	34	6	1031	130	4	3	36.82	13	–
Matthews, TJ	8	10	1	153	53	1	–	17.00	7	–
Mayne, LC	6	11	3	76	13	–	–	9.50	3	–
Mayne, RE	4	4	1	64	25*	–	–	21.33	2	–
McAlister, PA	8	16	1	252	41	–	–	16.80	10	–
McCabe, SJ	39	62	5	2748	232	13	6	48.21	42	–
McCool, CL	14	17	4	459	104*	1	1	35.31	14	–

Player	M	Inn	NO	Runs	H.S	50s	100s	Avrge	Ct	St
McCormick, EL	12	14	5	54	17*	–	–	6.00	8	–
McCosker, RB	25	46	5	1622	127	9	4	39.56	21	–
McDermott, CJ	17	23	1	189	36	–	–	8.59	5	–
McDonald, CC	47	83	4	3107	170	17	5	39.33	14	–
McDonald, EA	11	12	5	116	36	–	–	16.57	3	–
McDonnell, PS	19	34	1	950	147	2	3	28.79	6	–
McIlwraith, J	1	2	–	9	7	–	–	4.50	1	–
McKenzie, GD	61	89	12	945	76	2	–	12.27	34	–
McKibbin, TR	5	8	2	88	28*	–	–	14.67	4	–
McLaren, JW	1	2	2	–	0*	–	–	–	–	–
McLeod, CE	17	29	5	573	112	4	1	23.88	9	–
McLeod, RW	6	11	–	146	31	–	–	13.27	3	–
McShane, PG	3	6	1	26	12*	–	–	5.20	2	–
Meckiff, I	18	20	7	154	45*	–	–	11.85	9	–
Meuleman, KD	1	1	–	0	0	–	–	0.00	1	–
Midwinter, WE	8	14	1	174	37	–	–	13.38	5	–
Miller, KR	55	87	7	2958	147	13	7	36.98	38	–
Minnett, RB	9	15	–	391	90	3	–	26.07	–	–
Misson, FM	5	5	3	38	25*	–	–	19.00	6	–
Moroney, JR	7	12	1	383	118	1	2	34.82	–	–
Morris, AR	46	79	3	3533	206	12	12	46.49	15	–
Morris, S	1	2	1	14	10*	–	–	14.00	–	–
Moses, H	6	10	–	198	33	–	–	19.80	1	–
Moss, JK	1	2	1	60	38*	–	–	60.00	–	–
Moule, WH	1	2	–	40	34	–	–	20.00	1	–
Murdoch, WL	18	33	5	896	211	1	2	32.00	13	1
Musgrove, H	1	2	–	13	9	–	–	6.50	–	–
Nagel, LE	1	2	1	21	21*	–	–	21.00	–	–
Nash, LJ	2	2	–	30	17	–	–	15.00	6	–
Nitschke, HC	2	2	–	53	47	–	–	26.50	3	–
Noble, MA	42	73	7	1997	133	16	1	30.26	26	–
Noblet, G	3	4	1	22	13*	–	–	7.33	1	–
Nothling, OE	1	2	–	52	44	–	–	26.00	–	–
O'Brien, LPJ	5	8	–	211	61	2	–	26.38	3	–
O'Connor, JDA	4	8	1	86	20	–	–	12.29	3	–
O'Donnell, SP	6	10	3	206	48	–	–	29.43	4	–
O'Keeffe, KJ	24	34	9	644	85	1	–	25.76	15	–
O'Neill, NC	42	69	8	2779	181	15	6	45.56	21	–
O'Reilly, WJ	27	39	7	410	56*	1	–	12.81	6	–

Player	M	Inn	NO	Runs	H.S	50s	100s	Avrge	Ct	St
Ogilvie, AD	5	10	–	178	47	–	–	17.80	5	–
Oldfield, WAS	54	80	17	1427	65*	4	–	22.65	78	52
Oxenham, RK	7	10	–	151	48	–	–	15.10	4	–
Palmer, GE	17	25	4	296	48	–	–	14.10	13	–
Park, RL	1	1	–	0	0	–	–	0.00	–	–
Pascoe, LS	14	19	9	106	30*	–	–	10.60	2	–
Pellew, CE	10	14	1	484	116	1	2	37.23	4	–
Phillips, WB	27	48	2	1485	159	7	2	32.28	52	–
Philpott, PI	8	10	1	93	22	–	–	10.33	5	–
Ponsford, WH	29	48	4	2122	266	6	7	48.23	21	–
Pope, RJ	1	2	–	3	3	–	–	1.50	–	–
Rackemann, CG	5	5	–	16	12	–	–	3.20	2	–
Ransford, VS	20	38	6	1211	143*	7	1	37.84	10	–
Redpath, IR	67	120	11	4737	171	31	8	43.46	83	–
Reedman, JC	1	2	–	21	17	–	–	10.50	1	–
Reid, BA	13	16	8	45	13	–	–	5.62	1	–
Renneberg, DA	8	13	7	22	9	–	–	3.67	2	–
Richardson, AJ	9	13	–	403	100	2	1	31.00	1	–
Richardson, VY	19	30	–	706	138	1	1	23.53	24	–
Rigg, KE	8	12	–	401	127	1	1	33.42	5	–
Ring, DT	13	21	2	426	67	4	–	22.42	5	–
Ritchie, GM	30	53	5	1690	146	7	3	35.21	14	–
Rixon, SJ	13	24	3	394	54	2	–	18.76	42	5
Robertson, WR	1	2	–	2	2	–	–	1.00	–	–
Robinson, RD	3	6	–	100	34	–	–	16.67	4	–
Robinson, RH	1	2	–	5	3	–	–	2.50	1	–
Rorke, GF	4	4	2	9	7	–	–	4.50	1	–
Rutherford, JW	1	1	–	30	30	–	–	30.00	–	–
Ryder, J	20	32	5	1394	201*	9	3	51.63	17	–
Saggers, RA	6	5	2	30	14	–	–	10.00	16	8
Saunders, JV	14	23	6	39	11*	–	–	2.29	5	–
Scott, HJH	8	14	1	359	102	1	1	27.62	8	–
Sellers, RHD	1	1	–	0	0	–	–	0.00	1	–
Serjeant, CS	12	23	1	522	124	2	1	23.73	13	–
Sheahan, AP	31	53	6	1594	127	7	2	33.91	17	–
Shepherd, BK	9	14	2	502	96	5	–	41.83	2	–
Sievers, MW	3	6	1	67	25*	–	–	13.40	4	–
Simpson, RB	62	111	7	4869	311	27	10	46.82	110	–
Sincock, DJ	3	4	1	80	29	–	–	26.67	2	–

Player	M	Inn	NO	Runs	H.S	50s	100s	Avrge	Ct	St
Slater, KN	1	1	1	1	1*	–	–	–	–	–
Sleep, PR	7	12	–	149	64	1	–	12.42	1	–
Slight, J	1	2	–	11	11	–	–	5.50	–	–
Smith, DBM	2	3	1	30	24*	–	–	15.00	–	–
Smith, SB	3	5	–	41	12	–	–	8.20	1	–
Spofforth, FR	18	29	6	217	50	1	–	9.43	11	–
Stackpole, KR	44	80	5	2807	207	14	7	37.43	46	–
Stevens, GB	4	7	–	112	28	–	–	16.00	2	–
Taber, HB	16	27	5	353	48	–	–	16.05	56	4
Tallon, D	21	26	3	394	92	2	–	17.13	50	8
Taylor, JM	20	28	–	997	108	8	1	35.61	11	–
Taylor, PL	1	2	–	53	42	–	–	26.50	–	–
Thomas, G	8	12	1	325	61	3	–	29.55	3	–
Thompson, N	2	4	–	67	41	–	–	16.75	3	–
Thoms, GR	1	2	–	44	28	–	–	22.00	–	–
Thomson, AL	4	5	4	22	12*	–	–	22.00	–	–
Thomson, JR	51	73	20	679	49	–	–	12.81	20	–
Thurlow, HM	1	1	–	0	0	–	–	0.00	1	–
Toohey, PM	15	29	1	893	122	7	1	31.89	9	–
Toshack, ERH	12	11	6	73	20*	–	–	14.60	4	–
Travers, JPF	1	2	–	10	9	–	–	5.00	1	–
Tribe, GE	3	3	1	35	25*	–	–	17.50	–	–
Trott, AE	3	5	3	205	85*	2	–	102.50	4	–
Trott, GHS	24	42	–	921	143	4	1	21.93	21	–
Trumble, H	32	57	14	851	70	4	–	19.79	45	–
Trumble, JW	7	13	1	243	59	1	–	20.25	3	–
Trumper, VT	48	89	8	3163	214*	13	8	39.05	31	–
Turner, A	14	27	1	768	136	3	1	29.54	15	–
Turner, CTB	17	32	4	323	29	–	–	11.54	8	–
Veivers, TR	21	30	4	813	88	7	–	31.27	7	–
Waite, MG	2	3	–	11	8	–	–	3.67	1	–
Walker, MHN	34	43	13	586	78*	1	–	19.53	10	–
Wall, TW	18	24	5	121	20	–	–	6.37	11	–
Walters, FH	1	2	–	12	7	–	–	6.00	2	–
Walters, KD	75	125	14	5357	250	33	15	48.26	43	–
Ward, FA	4	8	2	36	18	–	–	6.00	1	–
Watkins, JR	1	2	1	39	36	–	–	39.00	1	–
Watson, GD	5	9	–	97	50	1	–	10.78	1	–
Watson, WJ	4	7	1	106	30	–	–	17.67	2	–

Player	M	Inn	NO	Runs	H.S	50s	100s	Avrge	Ct	St
Waugh, SR	13	21	4	482	79*	4	–	28.35	12	–
Wellham, DM	6	11	–	257	103	–	1	23.36	5	–
Wessels, KC	24	42	1	1761	179	9	4	42.95	18	–
Whatmore, DF	7	13	–	293	77	2	–	22.54	13	–
Whitney, MR	2	4	–	4	4	–	–	1.00	–	–
Whitty, WJ	14	19	7	161	39*	–	–	13.42	4	–
Wiener, JM	6	11	–	281	93	2	–	25.55	4	–
Wilson, JW	1	–	–	–	–	–	–	–	–	–
Wood, GM	53	101	5	3109	172	13	8	32.39	38	–
Woodcock, AJ	1	1	–	27	27	–	–	27.00	1	–
Woodfull, WM	35	54	4	2300	161	13	7	46.00	7	–
Woods, SMJ	3	6	–	32	18	–	–	5.33	1	–
Woolley, RD	2	2	–	21	13	–	–	10.50	7	–
Worrall, J	11	22	3	478	76	5	–	25.16	13	–
Wright, KJ	10	18	5	219	55*	1	–	16.85	31	4
Yallop, GN	39	70	3	2756	268	9	8	41.13	23	–
Yardley, B	33	54	4	978	74	4	–	19.56	31	–
Zoehrer, TJ	10	14	2	246	52*	1	–	20.50	18	1

AUSTRALIAN TEST BOWLING RECORDS

Player	M	Balls	Mdns	Runs	Wkts	Avrge	5WI	10WM	Best
A'Beckett, EL	4	1062	47	317	3	105.67	–	–	1/41
Alderman, TM	22	5373	217	2597	79	32.87	5	–	6/128
Alexander, G	2	168	13	93	2	46.50	–	–	2/69
Alexander, HH	1	276	3	154	1	154.00	–	–	1/129
Allan, FE	1	180	15	80	4	20.00	–	–	2/30
Allan, PJ	1	192	6	83	2	41.50	–	–	2/58
Andrews, TJE	16	156	5	116	1	116.00	–	–	1/23
Archer, RG	19	3576	160	1318	48	27.46	1	–	5/53
Armstrong, WW	50	8022	407	2923	87	33.60	3	–	6/35
Bannerman, AC	28	292	17	163	4	40.75	–	–	3/111
Barnes, SG	13	594	11	218	4	54.50	–	–	2/25
Beard, GR	3	259	17	109	1	109.00	–	–	1/26
Benaud, J	3	24	1	12	2	6.00	–	–	2/12
Benaud, R	63	19108	805	6704	248	27.03	16	1	7/72
Bennett, MJ	3	665	24	325	6	54.17	–	–	3/79

Player	M	Balls	Mdns	Runs	Wkts	Avrge	5WI	10WM	Best
Blackie, DD	3	1260	51	444	14	31.71	1	–	6/94
Bonnor, GJ	17	164	16	84	2	42.00	–	–	1/05
Boon, DC	23	12	1	5	–	–	–	–	–
Booth, BC	29	436	27	146	3	48.67	–	–	2/33
Border, AR	89	1781	82	699	16	43.69	–	–	3/20
Boyle, HF	12	1744	175	641	32	20.03	1	–	6/42
Bradman, DG	52	160	3	72	2	36.00	–	–	1/08
Bright, RJ	25	5541	298	2180	53	41.13	4	1	7/87
Bromley, EH	2	60	4	19	–	–	–	–	0/19
Bruce, W	14	988	71	440	12	36.67	–	–	3/88
Burke, JW	24	814	40	230	8	28.75	–	–	4/37
Callaway, ST	3	471	33	142	6	23.67	1	–	5/37
Callen, IW	1	440	5	191	6	31.83	–	–	3/83
Carlson, PH	2	368	10	99	2	49.50	–	–	2/41
Chappell, GS	88	5327	208	1913	47	40.70	1	–	5/61
Chappell, IM	76	2873	86	1316	20	65.80	–	–	2/21
Charlton, PC	2	45	1	24	3	8.00	–	–	3/18
Chipperfield, AG	14	924	28	437	5	87.40	–	–	3/91
Clark, WM	10	2793	63	1264	44	28.73	–	–	4/46
Colley, DJ	3	729	20	312	6	52.00	–	–	3/83
Collins, HL	19	654	31	252	4	63.00	–	–	2/47
Coningham, A	1	186	9	76	2	38.00	–	–	2/17
Connolly, AN	30	7818	289	2981	102	29.23	4	–	6/47
Cooper, WH	2	466	31	226	9	25.11	1	–	6/120
Corling, GE	5	1159	50	447	12	37.25	–	–	4/60
Cosier, GJ	18	899	30	341	5	68.20	–	–	2/26
Cotter, A	21	4633	86	2549	89	28.64	7	–	7/148
Cowper, RM	27	3005	138	1139	36	31.64	–	–	4/48
Crawford, WPA	4	437	27	107	7	15.29	–	–	3/28
Darling, LS	12	162	7	65	–	–	–	–	–
Davidson, AK	44	11587	431	3819	186	20.53	14	2	7/93
Davis, SP	1	150	4	70	–	–	–	–	–
Dell, AR	2	559	18	160	6	26.67	–	–	3/65
Donnan, H	5	54	2	22	–	–	–	–	–
Dooland, B	3	880	9	419	9	46.56	–	–	4/69
Duff, RA	22	180	8	85	4	21.25	–	–	2/43
Duncan, JRF	1	112	4	30	–	–	–	–	–
Dymock, G	21	5545	179	2116	78	27.13	5	1	7/67
Eady, CJ	2	223	14	112	7	16.00	–	–	3/30

Player	M	Balls	Mdns	Runs	Wkts	Avrge	5WI	10WM	Best
Eastwood, KH	1	40	–	21	1	21.00	–	–	1/21
Ebeling, HI	1	186	9	89	3	29.67	–	–	3/74
Edwards, R	20	12	–	20	–	–	–	–	–
Emery, SH	4	462	13	249	5	49.80	–	–	2/46
Evans, E	6	1247	166	332	7	47.43	–	–	3/64
Fairfax, AG	10	1520	54	645	21	30.71	–	–	4/31
Ferris, JJ	8	2030	224	684	48	14.25	4	–	5/26
Fleetwood-Smith, LO	10	3093	78	1570	42	37.38	2	1	6/110
Freeman, EW	11	2183	58	1128	34	33.18	–	–	4/52
Freer, FW	1	160	3	74	3	24.67	–	–	2/49
Gannon, JB	3	726	13	361	11	32.82	–	–	4/77
Garrett, TW	19	2708	297	970	36	26.94	2	–	6/78
Gaunt, RA	3	716	14	310	7	44.29	–	–	3/53
Gehrs, DRA	6	6	–	4	–	–	–	–	–
Giffen, G	31	6391	434	2791	103	27.10	7	1	7/117
Gilbert, DR	9	1647	49	843	16	52.69	–	–	3/48
Gilmour, GJ	15	2661	50	1406	54	26.04	3	–	6/85
Gleeson, JW	30	8857	378	3367	93	36.20	3	–	5/61
Gregory, DW	3	20	1	9	–	–	–	–	–
Gregory, JM	24	5582	138	2648	85	31.15	4	–	7/69
Gregory, RG	2	24	–	14	–	–	–	–	–
Gregory, SE	58	30	–	33	–	–	–	–	–
Grimmett, CV	37	14513	736	5231	216	24.22	21	7	7/40
Guest, CEJ	1	144	–	59	–	–	–	–	–
Hammond, JR	5	1031	47	488	15	32.53	–	–	4/38
Hartigan, RJ	2	12	–	7	–	–	–	–	–
Hartkopf, AEV	1	240	2	134	1	134.00	–	–	1/120
Harvey, RN	79	414	23	120	3	40.00	–	–	1/08
Hassett, AL	43	111	2	78	–	–	–	–	–
Hawke, NJN	27	6974	238	2677	91	29.42	6	1	7/105
Hazlitt, GR	9	1563	74	623	23	27.09	1	–	7/25
Hendry, HSTL	11	1706	73	640	16	40.00	–	–	3/36
Higgs, JD	22	4752	175	2057	66	31.17	2	–	7/143
Hill, JC	3	606	29	273	8	34.12	–	–	3/35
Hoare, DE	1	232	–	156	2	78.00	–	–	2/68
Hodges, JH	2	136	9	84	6	14.00	–	–	2/07
Hogan, TG	7	1436	54	706	15	47.07	1	–	5/66
Hogg, RM	38	7633	231	3503	123	28.48	6	2	6/74
Hole, GB	18	398	14	126	3	42.00	–	–	1/09

Player	M	Balls	Mdns	Runs	Wkts	Avrge	5WI	10WM	Best
Holland, RG	11	2889	124	1352	34	39.76	3	2	6/54
Hookes, DW	23	96	4	41	1	41.00	–	–	1/04
Hopkins, AJY	20	1327	49	696	26	26.77	–	–	4/81
Horan, TP	15	373	45	143	11	13.00	1	–	6/40
Hordern, HV	7	2148	50	1075	46	23.37	5	2	7/90
Hornibrook, PM	6	1579	63	664	17	39.06	1	–	7/92
Howell, WP	18	3892	245	1407	49	28.71	1	–	5/81
Hughes, KJ	70	85	4	28	–	–	–	–	–
Hughes, MG	5	1047	32	567	11	51.55	–	–	3/134
Hunt, WA	1	96	2	39	–	–	–	–	–
Hurst, AG	12	3054	74	1200	43	27.91	2	–	5/28
Hurwood, A	2	517	28	170	11	15.45	–	–	4/22
Inverarity, RJ	6	372	26	93	4	23.25	–	–	3/26
Iredale, FA	14	12	–	3	–	–	–	–	–
Ironmonger, H	14	4695	328	1330	74	17.97	4	2	7/23
Iverson, JB	5	1108	29	320	21	15.24	1	–	6/27
Jenner, TJ	9	1881	62	749	24	31.21	1	–	5/90
Johnson, IW	45	8780	329	3182	109	29.19	3	–	7/44
Johnson, LJ	1	282	10	74	6	12.33	–	–	3/08
Johnston, WA	40	11048	369	3826	160	23.91	7	–	6/44
Jones, DM	10	6	1	–	–	–	–	–	–
Jones, E	19	3748	160	1857	64	29.02	3	1	7/88
Jones, SP	12	262	26	112	6	18.67	–	–	4/47
Kelleway, C	26	4363	146	1683	52	32.37	1	–	5/33
Kendall, T	2	563	56	215	14	15.36	1	–	7/55
Kippax, AF	22	72	5	19	–	–	–	–	–
Kline, LF	13	2385	113	776	34	22.82	1	–	7/75
Laird, BM	21	18	1	12	–	–	–	–	–
Laughlin, TJ	3	516	16	262	6	43.67	1	–	5/101
Laver, F	15	2361	122	964	37	26.05	2	–	8/31
Lawry, WM	68	14	1	6	–	–	–	–	–
Lawson, GF	37	8705	283	4420	145	30.48	10	2	8/112
Lee, PK	2	436	19	212	5	42.40	–	–	4/111
Lillee, DK	70	18467	652	8493	355	23.92	23	7	7/83
Lindwall, RR	61	13642	419	5251	228	23.03	12	–	7/38
Loxton, SJE	12	906	20	349	8	43.62	–	–	3/55
Lyons, JJ	14	316	17	149	6	24.83	1	–	5/30
Macartney, CG	35	3615	175	1240	45	27.56	2	1	7/58
Mackay, KD	37	5792	267	1721	50	34.42	2	–	6/42

Player	M	Balls	Mdns	Runs	Wkts	Avrge	5WI	10WM	Best
Maguire, JN	3	616	21	323	10	32.30	–	–	4/57
Mailey, AA	21	6119	115	3358	99	33.92	6	2	9/121
Mallett, AA	39	9990	419	3940	132	29.85	6	1	8/59
Malone, MF	1	342	24	77	6	12.83	1	–	5/63
Mann, AL	4	552	4	316	4	79.00	–	–	3/12
Marr, AP	1	48	6	14	–	–	–	–	–
Marsh, RW	97	72	1	54	–	–	–	–	–
Martin, JW	8	1846	57	832	17	48.94	–	–	3/56
Massie, RAL	6	1739	74	647	31	20.87	2	1	8/53
Matthews, CD	2	421	14	233	6	38.83	–	–	3/95
Matthews, GRJ	21	3500	140	1707	39	43.77	2	1	5/103
Matthews, TJ	8	1111	46	419	16	26.19	–	–	4/29
Mayne, LC	6	1251	37	628	19	33.05	–	–	4/43
Mayne, RE	4	6	–	1	–	–	–	–	–
McCabe, SJ	39	3746	127	1543	36	42.86	–	–	4/13
McCool, CL	14	2512	45	958	36	26.61	3	–	5/41
McCormick, EL	12	2107	50	1079	36	29.97	–	–	4/101
McDermott, CJ	17	3352	79	1935	53	36.51	2	–	8/141
McDonald, CC	47	8	–	3	–	–	–	–	–
McDonald, EA	11	2885	90	1431	43	33.28	2	–	5/32
McDonnell, PS	19	52	1	53	–	–	–	–	–
McKenzie, GD	61	17684	547	7328	246	29.79	16	3	8/71
McKibbin, TR	5	1032	41	496	17	29.18	–	–	3/35
McLaren, JW	1	144	3	70	1	70.00	–	–	1/23
McLeod, CE	17	3374	172	1325	33	40.15	2	–	5/65
McLeod, RW	6	1089	67	384	12	32.00	1	–	5/55
McShane, PG	3	108	9	48	1	48.00	–	–	1/39
Meckiff, I	18	3780	118	1414	45	31.42	2	–	6/38
Midwinter, WE	8	949	102	333	14	23.79	1	–	5/78
Miller, KR	55	10474	335	3905	170	22.97	7	1	7/60
Minnett, RB	9	589	26	290	11	26.36	–	–	4/34
Misson, FM	5	1197	30	616	16	38.50	–	–	4/58
Morris, AR	46	111	1	50	2	25.00	–	–	1/05
Morris, S	1	136	14	73	2	36.50	–	–	2/73
Moule, WH	1	51	4	23	3	7.67	–	–	3/23
Nagel, LE	1	262	9	110	2	55.00	–	–	2/110
Nash, LJ	2	311	12	126	10	12.60	–	–	4/18
Noble, MA	42	7109	361	3027	121	25.02	9	2	7/17
Noblet, G	3	774	25	183	7	26.14	–	–	3/21

Player	M	Balls	Mdns	Runs	Wkts	Avrge	5WI	10WM	Best
Nothling, OE	1	276	15	72	–	–	–	–	–
O'Connor, JDA	4	692	24	340	13	26.15	1	–	5/40
O'Donnell, SP	6	940	37	504	6	84.00	–	–	3/37
O'Keeffe, KJ	24	5384	190	2018	53	38.08	1	–	5/101
O'Neill, NC	42	1392	49	667	17	39.24	–	–	4/41
O'Reilly, WJ	27	10024	585	3254	144	22.60	11	3	7/54
Oxenham, RK	7	1796	112	522	14	37.29	–	–	4/39
Palmer, GE	17	4519	452	1678	78	21.51	6	2	7/65
Park, RL	1	6	–	9	–	–	–	–	–
Pascoe, LS	14	3403	112	1668	64	26.06	1	–	5/59
Pellew, CE	10	78	3	34	–	–	–	–	–
Philpott, PI	8	2262	67	1000	26	38.46	1	–	5/90
Rackemann, CG	5	936	31	540	23	23.48	3	1	6/86
Ransford, VS	20	43	3	28	1	28.00	–	–	1/09
Redpath, IR	67	64	2	41	–	–	–	–	–
Reedman, JC	1	57	2	24	1	24.00	–	–	1/12
Reid, BA	13	2959	116	1368	41	33.37	–	–	4/64
Renneberg, DA	8	1598	40	830	23	36.09	2	–	5/39
Richardson, AJ	9	1812	91	521	12	43.42	–	–	2/20
Ring, DT	13	3024	69	1305	35	37.29	2	–	6/72
Ritchie, GM	30	6	–	10	–	–	–	–	–
Robertson, WR	1	44	3	24	–	–	–	–	–
Rorke, GF	4	703	27	203	10	20.30	–	–	3/23
Rutherford, JW	1	36	2	15	1	15.00	–	–	1/11
Ryder, J	20	1897	71	743	17	43.71	–	–	2/20
Saunders, JV	14	3565	116	1796	79	22.73	6	–	7/34
Scott, HJH	8	28	1	26	–	–	–	–	–
Sellers, RHD	1	30	1	17	–	–	–	–	–
Shepherd, BK	9	26	1	9	–	–	–	–	–
Sievers, MW	3	602	25	161	9	17.89	1	–	5/21
Simpson, RB	62	6881	253	3001	71	42.27	2	–	5/57
Sincock, DJ	3	724	7	410	8	51.25	–	–	3/67
Slater, KN	1	256	9	101	2	50.50	–	–	2/40
Sleep, PR	7	1405	56	697	13	53.62	1	–	5/72
Spofforth, FR	18	4185	416	1731	94	18.41	7	4	7/44
Stackpole, KR	44	2321	86	1001	15	66.73	–	–	2/33
Taylor, JM	20	114	5	45	1	45.00	–	–	1/25
Taylor, PL	1	330	17	154	8	19.25	1	–	6/78
Thompson, N	2	112	16	31	1	31.00	–	–	1/14

Player	M	Balls	Mdns	Runs	Wkts	Avrge	5WI	10WM	Best
Thomson, AL	4	1520	33	654	12	54.50	–	–	3/79
Thomson, JR	51	10535	301	5602	200	28.01	8	–	6/46
Thurlow, HM	1	234	7	86	–	–	–	–	–
Toohey, PM	15	2	–	4	–	–	–	–	–
Toshack, ERH	12	3140	155	989	47	21.04	4	1	6/29
Travers, JPF	1	48	2	14	1	14.00	–	–	1/14
Tribe, GE	3	760	9	330	2	165.00	–	–	2/48
Trott, AE	3	474	17	192	9	21.33	1	–	8/43
Trott, GHS	24	1890	48	1019	29	35.14	–	–	4/71
Trumble, H	32	8099	452	3072	141	21.79	9	3	8/65
Trumble, JW	7	600	59	222	10	22.20	–	–	3/29
Trumper, VT	48	546	19	317	8	39.62	–	–	3/60
Turner, CTB	17	5195	457	1670	101	16.53	11	2	7/43
Veivers, TR	21	4191	196	1375	33	41.67	–	–	4/68
Waite, MG	2	552	23	190	1	190.00	–	–	1/150
Walker, MHN	34	10094	380	3792	138	27.48	6	–	8/143
Wall, TW	18	4812	154	2010	56	35.89	3	–	5/14
Walters, KD	75	3295	79	1425	49	29.08	1	–	5/66
Ward, FA	4	1268	30	574	11	52.18	1	–	6/102
Watkins, JR	1	48	1	21	–	–	–	–	–
Watson, GD	5	552	23	254	6	42.33	–	–	2/67
Watson, WJ	4	6	–	5	–	–	–	–	–
Waugh, SR	13	1185	45	618	19	32.53	1	–	5/69
Wessels, KC	24	90	3	42	–	–	–	–	–
Whatmore, DF	7	30	2	11	–	–	–	–	–
Whitney, MR	2	468	16	246	5	49.20	–	–	2/50
Whitty, WJ	14	3357	163	1373	65	21.12	3	–	6/17
Wiener, JM	6	78	4	41	–	–	–	–	–
Wilson, JW	1	216	17	64	1	64.00	–	–	1/25
Woods, SMJ	3	217	18	121	5	24.20	–	–	2/35
Worrall, J	11	255	29	127	1	127.00	–	–	1/97
Yallop, GN	39	192	5	116	1	116.00	–	–	1/21
Yardley, B	33	8909	379	3986	126	31.63	6	1	7/98

PART 2:

AUSTRALIA INTERNATIONAL LIMITED OVER CRICKET

THE GAMES

SUMMARY

Series	Opponent	Venue	Played	Won	Lost	No-result	Tie
1970-71	England	AUS	1	1	–	–	–
1972	England	ENG	3	1	2	–	–
1973-74	New Zealand	NZ	2	2	–	–	–
1974-75	England	AUS	1	–	1	–	–
1975	World Cup	ENG	5	3	2	–	–
1975-76	West Indies	AUS	1	1	–	–	–
1977	England	ENG	3	1	2	–	–
1977-78	West Indies	WI	2	1	1	–	–
1978-79	England	AUS	4	2	1	1	–
1979	World Cup	ENG	3	1	2	–	–
1979-80	B & H World Series Cup	AUS	8	3	5	–	–
1980	England	ENG	2	–	2	–	–
1980-81	B & H World Series Cup	AUS	14	9	4	1	–
1981	England	ENG	3	2	1	–	–
1981-82	B & H World Series Cup	AUS	14	5	9	–	–
1981-82	New Zealand	NZ	3	2	1	–	–
1982-83	Pakistan	PAK	3	–	2	1	–
1982-83	B & H World Series Cup	AUS	12	7	5	–	–
1982-83	New Zealand	AUS	1	–	1	–	–
1982-83	Sri Lanka	SL	4	–	2	2	–
1983	World Cup	ENG	6	2	4	–	–
1983-84	B & H World Series Cup	AUS	13	5	6	1	1
1983-84	West Indies	WI	4	1	3	–	–
1984-85	India	IND	5	3	–	2	–
1984-85	B & H World Series Cup	AUS	13	5	8	–	–
1984-85	World Championship	AUS	3	1	2	–	–
1984-85	4 Nation Tournament	SHJ	2	1	1	–	–
1985	England	ENG	3	2	1	–	–

Series	Opponent	Venue	Played	Won	Lost	No-result	Tie
1985-86	B & H World Series Cup	AUS	12	8	3	1	–
1985-86	New Zealand	NZ	4	2	2	–	–
1985-86	Australasia Cup	SHJ	1	–	1	–	–
1986-87	India	IND	6	2	3	1	–
1986-87	Challenge Cup	AUS	3	–	3	–	–
1986-87	B & H World Series Cup	AUS	10	5	5	–	–
1986-87	4 Nation Tournament	SHJ	3	–	3	–	–
Total			**177**	**78**	**88**	**10**	**1**

RESULTS SUMMARY

	Played	Won	Lost	No-result	Tie
Opponent:					
Canada	1	1	–	–	–
England	41	18	22	1	–
India	28	15	10	3	–
New Zealand	31	18	11	2	–
Pakistan	19	7	10	2	–
Sri Lanka	10	5	3	2	–
West Indies	45	13	31	–	1
Zimbabwe	2	1	1	–	–
Total	**177**	**78**	**88**	**10**	**1**
Venue:					
Australia	110	52	53	4	1
England	28	12	16	–	–
India	11	5	3	3	–
New Zealand	9	6	3	–	–
Pakistan	3	–	2	1	–
Sharjah (UAE)	6	1	5	–	–
Sri Lanka	4	–	2	2	–
West Indies	6	2	4	–	–
Total games abroad	67	26	35	6	–
Total	**177**	**78**	**88**	**10**	**1**

	Success Rate	Played	Won	Lost	No-result	Tie
Success Rate:						
AUS Batted first	40.23%	87	35	47	5	–
OPP Batted first	47.78%	90	43	41	5	1

	Games	From	To
Most wins in succession:			
	4	7 Dec 1980	11 Jan 1981
	4	26 Jan 1987	6 Feb 1987
Most losses in succession:			
	5	17 Mar 1983	11/12 Jun 1983
	5	8 Feb 1987	9 Apr 1987

TEAM SCORING DETAILS

Opponent	M	Inn	NO	Runs	H.S	50	100	Avrge	Ct/St	Won	Lost	Drawn	Tie
Sri Lanka	10	70	20	2224	118*	18	2	44.48	29/4	5	3	2	–
Zimbabwe	2	18	4	498	76	3	–	35.57	7/-	1	1	–	–
Canada	1	5	2	106	27*	–	–	35.33	5/-	1	–	–	–
India	28	214	46	5278	111	24	6	31.42	97/3	15	10	3	–
Pakistan	19	163	29	3706	121	20	2	27.66	70/2	7	10	2	–
England	41	363	70	7912	125*	38	5	27.00	161/5	18	22	1	–
New Zealand	31	255	47	5612	138*	33	3	26.98	145/2	18	11	2	–
West Indies	45	431	73	8820	127*	49	3	24.64	156/-	13	31	–	1
Total	**177**	**1519**	**291**	**34156**	**138***	**184**	**21**	**27.81**	**670/16**	**78**	**88**	**10**	**1**

TEAM BOWLING DETAILS

Opponent	M	Balls	Mdns	Runs	Wkts	Avrge	5WI	Best	Stk/rt
Canada	1	200	9	105	10	10.50	1	5/21	20.00
New Zealand	31	8378	141	5765	247	23.34	3	5/17	33.92
India	28	7003	101	5088	191	26.64	3	6/39	36.66
England	41	11604	188	8047	302	26.65	3	6/14	38.42
Sri Lanka	10	2257	36	1629	57	28.56	–	3/27	39.59
Zimbabwe	2	719	10	479	16	29.93	–	3/40	44.93
Pakistan	19	5181	78	3772	126	29.94	2	5/16	41.12
West Indies	45	12676	180	9610	282	34.08	1	5/48	44.95
Total	**177**	**48018**	**743**	**34495**	**1231**	**28.02**	**13**	**6/14**	**39.01**

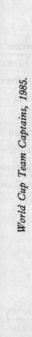

World Cup Team Captains, 1985.

ONE-DAY MATCHES

The introduction of one-day matches has been the most revolutionary change in cricket in this century. It does not please some of the diehards, who determinedly stay away, and it can make even the most stylish stroke-makers look foolish as they swing the bat awkwardly in the search for quick runs.

But the money it attracts through the turnstiles and the audiences who follow it on television are vital to Australian cricket's future. By producing a winner after a limited number of overs, these games have attracted a new audience to our cricket grounds—an audience the game needs.

Nobody could have predicted that limited-over cricket played at night would succeed as it has in Australia. Every summer Australian night games provide a spectacle unequalled in world cricket. Traditionalists dislike the coloured equipment and the coloured clothing, and the Members' stands at some of the grounds are noticeably empty on some nights, but crowds in excess of 50,000 cause no surprise.

One of the reasons for this sustained success—limited-over matches are now more than a decade old in Australia—is the admission charge. Families can afford a night out together at the cricket, whereas five days at a traditional Test is too expensive.

Another reason is the lights. Who would have believed 20 years ago that cricket could be played at night with every incident so vividly seen, every drop of sweat on the batsmen's faces clearly visible? Somehow those lights bring the players closer than they seem in a Test played in daylight, optical illusion though it may be.

One-day matches have brought many improvements to playing standards. Before English cricketers began to play one-day matches regularly, Australia could always count on having a big advantage in the field when the countries met in Tests. That has all changed since the advent of one-day games. Indeed, English teams are showing an unprecedented athleticism and hold just as many spectacular catches as their Australian opponents.

The major problem with one-day cricket is that it has been too successful. Programs for Australia's first-class players have become so heavily loaded with one-day matches that the career span of an average

An enthusiastic crowd of one-day cricket supporters.

international will soon be markedly shorter than in the years before the one-day wonders.

Australian captain Allan Border is only one of many prominent players who have called for a curtailing of the one-day schedules. A packed program of one-dayers gives players little time to recover from muscle tear, and there is a high emotional toll not experienced in traditional cricket.

A close scrutiny of the notorious underarm ball incident in Melbourne, when Greg Chappell instructed his brother to deliver the last ball against New Zealand below the waist, suggests such an error of judgment was due to emotional strain. Chappell had played his hardest throughout a long and tiring day and in his own words was totally exhausted. There was no time to consider the factors involved, no time for consultation.

Very few of the players involved in a tense limited-over match under lights can get to sleep easily when they return to their hotels. They are too agitated, still on mental highs, and for some of them sleep takes hours to arrive. A visit to the dressing-rooms immediately after one of these limited-over thrillers is a memorable experience. The fielding side slumps on benches utterly drained and it's cruel even to approach the players for a comment.

"One-day cricket is injecting a dementia into the souls of all those who play it," former Test spinner Bill O'Reilly wrote in the *Sydney Morning Herald*. "The whole thing is cancerous." Bill is not alone in his fierce condemnation of commentators who praise bowlers for containing batsmen , when their traditional job has been to get them out.

Limited-over cricket has been played in Australia almost from the time the game began in Australia, but while spectators and sponsors queue eagerly for more, there is no way it can be discarded. What other form of cricket can produce five run-outs in one innings, as Australia suffered in her first World Cup final against the West Indies in 1975?

RESULTS OF ALL GAMES

Game	Date	Venue	Australia Total	Ovrs	Opponent	Total	Ovrs	Result	Captain
1	5 Jan 1971	Melbourne	5-191	34.6	England	190*	39.4	AUS by 5 wkts	Lawry, WM
2	24 Aug 1972	Manchester	8-222*	55.0	England	4-226	49.1	ENG by 6 wkts	Chappell, IM
3	26 Aug 1972	Lord's	5-240	51.3	England	9-236*	55.0	AUS by 5 wkts	Chappell, IM
4	28 Aug 1972	Birmingham	9-179*	55.0	England	8-180	51.3	ENG by 2 wkts	Chappell, IM
5	30 Mar 1974	Dunedin	3-195	24.3	New Zealand	9-194*	35.0	AUS by 7 wkts	Chappell, IM
6	31 Mar 1974	Christchurch	5-265*	35.0	New Zealand	6-234	35.0	AUS by 31 runs	Chappell, IM
7	1 Jan 1975	Melbourne	190*	34.5	England	7-191	37.1	ENG by 3 wkts	Chappell, IM
8	7 Jun 1975	Leeds	7-278*	60.0	Pakistan	205	53.0	AUS by 73 runs	Chappell, IM
9	11 Jun 1975	The Oval	5-328*	60.0	Sri Lanka	4-276	60.0	AUS by 52 runs	Chappell, IM
10	14 Jun 1975	The Oval	192*	53.4	West Indies	3-195	46.0	WI by 7 wkts	Chappell, IM
11	18 Jun 1975	Leeds	6-94	28.4	England	93*	36.2	AUS by 4 wkts	Chappell, IM
12	21 Jun 1975	Lord's	274	60.0	West Indies	8-291*	58.4	WI by 17 runs	Chappell, IM
13	20 Dec 1975	Adelaide	5-225	31.5	West Indies	224*	37.6	AUS by 5 wkts	Chappell, GS
14	2 Jun 1977	Manchester	9-169*	55.0	England	8-173	45.2	ENG by 2 wkts	Chappell, GS
15	4 Jun 1977	Birmingham	70	25.2	England	171*	53.5	ENG by 99 runs	Chappell, GS
16	6 Jun 1977	The Oval	8-246	53.2	England	242*	54.2	AUS by 2 wkts	Chappell, GS
17	22 Feb 1978	St. John's	7-181	36.0	West Indies	9-313*	50.0	WI on run rate	Simpson, RB
18	12 Apr 1978	Castries	8-140	35.0	West Indies	139*	34.4	AUS by 2 wkts	Simpson, RB
19	13 Jan 1979	Sydney	1-17*	7.2	England	–		No result	Yallop, GN
20	24 Jan 1979	Melbourne	101*	33.5	England	3-102	28.2	ENG by 7 wkts	Yallop, GN

No.	Date	Venue	Score	Overs	Opponent	Score	Overs	Result	Captain
21	4 Feb 1979	Melbourne	6-215	38.6	England	6-212*	40.0	AUS by 4 wkts	Yallop, GN
22	7 Feb 1979	Melbourne	4-95	21.5	England	94*	31.7	AUS by 6 wkts	Yallop, GN
23	9 Jun 1979	Lord's	9-159*	60.0	England	4-160	47.1	ENG by 6 wkts	Hughes, KJ
24	13/14 Jun 1979	Nottingham	197	57.1	Pakistan	7-286*	60.0	PAK by 89 runs	Hughes, KJ
25	16 Jun 1979	Birmingham	3-106	26.0	Canada	105*	33.2	AUS by 7 wkts	Hughes, KJ
26	27 Nov 1979	Sydney	5-196	47.1	West Indies	193*	49.3	AUS by 5 wkts	Chappell, GS
27	8 Dec 1979	Melbourne	9-207*	50.0	England	7-209	49.0	ENG by 3 wkts	Chappell, GS
28	9 Dec 1979	Melbourne	8-191	48.0	West Indies	2-271*	48.0	WI by 80 runs	Chappell, GS
29	11 Dec 1979	Sydney	192	47.2	England	7-264*	49.0	ENG by 72 runs	Chappell, GS
30	21 Dec 1979	Sydney	6-176*	50.0	West Indies	169	42.5	AUS by 7 runs	Chappell, GS
31	26 Dec 1979	Sydney	6-194*	47.0	England	6-195	45.1	ENG by 4 wkts	Chappell, GS
32	14 Jan 1980	Sydney	163*	48.4	England	8-164	48.5	ENG by 2 wkts	Chappell, GS
33	18 Jan 1980	Sydney	190*	48.3	West Indies	181	49.1	AUS by 9 runs	Chappell, GS
34	20 Aug 1980	The Oval	8-225	55.0	England	6-248*	55.0	ENG by 23 runs	Chappell, GS
35	22 Aug 1980	Birmingham	5-273	55.0	England	8-320*	55.0	ENG by 47 runs	Chappell, GS
36	23 Nov 1980	Adelaide	9-217*	50.0	New Zealand	7-219	49.1	NZ by 3 wkts	Chappell, GS
37	25 Nov 1980	Sydney	3-289*	50.0	New Zealand	195	42.5	AUS by 94 runs	Chappell, GS
38	6 Dec 1980	Melbourne	142	42.1	India	9-208*	49.0	IND by 66 runs	Chappell, GS
39	7 Dec 1980	Melbourne	6-159	47.2	New Zealand	156*	49.5	AUS by 4 wkts	Chappell, GS
40	18 Dec 1980	Sydney	1-183	42.2	India	9-180*	49.0	AUS by 9 wkts	Chappell, GS
41	8 Jan 1981	Sydney	1-64	21.0	India	63*	25.5	AUS by 9 wkts	Chappell, GS
42	11 Jan 1981	Melbourne	3-193	47.2	India	5-192*	50.0	AUS by 7 wkts	Chappell, GS
43	13 Jan 1981	Sydney	7-219	50.0	New Zealand	8-220*	50.0	NZ by 1 run	Chappell, GS

Game	Date	Venue	Australia Total	Ovrs	Opponent	Total	Ovrs	Result	Captain
44	15 Jan 1981	Sydney	8-242*	50.0	India	8-215	50.0	AUS by 27 runs	Chappell, GS
45	21 Jan 1981	Sydney	180*	43.1	New Zealand	1-23	8.0	No result	Chappell, GS
46	29 Jan 1981	Sydney	155	39.3	New Zealand	6-233*	50.0	NZ by 78 runs	Chappell, GS
47	31 Jan 1981	Melbourne	3-130	39.3	New Zealand	126*	46.4	AUS by 7 wkts	Chappell, GS
48	1 Feb 1981	Melbourne	4-235*	50.0	New Zealand	8-229	50.0	AUS by 6 runs	Chappell, GS
49	3 Feb 1981	Sydney	4-218	47.4	New Zealand	8-215*	50.0	AUS by 6 wkts	Chappell, GS
50	4 Jun 1981	Lord's	7-210*	55.0	England	4-212	51.4	ENG by 6 wkts	Hughes, KJ
51	6 Jun 1981	Birmingham	8-249*	55.0	England	247	54.5	AUS by 2 wkts	Hughes, KJ
52	8 Jun 1981	Leeds	8-236*	55.0	England	165	46.5	AUS by 71 runs	Hughes, KJ
53	21 Nov 1981	Melbourne	9-209*	50.0	Pakistan	6-210	49.2	PAK by 4 wkts	Chappell, GS
54	24 Nov 1981	Sydney	3-237	47.0	West Indies	8-236*	49.0	AUS by 7 wkts	Chappell, GS
55	6 Dec 1981	Adelaide	208*	48.3	Pakistan	8-170	50.0	AUS by 38 runs	Chappell, GS
56	17 Dec 1981	Sydney	6-222*	50.0	Pakistan	4-223	43.2	PAK by 6 wkts	Chappell, GS
57	20 Dec 1981	Perth	9-188*	50.0	West Indies	2-190	30.0	WI by 8 wkts	Chappell, GS
58	20 Jan 1982	Melbourne	193	49.0	Pakistan	6-218*	50.0	PAK by 25 runs	Chappell, GS
59	10 Jan 1982	Melbourne	146*	42.5	West Indies	5-147	47.1	WI by 5 wkts	Chappell, GS
60	14 Jan 1982	Sydney	5-230*	50.0	Pakistan	9-154	40.3	AUS by 76 runs	Chappell, GS
61	17 Jan 1982	Brisbane	9-185*	40.0	West Indies	5-186	38.4	WI by 5 wkts	Chappell, GS
62	19 Jan 1982	Sydney	7-168	43.1	West Indies	189*	50.0	AUS on run rate	Chappell, GS
63	23 Jan 1982	Melbourne	130	37.4	West Indies	8-216*	49.0	WI by 86 runs	Chappell, GS
64	24 Jan 1982	Melbourne	107	32.2	West Indies	9-235*	50.0	WI by 128 runs	Chappell, GS
65	26 Jan 1982	Sydney	8-214*	50.0	West Indies	168	42.5	AUS by 46 runs	Chappell, GS

66	27 Jan 1982	Sydney	9-216	50.0	West Indies	6-234*	50.0	WI by 18 runs	Chappell, GS
67	13 Feb 1982	Auckland	194	44.5	New Zealand	6-240*	50.0	NZ by 46 runs	Chappell, GS
68	17 Feb 1982	Dunedin	4-160	45.0	New Zealand	9-159*	49.0	AUS by 6 wkts	Chappell, GS
69	9 Feb 1982	Wellington	2-75	20.3	New Zealand	74*	29.0	AUS by 8 wkts	Chappell, GS
70	20 Sep 1982	Hyderabad	9-170	40.0	Pakistan	6-229*	40.0	PAK by 59 runs	Hughes, KJ
71	8 Oct 1982	Lahore	4-206	40.0	Pakistan	3-234*	40.0	PAK by 28 runs	Hughes, KJ
72	22 Oct 1982	Karachi	–	–	Pakistan	1-44*	12.0	No result	Hughes, KJ
73	9 Jan 1983	Melbourne	2-182	46.4	New Zealand	181*	44.5	AUS by 8 wkts	Hughes, KJ
74	11 Jan 1983	Sydney	180*	46.4	England	149	41.1	AUS by 31 runs	Hughes, KJ
75	16 Jan 1983	Brisbane	3-184	41.0	England	182*	46.4	AUS by 7 wkts	Hughes, KJ
76	18 Jan 1983	Sydney	179	45.3	New Zealand	8-226*	50.0	NZ by 47 runs	Hughes, KJ
77	22 Jan 1983	Melbourne	9-188	44.1	New Zealand	6-246*	50.0	NZ by 58 runs	Hughes, KJ
78	23 Jan 1983	Melbourne	5-217	34.4	England	5-213*	37.0	AUS by 5 wkts	Hughes, KJ
79	26 Jan 1983	Sydney	109	27.3	England	207*	41.0	ENG by 98 runs	Hughes, KJ
80	30 Jan 1983	Adelaide	7-214	47.0	England	6-228*	47.0	ENG by 14 runs	Hughes, KJ
81	31 Jan 1983	Adelaide	153	44.0	New Zealand	9-199*	50.0	NZ by 46 runs	Hughes, KJ
82	6 Feb 1983	Perth	9-191*	50.0	New Zealand	164	44.5	AUS by 27 runs	Hughes, KJ
83	9 Feb 1983	Sydney	4-155	31.1	New Zealand	7-193*	49.0	AUS by 6 wkts	Hughes, KJ
84	13 Feb 1983	Melbourne	8-302*	50.0	New Zealand	153	39.5	AUS by 149 runs	Hughes, KJ
85	17 Mar 1983	Sydney	124	35.0	New Zealand	8-138*	34.0	NZ by 14 runs	Hughes, KJ
86	13 Apr 1983	Colombo1	9-168*	45.0	Sri Lanka	8-169	44.1	SL by 2 wkts	Chappell, GS
87	16 Apr 1983	Colombo1	5-207*	45.0	Sri Lanka	6-213	43.2	SL by 4 wkts	Chappell, GS
88	20 Apr 1983	Colombo2	5-194*	39.2	Sri Lanka	–	–	No result	Chappell, GS

Game	Date	Venue	Australia Total	Ovrs	Opponent	Total	Ovrs	Result	Captain
89	30 Apr 1983	Colombo2	3-124*	19.2	Sri Lanka	–	–	No result	Chappell, GS
90	9 Jun 1983	Nottingham	7-226	60.0	Zimbabwe	6-239*	60.0	ZIM by 13 runs	Hughes, KJ
91	11/12 Jun 1983	Leeds	9-151	30.3	West Indies	9-252*	60.0	WI by 101 runs	Hughes, KJ
92	13 Jun 1983	Nottingham	9-320*	60.0	India	158	37.5	AUS by 162 runs	Hughes, KJ
93	16 Jun 1983	Southampton	7-272*	60.0	Zimbabwe	240	59.5	AUS by 32 runs	Hughes, KJ
94	18 Jun 1983	Lord's	6-273*	60.0	West Indies	3-276	57.5	WI by 7 wkts	Hughes, KJ
95	20 Jun 1983	Chelmsford	129	38.2	India	247*	55.5	IND by 118 runs	Hookes, DW
96	8 Jan 1984	Melbourne	194	46.0	West Indies	7-221*	50.0	WI by 27 runs	Hughes, KJ
97	10 Jan 1984	Sydney	264*	50.0	Pakistan	9-230	50.0	AUS by 34 runs	Hughes, KJ
98	15 Jan 1984	Brisbane	0-15	3.5	Pakistan	6-184*	42.0	No result	Hughes, KJ
99	17 Jan 1984	Sydney	9-195	49.0	West Indies	7-223*	49.0	WI by 28 runs	Hughes, KJ
100	21 Jan 1984	Melbourne	8-209*	50.0	Pakistan	166	45.0	AUS by 45 runs	Hughes, KJ
101	22 Jan 1984	Melbourne	226	49.5	West Indies	6-252*	50.0	WI by 26 runs	Hughes, KJ
102	25 Jan 1984	Sydney	8-244*	50.0	Pakistan	157	47.2	AUS by 87 runs	Hughes, KJ
103	29 Jan 1984	Adelaide	7-165*	50.0	West Indies	4-169	45.1	WI by 6 wkts	Hughes, KJ
104	30 Jan 1984	Adelaide	8-210*	50.0	Pakistan	140	45.2	AUS by 70 runs	Hughes, KJ
105	5 Feb 1984	Perth	8-211*	50.0	West Indies	197	43.3	AUS by 14 runs	Hughes, KJ
106	8 Feb 1984	Sydney	160*	44.4	West Indies	1-161	43.1	WI by 9 wkts	Hughes, KJ
107	11 Feb 1984	Melbourne	9-222	50.0	West Indies	5-222*	50.0	Tie	Hughes, KJ
108	12 Feb 1984	Melbourne	8-212*	50.0	West Indies	4-213	45.3	WI by 6 wkts	Hughes, KJ
109	29 Feb 1984	Berbice	5-231*	50.0	West Indies	2-232	48.0	WI by 8 wkts	Hughes, KJ
110	14 Mar 1984	Port-of-Spain	6-194	36.4	West Indies	6-190*	37.0	AUS by 4 wkts	Hughes, KJ

111	19 Apr 1984	Castries	9-206*	45.0	West Indies	3-208	41.4	WI by 7 wkts	Hughes, KJ
112	26 Apr 1984	Kingston	7-209*	50.0	West Indies	1-211	47.4	WI by 9 wkts	Hughes, KJ
113	28 Sep 1984	New Delhi	9-220*	48.0	India	172	40.5	AUS by 48 runs	Hughes, KJ
114	1 Oct 1984	Trivandrum	1-29	7.4	India	175*	37.0	No result	Hughes, KJ
115	3 Oct 1984	Jamshedpur	–	–	India	2-21*	5.1	No result	Hughes, KJ
116	5 Oct 1984	Ahmedabad	3-210	43.5	India	6-206*	46.0	AUS by 7 wkts	Hughes, KJ
117	6 Oct 1984	Indore	4-236	40.1	India	5-235*	44.0	AUS by 6 wkts	Hughes, KJ
118	6 Jan 1985	Melbourne	6-240*	50.0	West Indies	3-241	44.5	WI by 7 wkts	Border, AR
119	8 Jan 1985	Sydney	4-240	46.2	Sri Lanka	7-239*	49.0	AUS by 6 wkts	Border, AR
120	13 Jan 1985	Brisbane	191	50.0	West Indies	5-195	37.4	WI by 5 wkts	Border, AR
121	15 Jan 1985	Sydney	5-200*	50.0	West Indies	5-201	43.3	WI by 5 wkts	Border, AR
122	19 Jan 1985	Melbourne	9-226*	50.0	Sri Lanka	6-230	49.2	SL by 4 wkts	Border, AR
123	20 Jan 1985	Melbourne	9-206	50.0	West Indies	7-271*	50.0	WI by 65 runs	Border, AR
124	23 Jan 1985	Sydney	7-242	47.1	Sri Lanka	6-240*	50.0	AUS by 3 wkts	Border, AR
125	27 Jan 1985	Adelaide	9-200*	50.0	West Indies	4-201	43.4	WI by 6 wkts	Border, AR
126	28 Jan 1985	Adelaide	2-323*	50.0	Sri Lanka	91	35.5	AUS by 232 runs	Border, AR
127	3 Feb 1985	Perth	1-172	23.5	Sri Lanka	171	44.3	AUS by 9 wkts	Border, AR
128	6 Feb 1985	Sydney	6-247*	50.0	West Indies	221	47.3	AUS by 26 runs	Border, AR
129	10 Feb 1985	Melbourne	3-271*	50.0	West Indies	6-273	49.2	WI by 4 wkts	Border, AR
130	12 Feb 1985	Sydney	178*	50.0	West Indies	3-179	47.0	WI by 7 wkts	Border, AR
131	17 Feb 1985	Melbourne	3-215	45.2	England	8-214*	49.0	AUS by 7 wkts	Border, AR
132	24 Feb 1985	Melbourne	200	42.3	Pakistan	6-262*	50.0	PAK by 62 runs	Border, AR
133	3 Mar 1985	Melbourne	163	49.3	India	2-165*	36.1	IND by 8 wkts	Border, AR

Game	Date	Venue	Australia Total	Ovrs	Opponent	Total	Ovrs	Result	Captain
134	24 Mar 1985	Sharjah	8-178	50.0	England	8-177*	50.0	AUS by 2 wkts	Border, AR
135	29 Mar 1985	Sharjah	139*	42.3	India	7-140	39.2	IND by 3 wkts	Border, AR
136	30 May 1985	Manchester	7-220	54.1	England	219*	54.0	AUS by 3 wkts	Border, AR
137	1 Jun 1985	Birmingham	6-233	54.0	England	7-231*	55.0	AUS by 4 wkts	Border, AR
138	3 Jun 1985	Lord's	5-254*	55.0	England	2-257	49.0	ENG by 8 wkts	Border, AR
139	9 Jan 1986	Melbourne	–	–	New Zealand	7-161*	29.0	No result	Border, AR
140	12 Jan 1986	Brisbane	6-164	45.2	India	161*	43.0	AUS by 4 wkts	Border, AR
141	14 Jan 1986	Sydney	6-153	45.1	New Zealand	152*	49.2	AUS by 4 wkts	Border, AR
142	16 Jan 1986	Melbourne	161*	44.2	India	2-162	40.2	IND by 8 wkts	Border, AR
143	19 Jan 1986	Perth	6-161	45.1	New Zealand	6-159*	50.0	AUS by 4 wkts	Border, AR
144	21 Jan 1986	Sydney	6-292*	50.0	India	4-192	50.0	AUS by 100 runs	Border, AR
145	26 Jan 1986	Adelaide	8-262*	50.0	India	226	45.3	AUS by 36 runs	Border, AR
146	27 Jan 1986	Adelaide	70	26.3	New Zealand	7-276*	50.0	NZ by 206 runs	Border, AR
147	29 Jan 1986	Sydney	7-239*	50.0	New Zealand	140	42.4	AUS by 99 runs	Border, AR
148	31 Jan 1986	Melbourne	7-235*	50.0	India	4-238	48.5	IND by 6 wkts	Border, AR
149	5 Feb 1986	Sydney	8-170*	44.0	India	159	43.4	AUS by 11 runs	Border, AR
150	9 Feb 1986	Melbourne	3-188	47.2	India	187*	50.0	AUS by 7 wkts	Border, AR
151	19 Mar 1986	Dunedin	156	47.0	New Zealand	6-186*	50.0	NZ by 30 runs	Border, AR
152	22 Mar 1986	Christchurch	205	45.4	New Zealand	7-258*	49.0	NZ by 53 runs	Border, AR
153	26 Mar 1986	Wellington	7-232	49.3	New Zealand	9-229*	50.0	AUS by 3 wkts	Border, AR
154	29 Mar 1986	Auckland	231*	44.5	New Zealand	9-187	45.0	AUS by 44 runs	Border, AR
155	11 Apr 1986	Sharjah	7-202*	50.0	Pakistan	2-206	49.1	PAK by 8 wkts	Bright, RJ

No.	Date	Venue	Score	Overs	Opponent	Score	Overs	Result	Captain
156	7 Sep 1986	Jaipur	3-250*	47.0	India	3-251	41.0	IND by 7 wkts	Border, AR
157	9 Sep 1986	Srinagar	7-226	46.0	India	8-222*	47.0	AUS by 3 wkts	Border, AR
158	24 Sep 1986	Hyderabad	6-242*	47.0	India	1-41	10.4	No result	Border, AR
159	2 Oct 1986	Delhi	6-238*	45.0	India	7-242	43.3	IND by 3 wkts	Border, AR
160	5 Oct 1986	Ahmedabad	141	43.3	India	193*	47.4	IND by 52 runs	Border, AR
161	7 Oct 1986	Rajkot	3-263	46.3	India	6-260*	48.0	AUS by 7 wkts	Border, AR
162	1 Jan 1987	Perth	235	48.2	England	6-272*	49.0	ENG by 37 runs	Border, AR
163	2 Jan 1987	Perth	6-273*	50.0	Pakistan	9-274	49.5	PAK by 1 wkt	Border, AR
164	4 Jan 1987	Perth	91	35.4	West Indies	8-255*	50.0	WI by 164 runs	Border, AR
165	18 Jan 1987	Brisbane	4-261*	50.0	England	9-250	50.0	AUS by 11 runs	Border, AR
166	20 Jan 1987	Melbourne	6-181*	50.0	West Indies	3-182	48.2	WI by 7 wkts	Border, AR
167	22 Jan 1987	Sydney	8-233*	50.0	England	7-234	49.5	ENG by 3 wkts	Border, AR
168	25 Jan 1987	Adelaide	9-221	50.0	West Indies	5-237*	50.0	WI by 16 runs	Border, AR
169	26 Jan 1987	Adelaide	6-225*	50.0	England	192	48.1	AUS by 33 runs	Border, AR
170	28 Jan 1987	Sydney	194*	50.0	West Indies	158	46.1	AUS by 36 runs	Border, AR
171	1 Feb 1987	Melbourne	5-248*	50.0	England	139	47.3	AUS BY 109 runs	Border, AR
172	6 Feb 1987	Sydney	8-195	49.1	West Indies	192*	49.0	AUS by 2 wkts	Border, AR
173	8 Feb 1987	Melbourne	8-171*	44.0	England	4-172	36.0	ENG by 6 wkts	Border, AR
174	11 Feb 1987	Sydney	8-179	50.0	England	9-187*	50.0	ENG by 8 runs	Border, AR
175	3 Apr 1987	Sharjah	9-176*	50.0	Pakistan	4-180	46.4	PAK by 6 wkts	Border, AR
176	6 Apr 1987	Sharjah	6-176*	50.0	India	3-177	42.0	IND by 7 wkts	Marsh, GR
177	9 Apr 1987	Sharjah	9-219	50.0	England	6-230*	50.0	ENG by 11 runs	Border, AR

* Denotes batted first

RESULTS FOR EACH GROUND

Venue	1st game	Played	Won	Lost	No/Result	Tie
Australia:						
Adelaide	20 Dec 1975	13	6	7	–	–
Brisbane	17 Jan 1982	6	3	2	1	–
Melbourne	5 Jan 1971	40	14	24	1	1
Perth	20 Dec 1981	8	4	4	–	–
Sydney	13 Jan 1979	43	25	16	2	–
England:						
Birmingham	28 Aug 1972	6	3	3	–	–
Chelmsford	20 Jun 1983	1	–	1	–	–
Leeds	7 Jun 1975	4	3	1	–	–
Lord's	26 Aug 1972	6	1	5	–	–
Manchester	24 Aug 1972	3	1	2	–	–
Nottingham	13/14 Jun 1979	3	1	2	–	–
Southampton	16 Jun 1983	1	1	–	–	–
The Oval	11 Jun 1975	4	2	2	–	–
New Zealand:						
Auckland	13 Feb 1982	2	1	1	–	–
Christchurch	31 Mar 1974	2	1	1	–	–
Dunedin	30 Mar 1974	3	2	1	–	–
Wellington	9 Feb 1982	2	2	–	–	–
Pakistan:						
Hyderabad	20 Sep 1982	1	–	1	–	–
Karachi	22 Oct 1982	1	–	–	1	–
Lahore	8 Oct 1982	1	–	1	–	–
West Indies:						
Berbice	29 Feb 1984	1	–	1	–	–
Castries	12 Apr 1978	2	1	1	–	–
Kingston	26 Apr 1984	1	–	1	–	–
Port-of-Spain	14 Mar 1984	1	1	–	–	–
St. John's	22 Feb 1978	1	–	1	–	–
Sri Lanka:						
Colombo1	13 Apr 1983	2	–	2	–	–
Colombo2	20 Apr 1983	2	–	–	2	–

Venue	1st game	Played	Won	Lost	No/Result	Tie
India:						
Ahmedabad	5 Oct 1984	2	1	1	–	–
Delhi	2 Oct 1986	1	–	1	–	–
Hyderabad	24 Sep 1986	1	–	–	1	–
Indore	6 Oct 1984	1	1	–	–	–
Jaipur	7 Oct 1986	1	–	1	–	–
Jamshedpur	3 Oct 1984	1	–	–	1	–
New Delhi	28 Sep 1984	1	1	–	–	–
Rajkot	7 Oct 1986	1	1	–	–	–
Srinagar	9 Sep 1986	1	1	–	–	–
Trivandrum	1 Oct 1984	1	–	–	1	–
UAE:						
Sharjah	24 Mar 1985	6	1	5	–	–

LARGEST MARGINS OF VICTORY

Margin	Opponent	Venue	Date
Runs:			
232	Sri Lanka	Adelaide	28 Jan 1985
162	India	Nottingham	13 Jun 1983
149	New Zealand	Melbourne	13 Feb 1983
109	England	Melbourne	1 Feb 1987
100	India	Sydney	21 Jan 1986
Wkts:			
9	India	Sydney	18 Dec 1980
9	India	Sydney	8 Jan 1981
9	Sri Lanka	Perth	3 Feb 1985
8	New Zealand	Wellington	9 Feb 1982
8	New Zealand	Melbourne	9 Jan 1983

LARGEST MARGINS OF DEFEAT

Margin	Opponent	Venue	Date
Runs:			
206	New Zealand	Adelaide	27 Jan 1986
164	West Indies	Perth	4 Jan 1987
128	West Indies	Melbourne	24 Jan 1982
118	India	Chelmsford	20 Jun 1983
101	England	Birmingham	4 Jun 1977
101	West Indies	Leeds	11/12 Jun 1983
Wkts:			
9	West Indies	Sydney	8 Feb 1984
9	West Indies	Kingston	26 Apr 1984
8	West Indies	Perth	20 Dec 1981
8	West Indies	Berbice	29 Feb 1984
8	India	Melbourne	3 Mar 1985
8	England	Lord's	3 Jun 1985
8	India	Melbourne	16 Jan 1986
8	Pakistan	Sharjah	11 Apr 1986

NARROWEST MARGINS OF VICTORY

Margin	Opponent	Venue	Date
Runs:			
232	Sri Lanka	Adelaide	28 Jan 1985
Ties:			
1	West Indies	Melbourne	11 Feb 1984
Wkts:			
2	England	The Oval	6 Jun 1977
2	West Indies	Castries	12 Apr 1978
2	England	Birmingham	6 Jun 1981
2	England	Sharjah	24 Mar 1985

Margin	Opponent	Venue	Date
Runs:			
2	England	Birmingham	6 Jun 1981
6	New Zealand	Melbourne	1 Feb 1981
7	West Indies	Sydney	21 Dec 1979
9	West Indies	Sydney	18 Jan 1980

NARROWEST MARGINS OF DEFEAT

Margin	Opponent	Venue	Date
Wkts:			
1	Pakistan	Perth	2 Jan 1987
2	England	Birmingham	28 Aug 1972
2	England	Manchester	2 Jun 1977
2	England	Sydney	14 Jan 1980
2	Sri Lanka	Colombo1	13 Apr 1983
Runs:			
1	New Zealand	Sydney	13 Jan 1981
8	England	Sydney	11 Feb 1987

HIGHEST INNINGS TOTALS

Total	Overs	Opp	Venue	Date	Result
5-328*	60.0	SL	The Oval	11 Jun 1975	AUS by 52 runs
3-323*	50.0	SL	Adelaide	28 Jan 1985	AUS by 232 runs
9-320*	60.0	IND	Nottingham	13 Jan 1983	AUS by 162 runs
8-302*	50.0	NZ	Melbourne	13 Feb 1983	AUS by 149 runs
6-292*	50.0	IND	Sydney	21 Jan 1986	AUS by 100 runs
3-289*	50.0	NZ	Sydney	25 Nov 1980	AUS by 94 runs
7-278*	60.0	PAK	Leeds	7 Jun 1975	AUS by 73 runs
274	58.4	WI	Lord's	21 Jun 1975	WI by 17 runs
6-273*	60.0	WI	Lord's	18 Jun 1975	WI by 7 wkts
5-273	55.0	ENG	Birmingham	22 Aug 1980	ENG by 47 runs
6-273*	50.0	PAK	Perth	2 Jan 1987	PAK by 1 wkt

Total	Overs	Opp	Venue	Date	Result
7-272*	60.0	ZIM	Southampton	16 Jun 1983	AUS by 32 runs
3-271*	50.0	WI	Melbourne	10 Feb 1985	WI by 4 wkts
5-265*	35.0¢	NZ	Christchurch	31 Mar 1974	AUS by 31 runs
3-263	48.0	IND	Rajkot	7 Oct 1986	AUS by 7 wkts
8-262*	50.0	IND	Adelaide	26 Jan 1986	AUS by 36 runs
4-261*	50.0	ENG	Brisbane	18 Jan 1987	AUS by 11 runs
5-254*	55.0	ENG	Lord's	3 Jun 1985	ENG by 8 wkts
3-250*	47.0	IND	Jaipur	7 Sep 1986	IND by 7 wkts

LOWEST COMPLETED INNINGS TOTALS

Total	Overs	Opponent	Venue	Date	Result
70	25.2	ENG	Birmingham	4 Jun 1977	ENG by 99 runs
70	26.3	NZ	Adelaide	27 Jan 1986	NZ by 206 runs
91	35.4	WI	Perth	4 Jan 1987	WI by 164 runs
101*	33.5	ENG	Melbourne	24 Jan 1979	ENG by 7 wkts
107	32.2	WI	Melbourne	24 Jan 1982	WI by 128 runs
109	27.3	ENG	Sydney	26 Jan 1983	ENG by 98 runs
124	34.0	NZ	Sydney	17 Mar 1983	NZ by 14 runs
129	38.2	IND	Chelmsford	20 Jun 1983	IND by 118 runs
130	37.4	WI	Melbourne	23 Jan 1982	WI by 86 runs
139*	42.3	IND	Sharjah	29 Mar 1985	IND by 3 wkts
141	43.3	IND	Ahmedabad	5 Oct 1986	IND by 52 runs
142	42.1	IND	Melbourne	6 Dec 1980	IND by 66 runs
146	42.5	WI	Melbourne	10 Jan 1982	WI by 5 wkts

* Denotes batted first
¢ Denotes 8-ball overs

HIGHEST INNINGS TOTALS
FOR EACH GROUND

Venue	Total	Overs	Opp	Date	Result
Australia:					
Adelaide	2-323*	50.0	SL	28 Jan 1985	AUS by 232 runs
Brisbane	4-261*	50.0	ENG	18 Jan 1987	AUS by 11 runs
Melbourne	8-302*	50.0	NZ	13 Feb 1983	AUS by 149 runs
Perth	6-273*	50.0	PAK	2 Jan 1987	PAK by 1 wkt
Sydney	6-292*	50.0	IND	21 Jan 1986	AUS by 100 runs
England:					
Birmingham	5-273	55.0	ENG	22 Aug 1980	ENG by 47 runs
Chelmsford	129	38.2	IND	20 Jan 1983	IND by 118 runs
Leeds	7-278*	60.0	PAK	7 Jun 1975	AUS by 73 runs
Lord's	274	58.4	WI	21 Jun 1975	WI by 17 runs
Manchester	8-222*	55.0	ENG	24 Aug 1972	ENG by 6 wkts
Nottingham	9-320*	60.0	IND	13 Jun 1983	AUS by 162 runs
Southampton	7-272*	60.0	ZIM	16 Jun 1983	AUS by 32 runs
The Oval	5-328*	60.0	SL	11 Jun 1975	AUS by 52 runs
New Zealand:					
Auckland	231	44.5	NZ	29 Mar 1986	AUS by 44 runs
Christchurch	5-265*	35.0¢	NZ	31 Mar 1974	AUS by 31 runs
Dunedin	3-195	24.3¢	NZ	30 Mar 1974	AUS by 7 wkts
Wellington	231*	44.5	NZ	29 Mar 1986	AUS by 44 runs
Pakistan:					
Hyderabad	9-170	40.0	PAK	20 Sep 1982	PAK by 59 runs
Karachi	–	–	PAK	22 Oct 1982	No result
Lahore	4-206	40.0	PAK	8 Oct 1982	PAK by 28 runs
West Indies:					
Berbice	5-231*	50.0	WI	29 Feb 1984	WI by 8 wkts
Castries	9-206*	45.0	WI	19 Apr 1984	WI by 7 wkts
Kingston	7-209*	50.0	WI	26 Apr 1984	WI by 9 wkts
Port-of-Spain	6-194	36.4	WI	14 Mar 1984	AUS by 4 wkts
St. John's	7-181	36.0	WI	22 Feb 1978	WI on run rate

Venue	Total	Overs	Opp	Date	Result
Sri Lanka:					
Colombo1	5-194*	39.2	SL	20 Apr 1983	No result
Colombo2	5-207*	45.0	SL	16 Apr 1983	SL by 4 wkts
India:					
Ahmedabad	3-210	44.0	IND	5 Oct 1984	AUS by 7 wkts
Delhi	6-238*	45.0	IND	2 Oct 1986	IND by 3 wkts
Hyderabad	6-242*	47.0	IND	24 Sep 1986	No result
Indore	4-236	40.1	IND	6 Oct 1984	AUS by 6 wkts
Jaipur	3-250*	47.0	IND	7 Sep 1986	IND by 7 wkts
Jamshedpur	–	–	IND	3 Oct 1984	No result
New Delhi	9-220*	48.0	IND	28 Sep 1984	AUS by 48 runs
Rajkot	3-263	46.3	IND	7 Oct 1986	AUS by 7 wkts
Srinagar	7-226	46.0	IND	9 Sep 1986	AUS by 3 wkts
Trivandrum	1-29	7.4	IND	1 Oct 1984	No result
UAE:					
Sharjah	9-219	50.0	ENG	9 Apr 1987	ENG by 11 runs

* Denotes batted first
¢ Denotes 8-ball overs

BATTING

LEADING BATSMEN

Player	M	Inn	N.O	Runs	H.S	50	100	Avrge
Border, AR	153	143	20	3969	127*	26	3	32.27
Chappell, GS	74	72	14	2331	138*	14	3	40.18
Wood, GM	78	72	10	2140	114*	11	3	34.51
Hughes, KJ	97	88	6	1968	98	17	–	24.00
Wessels, KC	54	51	3	1740	107	14	1	36.25
Jones, DM	45	44	9	1424	121	7	3	40.69
Boon, DC	40	38	–	1280	111	8	1	33.68
Marsh, RW	92	76	15	1225	66	4	–	20.08
Marsh, GR	37	37	–	1179	125	4	2	31.86
Ritchie, GM	44	42	7	959	84	6	–	27.40
Waugh, SR	39	35	8	928	83*	6	–	34.37
Smith, SB	28	24	2	861	117	8	2	39.13
Phillips, WB	48	41	6	852	75*	6	–	24.34
Hookes, DW	39	36	2	826	76	5	–	24.29
Yallop, GN	30	27	6	823	66*	7	–	39.19
Dyson, J	29	27	4	755	79	4	–	32.83
Chappell, IM	16	16	2	673	86	8	–	48.07
Laird, BM	23	23	3	593	117*	2	1	29.65
O'Donnell, SP	37	32	9	552	74*	4	–	24.00
Walters, KD	28	24	6	513	59	2	–	28.50

HIGHEST INDIVIDUAL INNINGS FOR EACH GROUND

Venue	Score	Opp	Player	Date	Result
Australia:					
Adelaide	104*	WI	Wood, GM	27 Jan 1985	WI by 6 wkts
Brisbane	101	ENG	Jones, DM	18 Jan 1987	AUS by 11 runs
Melbourne	117	NZ	Smith, SB	13 Feb 1983	AUS by 149 runs
Perth	121	PAK	Jones, DM	2 Jan 1987	PAK by 1 wkt
Sydney	138*	NZ	Chappell, GS	25 Nov 1980	AUS by 94 runs
England:					
Birmingham	98	ENG	Hughes, KJ	22 Aug 1980	ENG by 47 runs
Chelmsford	36	IND	Border, AR	20 Jun 1983	IND by 118 runs
Leeds	108	ENG	Wood, GM	8 Jun 1981	AUS by 71 runs
Lord's	114*	ENG	Wood, GM	3 Jun 1985	ENG by 8 wkts
Manchester	59	ENG	Border, AR	30 May 1985	AUS by 3 wkts
Nottingham	110	IND	Chappell, GS	13 Jun 1983	AUS by 162 runs
Southampton	73	IND	Wood, GM	16 Jun 1983	AUS by 32 runs
The Oval	125*	ENG	Chappell, GS	6 Jun 1977	AUS by 2 wkts
New Zealand:					
Auckland	108	NZ	Chappell, GS	13 Feb 1982	NZ by 46 runs
Christchurch	86	NZ	Chappell, IM	31 Mar 1974	AUS by 31 runs
Dunedin	83	NZ	Chappell, IM	30 Mar 1974	AUS by 7 wkts
Wellington	71	NZ	Waugh, SR	26 Mar 1986	AUS by 3 wkts
Pakistan:					
Hyderabad	52	PAK	Wood, GM	9 Sep 1982	PAK by 59 runs
Karachi	–	PAK	–	22 Oct 1982	No result
Lahore	91*	PAK	Laird, BM	8 Oct 1982	PAK by 28 runs
West Indies:					
Berbice	60	WI	Smith, SB	29 Feb 1984	WI by 8 wkts
Castries	90	WI	Border, AR	19 Apr 1984	WI by 7 wkts
Kingston	84	WI	Ritchie, GM	29 Apr 1984	WI by 9 wkts
Port-of-Spain	67	WI	Wessels, KC	14 Mar 1984	AUS by 4 wkts
St. John's	84	WI	Cosier, GJ	22 Feb 1978	WI on run rate
Sri Lanka:					
Colombo1	60*	SL	Yallop, GN	30 Apr 1983	No result
Colombo2	59	SL	Yallop, GN	16 Apr 1983	SL by 4 wkts

Venue	Score	Opp	Player	Date	Result
India:					
Ahmedabad	62*	IND	Border, AR	5 Oct 1984	AUS by 7 wkts
Delhi	57*	IND	Waugh, SR	2 Oct 1986	IND by 3 wkts
Hyderabad	75	IND	Ritchie, GM	24 Sep 1986	No result
Indore	59*	IND	Ritchie, GM	6 Sep 1984	AUS by 6 wkts
Jaipur	111	IND	Boon, DC	7 Sep 1986	IND by 7 wkts
Jamshedpur	–	IND	–	3 Oct 1984	No result
New Delhi	107	IND	Wessels, KC	28 Sep 1984	AUS by 48 runs
Rajkot	91*	IND	Border, AR	7 Oct 1986	AUS by 7 wkts
Srinagar	90*	IND	Border, AR	9 Sep 1986	AUS by 3 wkts
Trivandrum	12	IND	Wessels, KC	1 Oct 1984	No result
UAE:					
Sharjah	84	ENG	Border, AR	9 Apr 1987	ENG by 11 runs

HIGHEST AGAINST OTHER NATIONS

Opponent	Score	Player	Venue	Date
Canada	27*	Hughes, KJ	Birmingham	16 Jun 1979
Zimbabwe	73	Wood, GM	Southampton	16 Jun 1983

HUNDREDS IN CONSECUTIVE INNINGS

Score	Player	Opponent	Venue	Date
118*	Border, AR	Sri Lanka	Adelaide	28 Jan 1985
127*		West Indies	Sydney	6 Feb 1985
104	Jones, DM	England	Perth	1 Jan 1987
121		Pakistan	Perth	2 Jan 1987

TWO OR MORE HUNDREDS IN THE ONE INNINGS

Score	Player	Opponent	Venue	Date
104	Marsh, GR	India	Jaipur	7 Sep 1986
111	Boon, DC			

TONY MANN, NIGHTWATCHMAN

Tony Mann was a left-hand batsman and right-arm leg-spinner whose cheery personality and gutsy approach to his cricket delighted fans for 21 Australian summers. He enjoyed every match he ever played, and his enjoyment conveyed itself to the crowd, big or small.

He was the son of the vigneron for the Houghton wine company, Jack Mann, who worked on the grapes in the Swan Valley through the week and bowled fast under-arm spinners for the Middle Swan Cricket Club each Saturday. Jack Mann's three sons, Dorham, Tony, and Bill all played for the club.

Tony made his debut for Western Australia in 1963-64, but failed to take a wicket in 15 overs and went in last. He was not picked again for his State for two years. Tony Lock was firmly entrenched in the State team, and there was a tense struggle for the second spinner's job between Mann, Terry Jenner and Ashley Mallett. Finally, Jenner and Mallett switched to South Australia, leaving Mann with a firm grasp on a State berth.

Mann took five wickets in an innings against New South Wales, Victoria and Queensland in the 1969-70 season, and with 25 wickets had strong claims for a place in the Australian Second Eleven's tour of New Zealand. The selectors preferred Jenner and the Sydney leg-spinner Kerry O'Keeffe. The following season Mann scored a century against the touring England team, but his State selectors sent him in well down the order, treating him solely as a bowler.

With Mallett, O'Keeffe and Jenner regularly preferred for Australian sides Mann spent three winters playing in the Lancashire League with Bacup, during which time he also played minor county cricket for Shropshire. He turned out frequently for the Cavaliers, a side that included Freddie Trueman, Ted Dexter and Graeme Pollock.

His big chance came in the Australian 1977-78 season when Kerry Packer launched World Series Cricket and the third Indian team toured Australia. Among the 28 Australians who defected to WSC were Mallett, O'Keeffe and the Victorian spinner Ray Bright.

Forced to completely rebuild the Australian side, the selectors chose Mann as their number 1 spinner, and in captain Bob Simpson, who came out of a ten-year retirement to aid Australian cricket, Mann found someone attuned to the demands of a leg-spinner.

India had won every State match leading up to the First Test when Mann made his international debut in Brisbane. The Indian attack was based on the spin of Bishen Bedi, Erapally Prasanna and Bhagwat Chandresekhar, who that summer provided Australians with a feast of quality spin bowling. They also gave Australia a torrid time on a dampish pitch in Brisbane, where only Peter Toohey's fine 82 enabled Australia to score 166 in the first innings.

Mann provided the Australian pace men, Jeff Thomson, Wayne Clark and Alan Hurst, with splendid support when India batted, and his 3 for 12 helped keep India down to a total of 153. Simpson (89), and Toohey (57) revived Australia after another bad start in the second innings and some thrilling slogging by Thomson and Hurst put on 50 for the last wicket. This took Australia to a lead of 340, which proved 16 runs too many for India. The teams went to Perth for the Second Test aware that they had a tense struggle on their hands.

India began the Perth Test with a first innings of 402, Chetander Chauhan (88), Mohinder Amarnath (90), Dillip Vengsarkar (49) and Sharma Madan Lal (43) all batting well. Simpson saved Australia with a dogged 176, which lasted for six hours and 41 minutes, with Dyson and Rixon the only other batsmen to make 50. India declared its second innings at 9 for 330 after centuries from Gavaskar (127) and Amarnath (100), leaving Australia to score 339 in 400 minutes for victory.

When the first Australian wicket fell at 13, Simpson had no hesitation in sending Mann in as nightwatchman. Mann not only survived until stumps but next morning stayed to play a historic innings. He defied the Indian attack for just over three hours, hammering anything loose to the leg or point boundaries with an authority and confidence rare in a tailender. His hometown crowd loved it, and when he was out for 105 they cheered him to the echo.

Mann's innings, the first century in Test cricket by a nightwatchman, gave Simpson and Toohey the chance to take Australia to victory. Only 58 runs were needed when the last hour began with the 15 mandatory overs to be bowled. Simpson was run out for 39 by Madan Lal, who then had Kim Hughes out for a duck. But Toohey played a studied, disciplined knock that steadied Australia until only 9 runs were needed from six overs. Here Toohey mishit a drive off Bedi and Rixon fell LBW in the same over, before Clark and Thomson took Australia to victory by two wickets, with only 22 balls remaining. In a match when 1468 runs were scored, Mann's century was decisive.

CENTURY MAKERS

Score	Player	Opp	Venue	Date	Result
138*	Chappell, GS	NZ	Sydney	25 Nov 1980	AUS by 94 runs
127*	Border, AR	WI	Sydney	6 Feb 1985	AUS by 26 runs
125*	Chappell, GS	ENG	The Oval	6 Jun 1977	AUS by 2 wkts
125	Marsh, GR	IND	Sydney	21 Jan 1986	AUS by 100 runs
121	Jones, DM	PAK	Perth	2 Jan 1987	PAK by 1 wkt
118*	Border, AR	SL	Adelaide	28 Jan 1985	AUS by 232 runs
117*	Laird, BM	WI	Sydney	24 Nov 1981	AUS by 7 wkts
117	Smith, SB	NZ	Melbourne	13 Feb 1983	AUS by 149 runs
114*	Wood, GM	ENG	Lord's	3 Jun 1985	ENG by 8 wkts
111	Boon, DC	IND	Jaipur	7 Sep 1986	IND by 7 wkts
110	Chappell, TM	IND	Nottingham	13 Jun 1983	AUS by 162 runs
108	Chappell, GS	NZ	Auckland	13 Feb 1982	NZ by 46 runs
108	Wood, GM	ENG	Leeds	8 Feb 1981	AUS by 71 runs
107	Wessels, KC	IND	New Delhi	28 Sep 1984	AUS by 48 runs
106	Smith, SB	PAK	Sydney	25 Jan 1984	AUS by 87 runs
105*	Border, AR	IND	Sydney	18 Dec 1980	AUS by 9 wkts
104*	Wood, GM	WI	Adelaide	27 Jan 1985	WI by 6 wkts
104	Marsh, GR	IND	Jaipur	7 Sep 1986	IND by 7 wkts
104	Jones, DM	ENG	Perth	1 Jan 1987	ENG by 37 runs
101	Turner, A	SL	The Oval	11 Jun 1975	AUS by 52 runs
101	Jones, DM	ENG	Brisbane	18 Jan 1987	AUS by 11 runs

HIGHEST SCORE ON DEBUT

Score	Player	Opponent	Venue	Date
79	Wessels, GS	New Zealand	Melbourne	9 Jan 1983
60	Chappell, IM	England	Melbourne	5 Jan 1971
57	Edwards, R	England	Manchester	24 Aug 1972
53	Woodcock, AJ	New Zealand	Christchurch	31 Mar 1974

HIGHEST WICKET PARTNERSHIPS

Wkt	Score	Opp	Players		Venue	Date
1st	212	IND	Marsh, GR	& Boon, DC	Jaipur	7 Sep 1986
2nd	178	ENG	Marsh, GR	& Jones, DM	Brisbane	18 Jan 1987
3rd	224*	SL	Jones, DM	& Border, AR	Adelaide	28 Jan 1985
4th	173	PAK	Jones, DM	& Waugh, SR	Perth	2 Jan 1987
5th	115*	NZ	Laird, BM	& Border, AR	Dunedin	17 Feb 1982
6th	99	WI	Edwards, R	& Marsh, GR	The Oval	14 Jun 1975
7th	102*	IND	Waugh, SR	& Dyer, GC	Delhi	2 Oct 1986
8th	50*	ZIM	Marsh, GR	& Hogg, RM	Nottingham	9 Jun 1983
9th	51	WI	O'Donnell, SP	& Wood, GM	Sydney	12 Feb 1985
10th	45	ENG	Laughlin, TJ	& Walker, MHN	Sydney	11 Dec 1979

* Denotes unbroken partnership

CENTURY WICKET PARTNERSHIPS

Wkt	Score	Opp	Players		Venue	Date
3rd	224*	SL	Jones, DM	& Border, AR	Adelaide	28 Jan 1985
1st	212	IND	Marsh, GR	& Boon, DC	Jaipur	7 Sep 1986
1st	182	SL	McCosker, RB	& Turner, A	The Oval	11 Jun 1975
2nd	178	ENG	Marsh, GR	& Jones, DM	Brisbane	18 Jan 1987
4th	173	PAK	Jones, DM	& Waugh, SR	Perth	2 Jan 1987
4th	164	ENG	Border, AR	& Waugh, SR	Adelaide	26 Jan 1987
3rd	159	ENG	Boon, DC	& Border, AR	Sharjah	9 Apr 1987
2nd	157*	SL	Smith, SB	& Phillips, WB	Perth	3 Feb 1985
4th	157*	ENG	Kerr, RB	& Jones, DM	Melbourne	17 Feb 1985
1st	154	NZ	Wessels, KC	& Dyson, J	Melbourne	9 Jan 1983
1st	152	IND	Marsh, GR	& Boon, DC	Sydney	21 Jan 1986
2nd	151	NZ	Dyson, J	Chappell, GS	Sydney	25 Nov 1980
4th	150	WI	Border, AR	& Hughes, KJ	Castries	19 Apr 1984
2nd	148	ENG	Robinson, RD	& Chappell, GS	The Oval	6 Jun 1977
4th	147*	WI	Laird, BM	& Hughes, KJ	Sydney	24 Nov 1981
1st	146	IND	Marsh, GR	& Boon, DC	Melbourne	31 Jan 1986
2nd	145	NZ	Wood, GM	& Chappell, GS	Melbourne	1 Feb 1981
2nd	144	IND	Chappell, GS	& Hughes, KJ	Nottingham	13 Jun 1983
1st	140	NZ	Wood, GM	& Smith, SB	Melbourne	13 Feb 1983

Wkt	Score	Opp	Players		Venue	Date
3rd	140	PAK	Wessels, KC	& Border, AR	Sydney	10 Jan 1984
2nd	136	NZ	Stackpole, KR	& Chappell, IM	Dunedin	30 Mar 1974
1st	135	WI	Smith, SB	& Wood, GM	Melbourne	10 Feb 1985
2nd	130	ENG	Wood, GM	& Yallop, GN	Leeds	8 Jun 1981
2nd	128	IND	Wessels, KC	& Hughes, KJ	New Delhi	28 Sep 1984
2nd	127*	IND	Border, AR	& Chappell, GS	Sydney	18 Dec 1980
2nd	121	IND	Marsh, GR	& Border, AR	Sydney	21 Jan 1986
3rd	119	WI	Wessels, KC	& Hughes, KJ	Perth	5 Feb 1984
4th	117	SL	Chappell, GS	& Walters, KD	The Oval	11 Jun 1975
4th	117	PAK	Laird, BM	& Hughes, KJ	Lahore	8 Oct 1982
4th	116	NZ	Wessels, KC	& Hookes, DW	Sydney	18 Jan 1983
5th	115*	NZ	Laird, BM	& Border, AR	Dunedin	17 Feb 1982
4th	115	WI	Border, AR	& Boon, DC	Melbourne	6 Jan 1985
4th	114	PAK	Boon, DC	& O'Donnell, SP	Sharjah	3 Apr 1987
3rd	112	SL	Yallop, GN	& Hookes, DW	Colombo2	30 Apr 1983
2nd	109	WI	Wessels, KC	& Hughes, KJ	Melbourne	11 Feb 1984
1st	109	ENG	Marsh, GR	& Wellham, DW	Sydney	22 Jan 1987
1st	106	WI	Wessels, KC	& Smith, SB	Berbice	29 Feb 1984
5th	105	WI	Border, AR	& Phillips, WB	Sydney	6 Feb 1985
1st	104	PAK	Laird, BM	& Wood, GM	Hyderabad	20 Sep 1982
1st	103	WI	Wiener, JM	& McCosker, RB	Sydney	18 Jan 1980
4th	103	ENG	Chappell, GS	& Sheahan, AP	Lord's	26 Aug 1972
4th	103	ENG	Hughes, KJ	& Yallop, GN	Birmingham	22 Aug 1980
3rd	103	ENG	Jones, DM	& Border, AR	Melbourne	8 Feb 1987
7th	102*	IND	Waugh, SR	& Dyer, GC	Delhi	2 Oct 1986
3rd	101	WI	Hughes, KJ	& Hookes, DW	Lord's	18 Jun 1983
3rd	100	IND	Border, AR	& Hughes, KJ	Sydney	15 Jan 1981
3rd	100	WI	Boon, DC	& Hughes, KJ	Melbourne	12 Feb 1984
5th	100	NZ	Ritchie, GM	& Matthews, GRJ	Auckland	29 Mar 1986

* Denotes unbroken partnership

BOWLING

LEADING WICKET-TAKERS

Player	M	Balls	Mdns	Runs	Wkts	Avrge	5WI	Best	Stk/rt
Lillee, DK	63	3593	80	2145	103	20.83	1	5/34	34.88
Hogg, RM	71	3677	57	2418	85	28.44	–	4/29	43.25
Lawson, GF	71	3790	88	2283	79	28.90	–	4/26	47.97
Chappell, GS	74	3108	41	2096	72	29.11	2	5/15	43.17
Thomson, JR	50	2696	37	1942	55	35.31	–	4/67	49.01
Pascoe, LS	29	1568	21	1066	53	20.11	1	5/30	29.58
Rackemann, CG	28	1489	32	1016	49	20.73	1	5/16	30.38
McDermott, CJ	39	2156	24	1591	43	37.00	–	3/20	50.14
O'Donnell, SP	37	1917	18	1406	43	32.70	–	4/19	44.58
Reid, BA	33	1782	26	1258	42	29.95	1	5/53	42.43
Waugh, SR	39	1643	12	1210	41	28.14	–	4/48	40.07
Matthews, GRJ	44	2083	19	1435	40	35.88	–	3/27	52.08

FIVE WICKETS IN AN INNINGS

Wkts	Bowler	Opponent	Venue	Date
6/14	Gilmour, GJ	England	Leeds	18 Jun 1975
6/39	Macleay, KH	India	Nottingham	13 Jun 1983
5/15	Chappell, GS	India	Sydney	8 Jan 1981
5/16	Rackemann, CG	Pakistan	Adelaide	30 Jan 1984
5/17	Alderman, TM	New Zealand	Wellington	20 Feb 1982
5/18	Cosier, GJ	England	Birmingham	4 Jun 1977
5/20	Chappell, GS	England	Birmingham	4 Jun 1977
5/21	Hurst, AG	Canada	Birmingham	16 Jun 1979
5/30	Pascoe, LS	New Zealand	Sydney	25 Nov 1980
5/34	Lillee, DK	Pakistan	Leeds	7 Jun 1975
5/46	Gilbert, DR	New Zealand	Sydney	14 Jan 1986
5/48	Gilmour, GJ	West Indies	Lord's	21 Jun 1975
5/53	Reid, BA	India	Adelaide	26 Jan 1986

HIGHEST AGAINST OTHER NATIONS

Opponent	Wkts	Player	Venue	Date
Sri Lanka	4/47	Hogg, RM	Sydney	8 Jan 1985
Zimbabwe	3/40	Hogg, RM	Southampton	16 Jun 1983

MOST EXPENSIVE BOWLING PERFORMANCE (Minimum 5 overs)

Runs per overs	O	M	R	W	Bowler	Opponent	Venue	Date
10.80	5	–	54	–	Matthews, GRJ	India	Delhi	2 Oct 1986

MOST ECONOMICAL BOWLING PERFORMANCE (Innings and/or overs completed)

Runs per overs	O	M	R	W	Bowler	Opponent	Venue	Date
0.60	5	2	3	1	Lillee, DK	India	Sydney	8 Jan 1981
0.71	7	5	5	2	Lawson, GF	Sri Lanka	Adelaide	28 Jan 1985
0.88	8	4	7	3	Rackemann, CG	India	Trivandrum	1 Oct 1984
0.90	10	5	9	–	Malone, MF	West Indies	Melbourne	10 Jan 1982

BEST BOWLING ON DEBUT

Wkts	Bowler	Opponent	Venue	Date
4/39	Rackemann, CG	New Zealand	Melbourne	9 Jan 1983
3/34	Mallett, AA	England	Melbourne	5 Jan 1971
3/40	Stackpole, KR	England	Melbourne	5 Jan 1971
3/54	Laughlin, TJ	West Indies	St. John's	22 Feb 1978

FIVE WICKETS IN SUCCESSIVE INNINGS

Wkts	Bowler	Opponent	Venue	Date
6/14	Gilmour, GJ	England	Leeds	18 Jun 1975
5/48	Gilmour, GJ	West Indies	Lord's	21 Jun 1975

HAT-TRICKS

Bowler	Opponent	Venue	Date	Batsman	Balls
Reid, BA	New Zealand	Sydney	14 Jan 1986	Blair, BR	6th Ball, 8th over
				McSweeney, EB	1st Ball, 9th over
				Gillespie, SR	2nd Ball, 9th over

BEST BOWLING PERFORMANCE FOR EACH GROUND

Venue	Opp	O	M	R	W	Player	Date	Result
Australia:								
Adelaide	PAK	8.2	2	16	5	Rackemann, CG	30 Jan 1984	AUS by 70 runs
Brisbane	ENG	8.4	1	28	3	Rackemann, CG	16 Jan 1983	AUS by 7 wkts
Melbourne	NZ	9.5	3	37	4	Pascoe, LS	26 Nov 1980	AUS by 94 runs
Perth	PAK	9.5	–	48	4	Waugh, SR	2 Jan 1987	PAK by 1 wkt
Sydney	IND	9.5	5	15	5	Chappell, GS	8 Jan 1981	AUS by 9 wkts
England:								
Birmingham	ENG	8.5	3	18	5	Cosier, GJ	4 Jun 1977	ENG by 99 runs
Chelmsford	IND	12.0	2	40	3	Hogg, RM	20 Jan 1983	IND by 118 runs
Leeds	ENG	12.0	6	14	6	Gilmour, GJ	18 Jun 1975	AUS by 4 wkts
Lord's	WI	12.0	2	48	5	Gilmour, GJ	21 Jun 1975	WI by 17 runs
Manchester	ENG	10.0	1	26	4	Lawson, GF	30 May 1985	AUS by 3 wkts
Nottingham	IND	11.5	3	39	6	Macleay, KH	13 Jun 1983	AUS by 162 runs
Southampton	ZIM	12.0	–	40	3	Hogg, RM	16 Jun 1983	AUS by 32 runs
The Oval	CAN	10.0	3	21	5	Hurst, AG	16 Jun 1979	AUS by 7 wkts

Venue	Opp	O	M	R	W	Player	Date	Result

New Zealand:

Venue	Opp	O	M	R	W	Player	Date	Result
Auckland	NZ	9.0	1	33	3	Matthews, GRJ	29 Mar 1986	AUS by 44 runs
Christchurch	NZ	7.0¢	–	47	3	Mallett, AA	31 Mar 1974	AUS by 31 runs
Dunedin	NZ	10.0	3	22	3	Alderman, TM	17 Feb 1982	AUS by 6 wkts
Wellington	NZ	10.0	2	17	5	Alderman, TM	20 Feb 1982	AUS by 8 wkts

Pakistan:

Venue	Opp	O	M	R	W	Player	Date	Result
Hyderabad	PAK	8.0	–	63	2	Alderman, TM	20 Sep 1982	PAK by 59 runs
Karachi	PAK	6.0	2	22	1	Alderman, TM	22 Oct 1982	No result
Lahore	PAK	8.0	–	40	1	Thomson, JR	8 Oct 1982	PAK by 28 runs

West Indies:

Venue	Opp	O	M	R	W	Player	Date	Result
Berbice	WI	10.0	1	54	1	Rackemann, CG	29 Feb 1984	WI by 8 wkts
Castries	WI	7.0	–	24	3	Callen, IW	12 Apr 1978	AUS by 2 wkts
Kingston	WI	6.0	1	16	1	Maguire, JN	29 Apr 1984	WI by 9 wkts
Port-of-Spain	WI	9.0	1	40	2	Lawson, GF	14 Mar 1984	AUS by 4 wkts
St. John's	WI	10.0	–	67	4	Thomson, JR	22 Feb 1978	WI on run rate

Sri Lanka:

Venue	Opp	O	M	R	W	Player	Date	Result
Colombo1	SL	–	–	–	–	–	30 Apr 1983	No result
Colombo2	SL	9.0	1	27	3	Hogan, TG	13 Apr 1983	SL by 2 wkts

India:

Venue	Opp	O	M	R	W	Player	Date	Result
Ahmedabad	IND	10.0	2	25	3	Lawson, GF	5 Oct 1984	AUS by 7 wkts
Delhi	IND	9.0	–	43	3	Reid, BA	2 Oct 1986	IND by 3 wkts
Hyderabad	IND	4.0	–	20	1	Reid, BA	24 Sep 1986	No result
Indore	IND	10.0	–	61	3	Maguire, JN	6 Oct 1984	AUS by 6 wkts
Jaipur	IND	8.0	1	27	1	Reid, BA	7 Sep 1986	IND by 7 wkts
Jamshedpur	IND	2.1	–	3	2	Rackemann, CG	3 Oct 1984	No result
New Delhi	IND	10.0	1	41	4	Rackemann, CG	28 Sep 1984	AUS by 48 runs
Rajkot	IND	10.0	1	45	2	Waugh, SR	7 Oct 1986	AUS by 7 wkts
Srinagar	IND	10.0	2	37	2	Reid, BA	9 Sep 1986	AUS by 3 wkts
Trivandrum	IND	8.0	–	33	4	Hogan, TG	1 Oct 1984	No result

UAE:

Venue	Opp	O	M	R	W	Player	Date	Result
Sharjah	ENG	7.0	–	21	3	Border, AR	24 Mar 1985	AUS by 2 wkts

¢ Denotes 8-ball overs

FIELDING

MOST CATCHES IN AN INNINGS

Catches	Player	Opponent	Venue	Date
3	Walters, KD	New Zealand	Dunedin	30 Mar 1974
3	Dyson, J	England	Sydney	25 Nov 1980
3	Darling, WM	Pakistan	Adelaide	6 Dec 1981
3	Border, AR	India	Adelaide	26 Jan 1986
3	Border, AR	New Zealand	Adelaide	27 Jan 1986

WICKET-KEEPING

MOST DISMISSALS IN AN INNINGS

Dismissals	Keeper	Opponent	Venue	Date
5 (5 ct)	Marsh, RW	England	Leeds	8 Jun 1981
4 (4 ct)	Marsh, RW	England	Birmingham	28 Aug 1972
4 (4 ct)	Marsh, RW	England	Birmingham	4 Jun 1975
4 (3 ct 1 st)	Robinson, RD	England	The Oval	6 Jun 1977
4 (4 ct)	Marsh, RW	India	Sydney	8 Jan 1981
4 (4 ct)	Marsh, RW	New Zealand	Perth	6 Feb 1983
4 (3 ct 1 st)	Marsh, RW	Pakistan	Sydney	25 Jan 1984
4 (3 ct 1 st)	Phillips, WB	India	New Delhi	28 Sep 1984
4 (3 ct 1 st)	Phillips, WB	Sri Lanka	Perth	3 Feb 1985
4 (2 ct 2 st)	Rixon, SJ	England	Sharjah	24 Mar 1985
4 (3 ct 1 st)	Phillips, WB	New Zealand	Sydney	14 Jan 1986
4 (4 ct)	Zoehrer, TJ	England	Perth	1 Jan 1987

THE PLAYERS

BATTING AVERAGES

Player	M	Inn	NO	Runs	HS	50	100	Avrge	Ct/St	Capt	W	L	D	T
Alderman, TM	23	9	3	27	9*	–	–	4.50	12					
Beard, GR	2	–	–	–	–	–	–	–	–					
Bennett, MJ	8	4	1	9	6*	–	–	3.00	1					
Bishop, GA	2	2	–	13	7	–	–	6.50	1					
Boon, DC	40	38	–	1280	111	8	1	33.68	9					
Border, AR	153	143	20	3969	127*	26	3	32.27	54		58	26	30	2 –
Bright, RJ	11	8	4	66	19*	–	–	16.50	2		1	–	1	– –
Callen, IW	5	3	2	6	3*	–	–	6.00	2					
Carlson, PH	4	2	–	11	11	–	–	5.50	–					
Chappell, GS	74	72	14	2331	138*	14	3	40.18	23		49	21	25	3 –
Chappell, IM	16	16	2	673	86	8	–	48.07	5		11	6	5	– –
Chappell, TM	20	13	–	229	110	–	1	17.62	8					
Clark, WM	2	–	–	–	–	–	–	–	–					
Colley, DJ	1	–	–	–	–	–	–	–	–					
Connolly, AN	1	–	–	–	–	–	–	–	–					
Cosier, GJ	9	7	2	154	84	1	–	30.80	4					
Darling, WM	18	18	1	363	74	1	–	21.35	6					
Davis, IC	3	3	1	12	11*	–	–	6.00	–					
Davis, SP	34	11	7	20	6	–	–	5.00	4					
Dyer, GC	4	2	1	51	45*	–	–	51.00	2					
Dymock, G	15	7	4	35	14*	–	–	11.67	1					
Dyson, J	29	27	4	755	79	4	–	32.83	12					
Edwards, R	9	8	1	255	80*	3	–	36.43	–					
Edwards, WJ	1	1	–	2	2	–	–	2.00	–					
Gilbert, DR	14	8	3	39	8	–	–	7.80	3					
Gilmour, GJ	5	2	1	42	28*	–	–	42.00	2					
Graf, SF	11	6	–	24	8	–	–	4.00	1					
Hammond, JR	1	1	1	15	15*	–	–	–	–					
Hilditch, AMJ	8	8	–	226	72	1	–	28.25	1					

Player	M	Inn	NO	Runs	HS	50	100	Avrge	Ct/St	Capt	W	L	D	T
Hogan, TG	16	12	4	72	27	–	–	9.00	10					
Hogg, RM	71	35	20	137	22	–	–	9.13	8					
Holland, RG	2	–	–	–	–	–	–	–	–					
Hookes, DW	39	36	2	826	76	5	–	24.29	11	1	–	1	–	–
Hughes, KJ	97	88	6	1968	98	17	–	24.00	27	49	21	23	4	1
Hurst, AG	8	4	4	7	3*	–	–	–	1					
Jenner, TJ	1	1	–	12	12	–	–	12.00	–					
Jones, DM	45	44	9	1424	121	7	3	40.69	11					
Kent, MF	5	5	1	78	33	–	–	19.50	4					
Kerr, RB	4	4	1	97	87*	1	–	32.33	1					
Laird, BM	23	23	3	593	117*	2	1	29.65	5					
Laughlin, TJ	6	5	1	105	74	1	–	26.25	–					
Lawry, WM	1	1	–	27	27	–	–	27.00	1	1	1	–	–	–
Lawson, GF	71	48	17	373	33*	–	–	12.03	17					
Lillee, DK	63	34	8	240	42*	–	–	9.23	10					
Maclean, JA	2	1	–	11	11	–	–	11.00	–					
Macleay, KH	16	13	2	139	41	–	–	12.64	2					
Maguire, JN	23	11	5	42	14*	–	–	7.00	2					
Mallett, AA	9	3	1	14	8	–	–	7.00	4					
Malone, MF	10	7	3	36	15*	–	–	9.00	1					
Marks, PH	–	–	–	–	–	–	–	–	1					
Marsh, GR	37	37	–	1179	125	4	2	31.86	12	1	–	1	–	–
Marsh, RW	92	76	15	1225	66	4	–	20.08	120/4					
Massie, RAL	3	1	1	16	16*	–	–	–	1					
Matthews, GRJ	44	37	7	473	54	1	–	15.77	19					
McCosker, RB	14	14	–	320	95	2	–	22.86	3					
McCurdy, RJ	11	6	2	33	13*	–	–	8.25	1					
McDermott, CJ	39	24	7	157	37	–	–	9.24	8					
McKenzie, GD	1	–	–	–	–	–	–	–	1					
Moss, JK	1	1	–	7	7	–	–	7.00	2					
O'Donnell, SP	37	32	9	552	74*	4	–	24.00	12					
O'Keeffe, KJ	2	2	1	16	16*	–	–	16.00	–					
Pascoe, LS	29	11	7	39	15*	–	–	9.75	6					
Phillips, WB	48	41	6	852	75*	6	–	24.34	42/7					
Porter, GD	2	1	–	3	3	–	–	3.00	1					
Rackemann, CG	28	11	4	20	9*	–	–	2.86	4					
Redpath, IR	5	5	–	46	24	–	–	9.20	2					
Reid, BA	33	13	4	35	10	–	–	3.89	1					
Ritchie, GM	44	42	7	959	84	6	–	27.40	9					

Player	M	Inn	NO	Runs	HS	50	100	Avrge	Ct/St	Capt	W	L	D	T
Rixon, SJ	6	6	3	40	20*	–	–	13.33	9/2					
Robinson, RD	2	2	–	82	70	1	–	41.00	3/1					
Serjeant, CJ	3	3	–	73	46	–	–	24.33	1					
Sheahan, AP	3	3	–	75	50	1	–	25.00	–					
Simpson, RB	2	2	–	36	23	–	–	18.00	4	2	1	1	–	–
Smith, SB	28	24	2	861	117	8	2	39.13	8					
Stackpole, KR	6	6	–	224	61	3	–	37.33	1					
Taylor, PL	12	8	4	26	14*	–	–	4.00	5					
Thomson, AL	1	–	–	–	–	–	–	–	–					
Thomson, JR	50	30	6	181	21	–	–	7.54	9					
Toohey, PM	5	4	2	105	54*	1	–	52.50	–					
Trimble, GS	2	2	1	4	4	–	–	4.00	–					
Turner, A	6	6	–	247	101	–	1	41.17	3					
Veletta, MRJ	2	2	–	5	5	–	–	2.50	–					
Walker, MH	17	11	3	79	20	–	–	9.88	6					
Walters, KD	28	24	6	513	59	2	–	28.50	10					
Watson, GD	2	2	1	11	11*	–	–	11.00	–					
Waugh, SR	39	35	8	928	83*	6	–	34.37	8					
Wellham, DM	17	17	2	379	97	1	–	25.27	8					
Wessels, KC	54	51	3	1740	107	14	1	36.25	19					
Whatmore, DF	1	1	–	2	2	–	–	2.00	–					
Whitney, MR	3	2	–	7	6	–	–	3.50	2					
Wiener, JM	7	7	–	140	50	1	–	20.00	2					
Wood, GM	78	72	10	2140	114*	11	3	34.51	17					
Woodcock, AJ	1	1	–	53	53	1	–	53.00	–					
Woolley, RD	4	3	2	31	16	–	–	31.00	1/1					
Wright, KJ	5	2	–	29	23	–	–	14.50	8/-					
Yallop, GN	30	27	6	823	66*	7	–	39.19	5	4	2	1	1	–
Yardley, B	7	4	–	58	28	–	–	14.50	1					
Zoehrer, TJ	21	14	3	121	50	1	–	11.00	20/1					

BOWLING AVERAGES

Player	M	Balls	Mdns	Runs	Wkts	Avrge	5WI	Best	Stk/rt
Alderman, TM	23	1290	28	803	29	27.68	1	5/17	44.48
Beard, GR	2	112	3	70	4	17.50	–	2/20	28.00
Bennett, MJ	8	408	12	275	4	68.75	–	2/27	102.00
Boon, DC	40	22	–	24	–	–	–	–	–
Border, AR	153	1026	5	814	23	35.39	–	3/21	44.61
Bright, RJ	11	462	3	350	3	116.67	–	1/28	154.00
Callen, IW	5	180	2	148	5	29.60	–	3/24	36.00
Carlson, PH	4	168	3	70	2	35.00	–	1/21	84.00
Chappell, GS	74	3108	41	2096	72	29.11	2	5/15	43.17
Chappell, IM	16	42	1	23	2	11.50	–	2/14	21.00
Chappell, TM	20	736	4	538	19	28.32	–	3/31	38.74
Clark, WM	2	100	3	61	3	20.33	–	2/39	33.33
Colley, DJ	1	66	1	72	–	–	–	–	–
Connolly, AN	1	64	–	62	–	–	–	–	–
Cosier, GJ	9	409	9	248	14	17.71	1	5/18	29.21
Davis, SP	34	1728	43	974	36	27.06	–	3/10	48.00
Dymock, G	15	806	16	412	15	27.47	–	2/21	53.73
Edwards, WJ	1	1	–	0	–	–	–	–	–
Gilbert, DR	14	684	4	552	18	30.67	1	5/46	38.00
Gilmour, GJ	5	320	9	165	16	10.31	2	6/14	20.00
Graf, SF	11	522	4	345	8	43.12	–	2/23	65.25
Hammond, JR	1	54	1	41	1	41.00	–	1/41	54.00
Hogan, TG	16	917	13	574	23	24.96	–	4/33	39.87
Hogg, RM	71	3677	57	2418	85	28.44	–	4/29	43.25
Holland, RG	2	126	2	99	2	49.50	–	2/49	63.00
Hookes, DW	39	29	–	28	1	28.00	–	1/02	29.00
Hughes, KJ	97	1	–	4	–	–	–	–	–
Hurst, AG	8	402	11	203	12	16.92	1	5/21	33.50
Jenner, TJ	1	64	1	28	–	–	–.	–	–
Jones, DM	45	19	–	12	1	12.00	–	1/4	19.00
Laughlin, TJ	6	308	3	224	8	28.00	–	3/54	38.50
Lawson, GF	71	3790	88	2283	79	28.90	–	4/26	47.97
Lillee, DK	63	3593	80	2145	103	20.83	1	5/34	34.88
Macleay, KH	16	857	8	626	15	41.73	1	6/39	57.13
Maguire, JN	23	1009	12	769	19	40.47	–	3/61	53.11
Mallett, AA	9	502	7	341	11	31.00	–	3/34	45.64
Malone, MF	10	612	16	315	11	28.64	–	2/09	55.64

Player	M	Balls	Mdns	Runs	Wkts	Avrge	5WI	Best	Stk/rt
Marsh, GR	37	6	–	4	–	–	–	–	–
Massie, RAL	3	183	5	129	3	43.00	–	2/35	61.00
Matthews, GRJ	44	2083	19	1435	40	35.88	–	3/27	52.08
McKenzie, GD	1	60	–	22	2	11.00	–	2/22	30.00
McCurdy, RJ	11	515	8	375	12	31.25	–	3/19	42.91
McDermott, CJ	39	2156	24	1591	43	37.00	–	3/20	50.14
O'Donnell, SP	37	1917	18	1406	43	32.70	–	4/19	44.58
O'Keeffe, KJ	2	132	3	79	2	39.50	–	1/36	66.00
Pascoe, LS	29	1568	21	1066	53	20.11	1	5/30	29.58
Porter, GD	2	108	5	33	3	11.00	–	2/13	36.00
Rackemann, CG	28	1489	32	1016	49	20.73	1	5/16	30.38
Reid, BA	33	1782	26	1258	42	29.95	1	5/53	42.43
Simpson, RB	2	102	–	95	2	47.50	–	2/30	51.00
Smith, SB	28	7	–	5	–	–	–	–	–
Stackpole, KR	6	77	–	54	3	18.00	–	3/40	25.67
Taylor, PL	12	565	4	409	13	31.46	–	3/29	43.46
Thomson, AL	1	64	2	22	1	22.00	–	1/22	64.00
Thomson, JR	50	2696	37	1942	55	35.31	–	4/67	49.01
Trimble, GS	2	24	–	32	–	–	–	–	–
Walker, MHN	17	1006	24	546	20	27.30	–	4/19	50.30
Walters, KD	28	314	3	273	4	68.25	–	2/24	78.50
Watson, GD	2	48	1	28	2	14.00	–	2/28	24.00
Waugh, SR	39	1643	12	1210	41	28.14	–	4/48	40.07
Wessels, KC	54	737	2	656	18	36.44	–	2/16	40.94
Whitney, MR	3	162	3	133	5	26.60	–	2/19	32.40
Wiener, JM	7	24	–	34	–	–	–	–	–
Yallop, GN	30	138	–	119	3	39.67	–	2/28	46.00
Yardley, B	7	198	4	130	7	18.57	–	3/28	28.29

McGILVRAY
The Game Is Not The Same . . .
As told to Norman Tasker

For many Australians the sound of Alan McGilvray's voice on ABC
Radio has been synonymous for decades with the start of the cricket
season and the Australian summer. He has been Australia's best-
known commentator and has been much decorated for his contribution
to the country's sporting life and entertainment.

When McGilvray made his last Test match broadcast from the
Sydney Cricket Ground in 1985 the Australian Prime Minister, Bob
Hawke, made a speech of farewell. Years earlier another Australian
Prime Minister, Sir Robert Menzies, a connoisseur of the game, had
also complimented McGilvray publicly on his commentary style. The
man who made such an impression on cricket lovers, Prime Ministers
and players alike has now put his memories and opinions into this
book which surveys the game's high points and outstanding players.

As a player himself McGilvray was associated with some of the
finest cricketers Australia has produced. His career in broadcasting
continued and extended that association to include the world's best
known players over the next fifty years.

His recollections of famous innings and famous events make
marvellous reading not only for devotees of the game but also for
those who are interested in the changing nature of sport in society.

McGILVRAY
The Game Goes On . . .
As told to Norman Tasker

'Since I retired as a broadcaster, I am continually embroiled in discussing this player and that with people who love to remember', says Alan McGilvray in *The Game Goes On* . . ., his second book based on more than fifty years' involvement with the game. 'As people have so often asked me to consider and compare generations of cricketers, I have come to realise how much I enjoy doing so.'

He does it masterfully in this book which includes his recollections of games he has witnessed through his life as a commentator and, in his young days, as a player associated with Australian cricketers like Bradman, Oldfield, McCabe, Kippax and O'Reilly.

Alan McGilvray has kept detailed records of the games he described for generations of Australian and English cricket fans. These records complement his gift for bringing alive the excitement of past matches as he analyses for Norman Tasker outstanding bowlers and batsmen, memorable Ashes series, his favourite grounds, the future for the West Indies, the role of selectors and the practicalities of being a commentator.

He also names his England and Australian 'teams' containing the players he considers to be the best since World War II.

BRADMAN TO BORDER (revised edition)
A History of Australia-England Test Matches from 1946

The eleven captains who led Australia describe the Australia/England
Test Matches played since 1946-47. Australia won 40 to England's
33 Tests and the Ashes changed hands seven times.

Details of scores in all these Tests provide accurate accounts, but
they do not tell of the joy, hope, despair, frustrations and changing
fortunes. Nor the dropped catch, the weather, the luck of the toss
which might well have changed the result.

The captains' stories bring memories of England's captains . . .
Walter Hammond, Norman Yardley, Freddie Brown, Len Hutton,
Peter May, Colin Cowdrey, Ted Dexter, Mike Smith, Ray
Illingworth, Tony Greig, Mike Denness, Mike Brearley, Ian Botham,
Bob Willis, David Gower and Mike Gatting and the many great
players of both sides in this period.